Interrogating Sources

Questions: Any time you encounter a source, you will want to ask the same questions historians ask. Depending on the nature of the source you are working with, the answers may range from the obvious to the unobtainable.

- *When was this source produced and under what circumstances?*
- *Who produced this source?*
- *What purpose was this source created to serve?*
- *Who was the audience for this source?*
- *What is the point of view in this source?*

Checklists in each chapter help you dig deeper and ask the right questions of specific source types:

Limitations: When working with any source, follow the same principles that historians do and be aware of the limitations of historical evidence:

- *Sources are incomplete.* You will never have all the sources for any single historical moment, and no single source can tell the whole story.
- *Sources have limits to what they can tell you.* You must consider what you can and cannot logically conclude from a source.
- *Sources have biases, which must be accounted for.* Do not dismiss the source's bias or adopt it in your interpretation. Instead, identify the bias and use it as evidence of one viewpoint.
- *Sources can conflict.* Never hide or dismiss sources that complicate or contradict your interpretation. Either revise your interpretation or explain why conflicting evidence does not alter your interpretation.

Additional Resources

Refer to Appendix I for help **avoiding plagiarism** when writing about sources. See Appendix II for help **documenting your sources**.

Going to the Source

The Bedford Reader in American History

FOURTH EDITION

Going to the Source

The Bedford Reader in American History

VOLUME 1: TO 1877

Victoria Bissell Brown

Grinnell College

Timothy J. Shannon

Gettysburg College

Bedford/St. Martin's

A Macmillan Education Imprint

Boston • New York

For Bedford/St. Martin's

Vice President, Editorial, Macmillan Higher Education Humanities: Edwin Hill
Publisher for History: Michael Rosenberg
Senior Executive Editor for History: William J. Lombardo
Director of Development for History: Jane Knetzger
Developmental Editor: Tess Fletcher
Production Editor: Louis C. Bruno Jr.
Production Supervisor: Robert Cherry
Executive Marketing Manager: Sandra McGuire
Copy Editor: Lisa Wehrle
Director of Rights and Permissions: Hilary Newman
Photo Editor: Felice Pilchik
Senior Art Director: Anna Palchik
Text Design: Claire Seng-Niemoeller
Cover Design: William Boardman
Cover Art: Advertisement for twenty pounds reward for the capture of William Burns, printed in a Charleston, South Carolina newspaper, 1767 (print), American School, (18th century) / American Antiquarian Society, Worcester, Massachusetts, USA / Bridgeman Images
Composition: Achorn International, Inc.
Printing and Binding: RR Donnelley and Sons

Manufactured in the United States of America.

0   9   8   7   6   5
f   e   d   c   b   a

For information, write: Bedford/St. Martin's, 75 Arlington Street, Boston, MA 02116 (617-399-4000)

ISBN 978-1-319-02749-0

Acknowledgments

Acknowledgments and copyrights appear on the same page as the text and art selections they cover; these acknowledgments and copyrights constitute an extension of the copyright page. Text acknowledgments continue on page 356. It is a violation of the law to reproduce these selections by any means whatsoever without the written permission of the copyright holder. At the time of publication all Internet URLs published in this text were found to accurately link to their intended Web site. If you do find a broken link, please forward the information to history@macmillan.com so that it can be corrected for the next printing.

Preface

We live in an age of raw data. Every day we are bombarded with unexpurgated leaks, unfiltered images, and unedited texts. That access has fueled even our students' skepticism about how others—experts, officials, scholars, the press—use sources, and how they interpret and present them to us. Increasingly, we doubt the reliability of others' interpretation; we want to see the sources ourselves, whether we are studying the present or the past. *Going to the Source* recognizes that students need tools for interpreting historical sources, and that acquiring those tools can give students an appreciation for the ethical methods we all can use to produce trustworthy interpretations of documents.

Collections of historical documents can no longer claim to provide a pedagogical service simply by making primary sources from the past available to faculty and students. The problem students face today is not getting their hands on documents; the problem is learning how to sift through them, assess them, and understand them. *Going to the Source* is designed to assist teachers with that problem in at least three ways:

First, each chapter centers on a very specific event or definable era so that students can immediately see the importance of context when analyzing any document.

Second, each chapter offers only one type of source, such as newspaper articles, diaries, or song lyrics, so that students can focus on the qualities unique to each type of source. Each chapter is designed to expose students to historians' processes and to encourage active interrogation of the sources at hand. Toward that end, we include a chapter on how to use and interpret secondary sources. We also give students the opportunity to work with a variety of source types on one topic by providing a "capstone" chapter in each volume where students can engage in historical analysis on an issue that spans several decades and draws from the different sorts of documents discussed in earlier chapters.

Finally, the architecture of every chapter guides students toward a disciplined analysis of sources by offering a contextual introduction; a discussion of "Using the Source," which focuses on both the value and the limitations of the type of source in the given chapter; and a "Source Analysis Table," which offers an analytical grid intended to push students beyond the cherry-picking approach to data analysis that they instinctively distrust (but often replicate). "The Source" section then presents that chapter's selection of documents or images, followed by a set of analytical questions that can stimulate both written assignments and class discussion. The Source Analysis Tables for each chapter are available for download on the Instructor Resources tab on our catalog page: macmillanhighered.com/brownshannon/catalog.

Underscoring our message that document analysis demands understanding of the broader context, we conclude each chapter with two sections: "The Rest of the Story," which reveals later developments in the chapter's story and connects it to larger themes in U.S. history; and "To Find Out More," which points students to additional primary, secondary, and online sources for further study of that chapter's topic.

Two appendices give students an edge when writing papers, whether brief homework assignments or full-length research papers. Appendix I, "Avoiding Plagiarism," shows students how and why they need to keep track of sources, take careful notes, and acknowledge sources where appropriate. Appendix II, "Documenting the Source," provides guidelines and examples for following *Chicago Manual of Style* citation methods.

NEW TO THIS EDITION

This new edition of *Going to the Source* reflects several changes in the book's content and structure inspired by feedback we received from more than two dozen U.S. survey instructors. Each volume of this new edition offers one entirely new chapter topic and one chapter revised to include fresh sources. In Volume 1, a new Chapter 4 introduces students to the use of secondary sources by examining the material culture of the Great Lakes borderlands through a journal article from the *William and Mary Quarterly*. Chapter 5, now titled "The Sound of Rebellion," has been updated with five new songs from Revolutionary America. In Volume 2, a new Chapter 12 explores secondary sources by examining economic decline in the 1970s while demonstrating the value of historians' introductions in professional works of history. Chapter 4 has been streamlined to provide a broader view of ethnic females' experiences with settlement houses through three immigrant memoirs from the progressive era. We hope these revisions enhance the value of this reader for both faculty and students.

ACKNOWLEDGMENTS

We would like to thank the following reviewers who guided us in our revisions with their suggestions and comments: Elliott Bowen, Binghamton University; Margaret Brown, Brevard College; Mary Ann Caton, University of Pittsburgh at Titusville; Amy Curry, Lone Star College at Montgomery; Benjamin Dettmar, Adrian College; Neal Dugre, University of Houston-Clear Lake; Amy Foster, University of Central Florida; Aram Goudsouzian, University of Memphis; Martin Halpern, Henderson State University; Jay Hester, Sierra College; Dave Hochfelder, University at Albany; George Jarrett, Cerritos College; Greg Kaster, Gustavus Adolphus College; Kelly Kennington, Auburn University; April Merleaux, Florida International University; Matthew Osborn, University of Missouri-Kansas City; Kathryn Ostrofsky, Angelo State University; Emily Rader, El Camino College; Thaddeus Romansky, Sam Houston State University; Paul Rubinson, Bridgewater State University; Scott Stephan, Ball State University; Jeremy Vetter, University of Arizona; and Andrew Wehrman, Marietta College.

We extend our thanks to the editorial staff at Bedford/St. Martin's: Michael Rosenberg, publisher for history; Jane Knetzger, director of development for history; Bill Lombardo, executive editor; Emily DiPietro, our encouraging developmental editor for this edition; Tess Fletcher, the editor who patiently brought this edition into home port; Mary Posman, our deft editorial assistant; our copyeditor, Lisa Wehrle; the book's designer, Claire Seng-Niemoeller: and Lou Bruno, our efficient production editor. In thanking our current colleagues at Bedford we do not forget our previous editors, including Laura Arcari, Heidi Hood, and Sara Wise, and Michelle McSweeny whose work was so valuable in earlier editions. A very special thanks also to Katherine Kurzman, our original sponsoring editor. This book never would have happened without her impetus and the sponsorship of Charles H. Christensen, former president of Bedford/St. Martin's.

We have been greatly aided in our endeavors by the librarians at Gettysburg College, including Chris Amadure, Karen Drickamer, Linda Isenberger, and Susan Roach, as well as the Government Documents librarians at the University of Iowa, Marianne Mason and John Elson, and the staff in the archives section of the Minnesota Historical Society. Staff assistance from Rebecca Barth and Marna Montgomery is gratefully acknowledged, as is the advice we received from colleagues who answered questions and read drafts of chapters. We are particularly grateful to Brendan Cushing-Daniels, Tom Dublin, William Farr, Matt Gallman, Jim Jacobs, Mary Lou Locke, Gerald Markowitz, Barbara Sommer, Char Weise, Mark Weitz, and Robert Wright. The assistance of students and former students was invaluable in this project, and we owe much to Maggie Campbell, David Fictum, Katie Mears, April Mohler, Amy Scott, Lauren Rocco, and Meg Sutter.

Finally, of course, we owe thanks to our families, who encouraged us throughout this process and regularly offered much-needed relaxation from our labors. Thanks to Jim, Colleen, Caroline, Daniel, and both of our Elizabeths.

Victoria Bissell Brown
Timothy J. Shannon

About the Authors

Victoria Bissell Brown (Ph.D., University of California, San Diego) is Professor Emeritus, Grinnell College. In addition to editing Jane Addams's autobiography, *Twenty Years at Hull-House* for Bedford/St. Martin's, she is the author of *The Education of Jane Addams* and articles on Addams, on Woodrow Wilson and gender, and on female adolescents in the Progressive Era. She is currently working on a social history of the American grandmother in the twentieth century.

Timothy J. Shannon (Ph.D., Northwestern University) is professor of history at Gettysburg College, where he teaches Early American, Native American, and British history. His books include *Iroquois Diplomacy on the Early American Frontier*, *Atlantic Lives: A Comparative Approach to Early America*, and *Indians and Colonists at the Crossroads of Empire: The Albany Congress of 1754*, which received the Dixon Ryan Fox Prize from the New York State Historical Association and the Distinguished Book Award from the Society of Colonial Wars. He is also the editor of *The Seven Years' War in North America: A Brief History with Documents* for Bedford/St. Martin's. His articles have appeared in the *William and Mary Quarterly*, the *New England Quarterly*, and *Ethnohistory*.

Brief Contents

Contents

Sir Walter Raleigh: The Discovery of the Large, Rich and Beautiful Empire of Guiana, from 'Newe Weld un Americanische Historien,' by Johann Ludwig Gottfried, 1631 (litho), Bry, Theodore de (1528–98) (after) / Private Collection / The Stapleton Collection / Bridgeman Images.

Art Resource, NY.

The Connecticut Historical Society.

Hulton Archive/Getty Images.

8	**Family Values: Advice Literature for Parents and Children in the Early Republic** 160

Courtesy of Special Collections / Musselman Library, Gettysburg College.

© Photri / Topham / The Image Works.

12 The Illustrated Civil War: Photography on the Battlefield *245*

Library of Congress, Prints and Photographs Division.

Using the Source: Civil War Photographs   *248*

What Can Civil War Photographs Tell Us?   *249*

CHECKLIST: *Interrogating Photographs*   *253*

Source Analysis Table   *253*

The Source: Photographs of Civil War Battlefields and Military Life, 1861–1866   *256*

MILITARY PORTRAITS   *256*

1. "Lieut. Washington, a Confederate Prisoner, and Capt. Custer, U.S.A.," James F. Gibson, 1862   *256*

2. "Gen. Robert B. Potter and Staff of Seven, Recognized Capt. Gilbert H. McKibben, Capt. Wright, A.A.G. Also Mr. Brady, Photographer," Mathew Brady, c. 1863   *257*

3. "Portrait of a Soldier Group," photographer unknown, c. 1861–1865   *258*

4. "President Lincoln on Battle-Field of Antietam," Alexander Gardner, 1862   *259*

BATTLEFIELD LANDSCAPES AND CITYSCAPES   *260*

5. "Pennsylvania, Gettysburg 07/1863," Timothy O'Sullivan, 1863   *260*

6. "Ruins of Charleston, S.C.," George P. Barnard, 1866   *261*

AFRICAN AMERICANS IN MILITARY LIFE   *262*

7. "Portrait of Brig. Gen. Napoleon B. McLaughlin, Officer of the Federal Army, and Staff, Vicinity of Washington, D.C.," Mathew Brady, 1861   *262*

8. "Culpeper, Va. 'Contrabands,'" Timothy O'Sullivan, 1863   *263*

9. "African American Soldiers with Their Teachers and Officers," photographer and date unknown   *264*

BATTLEFIELD DEAD   *265*

10. "Antietam, Md. Bodies of Dead Gathered for Burial," Alexander Gardner, 1862   *265*

11. "A Contrast. Federal Buried; Confederate Unburied, Where They Fell on the Battle Field of Antietam," Alexander Gardner, 1862   *266*

12. "He Sleeps His Last Sleep," Alexander Gardner, 1862   *267*

Library of Congress, Prints and Photographs Division.

Library of Congress, Prints and Photographs Division.

Going to the Source

The Bedford Reader in American History

CHAPTER 1

Monsters and Marvels

Images of Animals from the New World

Sir Walter Ralegh was in deep trouble in 1595. An expedition he had led to South America in search of Manoa, a fabled city of gold in the continent's interior, had not gone as planned. Instead of finding a civilization with wealth and population to rival that of the Incas, he had sailed fruitlessly around the Orinoco River basin (in present-day Venezuela and Guyana), bumping into people who kept telling him that what he was looking for was around the next bend. As he returned home, Ralegh must have known that Queen Elizabeth I and the investors who had financed his expedition were not going to be happy. To keep their political and financial support, Ralegh would have to put the best possible spin on a bad situation.

Fortunately, he was up to the task. Shortly after returning to England, Ralegh published a narrative of his voyage titled *The Discoverie of the Large, Rich and Bewtiful Empyre of Guiana*. Ralegh might not have found Manoa, but he did capture the imagination of his readers. Within a few years, *The Discoverie* had been published in five languages throughout western Europe. Part of its appeal no doubt came from images that a German publisher named Theodore de Bry used to illustrate Ralegh's story. Readers could see Indians casting gold, decorating their bodies with the precious metal, and greeting Ralegh as their lord and friend. In word and image, the New World depicted by Ralegh was a ripe piece of fruit just waiting to be picked.

The Discoverie also included images of some of the animals and fantastical creatures that inhabited the New World. As with the scenes of the gold-laden Indians, these pictures illustrated passages from Ralegh's text. One scene depicted deer grazing along a riverbank while man-eating *lagartos* (alligators) swam nearby. Other exotic creatures included monkeys, manatees, and parrots, but the strangest of all were the *Ewaipanoma*, headless men "reported to have their eyes in their shoulders, and their mouths in the middle of their breasts . . . [with] a long train of haire grow[ing] backward between their shoulders." Ralegh admitted that he had not seen the *Ewaipanoma* himself, but he believed them to be real because so many of the local Indians "affirme the same." Nor had he personally met any *Amazones*, the tribe of warlike women who lived near the river named after them, but he relayed reports he had heard, perhaps a bit enviously, about their annual mating ritual with male neighbors. A map of Guiana included in Ralegh's narrative included depictions of the *Ewaipanoma* and *Amazones*, along with pictures of the armadillos, tigers, lions, deer, and "other sortes of beastes [fit] eyther for chace [i.e., hunting] or foode."

As Ralegh's book indicated, early European descriptions of the New World liberally blended fact with fiction. It comes as no surprise that explorers and colonizers trying to enrich their own reputations and bank accounts exaggerated the wealth of the land or the docility of the natives they encountered. They commonly depicted the oceans, rivers, and forests of the Americas as a new Eden teeming with natural bounty, but more was at work here than tall tales and outright lies. In some instances, Ralegh and his contemporaries described the creatures they found in the New World with the careful observation of a modern biologist, detailing an animal's anatomy, diet, and habits. At other times, they exhibited the pragmatism of an experienced survivalist: Could you eat this animal? What did it taste like? In other passages, these same writers appeared as gullible as children, ascribing magical powers or mythical origins to the creatures they encountered. It is easy for modern-day readers to understand why someone like Ralegh might have fabricated stories about Indians covered in gold; it is much harder to explain why his book also included pictures of headless warriors and man-eating sea monsters.

When Ralegh and his contemporaries wrote about the New World's environment, they relied on a mental framework inherited from Europe's medieval past. The best way to begin understanding that framework is to examine its vocabulary. The words early explorers and colonizers used to describe what they found in America are familiar to us today but had different meanings in their era. While we use "wonderful" and "marvelous" as synonyms for "good" and "pleasing," they used these words to describe things or events of such jaw-dropping strangeness that they could only be the handiwork of God. We tend to describe only positive things as a "marvel" or a "wonder," but Ralegh and his contemporaries applied these terms more broadly to mean anything extraordinary, be it good or bad. They also used "monstrous" to describe strange and grotesque deviations in the natural world, such as odd combinations of different animals into a single creature. What marvels, wonders, and monsters had in common was that they all testified to God's continuing intervention in his creation.

Another important component of Ralegh's mental world was the revival of classical learning in late medieval Europe. The artistic and intellectual movement known as the Renaissance dramatically changed how Europeans thought about the natural world. A key element of this transformation was the recovery, translation, and publication of ancient Greek and Roman texts on geography, biology, and philosophy that formed the foundation of the natural sciences in the Western world. Columbus's voyages to the New World were inspired by his reading of the Greek geographer Ptolemy, whose maps and writings were made available in print for the first time in 1477. Likewise, the Roman scholar Pliny the Elder's *Natural History* provided Renaissance Europeans with their most complete encyclopedia of the world's plant and animal life. When Columbus, Ralegh, and others sailed across the Atlantic, they relied on these ancient authorities to make sense of what they found there, but also recognized for the first time the limits of what the Greeks and Romans had known about the natural world. Pliny, for example, had described monstrous peoples very similar to the *Ewaipanoma* and *Amazones*, but nowhere did he mention an armadillo or many of the other exotic animals Ralegh found in South America.

Folklore also shaped how Europeans perceived the New World. Greek and Roman mythology provided many examples of mythical creatures whose bodies combined different animal and human parts and who were endowed with magical powers: Medusa, the snake-headed woman who could turn men to stone; the hydra, which could regenerate and multiply its heads; the chimera, a fire-breathing combination of goat, lion, and serpent. Many European explorers, when confronted with the strange anatomies and habits of American animals, described them as amalgams of different Old World animals that resembled these mythological beasts. Thus, one early description rendered an opossum as a "strange Monster, the foremost part resembling a Fox, the hinder a Monkey, the feet were like a mans, with ears like an owl, under whose Belly hung a great Bag, in which it carry'd the young." There was also a tradition in European travel literature of placing monstrous races of people at the edge of the known world. The most widely read travel narrative of Ralegh's time (he cited it as an authority) was authored by a thirteenth-century English knight known as Sir John Mandeville, who claimed to have traveled to the far corners of Asia, India, and Africa during the Crusades. Mandeville told of encountering many of the same monstrous peoples described centuries earlier by Pliny: Amazons, pygmies, cannibals, dog-headed men, and men with heads in their chests. Historians are now certain that Mandeville never existed, but the anonymous writer who fabricated his travels exerted a tremendous influence on Europe's imaginative perception of the New World.

Ancient scholarship, mythology, and folklore could go only so far in helping Ralegh and his contemporaries make sense of what they encountered in the Americas. Here was a world that contained marvels that Ptolemy, Pliny, and Mandeville had not known. Even Holy Scripture, Renaissance Europe's most authoritative text on creation, did not offer an explanation for America. If all humans had inherited the original sin of Adam and Eve, then why did Native Americans walk around naked without shame? If Noah's three sons and their wives had repopulated Africa, Asia, and Europe after the flood, then who were the biblical ancestors of the Americans? And how could the story of Noah's ark account for the innumerable new species of animals found on the other side of the Atlantic? The mere existence of America threw the inherited wisdom of the ages into question and encouraged a new spirit of inquiry and observation.

The monsters and marvels of the New World were a wonder in their own right, one that challenged the very foundations of all that Europeans knew about the world around them.

Using the Source: Images of Animals

The first images of the New World seen by Europeans were made possible by technological innovations in book publishing that had occurred in the decades preceding Columbus's first voyage to the Americas in 1492. Before the invention of the printing press in the mid-fifteenth century, books were a rare commodity in Europe. Monks and other trained copyists painstakingly reproduced important works one at a time. Such books are known as illuminated manuscripts because of the elaborate and colorful ink work that filled their pages, but they were rare and expensive, available to only the wealthy and learned.

The invention of the printing press changed all that. Movable type meant that books, maps, and other printed materials could be produced in greater quantities and at lower cost than previously imaginable. Furthermore, the efforts of religious reformers to translate the Bible from Latin into vernacular languages encouraged the growth of literacy, especially in regions where the Protestant Reformation took root. The expansion of Europe's trade with the outside world also created a market for consumer goods among merchants and other people with disposable income. All these changes brought books out of the monasteries and university libraries and into the retail stalls of urban printers and booksellers, and a growing number of people had the financial means and intellectual ability to make use of them.

Even the illiterate and semiliterate were drawn to these texts, especially if they contained images. In the medieval era, the Catholic Church had relied on all sorts of visual images and artifacts—paintings, sculptures, relics, stained glass—to convey spiritual messages to the faithful. That same visual tradition carried over into early book illustrations, which often borrowed symbols and scenes from religious art to convey their messages. Early book illustrations were generally of two types, woodcuts and engravings. As its name implies, a woodcut was manufactured by carving an image into a block of wood, inking it, and then pressing it to a piece of paper. Such images tended to be rudimentary, lacking detail and color, but unlike the illuminated manuscripts of the medieval era, they could be mass-produced; the same woodcut could produce hundreds, even thousands, of copies. In a similar manner, printers and artists engraved images on copper plates that could be inked and reproduced on paper. Copperplate engravings featured greater detail than woodcuts and gradually supplanted them as book illustrations. Some were hand-colored before being bound into books, creating images that rivaled illuminated manuscripts for their beauty.

Illustrating the New World animal life that Ralegh and other explorers described in their books presented a special problem to printers because they typically had no models from which to work. Live animals rarely survived the voyage back to Europe, and preserved dead ones usually ended up in the "cabinets of curiosities" maintained by wealthy collectors of such exotica. Some expeditions did include artists who drew or painted New World scenes, and if such works survived, they were occasionally reproduced as illustrations for books. Most often, however, the artist producing a woodcut or engraving had to apply his imagination to the words he read in a traveler's account, much like a police sketch artist who creates a visual image from a witness's spoken recollections. The results could be startling to the eye: grotesque or exaggerated features, monstrous combinations of human and animal body parts, even some beasts utterly unrecognizable then or now. These images, when examined alongside some of the written descriptions that inspired them, open a fascinating window into the European imagination as it struggled to make sense of the New World's environment.

What Can Images of Animals Tell Us?

If, as the old saying goes, a picture is worth a thousand words, then it demands the same critical eye and careful attention a historian brings to a written source. Images also have their own particular strengths and weaknesses as historical sources. Consider, for example, Figure 1.1, an image that appeared in an edition of Ralegh's *Discoverie* published by de Bry. The image was used to illustrate Ralegh's written description of the Orinoco River basin, which he called "the most beautifull countrie that ever mine eies beheld." Ralegh wrote of deer "feeding by the waters side," so tame that they seemed "used to a keepers call," as well as a "great store of fowle . . . of many sorts" and "divers sorts of strange fishes . . . of marvellous bignes." He also warned his readers about the "*lagartos*" (alligators), one of which had "devoured" a member of his party who had fallen into the water.

Although derived from a passage in Ralegh's text, this image elaborates on it in ways that show the imaginative license taken by de Bry, one of Europe's most prolific publishers of American scenes. De Bry has taken Ralegh's verbal description of a New World Eden and rendered it visually, with grazing deer and plump turkeys standing idly by as Ralegh's men move upriver. De Bry has also inserted some exotic animals not mentioned in Ralegh's narrative. The monkey was commonly associated with South America, but the ostrich was native to Africa (in other engravings, de Bry used ostriches to represent peacocks). The long-eared beast tucked behind a tree on the right appears to be a figment of de Bry's imagination. De Bry has rendered the river's left bank as a landscaped park, with trees planted in parallel rows. Most interesting of all, de Bry has chosen to present the *lagartos* as legless sea monsters. In earlier engravings, he had depicted alligators more realistically; perhaps his aim in this print was to link Ralegh's description of Guiana even more closely to the biblical account of Eden, in which evil took the form of a serpent.

When read as closely as Ralegh's text, de Bry's image tells us something about the artistic conventions used to present the New World to Europeans, about the pervasive influence of biblical themes in this art, and about the artists' willingness to play fast and loose with the facts to achieve a desired end. In such

Rows of trees create an open, parklike landscape

Turkey and deer suggest plentiful hunting

A monkey and ostriches indicate exotic animal life

A fish of "marvellous bignes"

What is this long-eared creature?

The *lagarto* that consumed one of Ralegh's men

Figure 1.1 *Untitled engraving from a Latin edition of Ralegh's* Discoverie, *depicting Ralegh and his men entering the Orinoco River.* Source: Sir Walter Raleigh: The Discovery of the Large, Rich and Beautiful Empire of Guiana, from 'Newe Weld un Americanische Historien,' by Johann Ludwig Gottfried, 1631 (litho), Bry, Theodore de (1528-98) (after) / Private Collection / The Stapleton Collection / Bridgeman Images.

images, realism took a backseat to eliciting awe, terror, or excitement from the viewer. Images of animals in early accounts of the New World also served as a sort of visual shorthand for conveying geographic information. Animals on maps indicated what natural resources were available to colonial enterprises. Plump turkeys, tame deer, and fish of "marvellous bignes" would help fill the bellies of hungry colonists, whereas beaver, bear, and deer would supply European markets with a new source of furs.

The disadvantages of using images of animals to study the European encounter with the New World derive mainly from the manner in which these images were produced. Europe's printing industry at the time of Ralegh and de Bry was centered in Germany and the Netherlands. Spain, which dominated the exploration and colonization of the Americas for the first two hundred years after Columbus, carefully guarded its growing knowledge of the New World. Much of what was published about the Americas during this period came to printers as hearsay, exaggeration, and fabrication (Ralegh being an excellent example). Images of New World animals show evidence of this loose grip on reality. They could also be heavily derivative of other sources. Making new woodcuts and copperplates was expensive and time-consuming; many printers cut costs by using old prints to illustrate new books or by borrowing willy-nilly from previous publications for their models. De Bry's work, most of which was published in the 1590s, was so influential that it was still being used by printers to illustrate books about the Americas two centuries later. Finally, it is worth noting that the people who knew the New World best, the Native Americans, never participated in the production of these images. In many respects, this source tells us much more about what Europeans hoped or expected to find in the New World than about what was actually there.

To get the most out of these images, you need to approach them critically and to take the same time with them that you would with a written source. As you work through the images on the following pages, you will want to keep in mind the questions in the Checklist below, which provide general guidelines for examining images as historical texts.

CHECKLIST: Interrogating Images

☐ When and where was the image published? In what kind of source did the image appear?

☐ What artist or printer published the image? Did the producer of the image have any inherent bias about the subject or any agenda to promote?

☐ What source did the artist use when creating the image: a painting or drawing? an oral or written account? a firsthand view?

☐ What is the artist trying to convey about the subject of the image? How is the artist using other elements in the image, such as perspective or background, to convey that information?

☐ Who was the audience for the image? What kind of response do you think the image elicited from its viewers?

Source Analysis Table

Once you have considered the basic questions about the image you are examining, turn your attention to the details of the subject being depicted. How would you describe the presentation of this animal or creature: realistic, grotesque, fantastic? What attributes does the image or its accompanying text ascribe to the beast? Does the image or its accompanying text convey a particular use for the animal, such as food, transportation, or medicine? What does the information conveyed in this image tell you about how Europeans perceived the New World's environment? The table on the following pages can help you organize your notes.

Source	Origin of the Image: Author/Artist, Date, Region the Animal(s) Inhabits	Distinguishing Characteristics of the Animal(s)	Potential Uses and Dangers of the Animal(s)
1. Succarath			
2. Hoga [Manatee]			
3. Whale			
4. Alligator			
5. Llama			
6. Birds and Fish of New England			

Source	Origin of the Image: Author/Artist, Date, Region the Animal(s) Inhabits	Distinguishing Characteristics of the Animal(s)	Potential Uses and Dangers of the Animal(s)
7. Animals of the Carolinas: *Buffalo*			
Opossum			
Rattlesnake			
8. Beaver			
9. The Vampire, or Spectre of Guiana [Vampire Bat]			
10. The Aboma Snake [Anaconda]			

The Source: Images of Animals from the New World

The images you are going to examine come from books about the Americas published in Europe between 1550 and 1800. They are arranged chronologically so that you can look for changes over time in the way European writers and artists described New World animals and their environment. Each image is also accompanied by some descriptive text about its subject excerpted from the source in which the image appeared.

1   *Succarath* (above right)

One of the earliest illustrated books about the New World was French geographer André Thevet's *Cosmographie universelle*, published in 1575. Thevet had traveled extensively in Turkey, Arabia, and Egypt, but his firsthand experience with the Americas was limited to a brief visit to Brazil in 1555, most of which he spent incapacitated by illness. He claimed to have visited North America on his voyage home from Brazil, but many of his peers thought him little more reliable than the fabled medieval traveler Sir John Mandeville. Thevet probably relied on reports and stories he gathered from sailors and fishermen for his descriptions of Mexico, Florida, and Canada.

Cosmographie universelle included descriptions of several exotic beasts of the New World, illustrated with woodcuts. One such creature was the succarath, which may have been a species of sloth. According to Thevet, it lived in Florida.

> There is also found another kind of beast (which for its rarity as well as for its deformity I should much dislike to omit) named by this people [local Indians] *Succarath* and by the cannibals *Su*. That animal mostly inhabits the banks of rivers and is rapacious, and is very strangely built, such as you see pictured above. If it is pursued, it takes its young on its back and covers them with its tail which is rather long and wide, and flees.

Source: André Thevet, *André Thevet's North America: A Sixteenth-Century View*, ed. Roger Schlesinger and Arthur P. Stabler (Kingston: McGill-Queen's University Press, 1986), 140–41.

2   *Hoga [Manatee]* (below right)

In his material on Mexico, Thevet included this description of a *Hoga*, an aquatic mammal. It was probably a manatee.

> It has a head and ears little different from a terrestrial pig, and five moustaches a half-foot long or thereabouts. . . . Its flesh is as tasty as that of the albacore of which I have already spoken. Formerly I had the skin of one in my cabinet, but because it was badly cured it was spoiled by vermin, which gave me the occasion to picture it for you here as I saw it from life. . . . This *Hoga* gives birth to its young alive as do whales and some others, which I have discussed previously. . . . If you look at it when it is frolicking [and] swimming in the water you would say that it is sometimes green, sometimes yellow, and then red like a chameleon. . . . It has many teeth and is ferocious, killing and devouring the other fish, even those twice as large as it is.

Source: André Thevet, *André Thevet's North America: A Sixteenth-Century View*, ed. Roger Schlesinger and Arthur P. Stabler (Kingston: McGill-Queen's University Press, 1986), 196–97.

Source: Courtesy of the John Carter Brown Library at Brown University.

Source: Courtesy of the John Carter Brown Library at Brown University.

Source: Courtesy of the John Carter Brown Library at Brown University.

3 *Whale*

Whalers and fishermen working off the coast of Canada and Newfoundland were some of the first Europeans to become familiar with the American environment. In his commentary on Canada, Thevet offered the following description to accompany an illustration of a female whale being slaughtered:

> The female of this Behemoth has only one little one at a time, to which she gives birth as do the quadrupeds, without eggs, contrary to the nature of all other fishes. Furthermore, the whale gives milk to her little whalelet once he is on the outside: and for this reason she has breasts on her stomach under the navel, which no other fish does either in the sea or in freshwater. . . .
>
> Moreover the whale is a dangerous beast for sailors to meet up with because of its hugeness. . . . I remember that when I was in the Antarctic it happened that a merchant who was going by boat from one land to another with fourteen sailors to trade was sunk by meeting up with this sea animal, which struck the boat with his tail and upset it in the depths of the sea, so that all of the men who were in it were lost except one who survived on a plank, who told us his story.

Source: André Thevet, *André Thevet's North America: A Sixteenth-Century View*, ed. Roger Schlesinger and Arthur P. Stabler (Kingston: McGill-Queen's University Press, 1986), 55–57.

4 | *Alligator*

This engraving is based on one originally published by the German engraver Theodore de Bry, who never visited the New World but whose monumental *Historia Americae*, published in fourteen volumes between 1590 and 1634, provided Europeans with their most widely circulated images of America before the eighteenth century. When possible, de Bry used paintings and drawings done by artists who had visited America as his models, but he also worked from textual descriptions and his own imagination.

De Bry's engraving and description of an alligator were based on the artwork and account of Jacques le Moyne, a Frenchman who had participated in an aborted attempt by French Protestants to colonize Florida in the 1560s. Europeans were familiar with African crocodiles, but those beasts seemed to pale in comparison to their monstrous American cousins.

> These creatures, driven by hunger, climb up out of rivers and crawl about on the islands in search of prey. When they find none they make such a ghastly noise that it can be heard half a mile away. At this moment the watchman calls the hunters who are in readiness. Grasping a pointed tree trunk ten or twelve feet long, they advance toward the animal, who usually crawls along with open mouth, and when he opens his mouth they quickly plunge the thinnest part of the pole into it in such a way that he cannot get it out because of the roughness and irregularity of the bark. Turning the crocodile over, they pound and pierce his belly, which is the softest part of his body, with blows from clubs and arrows. The backs of these animals, particularly those of the old ones, are impenetrable, covered as they are with hard scales. Such is the Indians' method of hunting the crocodile. These animals trouble them so much that they have to keep a watch against them at night and sometimes even in the day, as if they were guarding against some dreadful enemy.

Source: Erasmus Francisci, *Erasmi Francisci Guineischer und americanischer Blumen-Pusch* (Nuremberg: Christoph Gerhard, 1669), plate 1; and Michael Alexander, ed., *Discovering the New World: Based on the Works of Theodore de Bry* (New York: Harper and Row, 1976), 43.

Source: Courtesy of the John Carter Brown Library at Brown University.

5   *Llama*

De Bry's *Historia Americae* included an illustrated account of Peru adapted from the narrative of Spanish missionary José de Acosta. Like many European visitors to South America, Acosta was intrigued by the llama and its cousin the alpaca, both of which had been domesticated by native Peruvians, who used them for their wool and as beasts of burden. This description accompanied de Bry's engraving.

> A very particular sort of sheep exists in Peru, which the Indians called *llamas*. They used these animals to transport goods and silver from the mines, they ate their meat and used their wool for making blankets. These sheep were not expensive to keep because saddles were not necessary and they ate whatever they found in the fields. However, the llamas were supposed to be very stubborn. If they did not want to advance, nothing could be done save lie next to them for two or three hours until they were prepared to continue. If sometimes they refused to come down a mountain, and it was necessary to regain the merchandise they were transporting, they were shot so they would fall down the mountain.

Source: Michael Alexander, ed., *Discovering the New World: Based on the Works of Theodore de Bry* (New York: Harper and Row, 1976), 157.

Source: Courtesy of the John Carter Brown Library at Brown University.

Source: Courtesy of the John Carter Brown Library at Brown University.

6   *Birds and Fish of New England*

De Bry died in 1598, but his sons and grandsons continued publishing narratives and engravings under the family name. One author with whom they worked was Captain John Smith, the Englishman who had played an instrumental role in the founding of Jamestown, Virginia. Smith left Virginia in 1609, but he returned to North America several years later to map the coast of the region he named "New England." The de Bry family published Smith's travel narratives with engravings that illustrated his verbal descriptions of America's natural splendor.

> Here, in New England, nature and liberty furnish us freely that which in England costs us dearly. Men, women, and children, with a small hook and line, may take many kinds of excellent fish. . . . [H]e is a very bad fisher who cannot kill in a day with his hook and line one, two, or three hundred cod.
>
> For gentlemen, what exercise should more delight them than ranging daily these unknown parts for fowling, fishing, and hawking. And taking pleasure from seeing the wild hawks stoop six or seven times after one another in an hour or two at the fish in their fair harbours as those ashore at the fowl. For hunting, also, the woods, lakes, and rivers afford not only sufficient chase for those that enjoy such pleasure, but such beasts as not only are their bodies delicate food but also their skins are so rich that they will recompense a day's work with captain's pay.

Source: Michael Alexander, ed., *Discovering the New World: Based on the Works of Theodore de Bry* (New York: Harper and Row, 1976), 202.

7   *Animals of the Carolinas*

John Lawson, a native Englishman, arrived in Charles Town (present-day Charleston), South Carolina, in 1700 and spent the next ten years traveling throughout the Carolina backcountry, working as a surveyor, land speculator, and fur trader. In 1709, he returned to London, where he published a narrative titled *A New Voyage to Carolina*. It included a long section on the insects, reptiles, and mammals of North America, several of which were illustrated in an engraving for the book. He returned to Carolina in 1710 but was captured by Indians in a war that broke out shortly thereafter and was killed.

Lawson wrote with the detached tone of a scientist, but he was also fascinated by some of the oddities of New World animal life, including the buffalo, opossum, and rattlesnake.

Today we associate the buffalo with the American West, but in the colonial era, this beast ranged east of the Mississippi. Among other uses, Lawson believed it might be successfully crossbred with European cattle.

> 1. The *Buffelo* is a wild Beast of *America*, which has a Bunch on his Back. . . . I have eaten of their Meat, but do not think it so good as our Beef; yet the younger Calves are cry'd up for excellent Food, as very likely they may be. It is conjectured, that these Buffelos, mixt in Breed with our tame Cattle, would much better the Breed for Largeness and Milk, which seems very probable. . . . The *Indians* cut the Skins into Quarters for the Ease of their Transportation, and make Beds to lie on. They spin the Hair into Garters, Girdles, Sashes, and the like, it being long and curled, and often of chesnut or red Colour. These Monsters are found to weigh (as I am informed by a Traveller of Credit) from 1600 to 2400 Weight.

The opossum is the only marsupial indigenous to the Americas, and it was the first such animal encountered by Europeans. Travelers were fascinated by this animal's singular anatomy, which seemed to be such an odd amalgam of other beasts.

> 2. The *Possum* is found no where but in *America*. He is the Wonder of all the Land-Animals, being the size of a Badger, and near that Colour. The Male's Pizzle [penis] is placed retrograde; and in time of Coition, they differ from all other Animals, turning Tail to Tail, as Dog and Bitch when ty'd. The Female, doubtless, breeds her Young at her Teats; for I have seen them stick fast thereto, when they have been no bigger than a small Rasberry, and seemingly inanimate. She has a Paunch, or false Belly, wherein she carries her Young, after they are from those Teats, till they can shift for themselves. . . . They have no Hair on their Tails, but a sort of a Scale, or hard Crust, as the Bevers have. If a Cat has nine Lives, this Creature surely has nineteen; for if you break every Bone in their Skin, and mash their Skull, leaving them for Dead, you may come an hour after, and they will be gone quite away, or perhaps you meet them creeping away. They are a very stupid Creature, utterly neglecting their Safety. They are most like Rats of any thing.

The rattlesnake was another singular creature to Europeans. Observers such as Lawson were fascinated by how it gave a warning before striking by rattling its tail, and so it acquired a reputation for attacking only when provoked. Like his contemporaries, Lawson also believed this snake had hypnotic powers, which it used to charm its prey.

> 3. The Rattle-Snakes are accounted the peaceablest in the World; for they never attack any one, or injure them, unless they are trod upon, or molested. . . . They have the Power, or Art (I know not which to call it) to charm Squirrels, Hares, Partridges, or any such thing, in such a manner, that they run directly into their Mouths. This I have seen by a Squirrel and one of these Rattle-Snakes; and other Snakes have, in some measure, the same Power. . . . They cast their Skins every Year, and commonly abide near the Place where the old Skin lies. These Skins are used in Physick [medicine], and the Rattles are reckon'd good to expedite the Birth. The Gall [bile] is made up into Pills, with Clay, and kept for Use; being given in Pestilential Fevers and the Small-Pox. It is accounted a noble Remedy.

Source: John Lawson, *A New Voyage to Carolina* (London, 1709), 115–16, 120–21, 128–29.

8 *Beaver*

The beaver was indigenous to the Old World as well as the New, but by the time of Columbus it had been hunted to near extinction in many regions of Europe. Travelers' accounts from North America, therefore, made much of this creature's appearance and behavior. Europeans valued beaver fur, but they also saw these industrious creatures as model colonizers of the animal world because they worked cooperatively to alter the environment to their use, building comfortable homes and achieving group security.

Herman Moll, a German geographer and engraver living in London, captured this impression perfectly in an illustration he completed for a map of British North America in 1715. Moll based his description of the beavers' engineering skills on the accounts of French missionaries in the Great Lakes region.

> A View of ye [the] Industry of ye Beavers of Canada in making Dams to stop ye Course of a Rivulet, in order to form a great Lake, about which they build their Habitations. To Effect this: they fell large Trees with their Teeth, in such a manner as to make them come Cross ye Rivulet, to lay ye foundation for the Dam; they make Mortar, work up, and finish ye whole with great order and wonderfull Dexterity. The Beavers have two Doors to their Lodges, one to the Water and the other to the Land side. According to ye French Accounts.

Source: Herman Moll, "A New and Exact Map of the Dominions of the King of Great Britain on ye Continent of America" (1715), in *The World Discovered* (London, 1708–20).

The Cataract of NIAGARA, some make this Water-Fall to be half a League while others reckon it no more than a hundred Fathom.

Source: Courtesy of the John Carter Brown Library at Brown University.

Source: Courtesy of the John Carter Brown Library at Brown University.

9   *The Vampire, or Spectre of Guiana [Vampire Bat]*

John Gabriel Stedman was a Scottish mercenary who spent five years fighting rebellious slaves in Surinam, a South American sugar colony in the region Ralegh had originally called the "Empyre of Guiana." Like Ralegh before him, Stedman published a narrative of his South American sojourn, lavishly illustrated by engravings based on his own drawings. The quest for a city of gold was long dead; sugar and slaves had long since replaced *Ewaipanoma* and *Amazones* in European designs for this region. Stedman still had a keen eye for the monsters and marvels of the New World, one of which was the vampire bat.

> Waking about 4 OClock in my Hammock, I was Extremely Alarmed at Finding Myself . . . Weltering in Congealed Blood. . . . In Short the Mystery Was that I had Been Bit by the *Vampire* or *Spectre of Guiana* Also Call'd the *Flying Dog* of New Spain Which is no Other than a Monstrous Large Bat, that Sucks the Blood from Men and Cattle When they are a Sleep Sometimes till they Die; and as the Manner in Which they Proceed is Truly Wonderful I Will give an Account of it—Knowing by instinct that the Person they intend to Attack is in a very Sound Slumber they Pitch Generally near the Feet, Where, While they keep Fanning with theyr Enormous Wings to keep them Cool, they Bite a Small Piece out of The Tip of the Great Toe, Which Orifice is so Very Small that the Head of a Pin Could not be Received into it, And Consequently not painful, yet through which Opening they keep on Sucking Blood till they Degorge it, then begin Again and thus Continue Sucking And Degorging till they are Scarce Able to Fly and the Sufferer Sometimes Sleeps from time into Eternity.

Source: John Gabriel Stedman, *Narrative of a Five Years Expedition against the Revolted Negroes of Surinam,* ed. Richard Price and Sally Price (1796; Baltimore: Johns Hopkins University Press, 1988), 427–29.

Source: Courtesy of the John Carter Brown Library at Brown University.

10 | *The Aboma Snake [Anaconda]*

Stedman also described and illustrated several kinds of snakes he encountered in Surinam. The largest of these was the *aboma*, or anaconda. After
shooting one from his canoe, Stedman told of how a group of slaves slaughtered the beast.

> The negroe David having climb'd up a Tree with the end of a rope,
> let it down over a strong forked branch, and the other Negroes

hoisted the Snake up in the Suspence, this done David with a sharp knife between his teeth now left the Tree, and clung fast upon the Monster, which was still twisting, and began his Operations by ripping it up and stripping down the Skin as he descended, which though the Animal could now do him no hurt, I acknowledge had a terrible appearance . . . to See a Man Stark naked, black and bloody, clung with Arms and legs around the Slimy yet living Monster—however, his labour was not in vain since he not only dextrously finished the operation, but provided me with, besides the Skin, above 4 Gallons of fine Clerified fat or rather Oil . . . which I delivered to the Surgeons . . . for the use of the wounded Men in the Hospital . . . it being deem'd, particularly for Bruises, a verry excellent Remedy—at Signifying my Surprize to see the Snake still living after he was deprived of his Intestines and Skin, *Cramaca* the old Negro assured me, he would not die till after Sun Set.

Source: John Gabriel Stedman, *Narrative of a Five Years Expedition against the Revolted Negroes of Surinam*, ed. Richard Price and Sally Price (1796; Baltimore: Johns Hopkins University Press, 1988), 147–48.

Analyzing Images of Animals

1. What types of animals attracted the attention of European writers and artists? Judging from the examples you have seen here, what characteristics of an animal were most likely to catch a writer's or artist's attention?

2. What were some of the practical reasons Europeans had for paying attention to the animals of the New World? How do you think their perceptions of animals affected their overall interest in colonizing a particular region of the New World?

3. Which of the animals you have examined here reflect the European folklore of monstrous creatures? Do any of the verbal or visual depictions of these animals call to mind creatures from biblical accounts or ancient Greek or Roman mythology? Which of these animals were believed to have special powers? Were these powers generally helpful or harmful to humans?

4. Which of these creatures have anthropomorphic (humanlike) features or qualities? Why do you think early explorers and writers tended to anthropomorphize the new creatures they encountered?

5. Do these images reflect change or consistency in European perceptions of the New World and its natural environment over time? Does the tone of description or the visual presentation of animals change in any significant way between 1550 and 1800?

6. Imagine yourself as a semiliterate European contemplating migration to the New World in 1650. Explain how your exposure to these images would affect your decision. Based on these images, would you find one region more attractive than another? Why?

The Rest of the Story

Shifting political fortunes kept Ralegh from returning to South America for quite some time. In fact, he spent more than ten years locked up in the Tower of London after falling out of favor with Elizabeth I's successor, James I. Never one for small projects, Ralegh used the time to write another book, *The History of the World*. In 1616, he was freed from the tower so that he could lead another expedition to America, but the king forbade him from engaging in any hostilities with the Spanish. Nevertheless, Ralegh spent most of the expedition's time and resources unsuccessfully pursuing Spanish plunder. When he returned home empty-handed, he was arrested and executed for treason.

Monsters and marvels in the New World died much more slowly. As the images you have just examined indicate, the animal life of the Americas remained a source of European fascination for a long time. Gradually, however, the new science inspired by the Enlightenment changed the manner in which Europeans approached such phenomena. Tales of monsters and marvels gave way to more clinical descriptions by observers trained in scientific methods of observation. Swedish botanist Carl Linnaeus's system for classifying plant and animal life encapsulated a revolution in the way Europeans thought about nature in the eighteenth century, taking a world of wonders and turning it into an orderly universe in which every creature was somehow linked to another in a grand design. In the Linnaean system, there were no monstrous races or magical beasts living on the edge of the known world, only organisms awaiting their proper identification and classification.

An orderly environment was also one that could be mastered and exploited by humans. From the moment of their arrival, Europeans began altering the American environment by both intentionally and inadvertently introducing new plants and animals that had a profound effect on native species. Large domestic animals brought over by Europeans—cattle, horses, pigs, sheep, and goats—reproduced rapidly in an environment where they had few natural predators. The colonizers' search for "merchantable commodities"—goods that could be exported for a profit—also had a negative effect on indigenous animals. Codfish, whales, beaver, and deer were all hunted almost to the point of extinction for their value in the marketplace, and other species, such as the wolf, alligator, and rattlesnake, were attacked whenever possible because they threatened the newly arrived species, including humans. In some cases, local governments encouraged the destruction of such creatures by paying cash bounties, making them another source of the gold that had proved so elusive to Ralegh and his contemporaries.

The monsters and marvels of Europe's first contact with the Americas have never entirely left our consciousness. Thomas Jefferson, one of America's great Enlightenment thinkers, had his imagination set afire by the eighteenth-century search for the "American *incognitum* or Mammoth," an elephant-like beast that some of his contemporaries believed roamed the interior of the continent. Reports of its existence can be traced to the discovery of mastodon fossils in the Ohio Valley in the 1730s. More recently, we have sought our monsters and marvels in our own new worlds. As any number of science fiction films will attest, the beasts we conjure from the farthest reaches of space or the deepest depths of the ocean occasionally bear more than a passing resemblance to Thevet's Succarath or Stedman's Vampire.

To Find Out More

Images of America from the Age of Exploration

Alexander, Michael, ed. *Discovering the New World: Based on the Works of Theodore de Bry*. London: London Editions, 1976.

Brown University. *Archive of Early American Images*. http://www.brown.edu/Facilities /John_Carter_Brown_Library/pages/ea_hmpg.html.

George, Wilma. *Animals and Maps*. London: Secker and Warburg, 1969.

Honour, Hugh. *The New Golden Land: European Images of America from the Discoveries to the Present Time*. London: Allen Lane, 1975.

Virginia Historical Society. "Theodore de Bry's Engravings." *Early Images of Virginia Indians: The William W. Cole Collection*. http:// www.vahistorical.org/cole/debry .htm.

Secondary Sources on Early European Perceptions of America

Elliott, J. H. *The Old World and the New, 1492–1650*. Cambridge: Cambridge University Press, 1992.

Grafton, Anthony. *New Worlds and Ancient Texts: The Power of Tradition and the Shock of Discovery*. Cambridge, MA: Belknap Press, 1992.

Greenblatt, Stephen. *Marvelous Possessions: The Wonder of the New World*. Oxford: Clarendon Press, 1991.

Secondary Sources on Colonists, Indians, and Animals in the American Environment

Anderson, Virginia DeJohn. *Creatures of Empire: How Domestic Animals Transformed Early America*. Oxford: Oxford University Press, 2004.

Coleman, Jon T. *Vicious: Wolves and Men in America*. New Haven, CT: Yale University Press, 2004.

Crosby, Alfred W. *Ecological Imperialism: The Biological Expansion of Europe, 900–1900*, 2nd ed. Cambridge: Cambridge University Press, 2004.

Parrish, Susan Scott. *American Curiosity: Cultures of Natural History in the Colonial British Atlantic World*. Chapel Hill: University of North Carolina Press, 2006.

CHAPTER 2

Tales of Captivity and Redemption

North American Captivity Narratives

In the winter of 1675–1676, war raged across the New England frontier. Metacomet, a Wampanoag Indian known to the English as King Philip, led an uprising of several Algonquian tribes against English colonists in Massachusetts, Connecticut, and Rhode Island. The Indians had a number of long-standing grievances that led to this violence, including encroachment on their lands, attempts to subject them to English law, and unfenced colonial livestock destroying their cornfields. Indian war parties attacked frontier settlements, killing their inhabitants, burning homes and barns, and taking away as many captives as possible. Colonial militias responded with search-and-destroy missions against Indian communities. They, too, killed noncombatants, burned homes and crops, and took captives, most of whom they sold into slavery in the West Indies.

At sunrise on the morning of February 10, 1676, this brutal war came to the isolated town of Lancaster, Massachusetts. Its inhabitants were poorly prepared for the attack because many of the local men were off fighting with the militia elsewhere. Residents took refuge in their homes, but the Indians set the buildings on fire, forcing the occupants out into the open. Of the thirty-seven people who crowded into the home of the local minister, Joseph Rowlandson, twelve were killed in the raid and twenty-four were taken prisoner; only one escaped. Among the captives were the minister's wife, Mary, and her three children. She was immediately separated from the older two children, but the third, who had been wounded by a bullet that had also passed through Mary's side, remained in her arms. She described it as "the dolefullest day that ever mine eyes saw."

Many more doleful days lay ahead of her. For the next eleven weeks, Mary remained a captive of the Narragansetts who had raided her town. Her wounded child died not long after the attack, and she was forced to leave the corpse unburied. The pain from her own wound was compounded by hunger and physical exhaustion as her captors moved constantly to avoid the pursuing English. She sought consolation among other captives and read a Bible given to her as a piece of discarded loot, but her captors threatened her with beatings and death. Occasionally, they tormented her with false news of her husband's and other children's deaths. Mary's circumstances put her religious faith and identity to the test. She found herself eating food she had considered repellent before, at one point sinking so low as to steal a horse's hoof from the mouth of a small child. Denied the chance to worship among fellow Christians, she lamented time previously wasted smoking her pipe rather than being engaged in prayer. Eventually, she was sold back to the Massachusetts authorities in exchange for cash and goods raised by her family and friends. Six years later, she told her story in a short book titled *The Soveraignty and Goodness of God . . . Being a Narrative of the Captivity and Restauration of Mrs. Mary Rowlandson.*

Hundreds of other Europeans experienced Indian captivity in colonial America. Many, like Mary, were able to return to colonial society, either by escaping or by being ransomed by their captors. Others never returned. Some were quickly murdered for being too much of a burden to their captors on the trail home.

Figure 2.1 Title Page of a 1773 Edition of Mary Rowlandson's Captivity Narrative
Rowlandson's narrative first appeared in 1682, but it remained popular with New England readers throughout the colonial era. This 1773 edition featured an illustration depicting the Indians' attack on Rowlandson's home. The image of Rowlandson brandishing a musket is in sharp contrast to her self-portrait in the pages that follow as a patient and passive sufferer of God's will. Source: Fotosearch/Getty Images

Others survived the trek back to their captors' village only to be tortured and executed there. Still others were adopted, acquiring new names and clothes, living and working alongside their new kin, and even marrying Indian spouses. Although the use and fate of captives varied from one Indian culture to the next, captivity was the chief method by which native peoples converted enemies into members of their families and communities.

North American Indians practiced captivity long before they encountered Europeans, but the newcomers' arrival altered this practice in important ways. Captivity was part of the customs that governed Indian warfare. Indians warred to gain control of people, not to gain territory or to plunder. A successful war party returned home with minimal casualties of its own but with many captives, who could be distributed among the families of the community. Adult male captives could expect to be tortured to death in a ritualized process that allowed the community to vent its rage against its enemies or to mourn the loss of its own dead. Captives who were women or young children were prime candidates for adoption to replace deceased kin. Women capable of bearing children would be expected to take husbands and help replenish the community's numbers. Children would find themselves living among new relations, all of whom contributed to their upbringing as members of an extended family. Indians did not attach the same meaning to skin color and other physical differences as did Europeans; race did not affect how they dealt with colonial captives. Europeans, however, did pay ransoms to have captives returned, creating a new economic incentive for Indians to take them. European diseases and warfare also caused increased mortality among Indians, which in turn led them to rely even more heavily on captivity to replenish their populations.

In brief, Indians had many reasons for taking captives and many uses for them. Although some were tortured and killed and others were ransomed, many others were put to work and in time became productive members of Indian society. Rowlandson literally knit herself into her captors' community by sewing shirts and other articles of clothing for them. European observers were struck at how effectively Native Americans were able to turn colonial captives into "white Indians," so much so that when given the chance for repatriation to their former families and friends, some captives chose to remain with their newly adopted kin. Rowlandson may have described her captivity as a divine judgment ordained by God, but it may also be interpreted as her captors' cultural response to the European colonization of their homelands.

Using the Source: Captivity Narratives

Indian captivity narratives, like Mary Rowlandson's, made up one of the most influential and enduring forms of popular literature in early America. Such narratives had precedents in Old World tales of Christians held against their will in strange lands, such as Crusaders taken prisoner in the Holy Land or sailors enslaved in the Islamic kingdoms of northern Africa. Like those Old World tales, Indian captivity narratives emphasized the spiritual as well as physical trials of captivity. Pain suffered at the hands of an infidel enemy was only the physical manifestation of a soul in imminent peril of renouncing God or succumbing to despair. The moment of redemption, when the captive was finally delivered out of captivity, had a twofold meaning. Not only did it return the captive to the safety and security of home, but it also represented a renewed and strengthened faith. Indian captivity narratives provided American women with their first acceptable avenue of literary expression. Although both men and women penned such narratives, those featuring female captives were the best sellers and achieved the greatest notoriety for their authors.

Like any literary genre, Indian captivity narratives followed a format determined by a shared set of expectations between authors and readers. The narrative typically began, as Rowlandson's did, with a detailed description of the attack that resulted in the captivity. Plots then followed captives on a journey into the wilderness, where they experienced more violence, ate disgusting food, and contemplated escape. The farther the captive moved from home, the more she became familiar with her captors' way of life, shedding old clothes for new ones, learning a new language, and acquiring skills for survival. The author would periodically temper a newfound appreciation for the Indian way of life with professions of Christian faith and more evidence of Indian savagery. Variations in this format did occur, however. Some narratives were unrelenting in the hatred they expressed for Indians, whereas others offered stinging criticism of Christian hypocrisy. No two were exactly the same, and the genre varied between time and place.

What Can Captivity Narratives Tell Us?

The use of captivity narratives as a source for studying the European-Indian encounter offers two great advantages. First, they offer an insider's view of Indian cultures undergoing the profound stress and change of colonization. Captives were, of course, far from objective in their observations about Indian culture. For the most part, they shared the same prejudices and stereotypes about Indians as did other Europeans, but their experiences also offered uncommon insight into Indian communities. Some captives, especially those held for months or years, developed the language skills and kinship ties necessary to gain a deeper understanding of Indian life and in their narratives tried to correct misperceptions and biases Europeans held against native peoples. Others offered detailed descriptions of Indian rites of adoption seldom witnessed by other Europeans.

The second advantage to working with captivity narratives is the insight they provide into the captives' own cultures. Captivity narratives were the best sellers of their day, and they helped shape colonial American attitudes about Indians, the frontier, and history. What became known in the nineteenth century as Manifest Destiny—a God-given mandate to white Protestants to conquer North America and the other races that inhabited it—first found expression in captivity narratives from the colonial era. Overwhelmingly, colonial captives interpreted their experiences through the lens of their religious beliefs, relating their suffering to the captivity of the Jews in the Old Testament, describing Indians as agents of the devil, and attributing all to God's divine plan. Even Spanish and French captives, whose Catholic beliefs differed sharply from those of English Protestants, used their identities as Christians to explain their sufferings at the hands of their captors.

In other words, a close reading of a captivity narrative will reveal as much about the author's culture and beliefs as it will about the Indians he or she is observing. Consider, for example, this passage from Mary Rowlandson's narrative, which offers insight into not only the Narragansetts' marriage practices but also the Puritan values at the core of Rowlandson's identity.

> **The Indian male who claimed Rowlandson as his captive**
>
> My master had three Squaws, living sometimes with one, and sometimes with another one, this old Squaw at whose Wigwam I was, and with whom my Master had been those three weeks. Another was Wettimore, with whom I had lived and served all this while; A severe and proud Dame she was, bestowing every day in dressing her self neat as much as any of the Gentry of the land, powdering her hair, and painting her face, going with Neck-laces, with Jewels in her ears, and Bracelets upon her hands. When she had dressed her self, her work was to make Girdles of Wampum and Beads. The third squaw was a younger one, by whom he had two Papooses. . . . I understood that Wettimore thought that if she should let me go and serve with the old Squaw, she would be in danger to lose not only my service but the redemption-pay also. And I was not a little glad to hear this, being by it raised in my hopes that in Gods due time there would be an end of this sorrowfull hour.
>
> **Rowlandson's distaste for Wettimore's dress and bodily decorations**
>
> **Belts and sashes made from marine shells and trade beads**
>
> **Rowlandson's captors intend to ransom her**
>
> *Source:* Mary Rowlandson, *The Soveraignty and Goodness of God . . . Being a Narrative of the Captivity and Restauration of Mrs. Mary Rowlandson . . . The Second Addition, Corrected and Amended* (Cambridge, MA: Samuel Green, 1682), in *Narratives of the Indian Wars*, ed. Charles H. Lincoln (New York: Charles Scribner's Sons, 1913).

In this passage, Rowlandson's observations tell us something about the practice of polygamy among her captors. Her master had three wives, varying in age from old to young. Although most Indians in New England at this time would have had only one marriage partner at a time, such polygamous relationships were not uncommon as long as the husband had the resources to support multiple wives and their children. This arrangement may also have reflected the Indians' adaptation to an imbalance in their sex ratios, possibly caused by an increased mortality rate among young males from warfare. Of course, a historian would need more evidence to support such a conclusion, but when read in conjunction with other sources, captivity narratives provide important clues about how Native American lives changed in the wake of European contact. Rowlandson's Puritanism is also evident in this passage. Note how she equates Wettimore's "severe and proud" character with her elaborate clothing, bodily decoration, and jewelry. The Puritan notion of "providential affliction," a period of trial imposed by God to test the faith of his chosen people, is also evident in the way Rowlandson phrases her hope for redemption ("in Gods due time there would be an end of this sorrowfull hour").

Reading even a small sample of captivity narratives reveals some common disadvantages to working with them as a source. First, some narrators and editors are more reliable than others. Many captives were barely literate and so told their tales through editors or journalists who took considerable liberty with the text, inventing speeches or dialogue as if such words were remembered verbatim or massaging the details to maximize dramatic effect. Some narratives were published years after the experience of captivity, when the passage of time may have dulled some memories or exaggerated others. Separating fact from fiction in captivity narratives can be difficult. As with any source, a historian will seek other materials, such as Indian oral traditions or archaeological data, to corroborate conclusions derived from them.

Another significant disadvantage to working with captivity narratives concerns the type of captives who wrote them. Historians value the eyewitness accounts these narratives provide of Indian life, but those captives who were most assimilated into Native American communities—the ones who never returned to colonial society—rarely wrote narratives of their experiences. The longer a captive stayed with her captors, the more immersed she became in Indian life, learning a new language, acquiring new kin, and ultimately learning to view the world through Indian eyes. These same captives were the ones most likely to forget their native language, never acquire literacy, and lose connection with colonial society. Unless they were purposely sought out by journalists or publishers, their stories were not likely to be told in print. Conversely, many captivity narratives were published by escaped or ransomed captives who never spent more than a few weeks in Indian company. Compared with what long-term captives underwent, their experience amounted to little more than that of tourists on a particularly bad trip. Each captive has a unique story to tell, and, as with any historical source, you will want to examine the narratives with a critical eye. The Checklist questions on page 31 provide general guidelines for interrogating captivity narratives.

CHECKLIST: Interrogating Captivity Narratives

☐ Who is the author of the narrative? Was the captive male or female, and at what age was he or she taken captive?

☐ When was the captivity narrative written? How much time elapsed between the captivity itself and the writing of the narrative? Did the captive write it himself or herself, or did someone else put the captive's story into writing?

☐ What were the circumstances of the captivity? For example, among which Indian groups (i.e., tribes, bands, towns) did the captive live? What use did the captive serve for his or her captors? How was the captive treated? How long did the captivity last? How did it end?

☐ For whom was the narrative written? How do you suppose the narrative's readers reacted to it?

☐ What does the narrative tell you about Indian culture and society? About the captive's own values and attitudes? What biases can you detect in the narrative?

Source Analysis Table

When reading a set of captivity narratives, you will want to compare information about the captives' backgrounds as well as the circumstances of their captivity. You may not be able to determine the same level of detail for every narrative, but keeping track of the information you do have will help you construct a "group portrait" of the captives. The table on the following page will help you assemble this information.

Source	Date, Region, Duration of Captivity	Indians' Treatment and Use of the Captive	Information about Indian Culture	Captive's Values, Attitudes toward Indians
1. Cabeza de Vaca				
2. Jogues				
3. Rowlandson				

The Source: North American Captivity Narratives

The following sources are from three of the earliest North American captivity narratives. Although the vast majority of published captivity narratives were Anglo-American in origin, examples from Spanish and French sources will allow you to compare and contrast the experience of captivity across ethnic, religious, and regional lines.

1   *Alvar Nuñez Cabeza de Vaca,* 1542

Alvar Nuñez Cabeza de Vaca sailed from Spain in 1527 as part of an expedition to Florida. After a storm-tossed passage through the Caribbean and losses sustained from desertion and a hurricane, about three hundred men reached Tampa Bay in April 1528. They immediately fell prey to poor leadership, hostilities with Indians, and disease. Living at times as captives and slaves of local Indians, an ever-dwindling remnant of the expedition made its way along the Gulf Coast until, eight years later, Cabeza de Vaca and three other survivors crossed paths with Spanish slave raiders in northern Mexico. Cabeza de Vaca returned to Spain in 1537 to seek rewards from the king and told his story in a book published five years later.

Cabeza de Vaca's story shows the Indian captivity narrative in its infancy. In some passages, it reads like a medieval travel tale, full of fantastic adventures, whereas in others it resembles the field notes of an anthropologist visiting a foreign culture. Cabeza de Vaca's treatment as a captive also varied as he traveled. In some instances, he was beaten and starved; in others, he was treated with respect and generosity. Throughout his ordeal, he remained dependent on Indians for food, shelter, and security. The passage below describes his life and work among the Karankawan Indians on the Texas Gulf Coast.

On an island of which I have spoken,[1] they wished to make us physicians without examination or inquiring for diplomas. They cure by blowing upon the sick, and with that breath and the imposing of hands they cast out infirmity. They ordered that we also should do this, and be of use to them in some way. We laughed at what they did, telling them it was folly, that we knew not how to heal. In consequence, they withheld food from us until we should practice what they required. Seeing our persistence, an Indian told me I knew not what I uttered, in saying that what he knew availed nothing; for stones and other

---

[1] Cabeza de Vaca was at this time stranded on an island off the coast of Texas, probably near Galveston Bay.

Source: "The Narrative of Cabeza de Vaca," in *Spanish Explorers in the Southern United States, 1528–1543,* ed. Frederick W. Hodge (New York: Charles Scribner's Sons, 1907), 52–54, 76–78, 81–82.

matters growing about in fields have virtue, and that passing a pebble along the stomach would take away pain and restore health, and certainly then we who were extraordinary men must possess power and efficacy over all other things. At last, finding ourselves in great want we were constrained to obey; but without fear lest we should be blamed for any failure or success.

Their custom is, on finding themselves sick, to send for a physician, and after he has applied the cure, they give him not only all they have, but seek among their relatives for more to give. The practitioner scarifies[2] over the seat of pain, and then sucks about the wound. They make cauteries[3] with fire, a remedy among them in high repute, which I have tried on myself and found benefit from it. They afterwards blow on the spot, and having finished, the patient considers that he is relieved.

Our method was to bless the sick, breathing upon them, and recite a Paternoster and an Ave-Maria,[4] praying with all earnestness to God our Lord that He would give health and influence them to make us some good return. In His clemency He willed that all those for whom we supplicated, should tell the others that they were sound and in health, directly after we made the sign of the blessed cross over them. For this the Indians treated us kindly; they deprived themselves of food that they might give to us, and presented us with skins and some trifles. . . .

The next morning, many Indians came, and brought five persons who had cramps and were very unwell. They came that Castillo[5] might cure them. Each offered his bow and arrows, which Castillo received. At sunset he blessed them, commending them to God our Lord, and we all prayed to Him the best we could to send health; for that He knew there was no other means, than through Him, by which this people would aid us, so we could come forth from this unhappy existence. He bestowed it so mercifully, that, the morning having come, all got up well and sound, and were as strong as though they never had a disorder. It caused great admiration, and inclined us to render many thanks to God our Lord, whose goodness we now clearly beheld, giving us firm hopes that He would liberate and bring us to where we might serve Him. For myself I can say that I ever had trust in His providence that He would lead me out from that captivity, and thus I always spoke of it to my companions.

. . . The Indians told me to go and heal them, as they liked me; they remembered that I had ministered to them in the walnut grove when they gave us nuts and skins. . . . Coming near their huts, I perceived that the sick man we went to heal was dead. Many persons were around him weeping, and his house was prostrate,[6] a sign that the one who dwelt in it is no more. When I arrived I found his eyes rolled up, and the pulse gone, he having all the appearances of

---

[2] Makes shallow cuts.

[3] Instruments to burn the wound.

[4] Our Father and Hail Mary, Christian prayers.

[5] A fellow survivor of Cabeza de Vaca's expedition.

[6] Torn down.

death. . . . I removed a mat with which he was covered, and supplicated our Lord as fervently as I could, that He would be pleased to give health to him, and to the rest that might have need of it. After he had been blessed and breathed upon many times, they brought me his bow, and gave me a basket of pounded prickly pears.[7]

The natives took me to cure many others who were sick of a stupor, and presented me two more baskets of prickly pears, which I gave to the Indians who accompanied us. We then went back to our lodgings. Those to whom we gave the fruit tarried, and returned at night to their houses, reporting that he who had been dead and for whom I wrought before them, had got up whole and walked, had eaten and spoken with them and that all to whom I had ministered were well and much pleased. This caused great wonder and fear, and throughout the land the people talked of nothing else. All to whom the fame reached, came to seek us that we should cure them and bless their children. . . .

I bartered with these Indians in combs that I made for them and in bows, arrows, and nets. We made mats, which are their houses, that they have great necessity for; and although they know how to make them, they wish to give their full time to getting food, since when otherwise employed they are pinched with hunger. Sometimes the Indians would set me scraping and softening skins; and the days of my greatest prosperity there, were those in which they gave me skins to dress. I would scrape them a very great deal and eat the scraps, which would sustain me two or three days. When it happened among these people, as it had likewise among others whom we left behind, that a piece of meat was given us, we ate it raw; for if we had put it to roast, the first native that should come along would have taken it off and devoured it; and it appeared to us not well to expose it to this risk; besides we were in such condition it would have given us pain to eat it roasted, and we could not have digested it so well as raw. Such was the life we spent there; and the meagre subsistence we earned by matters of traffic[8] which were the work of our hands.

---

[7] Fruit of a cactus that was Cabeza de Vaca's main source of food.
[8] Trade.

2 | *Father Isaac Jogues, S.J.,* 1647

Father Isaac Jogues, S.J., was a Catholic missionary in Canada. In 1642, he was taken captive by Mohawk Indians while traveling with a party of Indian converts to a religious mission among the Hurons. Jogues spent several months among the Mohawks before escaping to the Dutch settlement at Fort Orange (present-day Albany, New York). From there he made his way back to France. His story was told in the 1647 edition of *Jesuit Relations*, an annual publication devoted to raising support for the French Catholic missionary effort in the New World. This passage describes the treatment Jogues and his fellow captives received en route to and on arrival at their captors' village.

All their men being assembled, and the runners having come back from their hunt for men, those barbarians divided among themselves their booty, rejoicing in their prey with great shouts of mirth. As I saw them engrossed in examining and distributing our spoils, I sought also for my share. I visit all the captives; I baptize those who were not yet baptized; I encourage those poor wretches to suffer with constancy, assuring them that their reward would far exceed the severity of their torments. I ascertained, on this round of visits, that we were twenty-two captives, without counting three Hurons killed on the spot. An old man, aged eighty years, having just received holy Baptism, said to the Hiroquois[1] who were commanding him to embark: "It is no more for an old man like me to go and visit foreign countries; I can find death here, if you refuse me life." Hardly had he pronounced these words when they beat him to death.

So there we were, on the way to be led into a country truly foreign. Our Lord favored us with his Cross. It is true that, during thirteen days that we spent on that journey, I suffered in the body torments almost unendurable, and, in the soul, mortal anguish; hunger, the fiercely burning heat, the threats and hatred of those Leopards, the pain of our wounds—which, for not being dressed, became putrid even to the extent of breeding worms—caused us, in truth, much distress. But all these things seemed light to me in comparison with an inward sadness which I felt at the sight of our earliest and most ardent Christians of the Hurons. I had thought they were to be the pillars of that rising Church, and I saw them become the victims of death. The ways closed for a long time to the salvation of so many peoples, who perish every day for want of being succored, made me die every hour, in the depth of my soul. It is a very hard thing, or rather very cruel, to see the triumph of Demons over whole nations redeemed with so much love, and paid for in the money of a blood so adorable.

[1] Iroquois. The Mohawks were the easternmost of the five Iroquois nations and inhabited present-day upstate New York.

Source: Reuben G. Thwaites, ed., *The Jesuit Relations and Allied Documents: Travels and Explorations of the Jesuit Missionaries in New France, 1610–1791* vol. 31 (Cleveland: Burrows Brothers, 1896–1901), 29–35, 39–45, 49–51.

Eight days after our departure from the shores of the great river of Saint Lawrence, we met two hundred Hiroquois, who were coming in pursuit of the French and Savages, our allies. At this encounter we were obliged to sustain a new shock. It is a belief among those Barbarians that those who go to war are the most fortunate in proportion as they are cruel toward their enemies; I assure you that they made us thoroughly feel the force of that wretched belief.

Accordingly, having perceived us, they first thanked the Sun for having caused us to fall into the hands of their Fellow-countrymen; they next fired a salute with a volley of arquebus[2] shots, by way of congratulation for their victory. That done, they set up a stage on a hill; then, entering the woods, they seek sticks or thorns, according to their fancy. Being thus armed, they form in line—a hundred on one side and a hundred on the other—and make us pass, all naked, along that way of fury and anguish; there is rivalry among them to discharge upon us the most and heaviest blows; they made me march last, that I might be more exposed to their rage. I had not accomplished the half of this course when I fell to the earth under the weight of that hail and of those redoubled blows. I did not strive to rise again—partly because of my weakness, partly because I was accepting that place for my sepulchre. . . . Seeing me prostrate, they rush upon me; God alone knows for how long a time and how many were the blows that were dealt on my body; but the suffering undertaken for his love and his glory are filled with joy and honor.

Seeing then, that I had not fallen by accident, and that I did not rise again for being too near death, they entered upon a cruel compassion; their rage was not yet glutted, and they wished to conduct me alive into their own country; accordingly, they embrace me, and carry me all bleeding upon that stage they have prepared. When I am restored to my senses, they make me come down, and offer me a thousand and one insults, making me the sport and object of their reviling; they begin their assaults over again, dealing upon my head and neck, and all my body, another hailstorm of blows. I would be too tedious if I should set down in writing all the rigor of my sufferings. They burned one of my fingers, and crushed another with their teeth, and those which were already torn, they squeezed and twisted with a rage of Demons; they scratched my wounds with their nails; and when strength failed me, they applied fire to my arm and thighs. My companions were treated very nearly as I was. . . .

After they had glutted their cruelty, they led us in triumph into that first village; all the youth were outside the gates, arranged in line—armed with sticks, and some with iron rods, which they easily secure on account of their vicinity to the Dutch.[3] Casting our eyes upon these weapons of passion, we remembered what Saint Augustin says, that those who turn aside from the scourges of God, turn aside from the number of his children; on that account, we offered ourselves with great courage to his fatherly goodness, in order to be

[2] A seventeenth-century gun.

[3] The Mohawks acquired iron and other metal goods from their trade with the Dutch at Fort Orange (present-day Albany).

victims sacrificed to his good pleasure and to his anger, lovingly zealous for the salvation of these peoples.

Here follows the order that was observed at that funereal and pompous entry. They made one Frenchman march at the head, and another in the middle of the Hurons, and me the very last. We were following one another at an equal distance; and, that our executioners might have more leisure to beat us at their ease, some Hiroquois thrust themselves into our ranks in order to prevent us from running and from avoiding any blows. The procession beginning to enter this narrow way of Paradise, a scuffling was heard on all sides; it was indeed then that I could say with my Lord and master, *Supra dorsum meum fabricaverunt peccatores*—"Sinners have built and left monuments and marks of their rage upon my back." I was naked to my shirt, like a poor criminal; and the others were wholly naked, except poor René Goupil,[4] to whom they did the same favor as me.

The more slowly the procession marched in a very long road, the more blows we received. One was dealt above my loins, with the pommel of a javelin, or with an iron knob, the size of one's fist, which shook my whole body and took away my breath. Such was our entrance into that Babylon. Hardly could we arrive as far as the scaffold which was prepared for us in the midst of that village, so exhausted were we; our bodies were all livid, and our faces all stained with blood. But more disfigured than all was René Goupil, so that nothing white appeared in his face except his eyes. I found him all the more beautiful as he had more in common with him who, bearing a face most worthy of the regards and delight of the Angels, appeared to us, in the midst of his anguish, like a leper. Having ascended that scaffold, I exclaimed in my heart, *"Spectaculum factisumus mundo et Angelis et hominibus propter Christum"*—"We have been made a gazing-stock in the sight of the world, of Angels, and of men, for Jesus Christ." We found some rest in that place of triumph and glory. The Hiroquois no longer persecuted us except with their tongues—filling the air and our ears with their insults, which did us no great hurt; but this calm did not last long.

A Captain exclaims that the Frenchmen ought to be caressed. Sooner done than it is said—one wretch jumping on the stage, dealt three heavy blows with sticks, on each Frenchman, without touching the Hurons. Others, meanwhile drawing their knives and approaching us, treated me as a Captain—that is to say, with more fury than the rest. The deference of the French, and the respect which the Hurons showed me, caused me this advantage. An old man takes my left hand and commands a captive Algonquin woman to cut one of my fingers; she turns away three or four times, unable to resolve upon this cruelty; finally she has to obey, and cuts the thumb from my left hand; the same caresses are extended to the other prisoners. This poor woman having thrown my thumb on the stage, I picked it up and offered it to you, O my God! Remembering the sacrifices that I had presented to you for seven years past, upon the Altars of your Church, I accepted this torture as loving vengeance for the want of love and

---

[4] A fellow Frenchman taken captive with Jogues.

respect that I had shown, concerning your Holy Body; you heard the cries of my soul. One of my two French companions, having perceived me, told me that, if those Barbarians saw me keep my thumb, they would make me eat it and swallow it all raw; and that, therefore, I should throw it away somewhere. I obey him instantly. They used a scallop or an oyster-shell for cutting off the right thumb of the other Frenchman, so as to cause him more pain. The blood flowing from our wounds in so great abundance that we were likely to swoon, a Hiroquois—tearing off a little end of my shirt, which alone had been left to me—bound them up for us; and that was all the dressing and all the medical treatment applied to them. . . .

Word was brought that some warriors, or hunters of men, were conducting thither some Hurons, recently taken. I betook me to the place as best I could. I consoled those poor captives, and having sufficiently instructed them, I conferred upon them holy Baptism; in recompense, I am told that I must die with them. The sentence decreed in the Council is intimated to me; the following night is to be (as they say) the end of my torments and of my life. My soul is well pleased with these words, but not yet was my God—he willed to prolong my martyrdom. Those Barbarians reconsidered the matter, exclaiming that life ought to be spared to the Frenchmen, or rather, their death postponed. They thought to find more moderation at our forts,[5] on account of us. . . . Life being granted us, they did us no more harm. . . . Some women, more merciful, regarded us with much charity and were unable to look at our sores without compassion.

[5] The Mohawks believed they could use Jogues and his compatriots as bargaining chips with the French.

3   *Mary Rowlandson,* 1682

The most famous Indian captivity narrative of the colonial era was Mary Rowlandson's, first published in 1682 with the encouragement of Puritan clergyman Increase Mather. It was the first North American captivity narrative with a woman as the central character and the first to be published as a book of its own, rather than as part of a larger travel narrative or collection of stories. It quickly went through several editions in Massachusetts and London. Today, scholars regard it as a classic of early American literature. The following passages describe the Indian attack on Rowlandson's home, her relationship with her captors, and her spiritual reflections on the ordeal.

Source: Mary Rowlandson, *The Sovereignty and Goodness of God . . . Being a Narrative of the Captivity and Restauration of Mrs. Mary Rowlandson . . . The Second Addition, Corrected and Amended* (Cambridge, MA: Samuel Green, 1682), in *Narratives of the Indian Wars*, ed. Charles H. Lincoln (New York: Charles Scribner's Sons, 1913), 119–22, 130–31, 150–51, 166–67.

Now is the dreadfull hour come, that I have often heard of (in time of War as it was the case of others), but now mine eyes see it. Some in our house were fighting for their lives, others wallowing in their blood, the House on fire over our heads, and the bloody Heathen ready to knock us on the head, if we stirred out. Now might we hear Mothers and Children crying out for themselves, and one another, "Lord, what shall we do?" Then I took my Children (and one of my sisters, hers) to go forth and leave the House; but as soon as we came to the door and appeared, the Indians shot so thick that the bullets rattled against the House as if one had taken an handfull of stones and threw them so that we were fain to give back.[1] . . . But out we must go, the fire increasing and coming along behind us roaring, and the Indians gaping before us with their Guns, Spears, and Hatchets to devour us. No sooner were we out of the House, but my Brother in Law (being before wounded, in defending the house, in or near the throat) fell down dead, whereat the Indians scornfully shouted, halloed,[2] and were presently upon him, stripping off his cloaths, the bullets flying thick, one went through my side, and the same (as would seem) through the bowels and hand of my dear Child in my arms. One of my elder Sisters children, named William, had then his Leg broken, which the Indians perceiving, they knockt him on the head. Thus were we butchered by those merciless Heathen, standing amazed, with the blood running down to our heels.

My eldest Sister being yet in the House and seeing those woefull sights, the infidels hailing mothers one way and children another and some wallowing in their blood, and her elder Son telling that her Son William was dead and my self was wounded, she said, "And, Lord, let me die with them." Which was no sooner said, but she was struck with a Bullet, and fell down dead over the threshold. I hope she is reaping the fruit of her good labours, being faithfull to the service of God in her place. . . . The Indians laid hold of us, pulling me one way, and the Children another, and said, "Come go along with us." I told them they would kill me. They answered, if I were willing to go along with them they would not hurt me. . . .

I had often before this said that if the Indians should come, I should chuse rather to be killed by them than be taken alive, but when it came to the tryal, my mind changed; their glittering weapons so daunted my spirit, that I chose rather to go along with those (as I may say) ravenous beasts than that moment to end my dayes. . . .

A certain number of us[3] got over the river that night, but it was the night after the Sabbath before all the company was got over. On the Saturday they boyled an old Horse's leg which they had got, and so we drank of the broth as soon as they thought it was ready, and when it was almost all gone, they filled it up again.

[1] Wished to retreat.

[2] Gave the war cry.

[3] Rowlandson is traveling with a band of her captors and fellow captives, who were mostly women and children.

The first week of my being among them I hardly ate anything; the second week, I found my stomach grow very faint for want of something; and yet it was very hard to get down their filthy trash, but the third week, though I could think how formerly my stomach would turn against this or that, and I could starve and die before I could eat such things, yet they were sweet and savoury to my taste. I was at this time knitting a pair of white cotton stockins for my mistriss[4] and had not yet wrought[5] upon a Sabbath day; when the Sabbath came they bade me go to work; I told them it was the Sabbath day, and desired them to let me rest, and told them I would do as much more to morrow, to which, they answered me, they would break my face. And here I cannot but take notice of the strange providence of God in preserving the heathen. They were many hundreds, old and young, some sick, and some lame, many had Papooses[6] at their backs, the greatest number at this time with us were Squaws, and they travelled with all they had, bag and baggage, and yet they got over this River aforesaid. And on Munday they set their Wigwams on fire, and away they went. On that very day came the English Army after them to this River and saw the smoak of their Wigwams, and yet this River put a stop to them. God did not give them courage or activity to go over after us; we were not ready for so great a mercy as victory and deliverance; if we had been, God would have found out a way for the English to have passed this River, as well as for the Indians with their Squaws and Children and all their luggage. *"Oh that my People had hearkened to me, and Israel had walked in my ways, I should soon have subdued their Enemies and turned my hand against their Adversaries,"* Psal. 81:13, 14.[7] . . .

My master[8] had three Squaws, living sometimes with one, and sometimes with another one, this old Squaw at whose Wigwam I was, and with whom my Master had been those three weeks. Another was Wettimore, with whom I had lived and served all this while; A severe and proud Dame she was, bestowing every day in dressing her self neat as much as any of the Gentry of the land, powdering her hair, and painting her face, going with Neck-laces, with Jewels in her ears, and Bracelets upon her hands. When she had dressed her self, her work was to make Girdles of Wampum and Beads.[9] The third squaw was a younger one, by whom he had two Papooses. By that time I was refresht by the old Squaw with whom my master was. Wettimore's Maid came to call me home, at which I fell a weeping. Then the old Squaw told me, to encourage me, that if I wanted victuals, I should come to her, and that I should lie there in her Wigwam. Then I went with the maid and quickly came again and lodged there. The Squaw laid a Mat under me and a good Rugg over me; the first time I had any such kindness shewed me. I understood that Wettimore thought that if she

---

[4] One of the wives of the Indian who took Rowlandson captive.

[5] Worked.

[6] Infants and young children.

[7] Rowlandson's narrative often cited biblical passages as commentary on her experiences.

[8] The Indian who had taken Rowlandson captive.

[9] Belts and sashes made from marine shells and trade beads.

should let me go and serve with the old Squaw, she would be in danger to lose not only my service but the redemption-pay[10] also. And I was not a little glad to hear this, being by it raised in my hopes that in Gods due time there would be an end of this sorrowfull hour. Then came an Indian and asked me to knit him three pairs of stockins, for which I had a Hat and a silk Handkerchief. Then another asked me to make her a shift,[11] for which she gave me an Apron.

[10] At this point, colonial agents were negotiating with Rowlandson's master a price for her return.

[11] A loosely fitted dress.

Analyzing Captivity Narratives

1. How does the information you have assembled on each of these captives affect your judgment of them as sources? Which narrator—Cabeza de Vaca, Jogues, or Rowlandson—do you consider most truthful or reliable? Why?

2. What roles did each of these captives play in the Indian communities they encountered? Why do you think those roles differed from one time or place to another? How do you think the personal background of the individual captive affected his or her treatment and incorporation into Indian society?

3. What do these captivity narratives tell you about the Indians' practice of taking captives? Do you see any evidence in these sources of how contact with Europeans changed the Indians' practice of captivity?

4. How did gender shape the captivity experience? Does Rowlandson's narrative differ from that of Cabeza de Vaca or Jogues in any significant way because she is a woman? Why do you think female captivity narratives came to dominate this literary genre?

5. In these narratives, do you see any significant differences in the way Spanish, French, and English captives interpreted their experiences? What role did religion play in shaping the captives' interpretation of their experiences?

6. Imagine that the Indians who held Cabeza de Vaca, Jogues, or Rowlandson captive had the opportunity to tell their story. Explain how their version might have differed from the one you have read.

The Rest of the Story

Captives who returned to their society of origin often faced a difficult transition, depending on the age at which they were taken and the length of time they stayed among their captors. Young children assimilated quickly into Indian society, forgot European languages, and were reluctant to leave adopted parents and kin. Captive women who took Indian husbands were also less inclined to seek repatriation because they correctly suspected that former friends and neighbors would view them as sexually polluted and any children they had by Indian husbands as racially degenerate.

Some former captives used skills and knowledge they had acquired from Indians to work as traders, interpreters, and go-betweens. Jogues, for example, returned to North America after a short stay in France. His familiarity with the language and customs of his former captors led the governor of Canada to send him as an envoy to the Mohawks. Jogues's adopted Mohawk kin welcomed him back, but others blamed him for a crop failure that coincided with his return and murdered him. Like Jogues, Cabeza de Vaca returned to America after an interlude in Europe, but not to the site of his captivity. He acquired a commission from the Spanish king to serve as a governor in South America. His career as a colonial administrator was almost as disastrous as his first American expedition. Political rivals had him jailed and sent back to Spain, where he died under house arrest in 1557. Of the three captives featured in this chapter, we know the least about what happened to Mary Rowlandson after her redemption. Her husband died not long after her return, after which she remarried and slipped quietly back into colonial life, a fate indicative of her status as a Puritan woman, but also ironic for the most famous Indian captive of the colonial era.

During the eighteenth century, the captivity narrative grew in popularity. Initially, Puritan captives like Mary Rowlandson dominated the genre, telling tales of spiritual trial and physical torment along the New England frontier. During the French and Indian War (1754–1760), the captivity narrative shed some of its regional distinctiveness. Tales of captivity from the Pennsylvania and Virginia frontiers did not place the same emphasis on spiritual introspection as had those that originated in New England. Instead, the narratives became more secular and much more graphic and violent, lingering over descriptions of torture, scalpings, and hair-raising escapes. By the 1790s, frontier warfare in the Ohio region had given rise to hundreds of sensationalistic accounts of captivity that demonized Indians and mixed fact with fiction. The success of these sensationalistic accounts inspired early American novelists such as Charles Brockden Brown and James Fenimore Cooper to incorporate captivity stories into their plots. As the nation's Indian wars moved westward, so too did the setting for captivity narratives, real and imagined. From dime-store novels of the Old West to films such as *The Searchers* and *Dances with Wolves*, the "white Indian" has remained a stock character in American arts and literature, used to illustrate the gap between Indian and European cultures as well as the constant desire to pass between them.

To Find Out More

Captivity Narrative Anthologies

Campbell, Donna M. "Early American Captivity Narratives." *Literary Movements*. Department of English, Washington State University. http://www.wsu.edu /~campbelld/amlit/captive.htm.

Derounian-Stodola, Kathryn Zabelle, ed. *Women's Indian Captivity Narratives*. New York: Penguin Books, 1998.

The Jesuit Relations and the History of New France. Library and Archives Canada. http:// epe.lac-bac.gc.ca/100/206/301/lac-bac/jesuit_relations-ef/jesuit-relations/index -e.html.

Vaughan, Alden T., and Edward W. Clark, eds. *Puritans among the Indians: Accounts of Captivity and Redemption, 1676–1724*. Cambridge, MA: Belknap Press, 1981.

Secondary Sources on Indian Captivity and Captivity Narratives

Axtell, James. "The White Indians of Colonial America." *William and Mary Quarterly*, 3rd ser., 32 (1975): 55–88.

Brooks, James F. *Captives and Cousins: Slavery, Kinship, and Community in the Southwest Borderlands*. Chapel Hill: University of North Carolina Press, 2002.

Demos, John. *The Unredeemed Captive: A Family Story from Early America*. New York: Knopf, 1994.

Foster, William Henry. *The Captors' Narrative: Catholic Women and Their Puritan Men on the Early American Frontier*. Ithaca, NY: Cornell University Press, 2003.

Haefeli, Evan, and Kevin Sweeney. *Captors and Captives: The 1704 French and Indian Raid on Deerfield*. Amherst: University of Massachusetts Press, 2003.

Namias, June. *White Captives: Gender and Ethnicity on the American Frontier*. Chapel Hill: University of North Carolina Press, 1993.

Pearce, Roy Harvey. "The Significance of the Captivity Narrative." *American Literature* 19 (1947): 1–20.

Richter, Daniel K. "War and Culture: The Iroquois Experience." *William and Mary Quarterly*, 3rd ser., 40 (1983): 528–59.

Socolow, Susan Migden. "Spanish Captives in Indian Societies: Cultural Contact along the Argentine Frontier, 1600–1835." *Hispanic American Historical Review* 72 (1992): 73–99.

CHAPTER 3

Colonial America's Most Wanted

Runaway Advertisements in Colonial Newspapers

Between 1759 and 1766, a man named Bood appeared three times in runaway advertisements placed by his master in the *New-York Gazette*, a colonial newspaper. The first advertisement, from June 21, 1759, described Bood as a "Mulatto" who ran away with "three Negroe Men." The four fugitives took with them extra shirts, breeches, shoes and stockings, two guns, two or three hatchets, and several blankets. William Hunt, who claimed Bood and one of the other runaways as his property, believed the four men had planned their escape together and would likely head for "the Indian Towns upon the Sasquehannah [Susquehanna River]" in frontier Pennsylvania, because Bood had lived among the Indians there for "several months, some years ago."

Bood showed up next in a runaway advertisement on May 26, 1763. His owner, Wilson Hunt (the same William Hunt as before, or perhaps a relative?), described Bood as "of a yellowish Complexion," and this time Bood ran away without accomplices or goods other than the clothes on his back. Hunt warned anyone who apprehended Bood that he was a "smooth Tongued Fellow" who would surely try to escape again "if not well secured."

On December 25, 1766, Bood made his last appearance in the *New-York Gazette* (see Figure 3.1 on p. 46). This time Wilson Hunt added to his physical description of Bood, noting that the runaway "has had the Small Pox" and "his great Toes have been froze, and have only little Pieces of Nails on them." Hunt repeated his warning about Bood's penchant for evading capture, "as he is a remarkable stout, cunning, artful Fellow."

The historical record is silent as to whether Bood was caught again, and we do not know if he lived the rest of his life in bondage or freedom. These three advertisements, however, paint a fascinating portrait of a man who constantly

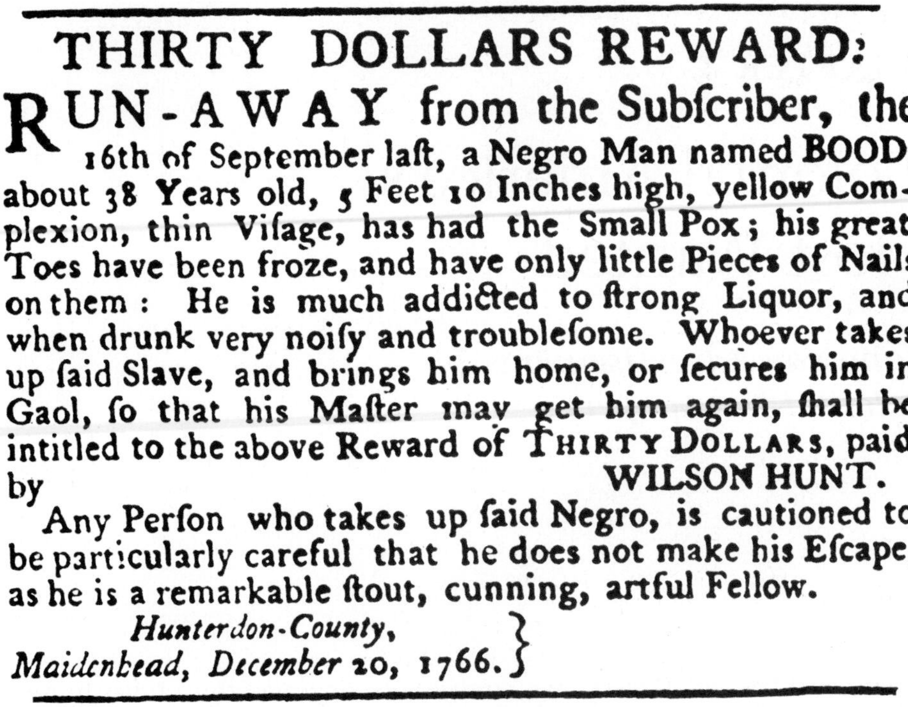

THIRTY DOLLARS REWARD:

RUN-AWAY from the Subscriber, the 16th of September last, a Negro Man named BOOD, about 38 Years old, 5 Feet 10 Inches high, yellow Complexion, thin Visage, has had the Small Pox; his great Toes have been froze, and have only little Pieces of Nails on them: He is much addicted to strong Liquor, and when drunk very noisy and troublesome. Whoever takes up said Slave, and brings him home, or secures him in Gaol, so that his Master may get him again, shall be intitled to the above Reward of THIRTY DOLLARS, paid by　　　　　　　　　　　　　　　　WILSON HUNT.

Any Person who takes up said Negro, is cautioned to be particularly careful that he does not make his Escape, as he is a remarkable stout, cunning, artful Fellow.

Hunterdon-County,
Maidenhead, December 20, 1766.

Figure 3.1 Runaway Advertisement from the New-York Gazette *This runaway advertisement appeared in the* New-York Gazette *on December 25, 1766. It is the last one in which Bood, a runaway from New Jersey, appeared. We do not know whether he was recaptured or remained free.*

resisted another person's effort to claim him as property. Moreover, Bood's story challenges the typical image of runaway slaves in American history, which depicts them as fugitives from cotton plantations in the Deep South running north to freedom. Nineteenth-century slave narratives and novels such as Harriet Beecher Stowe's *Uncle Tom's Cabin* have indelibly printed this image in the American mind, associating fugitive slaves with the coming of the Civil War. The Underground Railroad, with its secret network of "conductors" and "stations" that ferried runaway slaves to freedom, played an important role in the sectional crisis, but its story belongs to the nineteenth century. Before the American Revolution, slavery and servitude were legal throughout the colonies, and no clear geographic line or barrier separated freedom from bondage. When slaves such as Bood stole themselves, they were just as likely to run east, west, or south as north.

Bood's story also raises questions about the intersection of race, slavery, and servitude in eighteenth-century America. In each of the three advertisements placed for Bood, his master claimed him as property, but only in the last one did he refer to Bood as a slave. Many people lived and worked in eighteenth-century

America in a state of bondage; some were African slaves, but others were white indentured servants, apprentices, or convicted felons transported from the British Isles. The institutions of slavery and servitude were universal, and unfree laborers, whether servants or slaves, dominated the workforce. Black slaves and white servants toiled in the swamps of lowland Georgia, in the tobacco fields of Virginia, in workshops and iron forges in Pennsylvania, and in the homes and on the docks of Boston. Both called their bosses "master" and endured whipping as the most common form of discipline.

On the other hand, a clear racial barrier separated black slaves and white servants and made the conditions of their bondage different. Slavery was a hereditary, lifetime status that passed from mother to child. Servitude was contractual; people entered into it voluntarily, even convicts who chose it over the noose, for a fixed number of years. It was much harder for a runaway slave to pass unmolested into free society, and a suspected runaway slave faced much more severe punishment and fewer legal protections when apprehended than a white servant. A master could "outlaw" a runaway slave, giving license to others to kill the fugitive, but no such legal sanction existed for the murder of a runaway servant. Although the working lives of servants and slaves could be similar in many ways, race made the experience of running away much different for an African slave than for a white servant.

Using the Source: Runaway Advertisements

Few sources offer a more comprehensive or interesting look inside colonial American society than its newspapers. The first colonial newspaper appeared in 1690 in Boston, but it folded after one issue; a successful newspaper did not appear until the *Boston News-Letter* in 1704. Boston sustained its preeminence in newspaper publication throughout the colonial era, but during the 1720s newspapers appeared in New York and Philadelphia as well. The most significant growth in colonial newspapers occurred in the 1760s and 1770s. In 1764, there were twenty-three colonial newspapers; by the eve of the American Revolution, that figure had increased to thirty-eight.

Colonial newspapers were typically published once a week, on long sheets of paper that when folded in half, divided into columns, and printed on both sides made for four pages stuffed with information. Their publishers included local and international news they copied from other papers or received from private correspondents. As with modern newspapers, an important source of the newspaper's revenues was advertising. In columns of notices similar to the modern classifieds section, readers found announcements for the arrival and departure of ships, the importation and sale of goods, public auctions, and the like. Seaports such as Boston, New York, Philadelphia, and Charles Town were the nerve centers of colonial trade, and merchants and other business folk relied heavily on newspapers for this information. The smudged and tattered state of surviving editions of colonial newspapers testifies to their wide circulation and readership.

A common feature of colonial newspapers from Massachusetts to Georgia were advertisements for runaway servants and slaves, which numbered in the thousands. The ads could be found among other notices for lost or stolen goods, for debt collections and foreclosures, or for the sale of real estate, servants, slaves, or animals. One of the great advantages to reading these advertisements in their original context is to comprehend how casually colonial Americans bought and sold human laborers, subjecting them to public inspections and sales in the same way they traded livestock or any other goods. No one in colonial America thought it out of the ordinary to read an advertisement for a runaway servant or slave alongside one for a stray horse or to see a monetary reward offered for both.

Individually, these advertisements provide snapshots of men, women, and children who sought at least temporary respite from a life of working for others. Collectively, they provide scholars with a database that they can use to quantify the age, gender, place of origin, occupation, and destination of thousands of discontented workers who otherwise left no discernible trace in the historical record. By sampling runaway advertisements from a number of regions, you can recover the dynamics of unfree labor in colonial America: the living and working conditions of the slaves and servants, their relations with one another and their masters, and their masters' efforts to control their lives.

What Can Runaway Advertisements Tell Us?

By studying runaway advertisements, we can learn about the material circumstances of slaves and servants in colonial America and the physical and psychological tensions they had with their masters. The advertisements also tell us something about how masters viewed their human property, what physical characteristics and personality traits they attributed to them, and the techniques they relied on to recapture runaways and keep them in line.

The detailed descriptions of the runaways' physical appearance in such advertisements offer important clues about the day-to-day lives and material circumstances of the "lower sort" in colonial society: slaves and servants who lived and worked under the authority of someone else. The coarseness of the clothing these runaways wore serves as a metaphor for the hand-to-mouth existence so many of them endured. Likewise, descriptions of scars and physical disabilities are evidence of the dangers they endured from the elements, disease, malnutrition, hazardous working conditions, and brutal discipline meted out by their masters.

Runaway advertisements also offer a glimpse into the runaways' strategies and motives for resisting their masters. In many such advertisements, the master speculates about why the slave or servant ran away. Was the fugitive seeking a reunion with family members or perhaps trying to preserve a family that was about to be driven apart by the sale of a spouse or child? Labor was very scarce in colonial America. Many runaway advertisements hint that a servant or slave with a marketable skill—such as blacksmithing, woodworking, or seafaring—left to find more satisfactory work, perhaps at the instigation of another potential employer. Some advertisements, such as the one for Bood from the June 21, 1759, edition of the *New-York Gazette*, also indicate that runaways found living among neighboring Indians or backcountry settlements more appealing than their masters' accommodations; others suggest that runaways headed for seaports where they hoped to find work in workshops or on ships.

One disadvantage of working with runaway advertisements derives in part from the medium in which they appeared. Relatively few colonial newspapers existed before 1760, and those that did tended to be in northern cities, such as Boston, New York, and Philadelphia. Southern newspapers lagged behind northern ones in their founding and readership because the southern colonies lacked the urban centers and print shops necessary to sustain newspapers. New England had few servants and slaves but many newspapers; the colonies of the Chesapeake and Lower South had many slaves but few newspapers. The Middle Colonies had many servants and slaves as well as an active printing industry. Thus, historians interested in runaway advertisements have often focused their attention on New York, New Jersey, and Pennsylvania. Although this geographic bias shortchanges the southern colonies, especially before 1760, it does help shed light on the experience of northern and urban slaves and servants.

Another disadvantage is that runaway advertisements accounted for only a small portion of slaves and servants who ran away. Placing a newspaper advertisement cost money and required a master to post a reward and pay the charges of anyone who apprehended the runaway. Capturing a fugitive slave or servant was an expensive proposition, and many masters chose to wait a considerable time before placing a runaway advertisement in hopes that they would recover their property by some other means. Some slaves and servants used running away for short periods of time as a way of protesting their treatment or negotiating better working and living conditions. Such fugitives were less likely to be documented in runaway advertisements than those who absconded with stolen goods or left evidence that they were seeking permanent freedom. Masters were also less likely to post advertisements for runaways whom they did not consider worth the expense of retrieving. Therefore, runaway advertisements were more likely to describe valuable, skilled slaves and servants than old, sick, or unskilled ones.

Finally, in weighing the disadvantages of this source, one must consider that the advertisements' descriptions of the runaways came from the masters rather than the fugitives themselves. In composing advertisements, masters were anxious to dismiss any suggestion that a runaway's actions reflected mistreatment or abuse on their part. They were also inclined to attribute negative personality traits to the runaway in question. In the master's eyes, any servant or slave who ran away was by definition a person of questionable moral character. The standard words and phrases that masters used to describe runaways' personalities sound like a roll call of seven dwarfs Snow White would not want to meet: Surly, Insolent, Cunning, Lusty, Sour, Impudent, and Artful. In this respect, the advertisements do not tell us about the runaways themselves as much as they tell us about what their masters thought of them.

A review of even a small sample of runaway advertisements reveals a consistent pattern in their composition. This advertisement placed by Virginia slave owner Archibald Cary for three runaways in the *Virginia Gazette* on March 7, 1766, is typical of the style used in such ads. A close reading reveals important clues about the runaways' background, their relationship to one another, and their relationship with their master.

These runaways worked at an iron forge	RUN away from the subscriber's forge, on the 22d instant, at night, three Negro men; one of them named STEPHEN, by trade a carpenter, Virginia born, a black fellow, about 5 feet 8 or 9 inches high, very brisk and active, speaks quick, has a pleasant countenance, and walks very nimbly. Also NED, a fellow fire-man, a black fellow, remarkably well made for strength, about 5 feet 7 or 8 inches high, generally laughs when he speaks, has a large mouth, which is seldom shut, Virginia born, inclinable to be fat, has a sluggish walk, and broad shoulders. Also BRUMALL, a Gold Coast Negro, about the size and height of Ned; he is a fire-man, has remarkable broad shoulders, a roll in his walk, and had a hurt on his knee lately, from which he was lame a day or two before he went off; but whether any scar on it, I know not. Both the last mentioned fellows, have scars on their arms, from burns which they got by melted cinders flying on them when at work. Brumall is a yellow Negro, and has a very pleasant countenance. I can give no particular description of their clothes; I do not know of their carrying any more than their suits of cotton and osnabrugs. I will give £5 reward for each slave, if taken up in Virginia, and delivered to me; if in Carolina, £10 for each.	Born in coastal West Africa and therefore less familiar with colonial society
A skilled slave		
Born into slavery in North America and therefore assimilated into colonial society		The physical hazards these slaves faced in their work may have motivated their flight
Runaway advertisements often included details about the speech patterns of runaways, such as their proficiency with English or foreign languages, accents, or speech impediments		Suggests biracial parentage
		Suggests that someone other than Cary supervised these slaves
		Cary believes these slaves may have intended to run far from home

ARCHIBALD CARY

Details commonly found in runaway advertisements included the name, age, gender, ethnicity, and race of the fugitive, along with a description of his or her physical appearance and disposition followed by a description of the clothing he or she was wearing when last seen. Advertisements typically concluded with the offer of a reward for the fugitive's return and a warning against assisting the person in flight. More detailed advertisements provided a wealth of other information: occupations and skills; aliases, disguises, and motivations for running away; potential destinations or plans; distinctive habits or vices. As you work through the selection of runaway advertisements on the following pages, you will want to uncover these various details. In addition, the Checklist questions below provide general guidelines for examining print advertisements.

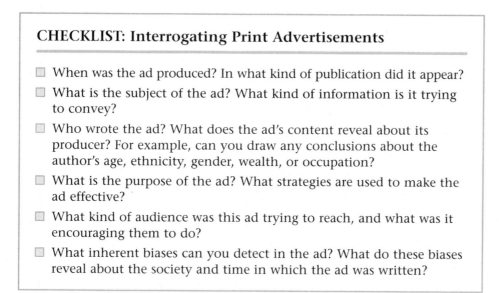

CHECKLIST: Interrogating Print Advertisements

☐ When was the ad produced? In what kind of publication did it appear?

☐ What is the subject of the ad? What kind of information is it trying to convey?

☐ Who wrote the ad? What does the ad's content reveal about its producer? For example, can you draw any conclusions about the author's age, ethnicity, gender, wealth, or occupation?

☐ What is the purpose of the ad? What strategies are used to make the ad effective?

☐ What kind of audience was this ad trying to reach, and what was it encouraging them to do?

☐ What inherent biases can you detect in the ad? What do these biases reveal about the society and time in which the ad was written?

Source Analysis Table

To get the most from using runaway advertisements as a source, it is helpful to devise a plan, such as the one in the following table, for classifying information. You can start by keeping track of the name, age, gender, and race of each runaway described. You can then look for more specific biographical information, such as proficiency in English and occupational skills, as well as information about the runaways' personalities and motives for pursuing freedom. After collecting information from many advertisements, you can begin to draw defensible conclusions about the experience of servitude and slavery in colonial America. The first two advertisements on the table on page 52 have been completed as examples.

	Number of Runaways	Runaway's Name	Servant or Slave	Ethnicity or Race	Sex	Age	Physical Features, Personality Traits, Occupational Skills, or Other Significant Information	Notes
Source 1	1	Quomino	servant	African	M	21	head half-shaved; speaks good English; carried away clothes and a scythe	carrying scythe as a weapon?
Source 2	1	Cuff	?	African	M	45	facial scars in "Negro Fashion"; could be carrying a forged pass	born in Africa?
Source 3								
Source 4								
Source 5								
Source 6								
Source 7								
Source 8								

Source 16	Source 15	Source 14	Source 13	Source 12	Source 11	Source 10	Source 9		
								Number of Runaways	
								Runaway's Name	
								Servant or Slave	
								Ethnicity or Race	
								Sex	
								Age	
								Physical Features, Personality Traits, Occupational Skills, or Other Significant Information	
								Notes	

53

The Source: Runaway Advertisements in Colonial Newspapers, 1747–1770

These runaway advertisements are reprinted in their entirety. They are arranged by region: New England, the Middle Colonies, the Chesapeake, and the Lower South.

As you will see, all runaway advertisements promised rewards, but it is hard to convert eighteenth-century values into their present-day equivalents. The colonies used a bewildering combination of monetary units they borrowed from the British and Spanish, not to mention their own paper currencies. Exchange rates varied substantially over time and between regions. The following table offers a roughly estimated conversion guide to help you understand the present-day equivalent of the reward amount most commonly cited in the advertisements you will read.

In 1766	1 pound (£) = in 2009 Dollars	£5 Reward = in 2009 Dollars
New England	$ 68.21	$ 341.03
Middle Colonies	$ 44.76	$ 223.78
Chesapeake	$ 76.55	$ 382.74
Lower South	$242.10	$1,210.51

Table based on values of local currency in 1766–1772 for Massachusetts, Pennsylvania, Virginia, and South Carolina listed in John J. McCusker, *How Much Is That in Real Money? A Historical Price Index for Use as a Deflator of Money Values in the Economy of the United States* (Worcester, MA: American Antiquarian Society, 1992), Table A-3, adjusted according to 2009 U.S. Consumer Price Index.

NEW ENGLAND

1   *Boston Evening-Post,* August 1, 1748

RAN away from his Master, John Allen, Merchant of Newton, a Negro Man named Quomino, about 21 Years of Age, a likely Fellow, of middling Stature, his Head shav'd half over, and speaks good English. Carried away with him, an Olive coloured Cloth Coat with Buttons of the same Colour, a new Jacket and Breeches, dark Cloth Colour, homespun, with Pewter Buttons on, two pair of Trousers, two Tow[1] Shirts, two Linnen Shirts, an old Bever Hat, and large Brass Buckles in his Shoes, &c. He also carried with him a Scythe.

    Whoever shall take him up and return him to his said Master, shall receive of him the Sum of Five Pounds, and all necessary Charges, in Old

---

[1] Fabric made from flax or hemp fibers.

Tenor Money[2]; and all Masters of Vessels are upon their Peril forbid concealing or carrying off said Servant.

NEWTON, JULY 26, 1748

[2] Paper currency used in Massachusetts.

2   *Boston Evening-Post,* May 19, 1755

RAN away from his Master William Bucknam, a Negro Man named Cuff, about 45 Years old, and pretty tall and slender, and has Scars on each Side of his Face, Negro Fashion,[1] and had on a streaked blue and white woollen Shirt, an under Jacket and Breeches, homespun woollen Cloth, streaked black and white about an Inch wide, mill'd Cloth; outside Jacket, homespun Kersey[2] grey colour'd, and grey yarn-Stockings, thick [illegible], worsted Cap, Felt Hat, and is suspected to have a forged Pass or Freedom for his Protection with him. Any Person that shall take up said Negro, and commit him to Gaol,[3] and secure the Papers, if any, and send me Tidings of the same, or to Messieurs Samuel Hewes and Son, Merchants in Boston, shall have Five Dollars Reward, and all necessary Charges paid. This likewise is to forbid all Masters of Vessels from carrying said Negro away.

FALMOUTH, APRIL 22, 1755   WILLIAM BUCKNAM

[1] A reference to ritual scarification found on slaves born in West Africa (also described as "country marks" in Source 14 on p. 61).
[2] Coarse woolen cloth from Yorkshire, England.
[3] Jail.

3   *Boston Evening-Post,* March 29, 1762

SIXTY DOLLARS Reward

RUN-away from Messi'rs Bodkin & Ferrall, of the Island of St. Croix,[1] on the 1st Day of July, 1760, a Negro Man named Norton Minors, is by Trade a Caulker and Ship-Carpenter, was born & bred up at Capt. Marquand's at Newbury,[2] who sold him to Mr. Craddock of Nevis,[3] from whom the above Gentleman bought him, is about 5 Feet 10 Inches high, about 30 Years of Age, speaks good English, can read and write, is a very sensible, smart, spry Fellow, has a remarkable bright Eye, he has been

[1] A Caribbean island.
[2] A Massachusetts port town.
[3] A Caribbean island.

seen at and about Newbury sundry Times since his Elopement.[4] Whoever takes up and secures the said Negro Man, so that he may be delivered to the Subscriber,[5] shall receive SIXTY DOLLARS Reward, and all necessary Charges paid by

BOSTON, MARCH 29, 1762   HENRY LLOYD

N.B. All Persons whatever are cautioned against harbouring or concealing said Negro, or carrying him off, as they may depend on being prosecuted with the utmost Rigour of the Law.

[4] Disappearance.
[5] The person placing the advertisement.

MIDDLE COLONIES

 Pennsylvania Gazette, November 26, 1747

RUN away the 22d instant, from James Greenfield, of Newlin township, Chester county, an Irish servant man named Robert Clinton, a weaver by trade. He is of middle stature, with black curled hair, swarthy complexion, and about twenty years of age. Had on when he went away, a new felt hat, a dark brown coat, green jacket, flaxen shirt, and fine stock, tow trowsers, black stockings, footed with brown worsted,[1] old brass shoes, with large brass buckles. He was enticed away by one Sylvester Eagon, an Irishman, by trade a weaver, and speaks very brogueish, but no servant. Whoever secures said servant, and sends word to his master, so as he may have him again, shall have Five Pounds reward, and reasonable charges, paid by

JAMES GREENFIELD

[1] Woolen fabric made in Worstead, England.

 Pennsylvania Gazette, July 8, 1756

RUN away on the 23rd of June last, from the subscriber, living in Vincent township, Chester county two Dutch[1] servants, husband and wife; the man named Jacob Hakaliver, about 24 years of age, 5 feet 4 inches high, has a pale complexion, and a down look: Had on and took with him, a coarse shirt and trowsers, a black coat, with white metal buttons on it, the fore skirts lined with red, an old

[1] When used in runaway advertisements from the eighteenth century, this ethnic designation usually refers to German-speaking servants from the Rhine River Valley.

blue jacket, old felt hat, and has no shoes; he has brown bushy hair. His wife is named Magdalen, a lusty woman, about 30 years of age, has fair hair and a sour look: Had on and took with her, an orange coloured linsey[2] bed-gown, three petticoats, one of linsey, striped red and brown, another of brown cloth, bound about the tail with black, and the third of black linen, a coarse shirt and apron, three black Dutch laced caps. She has with her a male child, named Michael, five months old, little of his age. They carried with them some bed clothes, and some Dutch books. Whoever takes up and secures said servants, so as their master may have them again, shall have Forty Shillings reward, and reasonable charges, paid by

ABRAHAM SMITH

[2] A wool-flax blend.

6   *Pennsylvania Gazette,* July 22, 1756

RUN away from the subscriber, living in Kent County, Maryland, two convict servant men; the one named Benjamin Shotton, a shoemaker by trade, about 5 feet 8 or 9 inches high, of a tawney complexion, large black beard, and curled hair; he is a talkative, pert, well-made fellow: Had on when he went away, An ozenbrigs[1] shirt, coarse country made trowsers, old brown cloth coat, with a cuff and slash sleeve, and broad metal buttons, old swanskin jacket, with red stripes, and an old beaver hat. He also got with him a pair of old fine blue broadcloth breeches, and probably has other clothes with him. He is a notorious villain, and this is the third time he has run away without the least reason. The other one is a young fellow, named Edward Phelps, about 22 years of age, a smooth faced fellow, about 5 feet ten inches high, slim made and thin faced, has light colour'd short hair, and a down look: Had on when he went away, An old white linen shirt, a country kersey jacket, a half-worn, dark colour'd, and almost black coat, trimmed with brass buttons with wood bottoms, ozenbrigs trowsers, and a pair of old pumps[2] much too big for him. He also took with him two new shirts, made of country linen. They have forged two passes; probably will change their names and cut their hair. Whoever takes up and secures abovesaid fellows, shall have Four Pistoles[3] reward, or two for each, paid by

THOMAS SMYTH

[1] Cheap linen made in Osnaburg, Germany.

[2] Thin-soled shoes.

[3] A Spanish coin commonly used in colonial North America.

7   *Pennsylvania Gazette,* August 11, 1757

Middletown, Monmouth County, East New Jersey, Aug. 1. 1757.
RUN away from the Subscriber the First of January, twelve Months past, a Negroe Man, named Cato, who has since his Elopement changed his Name several times: Had on when he went away, a Pair of Buckskin Breeches, fine brown Linen Shirt, a plain made whitish Camblet[1] Coat, dark Yarn Stockings, new Shoes, and a Wool Hat. He is a stout well set Fellow, understands Husbandry in all its Parts, an excellent Hand with a Scythe in Grass or Grain, speaks English as well as if Country born, and pretends to be free. Underneath his right-shoulder Blade he was branded in Jamaica when a Boy with the Letters BC, which are plain to be seen. He plays poorly on the Fiddle, and pretends to tell Fortunes. It is supposed he has a forged Pass. Whoever secures the said Negroe, so that his Master may have him again, shall receive a Reward of FIVE POUNDS and reasonable Charges, paid by

RICHARD STILLWELL

[1] A fabric made from different materials, including wool and silk.

8   *Pennsylvania Gazette,* November 29, 1764

RUN away from the Subscriber, in King and Queen, Virginia, two white indented Servants, a Man and his Wife. The Man is English, about 5 Feet 5 Inches high, of a red Complexion, wears his Hair, is much Sun-burnt, steps short and quick in his Walk, is a Brickmaker by Trade, and has a sett of Shoemaker's Tools; had a short red Coat, red Breeches with Metal Buttons, an old green lapelled Jacket, a Flannel Jacket with red Stripes, new Osenbrigs Trowsers, with other Clothes, as he stole Part of mine; his Name is James Marrington. His Wife is about 30 Years of Age, about 5 Feet high, very thick, looks well, and has got good Clothes; she is an Irish Woman, and her Name is Mary Marrington.

Run away likewise 4 Negroes, viz. Jack, a black thick Fellow, about 30 Years old, about 5 Feet 6 Inches high, speaks broken English, has been used to go by Water, but of late to Plantation Business; had on a blue Cotton Jacket and Breeches, Petticoat Trowsers, Stockings, Shoes with Buckles, and has a White-metal Button in his Hat. Dick, a dark Mulattoe, very lusty, about 25 Years old, about 5 Feet 8 Inches high, a Carpenter and Painter by Trade; had on Cotton Clothes, with Petticoat Trowsers, and he has got a red Jacket and Breeches, a good Felt Hat, and Buckles in his Shoes. Daniel, a well set black Fellow, about 5 Feet 10 Inches high, has been used to Plantation Business, and had on Cotton Clothes. Dorcas, a small Wench, about 5 Feet high, has been used to House Business, has got a new brown Linen Jacket and Petticoat, and sundry other Things that she stole. They have all large Bundles, as they stole several Sheets and Blankets, with other Things. They are supposed to be seen crossing from Point Comfort to Little River, in a small Boat, with a Blanket Sail, Last Saturday Morning, and I imagine will make for North-Carolina. Whoever apprehends the above Servants and Slaves, and delivers them to me, shall have Ten Pounds Reward, if taken in Virginia, if out thereof Twenty Pounds.

EDWARD VOSS

If the above Runaways are taken in Pennsylvania, and conveyed to Philadelphia, the above Reward will be paid by RITCHIE and CLYMER.

CHESAPEAKE

 9   *Virginia Gazette,* April 11, 1766

WARWICK county,
April 8, 1766.
RUN away from the subscriber, on or about the 10th of February last, a Virginia born Negro man named GEORGE AMERICA, about 5 feet 8 or 9 inches high, about 30 years old, of a yellow complexion, is a tolerable good shoemaker, and can do something of the house carpenters work, walks quick and upright, and has a scar on the back of his left hand; had on a cotton waistcoat and breeches osnbrugs shirt, and yarn stockings. As the said slave is outlawed,[1] I do hereby offer a reward of £5 to any person that will kill and destroy him, and 40s.[2] if taken alive.

THOMAS WATKINS

[1] An "outlawed" runaway slave was considered a threat to public safety, and he or she could be killed by another person without fear of legal prosecution.
[2] 20 shillings (s.) equaled 1 pound (£). Thus, in this advertisement, the reward for returning the runaway slave alive is £2, but the reward for killing him is £5.

10   *Virginia Gazette,* April 25, 1766

RUN away from the subscriber in Louisa county, the 24th of February last, 2 Negroes viz. POMPEY, a short thick fellow, 36 years old, Virginia born, very apt to wink his eyes quick, contract one corner of his mouth, and stammer in his speech when under any apprehension of fear; had on when he went away a cotton waistcoat and breeches, died of 2 brown colour, Virginia shoes and stockings; he carried with him some other clothes, but of what sort is not known; he pretends to something of the tailor's business, and sews well. ALICE, a tall slim wench, about 20 years old, and clothed in Negro cotton when she went away. Whoever secures them, or either of them, shall have 20s. reward, besides what the law allows, if taken in the colony and if out thereof 40s. They are both outlawed.

R. ARMISTEAD

11   *Virginia Gazette,* August 10, 1769

RUN away from the subscriber, in King & Queen county, a Negro man named BEN about six feet high, a very black fellow, his right knee so much bent in, that when he walks it knocks much against the other. Also, a Negro woman named ALICE, about five feet eight inches high, of a yellow complexion; and has remarkable large eyes. A few years ago she made an elopement, and passed for a free woman, in Williamsburg, and I suspect she may now do the like, or both of them attempt to get on board some vessel; if [this] should be the case, I beg of all persons they may apply to, to forward them (or either of them) to the most convenient gaol, and the gaoler is also begged to send an express immediately to the subscriber, which he will defray. As neither of those slaves have been ill used at my hands, I have had them outlawed in this county, and for their bodies without hurt, or a proper certificate of their death, a proper reward will be given; the fellow I suppose (for many reasons) will not be taken easily, as he has formerly made several overseers fear him.

EDWARD CARY

12   *Virginia Gazette,* May 31, 1770

RUN away from the subscriber, the first day of November last, (under pretence of suing for his freedom) a likely young fellow, named Bob, of a yellow complexion, slim made, near six feet high, has a remarkable down look, is a very good blacksmith, and, as supposed, is harboured by some white man of that trade. Whoever will bring the said fellow to my house in Dinwiddie county, near the court-house, shall receive a reward of FIVE POUNDS.

JOHN HARDAWAY

LOWER SOUTH

13   *Georgia Gazette,* May 26, 1763

Run away in January last, from my plantation near Savannah, A NEGROE called Primus, belonging to James Skirving, Esq; of Ponpon. As he has not been heard of since, I am apprehensive he might have gone away with a gang of Creek

Indians which were down at that time, or that he may be taken up by some of the back settlers, who, I am informed, frequently conceal runaway Negroes, and work them in their own fields, or change them in some of the northern colonies for horses; whoever delivers the said negroe to me, or gives information of his being concealed, shall be well rewarded; and whoever conceals him may expect to be prosecuted by

JOSEPH GIBBONS

N.B. He is a slim fellow, speaks tolerable good English, and had when he went away a new blanket, jacket and breeches.

14   *Georgia Gazette,* March 7, 1765

RUN AWAY FROM THE SUBSCRIBER
A YOUNG NEW NEGROE WENCH, named SIDNEY, has her country marks[1] on her breast and arms, and a mole under her left eye, talks no English, wore a blue negroe cloth gown and coat, a new oznaburg shirt, a cheque handkerchief on her head and another about her neck. A reward of TEN SHILLINGS will be given to any person who takes her up and delivers her in Savannah to

ELIZABETH ANDERSON

[1] See note 1 with Source 2, p. 55.

15   *Georgia Gazette,* January 14, 1767

RUN AWAY from the subscriber's brick-yard, the 19th August last, ONE NEW NEGROE MAN, named DAVID, of the Gambia country, about 5 feet nine inches high, can speak no English, has a large hole in each ear, had on when he went away a blanket, a hat, a pair of broad, cheque trowsers, and an old cheque shirt. Whoever takes up said negroe, and delivers him to me, or to the warden of the work-house, shall receive 40s. reward.

THOMAS LEE

16   *Georgia Gazette,* August 31, 1768

RUN AWAY from Mr. Robert Bradley's plantation at Pansacola, THREE NEW NEGROE MEN, called NEPTUNE, BACCHUS, and APOLLO, that can speak no English, and one STOUT SEASONED FELLOW called LIMERICK, speaks good English, and is very much marked on the back, &c. by severe whipping. It is imagined he has taken the conduct of the rest, and that they may have found their way through the Creek nation. Whoever takes up and will deliver the said Negroes, or any of them, to the Warden of the Work-House in Savannah, shall receive TWENTY SHILLINGS STERLING REWARD for each over and above all reasonable charges for bringing them any considerable distance from Savannah.

11TH AUGUST, 1768   T. NETHERCLIFT

Analyzing Runaway Advertisements

1. One striking feature of these advertisements is the detail they devoted to the physical appearance and dress of the runaways. Describe the composite portraits these advertisements paint of slaves and servants. What were the typical visual or spoken clues that indicated a person's status (slave, servant, or free)?

2. What evidence do these advertisements present of the techniques and strategies runaways used to make their way into free society? What skills or traits were helpful for doing so? Judging from the information conveyed in Sources 4, 12, and 13, who was likely to assist a runaway slave or servant, and why?

3. What types of racial and ethnic diversity are evident in the slaves and servants described in these advertisements? How does information about a runaway's place of origin (that is, born in America or elsewhere?) contribute to your understanding of his or her motive and method for running away?

4. Are there any significant differences in the structure and content of runaway advertisements from one region to another? If so, what do these differences tell you about regional variations in slavery and servitude in colonial America?

5. Where in these advertisements do you see evidence of different methods used to apprehend runaway slaves versus runaway servants? How was a runaway's race likely to affect the punishment he or she faced if caught?

6. Using what you have learned from these advertisements, compare the institutions of servitude and slavery in colonial America. In what ways were the worlds of servants and slaves similar? What were the most significant differences between them?

The Rest of the Story

The American Revolution changed the nature of unfree labor in North America. Indentured servitude gradually fell out of use in all regions after independence from Britain, in part because it was considered contrary to the democratic values of the new nation. Also, after 1790 the economy of the northern states began to industrialize, and wage labor gradually replaced other forms of labor in urban areas. Apprentices and journeymen, who in the colonial era typically received room, board, and clothing from their masters, now received cash payments instead. These wages allowed apprentices and journeymen to live independently of their masters' authority when not at work, but the wage economy also led to greater social and geographic segregation between employers and workers in the cities of nineteenth-century America.

The nature of slavery in the new nation also changed dramatically. Between 1780 and 1830, every state north of the Mason-Dixon Line, which divided Maryland and Pennsylvania, prohibited slavery within its borders. New York and New Jersey were the slowest in this regard, passing gradual emancipation laws that freed only slaves born after a certain date. As late as 1840, advertisements appeared in New Jersey newspapers for runaway slaves. Nevertheless, in the wake of the Revolution, slavery receded along with indentured servitude in the North.

Labor relations took a different course in the South. Southern states experienced a hemorrhaging of runaway slaves during the Revolution, but the invention of the cotton gin and expansion into new western territories after the war reinvigorated the plantation system. Rather than melting away as it had in the North, unfree labor in the South became the cornerstone of the new cotton economy. Runaway advertisements continued to appear in southern newspapers through the era of the Civil War.

During the 1840s and 1850s, runaway slaves became a political wedge between North and South. Free blacks and abolitionists encouraged slaves in the South to seek their freedom by fleeing north, and slave owners insisted that the federal government help them recover such human contraband. The United States Constitution included a fugitive slave clause (Article IV, Section 2) that prohibited states from passing laws that would confer freedom upon runaways from other states. In 1850, the federal Fugitive Slave Law strengthened the hand of slaveholders by denying accused runaways the right to trial by jury and by requiring U.S. citizens to assist federal marshals in apprehending runaways. Abolitionists and free blacks decried this law as a blatant violation of civil liberties, and even people unsympathetic to the plight of slaves found the law's extension of federal power repugnant, yet as long as there was slavery in America, slaves continued to challenge the institution by stealing themselves. Although the decision to run away was as singular as the person making it, the collective effect of runaways on the slave system is undeniable. Runaways made slavery less efficient and more costly, and their masters' efforts to recover them caused political repercussions that were not resolved until the Civil War.

To Find Out More

Runaway Advertisement Collections

Costa, Tom. *The Geography of Slavery Project*. University of Virginia. http://www.vcdh .virginia.edu/gos/. An archive of more than 4,000 runaway advertisements from Virginia and Maryland.

Hodges, Graham Russell, and Alan Edward Brown, eds. *"Pretends to Be Free": Runaway Slave Advertisements from Colonial and Revolutionary New York and New Jersey.* New York: Garland, 1994.

Meaders, Daniel, ed. *Advertisements for Runaway Slaves in Virginia, 1801–1820.* New York: Garland, 1997.

Smith, Billy G., and Richard Wojtowicz, eds. *Blacks Who Stole Themselves: Advertisements for Runaways in the* Pennsylvania Gazette, *1728–1790.* Philadelphia: University of Pennsylvania Press, 1989. Contains a small selection of runaway advertisements for servants.

Windley, Lathan A., ed. *Runaway Slave Advertisements: A Documentary History from the 1730s to 1790.* 4 vols. Westport, CT: Greenwood, 1983.

Colonial Newspapers (in General)

Accessible Archives. http://www.accessible.com/accessible. Provides full-text articles from eighteenth- and nineteenth-century American newspapers. By subscription only.

Brigham, Clarence. *History and Bibliography of American Newspapers, 1690–1820.* 2 vols. Worcester, MA: American Antiquarian Society, 1947. Identifies colonial newspapers according to region and time period.

Secondary Sources on Slavery, Servitude, and Runaways in Early America

Desrochers, Robert E., Jr. "Slave-for-Sale Advertisements and Slavery in Massachusetts, 1704–1781." *William and Mary Quarterly,* 3rd ser., 59 (July 2002): 623–64.

Franklin, John Hope, and Loren Schweninger. *Runaway Slaves: Rebels on the Plantation, 1790–1860.* New York: Oxford University Press, 1999.

Gomez, Michael A. *Exchanging Our Country Marks: The Transformation of African Identities in the Colonial and Antebellum South.* Chapel Hill: University of North Carolina Press, 1998.

Mullin, Gerald W. *Flight and Rebellion: Slave Resistance in Eighteenth-Century Virginia.* New York: Oxford University Press, 1972.

Parker, Freddie L. *Running for Freedom: Slave Runaways in North Carolina, 1775–1840.* New York: Garland, 1993.

Prude, Jonathan. "To Look upon the 'Lower Sort': Runaway Ads and the Appearance of Unfree Laborers in America, 1750–1800." *Journal of American History* 78, no. 1 (1991): 124–59.

Salinger, Sharon V. *To Serve Well and Faithfully: Labor and Indentured Servants in Pennsylvania, 1682–1800.* Cambridge: Cambridge University Press, 1987.

Waldstreicher, David. "Reading the Runaways: Self-Fashioning, Print Culture, and Confidence in Slavery in the Eighteenth-Century Mid-Atlantic." *William and Mary Quarterly,* 3rd ser., 56 (April 1999): 243–72.

CHAPTER 4

Material Culture of the Borderlands

An Article from the *William and Mary Quarterly*

Eighteenth-century Americans, whether European or Native American, rarely had their portraits painted by a first-rate artist. Such an opportunity arose, however, in 1776, when Guy Johnson and Karonghyontye traveled to London from Quebec on a diplomatic mission. Johnson was the British Crown's agent for Indian relations in the northern colonies. Karonghyontye (also known as Captain David Hill) was a Mohawk warrior with close ties to Johnson's family. Both men were part of a contingent of loyalist colonists and Indians who traveled to Britain at the outset of the American Revolution to seek aid from the Crown in fighting the rebellious patriots. In London, they met the painter Benjamin West, who was already well known for his works depicting Native Americans. West had Johnson and Karonghyontye pose for a dual portrait, and the finished product is widely considered to be one of the most striking paintings of his career (Figure 4.1).

In the portrait, Johnson is seated in the foreground, while Karonghyontye stands in a shadow behind him, pointing to a group of Indians near a waterfall in the background. Karonghyontye has an elaborately embroidered mantle (a type of cloak) draped around his body, and he wears wampum (marine shell beads made by Indians) around his wrists and neck and in his hair. In his right hand, he holds a long-stemmed Native calumet pipe, a symbol of peace. A knife sheath hangs from his neck. The rims of his ears have been partially severed and elongated in a style common among Native American males of his time and place. Johnson wears a fur robe around his upper body, as well as an eighteenth-century gentleman's jacket, waistcoat, neck cloth, and breeches. Native beadwork is evident in the sashes around his chest and waist and on the

Figure 4.1 *Benjamin West, Colonel Guy Johnson and Karonghyontye (Captain David Hill), 1776. Source:* Art Resource, NY.

cap that he holds in his right hand. On his lower legs, Johnson wears leather leggings held up by beaded garters and a pair of moccasins embroidered with Native quill work. Johnson's dress is a hybrid of European and Native American fashion, but below the knees, it is all Indian.

The Native American elements incorporated into Johnson's dress testified to his expertise in intercultural diplomacy. But Johnson's choice of footwear was hardly exceptional among Europeans who lived along the Great Lakes frontier of North America at this time. Moccasins were an item of Indian dress that colonists adopted into their own dress without hesitation. Manufactured from commonly available materials such as deer skins, moccasins had an elegantly simple design and were much less expensive to produce than the heeled boots or shoes made by European shoemakers. When waterproofed, they were also better suited for the all-weather extremes of the North American climate. The appeal of moccasins to Europeans did not end with their utilitarian value. Although colonists usually wore moccasins unadorned with the bead and quill work evident in the West portrait, they still made them objects of fashion. In Canada, they became part of the distinctive dress associated with *habitants*, the French-speaking settlers of the St. Lawrence Valley, and during the early nineteenth century, New England merchants marketed them to middle-class consumers as healthy footwear for walking outdoors. The story of the moccasin, in short, is one of adoption and innovation between Native and European peoples in early America, illustrating in material form how one culture borrowed and adapted from another.

The fur trade represented an important economic relationship between Native Americans and Europeans; Natives traded animal pelts and hides for manufactured goods, such as woven cloth, metal wares, and alcohol. This type of analysis emphasizes the technological differences between Native and European cultures: Indians became dependent on European goods produced on an industrial scale, which led them into debt and dispossession as the animal populations they relied on dwindled from overhunting. In this interpretation of the fur trade, change over time is unilateral and overwhelmingly negative: a technologically advanced group exploits the labor and resources of a less sophisticated one, leaving the latter mired in poverty and dependence.

Some objects from the fur trade tell a different, more nuanced story. This approach does not deny the obvious technological and economic disparities between Natives and Europeans, but it does illuminate how each side borrowed and adapted from the other, and thereby created new styles of dress, new methods of production, and even new ideas or values that were unique products of this encounter. Along the borderlands of early America, where Native and European peoples mixed with one another but neither side possessed unchallenged power over the other, the fur trade facilitated all kinds of intercultural exchange. Native Americans used items acquired from fur traders to dress in a manner that colonists called the "Indian fashion," an eclectic mixture of Native and European clothing that colonial observers associated with the Indians' pride of appearance. In another example, colonial blacksmiths produced for

Indian customers a combined smoking and striking device known as a pipe tomahawk. This fascinating object combined European iron-making technology with the Native American practice of smoking tobacco to create something that gave material form to the diplomatic metaphors of "taking up the hatchet" and "smoking the peace pipe."

Like these examples, the humble moccasin is a fit subject for closer study. As an object associated with the early American fur trade, it illustrates the material and cultural exchange that occurred between Native and colonial peoples along early America's borderlands. It also suggests the multilayered meanings human beings associate with material objects as they produce and use them. Moccasins were and remain a popular form of footwear in North America, but when we examine their production, distribution, and use at one particular place in time, they also tell us a surprising story about the economic origins of the city of Detroit.

Using the Source: Journal Articles

Historians interested in material culture need to use objects as they would any other source, and so often end up working with museum and archaeological collections, as well as with visual materials such as paintings, drawings, or advertisements. In the same manner that other historians use written texts to study the past, these historians read objects to recover what they can tell us about the people who created them. Was the item handmade or produced by a machine? What does the item tell us about how women and men divided work within their society? Did the object's makers and users invest it with any spiritual value or significance? These are all questions that historians use to unlock the meaning of objects within a particular time, place, and set of social relations. Of course, a student interested in material culture may not have the same access to such materials as a professional scholar and so may want to use what historians call "secondary sources." "Primary sources" are any sources that provide first-hand information about the topic you are studying (you have already encountered some of these in the form of woodcuts and engravings, captivity narratives, and runaway advertisements). Secondary sources are the result of a historian's interpretation of those primary materials, and they are most commonly found in the form of books and journal articles.

Within the historical profession, journals have long served the role of featuring the "breaking news" of the field, highlighting new scholarship, calling attention to new books, and providing a forum for current debates. Most of these journals are quarterlies, meaning that they are published four times a year. They typically feature two to three articles, book reviews, and sometimes round-tables in which historians offer opinions about a common topic. Articles in scholarly journals are the front lines of new historical interpretations, and a provocative article can often generate more excitement and controversy in the profession than a book, which takes much longer to reach its intended audience. If you want to jump into the middle of an argument between historians or to learn what the most recent scholarship has to say about a long-standing topic, reading an article in a history journal is a great place to start.

The article excerpted in this chapter first appeared in the *William and Mary Quarterly*, a journal of early American history, in April 2012. Its author, Catherine Cangany of the University of Notre Dame, uses material culture analysis to examine the role moccasins played in Detroit's economic development. Her work is an excellent example of how historians use a wide variety of sources to study material culture, as well as how they use journal articles to ask new questions and breathe life into old and familiar topics. Cangany is not the first scholar to take an interest in the fur trade, the Great Lakes borderlands, or even the footwear worn by the people who lived there, but by tying these three avenues of inquiry together, she does tell us something new about Detroit's growth from an isolated trading post to a center of industrial-style production, challenging and revising conventional wisdom about borderland economies along the way.

What Can Journal Articles Tell Us?

In our fast-paced society, it may seem strange that historians rely on quarterly journals as a method of engaging one another in conversation about the latest research in their fields. The scholarly journal persists, however, because it has important advantages over other forms of organizing and publishing historical scholarship.

First and most important, scholarly journals are peer-reviewed, which means that articles published by historians in scholarly journals undergo a rigorous editing process. The author of the piece and the reviewers who decide whether it merits publication remain anonymous to each other to ensure that all articles published in the journal are evaluated by experts in the field, working as freely as possible from the prejudices and biases that might result if they knew the author's identity. While no review process is foolproof, this method allows readers of a scholarly journal to assume that all of its article have met professional standards about research, documentation, and writing. You cannot make the same assumption about the "history" you find on the Internet. Although many Web sites that present historical sources or materials are vetted by professional organizations or editors, many others are not. Doing historical research on the Internet requires you to evaluate carefully the trustworthiness of the content you find there. When you read an article from a scholarly journal, that work has already been done for you.

A second advantage to working with scholarly articles is that they are concise. Generally, an article published in a history journal will run from 20 to 30 pages. Books written by historians, on the other hand, might run anywhere from 150 to 1,000 pages. Historians write articles and books to accomplish different things: an article is brief and to the point, focused on illuminating a particular question or topic; a book allows room for developing a narrative or synthesizing material with far greater chronological breadth or analytical depth. A good researcher will recognize the merits of each format and use articles and books accordingly. Scholarly articles, because of their brevity and focus, can be especially helpful to you in the early stages of your research, when you are casting your net for potential sources widely and trying to decide what to keep and what to throw back.

The third advantage of using journal articles in your research is that their documentation can lead you to the sources you will want to look at next. The quality of documentation on a Web site claiming to contain historical scholarship can vary widely, depending on the creator of the site. All scholarly journals, on the other hand, insist that their authors document their work. The footnotes that accompany a journal article offer you a road map to other sources that might be helpful in your research. Part of the architecture of any article in a history journal is a review of the relevant scholarship that has preceded it. Within the first few footnotes of an article, its author will identify the most significant previous articles or books on the topic and then situate his or her work in relation to it. Historians are avid footnote readers: they are always interested in seeing what new sources the author has identified or what previous interpretations the author is trying to refine or discredit. If you take the time to pay attention to an article's documentation, you will quickly identify the interpretive issues that occupy historians on any given topic.

The chief disadvantage to working with a journal article or any other secondary source is that someone else is interpreting the facts for you. In one sense, the author has done you a service by identifying, collecting, and analyzing the relevant materials — no small task, even for a thirty-page article — and synthesizing them into a persuasive argument. However, the author has done that in response to his or her own research question; in all likelihood, you will have a different one.

One other disadvantage of working with journal articles is that they often assume that the reader is already familiar with the topic at hand. Historians publish articles in scholarly journals to engage in conversation with one another. The authors of journal articles will assume that their readers bring some prior knowledge to the topic and are ready to plunge into finer points of interpretation and analysis. If you find yourself reading an article that has not provided you with enough background information, you may want to read up on the topic first in a textbook, encyclopedia, or other reference work.

Disadvantages aside, a journal article offers an excellent model for writing about history, and students can improve their own writing by paying close attention to how historians organize and present their arguments in their articles. For example, the introduction to any piece of persuasive writing must complete certain tasks. It must acquaint the reader with the topic at hand and provide necessary background information, articulate the author's research question, and present the thesis, a brief statement of the argument the author intends to prove. The following excerpt from Cangany's introduction gives the reader a concise forecast of her article's argument.

In turn, the business of moccasins challenges our understanding of eighteenth-century borderlands. It demonstrates one facet of the hybrid culture that existed on a number of North American frontiers, including at Detroit. Con-current with Detroit's establishment in 1701, the town's earliest colonists, including soldiers, fur traders, and farmers, appropriated native footwear. As new population groups arrived, the practice increased; by the 1780s virtually all types of residents, regardless of race, class, or gender, were wearing mocca-sins. Colonists who otherwise assumed European and European-style dress and customs and who had access to European shoes consciously chose to wear this component of native dress, for practical as well as political reasons.

The author situates Detroit as part of a larger "borderlands" frontier

A quick summary of the article's "who, what, when, and where"

The moccasin business also illustrates that Detroit was no mere cultural, political, or economic go-between. Although this particular manufacturing story, played out in a British colony long thought to have had no manufacturing, confirms on one level Detroit's ties to both "frontier" and "empire," it also establishes the town's status as an independent operator, one that capitalized on components of both west and east to capture some degree of commercial autonomy. The process of appropriating a western clothing item, modifying it to reflect its own cultural and aesthetic preferences, putting it through European-style manufacturing paces, and then shipping it east to supply an increasingly clamoring clientele was one way in which Detroit attempted to accomplish this.

The author connects her story about moccasins to a larger argument about Detroit's economic transformation from trading post to manufacturing center

Source: Catherine Cangany, "Fashioning Moccasins: Detroit, the Manufacturing Frontier, and the Empire of Consumption, 1701–1835," *William and Mary Quarterly*, 3rd ser., 69 (April 2012): 267.

Students are sometimes reluctant to challenge or question the argument a historian makes in an article or a book because they do not believe they have the expertise to do so, but you do not need a Ph.D. to distinguish good history from bad. When you read a journal article, think of yourself as a jury member listening to an attorney argue a case in court. Consider whether the argument is logical and whether the evidence offered supports it. The Checklist questions below will help you approach any journal article in a critical way by identifying its argument and evaluating its evidence.

CHECKLIST: Interrogating Journal Articles

☐ When was the article published?

☐ Who wrote the article, and what are the author's credentials?

☐ What research question does the author pose in the introduction?

☐ What is the author's thesis? What types of evidence does the author present to support the thesis? Is that evidence appropriately documented?

☐ What weaknesses or flaws do you find in the author's argument?

☐ What is the wider significance of the author's conclusion?

Source Analysis Table

The following table will help you identify and summarize the argument in Catherine Cangany's article. First, write down the research question and thesis she presents in the article's introduction. Then, as you read the article, take notes on how the production and consumption of moccasins changed over time.

Research Question:

Thesis:

Years	How Were Moccasins Produced?	Who More Moccasins?
1701–1780		
1780–1810		
1810–1835		

The Source: An Article from the *William and Mary Quarterly*, April 2012

Fashioning Moccasins: Detroit, the Manufacturing Frontier, and the Empire of Consumption, 1701–1835
by Catherine Cangany

During the final days of Odawa leader Pontiac's 176-day siege of Fort Detroit in 1763, an early winter settled over the town. Among those waiting out the long attack inside the beleaguered fort was John Montresor, a British military engineer stationed there. Two days after the siege broke on October 31, Montresor fired off a letter to fellow engineer Henry Bassett, stationed at Fort Pitt. In the letter Montresor recounted the end of the siege, worried that Pontiac and his allies might regroup in Illinois, and fretted over Britain's stake in the fur trade. He reviewed, in other words, Britain's political and economic relationships with local Indian groups. But at the close of the letter, there is a startling reminder that the cultural influences of the fur trade cut many ways. Remarking on the unseasonable winter grasping at Detroit, Montresor recorded of his fellow soldiers, "we are now in Snow in Blanket Coats & Mocasins."[1]

Although metropolitan military officials might have blanched at this picture of Montresor and his comrades sporting nonregulation winter apparel, Bassett, in rural Pennsylvania, and settlers in and around Detroit would have found nothing out of the ordinary in the moccasins' appearance. Indeed, by 1763 the appropriation of moccasins by nonnative peoples was a pervasive, century-old practice found throughout many of the borderlands of eastern North America: Bassett himself may well have been wearing moccasins while reading Montresor's message. But in Detroit the practice developed beyond mere appropriation. Almost certainly, the moccasins worn by Montresor and his comrades were manufactured and purchased within the town of Detroit. Moreover, their creation, from production to distribution, was likely overseen by Detroit's Euro-American residents. In the ensuing decades, as that process became increasingly routinized, moccasins manufactured in Detroit were shipped east, marking their transition from frontier culture to imperial fashion.

The transatlantic business of moccasins does not fit with the current view of eighteenth-century Detroit and, more broadly, eighteenth-century frontier settlements. Generally, we tend to emphasize their roles as collection and distribution centers for the commodities exchanged in the fur trade or as sites of

---

[1] John Montresor to Henry Bassett, Nov. 2,1763, in Clarence Walworth Alvord and Clarence Edwin Carter, eds., *The Critical Period: 1763–1765* (Springfield, Ill, 1915), 534–36, esp. 535–56 (quotation, 536).

political mediation between discordant Indian and European peoples. Both of these strands of analysis are useful. They convey something of the region's liminality, its state of being geographically, politically, and economically between (and thus distinct from) "east" and "west." But most studies provide only a partial picture, portraying Detroit and other settlements as if they were facing the frontier and doing the empire's bidding—to the diminishment, and at times exclusion, of northern, southern, hybrid, internal, and other types of connections. Moreover, accentuating the function of borderland towns as repositories and intermediaries can obscure their inhabitants' own ideas, motivations, and actions and cause us to overlook other roles filled by those inhabitants on local, regional, continental, and international stages.[2]

Focusing on the transatlantic fashioning of moccasins as it unfolded at Detroit highlights the economic, political, and cultural contours of one so-called frontier town. The footwear's transition among nonnative wearers from cultural borrowing to homecraft to manufactured commodity reveals not just the considerable influences of both west and east on this particular community but also the local commercial sector's considerable skill in employing them. The success of Detroit's moccasin manufactories, from their facilities and production to output and distribution, depended on the complementarity of native and Atlantic technologies. Nevertheless, fashion-conscious consumers on both sides of the ocean conceived of and used their moccasins in diverse and even divergent ways.

In turn, the business of moccasins challenges our understanding of eighteenth-century borderlands. It demonstrates, one facet of the hybrid culture that existed on a number of North American frontiers, including at Detroit. Concurrent with Detroit's establishment in 1701, the town's earliest colonists, including soldiers, fur traders, and farmers, appropriated native footwear. As new population groups arrived, the practice increased; by the 1780s virtually all types of residents, regardless of race, class, or gender, were wearing moccasins. Colonists who otherwise assumed European and European-style dress and customs and who had access to European shoes consciously chose to wear this component of native dress, for practical as well as political reasons.

---

[2] Influential scholarship on eastern North America's eighteenth-century frontiers includes Fred Anderson, *Crucible of War: The Seven Years' War and the Fate of Empire in British North America, 1754–1766* (New York, 2000); John Clarke, *Land, Power, and Economics on the Frontier of Upper Canada* (Montreal, 2001); R. Alan Douglas, *Uppermost Canada: The Western District and the Detroit Frontier, 1800–1850* (Detroit, 2001); Gregory Evans Dowd, *War under Heaven: Pontiac, the Indian Nations, and the British Empire* (Baltimore, 2002); Walter S. Dunn Jr., *Opening New Markets: The British Army and the Old Northwest* (Westport, Conn., 2002); Kim M. Gruenwald, *River of Enterprise: The Commercial Origins of Regional Identity in the Ohio Valley, 1790–1850* (Bloomington, Ind., 2002); Eric Hinderaker and Peter C. Mancall, *At the Edge of Empire: The Back-country in British North America* (Baltimore, 2003); Jane T. Merritt, *At the Crossroads: Indians and Empires on a Mid-Atlantic Frontier, 1700–1763* (Chapel Hill, N.C., 2003); William A. Pencak and Daniel K. Richter, eds., *Friends and Enemies in Penn's Woods: Indians, Colonists, and the Racial Construction of Pennsylvania* (University Park, Pa., 2004); William H. Bergmann, *Commerce and Arms: The Federal Government, Native Americans, and the Economy of the Old Northwest, 1783–1807* (Ph.D. diss., University of Cincinnati, 2005).

The moccasin business also demonstrates that Detroit was no mere cultural, political, or economic go-between. Although this particular manufacturing story, played out in a British colony long thought to have had no manufacturing, confirms on one level Detroit's ties to both "frontier" and "empire," it also establishes the town's status as an independent operator, one that capitalized on components of both west and east to capture some degree of commercial autonomy. The process of appropriating a western clothing item, modifying it to reflect its own cultural and aesthetic preferences, putting it through European-style manufacturing paces, and then shipping it east to supply an increasingly clamoring clientele was one way in which Detroit attempted to accomplish this.

More broadly, the fashioning of moccasins encourages a rethinking of the relationship between production and consumption during the transition from the colonial period to the American empire. Within early Detroit, as was typical during the consumer revolution, consumption compelled production: the small-scale homecraft of moccasin making developed into a full-fledged industry designed to keep pace with demand. By contrast, in the broader Atlantic world, moccasin imports fueled consumption. Only after frontier moccasins gained an eastern following did East Coast entrepreneurs begin to make and sell their own moccasins on a large scale, effectively shutting out western competitors from the market. The economic processes used on the frontier and across the empire to fashion moccasins constitute an early instance of the American interior shaping the Atlantic seaboard. In this time and place, fashion and the trappings of empire typically moved east to west. The business of moccasins essentially reversed this sequence: Detroit supplied the finished articles, helping to create through supply a progressively eastern demand. Thus production, distribution, consumption, and fashionability moved steadily from west to east. Though small, it was perhaps one of the most visible occasions in which Detroit attempted to secure more of a presence within the empire, which it did by drawing on its frontier character. . . .

Among the [Indian] nations of the Great Lakes basin, there were two different methods for constructing moccasins, each of which resulted in a different style of shoe. The center-seam or one-piece moccasin was constructed from a single piece of hide sewn into a tube, which produced a central line of stitching along the length of the upper, or vamp. The distinctive puckering that occurred on either side of the long vamp seam gave the style its contemporary French nickname: *soulier à plis*, pleated shoe (Figure. 4.2). The second construction method, the two-piece moccasin or *soulier à piéces*, required two pieces of leather: one for the sole and sides and a smaller, oval-shaped piece stitched on top to create the vamp. Stitching together the two pieces of leather produced a long seam curving around the vamp's perimeter (Figure 4.3). To these basic patterns, tailoring and decoration could be added to accommodate seasonal and aesthetic preferences, including side cuffs (flaps that could be pulled up and laced around the ankle in poor weather); botanical-inspired designs done in beading, quills, or natural dyes; and visually and aurally decorative sheet-metal "tinkle cones." More ornamental footwear, typified by Figure 4.3, was meant for

Figure 4.2 Native-made center-seam moccasins, Great Lakes, ca. 1790. *The puckered seams and side cuffs are covered with bands of red, black, and white quillwork and trimmed with white beads that are fashioned into scrolls and waves called double curves. The cuffs and vamps are also adorned with metal cones tied with red-dyed hair tassels.*
Copyright © 2015 Bata Shoe Museum, Toronto, Canada.

Figure 4.3 Huron two-piece moccasins, eastern Canada, ca. 1820. *The moccasins, dyed black, feature side cuffs adorned with intricate, floral-patterned, moose hair embroidery in shades of red, blue, and ivory. Influenced by European footwear, the shoes' fabricator used ribbons of magenta silk to bind the side-cuffs and serve as shoe ties.* Copyright © 2015 Bata Shoe Museum, Toronto, Canada.

ceremonial use and required no additional treatments. Moccasins destined for heavy use, on the other hand, called for waterproofing (a temporary expedient to combat brain-tanned leather's tendency to absorb water on contact), which was usually achieved by coating the shoes in fish oil or bear grease. The resulting everyday moccasins were well suited to the terrain of eastern North America. They afforded the wearer quieter footfalls, surer feet, and a more comfortable journey than other types of footwear. They dried quickly, could be kept relatively well waterproofed with minimal maintenance, and could be lined with fur to provide insulation against cold weather. In regions characterized by only a few rough roads and by lakes and rivers best navigated by canoes in summer and snowshoes in winter, many backcountry colonists found rigid, heeled European shoes (when they could be obtained) clumsy and impractical.[3] . . .

European priests, farmers, and soldiers living in any number of borderlands constitute three of the first population groups who appropriated native footwear. But despite the prevalence of the custom, these groups have not figured in the scholarship on moccasin wearing among nonnatives. Indeed, references to and discussions of this behavior are generally incidental to larger debates about what Beth Fowkes Tobin has termed "cultural cross-dressing," a practice in which members of one ethnic or cultural group don, often head to toe, the vestments of another.[4] Cultural cross-dressing has most often been studied through portraits of British Indian Department officers wearing fanciful Mohawk dress to display their own supremacy, white captives' involuntary appropriation of native garments as a symbolic and tangible beginning to the process of "Indianization," and fur traders' adoption of native dress as a part of a job-related uniform. Although the motivations (whether strategic, involuntary, or occupational) behind each group's wearing of native garb varied, scholars have emphasized the performative subtext of their sartorial appropriation: the projection of certain, often-political agendas through the adoption of native dress. But, as the prevalence of moccasin appropriation across a range of backcountry population groups suggests, there were many other reasons for cultural cross-dressing. Moccasins were part of a hybridized culture existing within the borderlands of the eighteenth century, one in which native and nonnative peoples combined the most useful and practical elements of at least

[3] F. G. Speck, "Notes on the Material Culture of the Huron," *American Anthropologist* II, no. 2 (April–June 1911): 208–28; Casse, *Dress* 10: 12–13, 17; Suzanne Gousse and André Gousse, *Costume in New France from 1740 to 1760: A Visual Dictionary* (Chambly, Québec, 1997), 29, 33; John Mack Faragher, " 'More Motley than Mackinaw': From Ethnic Mixing to Ethnic Cleansing on the Frontier of the Lower Missouri, 1783–1833," in *Contact Points: American Frontiers from the Mohawk Valley to the Mississippi, 1750–1830*, ed. Andrew R. L Cayton and Fredrika J. Teute (Chapel Hill, N.C., 1998), 304–26, esp. 309; Rountree, *Ethnohistory* 45: 1–29; [Timothy J.] Kent, *Ft. Pontchartrain at Detroit: A Guide to the Daily Lives of Fur Trade and Military Personnel, Settlers, and Missionaries at French Posts* (Ossineke, Mich., 2001), 2: 602–8. For other museum examples of one- and two-piece moccasins from the Great Lakes basin, see Christian Feest, *Premières nations, collections royalès: Les Indiens des forêts et des prairies d'Amérique du Nord* (Paris, 2007), 38, 54, 69, 79–80.

[4] Beth Fowkes Tobin, *Picturing: Imperial Power: Colonial Subjects in Eighteenth-Century British Painting* (Durham, N.C., 1999), 81–109 (quotation, 81).

three different cultural traditions (Indian, European, and French-Canadian) to create a distinctive set of local customs.[5] . . .

By the mid-seventeenth century across eastern Canada, French-Canadian habitants were making their own moccasins. They did so for many of the same reasons that they had appropriated them so quickly after the establishment of their settlements: close proximity to and integration with Indians, small numbers of colonists in comparison with Indians, the absence of a marked and enforced line of European settlement, the provisional and often migratory nature of the fur trade posts, the separateness of French notions of identity and appearance, the practicality of native-style footwear, and the geographic difficulties of transporting European imports so far inland. As the French names for native moccasin patterns (*soulier à plis* and *soulier à pièces*) suggest, backcountry habitants began the process of fabrication by studying and then copying native styles. Despite their manufacture, the resulting French-made shoes were often called by the same term used for native-made shoes: *souliers sauvages*, in a nod to their origin and in contrast to *souliers français* ("French shoes," or, rather, shoes made in a French style). In 1776 an anonymous German staff officer noticed that habitants were making their own *"souliers des sauvages."*[6] The officer did not describe the homemade shoes at all, suggesting that the fact of their fabrication was more interesting to him than the result and that the shoes were probably unremarkably plain, lacking the embroidery, tinkle cones, tufts, and other decorative elements that often appeared in moderation even on native people's everyday moccasins. The simple, utilitarian, French-made moccasins such as those the officer observed had been stripped of their native ornamentation and their ceremonial meaning.[7] . . .

[5] [Nehemiah How], *A Narrative of the Captivity of Nehemiah How in 1745–1747* (Cleveland, Ohio, 1904), 30; Charles Johnston, *Incidents Attending the Capture, Detention, and Ransom of Charles Johnston of Virginia*, ed. Edwin Erle Sparks (Cleveland, Ohio, 1905), 59; Milo Milton Quaife, *The Indian Captivity of O. M. Spencer* (Chicago, 1917), 45; Alden T. Vaughan and Edward W. Clark, eds., *Puritans among the Indians: Accounts of Captivity and Redemption, 1676–1724* (Cambridge, Mass., 1981); James Axtell, *The Invasion Within: The Contest of Cultures in Colonial North America* (New York, 1985), 251–52; James Fenimore Cooper, *The Last of the Mohicans* (New York, 1986), 216; Bruce M. White, "Montreal Canoes and Their Cargoes," in *"Le Castor Fait Tout": Selected Papers of the Fifth North American Fur Trade Conference, 1985*, ed. Bruce G. Trigger, Toby Morantz, and Louise Dechêne (Montreal, 1987), 164–92, esp. 185; John Demos, *The Unredeemed Captive: A Family Story from Early America* (New York, 1994); Timothy J. Shannon, "Dressing for Success on the Mohawk Frontier: Hendrick, William Johnson, and the Indian Fashion," *William and Mary Quarterly*, 3d ser., 53, no. 1 (January 1996): 13–42; Colin G. Calloway, *New Worlds for All: Indians, Europeans, and the Remaking of Early America* (Baltimore, 1997), 62–67; Sophie White, "Dress in French Colonial Louisiana, 1699–1769: The Evidence from Notarial Sources," *Dress* 24 (1997): 69–75, esp. 71; Ann M. Little, "'Shoot That Rogue, for He Hath an Englishman's Coat on!' Cultural Cross-Dressing on the New England Frontier, 1620–1760," *New England Quarterly* 74, no. 2 (June 2001): 238–73.

[6] Letter from Canada," Nov. 2, 1776, in [William L.] Stone, trans. *Letters of Brunswick and Hessian Officers [during the American Revolution* (Albany, N.Y., 1891)], 33.

[7] André Vachon with Victorin Chabot and André Desrosiers, *Dreams of Empire: Canada before 1700* (Ottawa, Ontario, 1982); W. J. Eccles, *The Canadian Frontier, 1534–1760* (Albuquerque,

The other type of native-inspired footwear that Europeans created in the eighteenth century was the shoepack, an enhanced moccasin, produced in much the same way but featuring a tongue piece and often a hard sole, which yielded more resilient, protective footwear. Borrowed from an Unami Delaware word for moccasin, "shoepack" entered the English language around 1755—at roughly the same time that outside observers began noticing this moccasin hybrid. A German staff officer recorded in 1776 that the habitant "also manufactures a kind of shoe from dressed leather, made without heels and straps, and which, when new, does not look so very badly. In the winter we will have to try this shoe; for they tell us that our feet will freeze in our ordinary boots."[8] As the officer's description of the nameless shoe suggests, application of the term "shoepack" to this style of footwear was rare outside of English sources. This may be in part a problem of vocabulary. The French-made moccasins and moccasin-type shoes enumerated in inventories and other compilations were all called *souliers*, whether *souliers sauvages* or *souliers de boeuf*, terms that obscure as much as they reveal. An October 21, 1799, letter written in English from Detroit merchant James Henry to a business partner may provide a better sense of shoepacks' widespread popularity and profitability in Canada: "I have now Persons employed making the common Canadian Shoe Pack, in which shape the worst Hide neats forty eight Shillings [New] Y[ork] C[urrency]."[9] Across eighteenth-century Canada, the fabrication of moccasins and moccasin-like shoes by nonnatives was prevalent. But in at least one part of this vast colony, the small-scale homecraft of moccasin making continued to develop—by the 1780s into a cottage industry for domestic consumption, and by the 1790s into a fully formed factory-like system designed to keep pace with eastern demand. That unlikely manufactory town was Detroit.[10] . . .

N.Mex., 1983); Vachon with Chabot and Desrosiers, *Taking Root: Canada from 1700 to 1760* (Ottawa, Ontario, 1985); Gilles Paquet and Jean-Pierre Wallot, "Nouvelle-France/Québec/ Canada: A World of Limited Identities," *Colonial Identity in the Atlantic World, 1500–1800*, ed. Nicholas Canny and Anthony Pagden (Princeton, N.J., 1987), 95–114; Bruce G. Wilson, *Colonial Identities: Canada from 1760 to 1815* (Ottawa, Ontario, 1988); Peter N. Moogk, "Reluctant Exiles: Emigrants from France in Canada before 1760," *WMQ* 46, no. 3 (July 1989): 463–505.

[8] "Letter from Canada," Nov. 2, 1776, in Stone, *Letters of Brunswick and Hessian Officers*, 32–33 (quotation, 33).

[9] James Henry to John Wilkins Jr., Oct. 21, 1799, Solomon Sibley MSS, Burton Historical Collection (hereafter BHC), Detroit Public Library.

[10] *Oxford English Dictionary Online*, s.v. "shoepack," http://www.oed.com. The first documented reference to "shoepack" appears in Adam Stephen's Sept. 27, 1755, letter to George Washington suggesting that military scouts be given "Shoe-packs or Moccosons," in James Surkamp, "Adam Stephen's Life, 1721–1791: Soldier, Statesman, Founder, and Farmer," accessed Jan. 6, 2012, http/www.libraries.wvu-edu/adamstephen/as955.html. Robert-Lionel Séguin suggests that moccasin fabrication at Montreal and Quebec did not involve professional shoemakers, remaining an amateur homecraft (Séguin, *La civilisation traditionelle*, 470–73). But given that these and other towns shared and even predated Detroit's habit of wearing and making moccasins, it seems likely that moccasin manufactories also existed there, although evidence for their existence, and for the shipping of Canadian moccasins to France, has yet to come to light.

If a market for nonnative-made moccasins did exist in Detroit in the years after 1701, it would have been comparable to what could have been found on other contemporary frontiers: a small-scale homecraft that may have developed into a cottage industry but certainly remained a small, domestic, and self-contained process, given the proximity of few colonist-consumers. But in the years after Montresor's 1763 letter about the military's winter apparel at Detroit (written three years after Britain took control of the settlement and appropriated the French custom of wearing moccasins), something quite different occurred. As documents of the British Indian Department and other fur-trading ventures reveal, government and trading officials were acquiring moccasins in bulk by the 1770s: trader John Porteous counted fourteen pairs of moccasins, each valued at two shillings, stored in his fur-trading company's warehouse in 1774, and trader William Edgar purchased thirty-two shillings' worth of moccasins for Native Americans working for the British Indian Department in 1777. The business transactions prompting these two documents point not only to an exchange of moccasins from native to colonial hands and vice versa but also to the recording of those particular exchanges and to the valuation of the merchandise. This moment marked the commodification of moccasins by Euro-Americans.[11]

The second step toward moccasin manufacture was the increasing marginalization of Indians' visible involvement in the shoes' production for a nonnative clientele. Although natives continued to supply a substantial portion of the deerskins collected at Detroit during the eighteenth century, their discernible participation in the manufacturing process seems to have diminished. Only one confirmed Indian artisan appears on the Detroit books in this period. Alexis, Charles Barthe's native slave, received four shillings from merchant John Askin for making a pair of shoepacks in November 1810. As moccasin making was the realm of native women, it is unclear why an enslaved native man was compensated for this kind of labor. Indeed, five years earlier, Alexis had purchased a pair of moccasins for five shillings from Askin's son, merchant Charles Askin, apparently unable to make them himself or to acquire them directly from a native source. There may have been other Indian artisans: George Herkimer, a lieutenant with the British Rangers, purchased from merchant Thomas Smith a pair of "fine-worked" moccasins on December 17, 1782, for a comparatively costly twelve shillings (New York currency).[12] Merchants George Meldrum and William Park's 1789–92 House Expense Book contains a purchase on May 8, 1790, of one pair of small "wrought" moccasins for four shillings.[13]

---

[11] Sept. 24, 1774, inventory, microfilm roll r-A, John Porteous MSS, microfilmed by the Buffalo and Erie County Historical Society (hereafter BECHS); Isidore Chêne, Apr. 26, 1777, invoice, vol. 7, William Edgar MSS, BHC.

[12] George Herkimer, Dec. 17, 1782, 1779–1800 ledger, Thomas Smith MSS, BHC (quotation); Apr. 16, 1810, store inventory, John R. Williams MSS, BHC; Alexis, Barthe's Panis, Nov. 23, 1810, Petty Ledger M (1806–12), John Askin MSS, BHC; Alexis, July 29, 1805, Pinery Ledger (1805–7), Charles Askin MSS, BHC.

[13] House Expense Book, 1789–92, George Meldrum and William Park MSS, BHC.

The descriptors "fine-worked" and "wrought" may allude to decorative embroidery, which may indicate native fabrication. But adjectives such as these are rare, suggesting not only that merchants infrequently stocked and Euro-American clients infrequently purchased embellished moccasins but also that natives' contributions may have become less visible in moccasins manufactured in town. This is not to imply that Indians were excluded from the labor force that fabricated moccasins. John Askin, for example, owned native slaves, including women and girls, who may have worked in his tannery or shop. But because production and distribution records listing moccasin laborers name only white men, it seems that over time Indian labor became subordinate and unrecorded in moccasins' town-based manufacturing process.[14] . . .

Increasingly available in Detroit merchants' shops from the 1780s, moccasins and shoepacks became immensely popular among Detroit's paying customers, expanding far beyond the priests, soldiers, and farmers who wore moccasins on other borderlands. A sampling of the native-shoe clientele at Detroit from 1784 to 1834 reveals that moccasins were purchased a pair or two at a time, for from two to sixteen shillings each, every few months by Scottish and German traders, gardeners, French farmers, merchants, schoolteachers, women who owned property, indentured servants, tailors, attorneys, carpenters and other tradesmen, black and Indian slaves, clerks, and sailors. In short moccasins were bought (and presumably worn) by all types of Detroit's residents.[15]

Another development of the 1780s was the merchant-endorsed production of shoepacks. Like moccasins, shoepacks were worn by an array of socioeconomic groups, perhaps best demonstrated by three customers who did business with Askin from 1787 to 1789. In this span Askin sold seven pairs of shoepacks to tailor Thomas McCrae, sold three pairs to Commodore of the Great Lakes Alexander Grant, and provided one pair to his black slave, Jupiter. Askin was one of the largest purveyors of shoepacks in town, selling the footwear to the

---

[14] For references to John Askin's native slaves, including Manette, an enslaved Indian woman by whom he had three children before manumitting her in 1766, see Milo M. Quaife, ed., *The John Askin Papers* (Detroit, 1928), 1: 12–13, 98. Ruth B. Phillips has shown that Indian women made moccasins (both plain and decorated) and other native cultural items as "souvenir arts" for whites in the mid-nineteenth century. She has also demonstrated that as early as 1700 French-Canadian Ursuline nuns in Quebec produced moose-hair-embroidered bark wares for the tourist trade. See Philips, *Trading Identities: The Souvenir in Native North American Art from the Northeast, 1700–1900* (Seattle, 1998), esp. 4, 104–9, 250–54.

[15] Moccasin purchasers were compiled from ledgers of Detroit merchants, including Jacques Campau, 1793–96 account with Joseph Campau, Campau Family Papers, CHL; Julien DuHammel, 1779–90 Thomas Smith ledger, Smith MSS, BHC; John Burrell, 1783, 1783–84 daybook, ibid.; John Askin, Mar. 8, Apr. 15, 1792, 1779–1800 ledger, ibid.; Gabriel Chêne, Félix Peltier, and Benoit Chapoton accounts, Ledger B (1805–1832), John R. Williams MSS, BHC; Summer 1776–April 1777 notebook, microfilm roll 1, Porteous MSS, BECHS; Jonathan Schieffelin, Mar. 27,1790; Petty Ledger A (1789–90), John Askin MSS, BHC; Joe Countryman, Mar. 6,1792, Petty Ledger C (1791–92), ibid.; Charles LaFleur, 1787, petty ledger (1786–87), Thomas Williams MSS, BHC; Henry Ramsay, 1783, 1782–83 ledger, Cornwall and Miller MSS, BHC; John Laughton, 1782–83 ledger, ibid.; Thomas Smith's account, 1782–83 ledger, ibid.; Solomon Sibley, Feb. 22, 1812, account with B. Campau, Sibley MSS, BHC.

Miamis Company (a short-lived conglomerate of five Detroit fur-trading firms formed in 1786 to compete with the colossal North West Company), his own servants and children, other merchants, male and female fur traders, sailors, carpenters, and farmers. As in other French-Canadian settlements, Askin's customers recognized the merits of this hardier footwear. But with their hard soles and tongue pieces, shoepacks were more complicated to create than moccasins, requiring more skill as well as cobbler's tools rather than only scissors, needle, and thread. As such, although moccasins and shoepacks may have found equal popularity among different groups of Detroiters, the number of shoepacks manufactured for and purchased from local merchant shops far outstripped the number of moccasins, a testament to residents' inability to make shoepacks themselves.[16]

To meet the considerable local demand for more moccasins, shoepacks, and other leather goods, the Detroit commercial populace kicked into a higher, entrepreneurial gear. This process was spearheaded by Askin, who noted that many of the town's unsold skins could be sold locally with little additional effort. He remarked in a June 1786 letter to his Montreal partners, Isaac Todd and James McGill, that "if there was Leather dressers & Breeches makers here we would get Rid of a large Quantity [of skins] on the Spott for Smoked Skins Sell or Exchange very fast with the Inhabitants from 12/ to 16/[.] There cannot be a better Remedy for the Disorder this Country is got into."[17] Shortly thereafter Askin opened what would be the first of the town's three tanneries, Tanning in Company. Because records for Askin's tanning operation do not seem to have survived (indeed, even monographs on Askin himself do not mention his tanyard), it is impossible to determine the origins of the skins that his tanner, Jacob Clemens, used to make leather saddles, bridles, shoepacks, and other finished goods. Nevertheless, references to the tannery appear in Askin's store

[16] From 1784 to 1834, customers purchased the following from seven Detroit merchants: 42 pairs of moccasins, 92 pairs of shoepacks, 3 pairs of *souliers sauvages*, and 3 pairs of *souliers de boeuf*. In the same period, Detroit merchants' employees and merchant-owned tanneries turned out 3 documented pairs of moccasins and 837 documented pairs of shoepacks. Tallies are culled from the ledgers of John Askin, Meldrum and Park, James Henry, Thomas Smith, Joseph Campau, John R. Williams, and Thomas Williams, all in the BHC. For other references to purchased pairs of moccasins not included in the tallies, see also the 1792–99 logbook of the *Beaver*, John Drake MSS, BHC; Sibley MSS, ibid.; Campau Family Papers, CHL; Thomas McCray, 1787 account, Ledger D (1787–89), John Askin MSS, BHC; Jupiter, 1787 account, ibid.; Commodore Alexander Grant, 1787 account, ibid.; Ledger D, ibid.; John Davidson, Petty Ledger A (1789–90), ibid.; Augustin Francoer, 1800 and 1801 accounts, 1800—1801 ledger, ibid.; John Askin Jr., 1789 account, Petty Ledger A (1789–90), ibid.; William Thorn, ibid.; Louis Moran, July 1800 account, 1800–1801 ledger, ibid.; Madame Vessina, 1790 account, Petty Ledger A (1789–90), 469, ibid.; Ambrose Berar, assorted 1808 accounts, Petty Ledger M (1806–12), ibid.; James Dennison, 1808 account, ibid; Louis Castonie, 1796 account, 1784–96 ledger, Alexander and William Macomb MSS, BHC. Merchant David Cooper's ledgers include an 1816 notation that he delivered five pairs of moccasins, worth £3.23.5, to the schooner *Jackson* "for the use of The Hands on Board" (Jan. 18, 1816, notation, vol. I, David Cooper MSS, BHC).

[17] Quaife, *John Askin Papers*, 1: 251–54 (quotation, 1: 253).

ledgers. From January 1787 to March 1788, Tanning in Company supplied 182 pairs of shoepacks to Askin's shop, averaging just more than 12 pairs per month. For a town whose 1782 population, taking in both sides of the Detroit River, was 2,191, the number of pairs of shoepacks stocked at this one shop was considerable.[18]

In the early 1790s, the final years of British control over Detroit, Askin's shop began partnering with various local shoemakers to turn out stitched shoepacks. This partnership effectively downgraded Askin's tannery from shoemaker to mere hide supplier. The first Detroit shoemaker to contract with Askin's store was George Setchsteel, who began purchasing hides from and making shoepacks for the shop in 1791. Setchsteel's compensation, from four to six shillings per pair, was not much less than the price at which Askin sold a pair of shoepacks, suggesting that Askin was paying the cobbler not only for his labor but also for materials (Askin repurchased the leather for which he originally charged Setchsteel). During the 1790s and early 1800s, Askin's store employed a number of local cobblers to make shoepacks, including Baptiste LaPierre, Matthew Myars, Antoine Latarre, and François Ivon, each of whom crafted a dozen pairs each month for a comparatively paltry one shilling and four- or sixpence per pair. This development marked the real beginning of the industrialization of shoepack manufacture: the lower wage suggests that Askin paid only for labor, not for materials, and that he gave contract employees few benefits. Indeed, one day after being compensated for stitching a batch of footwear, LaPierre purchased a pair of shoepacks from Askin for the full price of eight shillings.[19]

In 1798, two years after Detroit was ceded to the United States, merchant James Henry, in partnership with General John Wilkins Jr., opened Detroit's second and most successful tannery. Located southwest of the settlement on Campau's River, Henry's tanyard was on a plot of land known as Point Industry, the town's manufacturing corridor. Under the management of three experienced tanners from the East Coast, the Point Industry Tannery partnered with myriad small-scale local hide suppliers, including sailors, farmers, merchants, shopkeepers, tannery employees, tradesmen, and even Henry himself, but not with Indians. Undoubtedly, many of these men received the hides from an even wider group of suppliers, which included Indians. But from Henry's perspective, those were indirect transactions.[20] . . .

[18] Almon Ernest Parkins, *The Historical Geography of Detroit* (Chicago, 1918), 288; F. Clever Bald, *Detroit's First American Decade, 1796 to 1805* (Ann Arbor, Mich., 1948), 26; Donna Valley Russell, ed., *Michigan Censuses, 1710–1830, under the French, British, and Americans* (Detroit, 1982), 49.

[19] Ledger D (1787–89), John Askin MSS, BHC; George Setchsteel, 1792 account, Petty Ledger C (1791–92), ibid.; Baptiste LaPierre, Matthew Myars, and Antoine Latarre, 1795–96 accounts, Petty Ledger F (1795–58), ibid.; François Ivon, 1798–99 accounts, Petty Ledger G (1798–1800), ibid.

[20] Henry to Wilkins, Oct. 21, 1799, Sibley MSS, BHC; Ephraim S. Williams, "Personal Reminiscences," *Collections of the Pioneer Society of the State of Michigan* 8 (1886): 233–59, esp. 234; Clarence M. Burton, William Stocking, and Gordon K. Miller, eds., *The City*

This exploration of the rise of Detroit's tanneries reveals that in the space of twenty years, Detroit's merchants began to use their leather manufactories to conduct all facets of moccasin production. The consolidation facilitated by the tanneries demonstrates that the manufacturing of moccasins and shoepacks on the frontier moved steadily townward. In this process the shoes themselves became somewhat hybridized, a blend of old techniques and new conventions. The tannery laborers, likely a mix of natives and nonnatives, cured Indian- and white-supplied skins in European-style chemical tanning vats. They cut the skins with European scissors to fit native patterns, often supplementing the simple forms with European-style tongue pieces and soles. They then stitched the leather pieces with European needles and thread and sent the finished hybrid moccasins to merchants' shops for retail to local consumers. In short, the process of fabrication depended on both native knowledge and technique and European manufacturing methods and production structures for its success. And it allowed a small imperial settlement of relatively little consequence, best known for collecting and packaging furs, to become a minor but significant manufacturing town. Yet this was a time and place in which historians believe colonial manufacturing efforts to have been minimal or quickly suppressed by imperial administrators. Far from being stamped out, Detroit's moccasin manufactories endured and expanded as local merchants recognized this frontier commodity's potential to appeal to a much wider clientele.

As a result of the burgeoning industry's commercialization, Detroit's moccasins and shoepacks were not worn in Detroit alone. Due to the town's geographic position at the heart of the Great Lakes, many pairs of moccasins and shoepacks were distributed to other towns via these waterways and their connecting rivers. The necessity of portaging cargo between rivers meant that a substantial portion of moccasins' transport occurred in canoes, bateaux, and other small vessels. But because watercraft weighing less than five tons were not bound to carry manifests, cargo records for this vessel class are virtually nonexistent.[21] . . .

Shortly after these shipments to the East began in the 1780s, retailers there began placing notices and advertisements in local papers to publicize the arrival of imported moccasins. Before Detroit began exporting moccasins and shoepacks in the late eighteenth century, East Coast advertisements for frontier

---

of Detroit, Michigan, 1701–1922 (Detroit, 1922), 1: 530; Bald, *Detroit's First American Decade*, 123, 129–30. List of suppliers gathered from Point Industry Tannery ledgers, James Henry MSS, BHC.

[21] The one exception to this general five-ton rule concerned vessels that crossed into international waters, which were required to carry manifests. But before 1796, when it became an American holding, this rule did not apply at Detroit because the town was always part of the same empire as its chief trading partners (France before 1760, and Britain from 1760 to 1796). The U.S. government did not regulate trade between Detroit and British Canada until 1800, when it appointed Matthew Ernest as Detroit's first revenue collector. What few canoe and other small-craft manifests have survived are generally in the collections of the Clarke Historical Library. See also Detroit's 1815–23 Impost Book, William Woodbridge MSS, BHC.

footwear did not exist. From 1792 to 1826, moccasin advertisements ran in a number of Massachusetts newspapers, including several from Boston, Dedham, Haverhill, New Bedford, Newburyport, and Pittsfield, as well as in papers from Wiscasser and Portland, Maine; Keene and Portsmouth, New Hampshire; Providence, Rhode Island; Hartford, Connecticut; Albany and New York City, New York; Baltimore, Maryland; Alexandria, Virginia; and Charleston, South Carolina. Certainly not all of the moccasins advertised in these newspapers had been fabricated in Detroit. Some native-style shoes were likely manufactured in and exported from larger, older French-Canadian settlements, including Montreal, and many advertised moccasins were made of materials uncommon in Michigan. Boston importer Joseph Thayer proclaimed in 1823 the arrival of "seal skin Moccasins," made from an animal not indigenous to the Old Northwest.[22] The "25 [pairs] dog Moccasins" that Portland auctioneer John D. Gardner received also likely were made elsewhere, given Detroit's preference for cow- and deerskin shoes.[23] But the quantities of shoes that Detroit's merchant houses and tanneries produced suggest that a sizable portion of the moccasins imported into the eastern seaboard were fabricated in Detroit.[24] . . .

Despite a history of sartorial appropriation that was both geographically and temporally widespread, when moccasins were introduced into postrevolutionary eastern cities and towns, they appeared as fashion novelties, marketed to the middle classes. But instead of capitalizing on sensational or romantic "frontier" associations, East Coast vendors employed promotional strategies reminiscent of those used for other common household commodities with which a middling clientele would have been well acquainted. By drawing on these recognizable marketing schemes, which emphasized moccasins' healthful, gendered, seasonal, or fashionable qualities, sellers subtly linked this new

[22] Joseph Thayer, [Boston] *American Federalist Columbian Centinel*, Jan. 18,1823, [1].

[23] John D. Gardner, [Portland, Maine] *Eastern Argus*, Nov. 18, 1823, [1].

[24] Other moccasin advertisements include those by T. K. Jones and Co., [Boston] *Repertory and General Advertiser*, Jan. 21, 1812, [3]; A. Lansing and Co, *American Federalist Columbian Centinel*, Jan. 25, 1823, [3]; Whitwell, Bond, and Co., *Boston Patriot and Morning Advertiser*, May 11, 1816, [3]; A[bel] Moore, [Boston] *New-England Palladium and Commercial Advertiser*, Feb. 15, 1820, [4]; Moore, *New-England Palladium and Commercial Advertiser*, Apr. 7, 1820, [4]; Moore, [Boston] *Columbian Centinel*, Jan. 13,1821, [4]; "State Prison. Boot, Shoe, Overshoe, Last and Peg Establishment," *Boston Intelligencer and Evening Gazette*, Nov. 14, 1818, [3]; Jacob Kuhn Jr., *Boston Commercial Gazette*, Jan. 5, 1824, [3]; "[No.] 36 Newbury-Street," *American Federalist Columbian Centinel*, Oct. 16,1822, [4]; "No. 36 Newbury-Street," *Boston Daily Advertiser*, certain editions from Nov. 16 to Dec.5, 1822, [4]; "Lost" (lost article advertisement), [Boston] *Repertory*, May 7,1805, [4]; Joseph Bancroft, "New Goods," *Salem [Mass.] Gazette*, Jan. 29, 1822, [4]; R. S. Smith, *New-Bedford [Mass:] Mercury*, Jan. 17, 1823, [4]; Phelps and Olmsted, [Charleston] *City Gazette and Commercial Daily Advertiser*, Mar. 14,1818, [3]; A. Yarington glove manufactory, [Hudson, N.Y.] *Northern Whig*, Jan. 4, 1820, [4]; "Glove Factory . . . By Mrs. Yarrington," *Northern Whig*, Nov. 7, 1820, [3]; Ebenezer Hilton and Asa F. Hall, [Wiscasset, Maine] *Lincoln Intelligencer*, Dec. 20, 1820, [3]; N. S. Draper, [Providence] *Rhode Island American*, Nov. 12, 1824, [4]. Milliken, Primerose, and Co. of Charleston announced the sale of "a Quantity of *Damaged Military Clothing*, Consisting of, Uniform Coats, Jackets, Blankets, Gaiters, Stockings, Socks, Mockisins, Mittens, &c &c," in the Jan. 6, 1821, [Charleston] *City Gazette and Commercial Daily Advertiser*, [3].

and "foreign" product to familiar, popular, and quintessentially American merchandise. In consequence, moccasins became increasingly urbanized and "easternized," losing their remaining vestiges of native and even frontier cultures. As a somewhat extreme example of this type of marketing, in 1814 William "Mockasin" Jackson of New York City touted hide shoes as a health aid—comparable to other curious cures available for purchase—to be used as a treatment for various foot ailments as well as a preemptive measure for "preventing coughs, cold, asthmas and consumptions."[25]

Most moccasin purveyors and manufacturers in this period did not follow Jackson's lead, preferring instead to emphasize moccasins' similarities to other types of familiar footwear. By the early nineteenth century, moccasins had become gender-specific. Although Detroit shop ledgers did not distinguish between men's and women's hide shoes (since, given their lack of ornamentation, the only difference would have been size), on the East Coast frontier footwear was marketed separately to women and men, demonstrating that moccasins, as items of fashion, were becoming increasingly gendered. The distinction was made as early as 1801, when Sargent, Loring, and Seaver of Boston hawked "women's and men's Moccasins" separately.[26] More than twenty years later, the promotional scheme was still being used: importer Washington Haven of Portsmouth put forward "an assortment of Ladies' Moccasins" and also "Gentlemen's Fur Moccasins with stout soals" in December 1823.[27] The timing of Haven's advertisement was no accident. Beginning in the 1810s, many East Coast retailers were marketing moccasins particularly for outdoor use in winter, whether as standalone footwear or as overshoes. Emerson and Nelson of Providence stocked "Winter Shoes," including overshoes and moccasins, in February 1813.[28] B. and H. Mirick of Boston proclaimed in the winter of 1821 that they "now offer[ed] . . . Ladies' and Misses' Moccasins, cut high, and of a superior quality. . . suitable for the present season."[29] The description

[25] [William] Mockasin Jackson, *New-York Evening Post*, May 13, 1814, [3] (quotations); Jackson, [New York] *Commercial Advertiser*, May 13, 1811, [3]. For a discussion of how goods were often marketed to and received by women during the early Republic, see Caroline Winterer, *The Mirror of Antiquity: American Women and the Classical Tradition, 1750–1900* (Ithaca, N.Y., 2007).

[26] Sargent, Loring, and Seaver, [Boston] *Constitutional Telegraphe*, Dec. 19, 1801, [3]. The ad also repeated in the *Constitutional Telegraphe*, Jan. 2, 1802, [1], Jan. 6,1802, [4].

[27] Washington Haven, *Portsmouth [N.H.] Journal of Literature and Politics*, Dec. 27, 1823, [3]. Other "gendered" ads include Samuel Goodhue, *Newburyport [Mass.] Herald, and Country Gazette*, Jan. 29, 1802, [1]; F. G. Shaeffer, *Baltimore Patriot and Mercantile Advertiser*, Feb. 2, 1821, [3]; Henry Allen, [Dedham] *Village Register*, Jan. 12, 1826, [4]; John Goodwin, *Times, and Hartford Advertiser*, Nov. 4, 1823, [3].

[28] Emerson and Nelson, [Providence] *Columbian Phenix*, Feb. 6, 1813; [3].

[29] B. and H. Mirick, *Columbian Centinel*, Dec. 26, 1821, [3]. Wearing moccasins in winter was not exclusively an East Coast phenomenon. Native and nonnative peoples in the Great Lakes and Canada had been wearing winter moccasins for centuries. The use of moccasins as fashionable "winter overshoes" was not a new trend either. Elizabeth Russell, writing from York (present-day Toronto), gushed to a friend in England in November 1797, "The Indians here—make mawkinsons which all the Indians wear instead of shoes and they ornament

"cut high" may have been a reference to long side cuffs but, equally plausibly, could have been a shoe more like a *botte sauvage*. The fashion of moccasins as seasonal shoes caught on, making the jump across the Atlantic in the 1820s. The May 1828 issue of the English periodical *La Belle Assemblée* reported that in April stylish women in London had worn "Indian moccassins drawn over the dress shoe" to keep out the spring chill.[30]

Although references to the availability of moccasins for East Coast customers appear continuously in local newspapers from the 1790s through the 1830s, by the 1810s a major shift in the retailing of moccasins had occurred. In this decade announcements posted by importers and auctioneers for the arrival of moccasin shipments from the interior began to wane, replaced by advertisements for locally made moccasins. These local versions were crafted by entrepreneurs from New Hampshire to Maryland who capitalized on the popularity of native-style shoes by copying western exports. In December 1814 George Charles of Albany stocked sheeted leather, "particularly finished for Shoe-Packs or Moccosins."[31] Eaton and Wiggin of Portsmouth broadcast in 1822 that they were "*Constantly on hand and making . . .* Ladies' & Gentlemen's . . . Moggasins."[32] William Jackson of New York City declared himself as early as 1811 to be "*Mockasin Maker to the Inhabitants of this renowned City of Gotham.*"[33] Jackson was among the first to advertise locally made moccasins for both wholesale and retail markets, and his advertisements and merchandise were also to be found in other cities. In 1814 Baltimore entrepreneur Joseph K. Stapleton announced that he possessed two hundred pairs of "Jackson Moccasins, a very comfortable article at this season, and worth the attention of ladies and gentlemen travelling. Country merchants and others will find them a desirable article in the sleighing season."[34] As his advertisement attests, Stapleton marketed Jackson's moccasins not just to Baltimore residents but also to small-town vendors who might have wanted the shoes for their own customers. But for all his self-promotion and aggrandizement, Jackson failed to secure what other East Coast

---

them very nicely with beads, ribbons, and porcupine quills—I had a squaw spoken to make me some but I have not heard any more of her. Mrs. Simcoe [wife of John Graves Simcoe, first lieutenant governor of Upper Canada] used to wear them over her shoes and she looked very smart." Indeed, Elizabeth Simcoe's 1792 diary makes reference to sending moccasins to her daughter in England. See June Swann, *Shoes* (New York, 1982), 33. Russell's letter is quoted in Toronto's Bata Shoe Museum's online exhibit *On Canadian Ground: Stories of Footwear in Early Canada*, presented by the Virtual Museum of Canada, http://www .virtualmuseum.ca/Exhibitions/Ground/english/exhibition/csrtv/sums2.html. Other "winter" ads include Wm. Lawson Jr., [Keene] *New Hampshire Sentinel*, Nov. 28, 1823, [1]; David How Jr., [Haverhill, Mass.] *Essex Patriot*, Jan. 15, 1820, [3]; Elisha Vinton, [Portland, Maine] *Eastern Argus*, Jan. 8, 1822, [3]; "Francis' Patent Hair Soles," *Columbian Centinel*, Dec. 21, 1822, [4].

[30] *La Belle Assemblée*, quoted in Nancy E. Rexford, *Women's Shoes in America, 1795–1930* (Kent, Ohio, 2000), 151.

[31] George Charles, "Stolen," *Albany Gazette*, Dec. 22, 1814, [3].

[32] Eaton and Wiggin, *Portsmouth Journal of Literature and Politics*, Jan. 5, 1822, [3].

[33] William Jackson, *Commercial Advertiser*, May 13, 1811, [3].

[34] Jos[eph] K. Stapleton, "*Elegant Fenders—Jackson Moccasins*," *Baltimore Patriot and Evening Advertiser*, Dec. 5, 1816, [3].

moccasin makers obtained in this era: a patent. From 1814 to 1827, the U.S. government granted ten patents for moccasins and moccasin-making techniques. All ten patentees worked in the East.[35] . . .

The late eighteenth and early nineteenth centuries marked a time of transition in American men's and women's fashions. Men's form-fitting knee breeches, popular in the colonial period, gave way to less restrictive tailored pantaloons, often paired with vests and long-tailed coats. Women's clothing also became less structured in the early Republic: corseted bodices and cumbersome full skirts were replaced by high-waisted gowns that skimmed the body's contours. Footwear echoed this more relaxed mode. The buckled, heeled shoes of the eighteenth century, although persisting somewhat in the postrevolutionary period, became less stylish over time. American men turned increasingly to sleek leather boots; American women favored French-style slippers. The structural commonalities between slippers and moccasins were many. Both were generally thin-soled and flat-bottomed, were sewn from uncomplicated patterns, and either slid on or were fastened with laces. These similarities in form suggest that understated footwear, whether moccasins or slippers, complemented the simple, fluid lines of Regency clothing.[36]

The more comfortable gowns of the early nineteenth century facilitated what increasingly became a new pastime for women in this period: walking outdoors. This fashionable activity required sturdier shoes than the slippers women were accustomed to wearing. To accommodate this new pursuit, a new type of shoe made its way to American shop shelves: British-style boots. Despite their practicality, the boots could not shake their association with Britishness. Such a connection, at a time when America's fondness for its former mother country had reached its nadir, doomed them to limited popularity. Moreover, from 1807 to the end of the War of 1812, the United States enacted an embargo against, in particular, British and French goods, including boots and slippers. Such timing was fortuitous for America's cobblers, who were anxious, as June Swann has argued, to produce footwear that could compete with French and British styles. This crashing together of political events and cultural activities

[35] Nearly all U.S. patents issued from 1790 to 1836 were destroyed in the 1836 fire at the U.S. Patent Office in Washington, D.C. Beginning In 1837, some of the lost patents—excluding those for moccasins—were reconstructed from patentees' resubmitted materials and are now housed at the National Archives and Records Administration, College Park, Md. The Franklin Pierce Center for Intellectual Property at the University of New Hampshire Law School has created a list of all patents issued before 1830 from patent circulars and other publications, including the moccasin patents: http://ipmall.info/hosted_resources/PatentHistory/pointvtrs .htm, accessed Jan. 6, 2012. Note that several of the patents were issued on the same day to separate parties for what appear to be the same techniques, suggesting a degree of competition among moccasin entrepreneurs.

[36] Madeleine Ginsburg, "Women's Dress before 1900," in *Four Hundred Years of Fashion*, ed. Natalie Rothstein (London, 1984), 13–47; Avril Hart, "Men's Dress," ibid, 48–75; [Michael] Zakim, *Ready-Made Democracy:* [*A History of Men's Dress in the American Republic, 1760–1860* (Chicago, 2003)], 69–126; Nancy Rexford, "The Perils of Choice: Women's Footwear in Nineteenth-Century America," in *Shoes: A History from Sandals to Sneakers*, ed. Giorgio Riello and Peter McNeil (New York, 2006), 138–59, esp. 138–45; Swann, *Shoes*, 32–38.

may have created an opportunity for moccasins—a particularly "American" footwear designed for perambulation—to fill a particular void. The rising popularity of walking outdoors may also explain why moccasins were often marketed in East Coast newspapers for outside use.[37] . . .

As the nineteenth century approached its midpoint, moccasin production continued to develop in the East, becoming increasingly gendered, decorative, and Europeanized. Nancy E. Rexford has shown that although they were still worn by both men and women, moccasins by 1830 had become casual house shoes and boudoir slippers, often fashioned from velvet and featuring the square toe popular in that decade. By the American Civil War, moccasins had been transformed into women's carriage shoes, made of heavily embroidered velvet, trimmed and lined with satin. How remarkable that a native shoe once prized, indeed appropriated, for its suitability for rough terrain had become an ornamental indoor slipper worn by elite white women.[38] . . .

The native-style moccasins that John Montresor, the British military engineer, wore during the hard winter at Fort Detroit in 1763 were likely made by the town's nonnative fabricators. He probably purchased them from a local merchant's shop. Montresor's moccasins challenge what we have thought about the economies and cultures of the supposedly peripheral frontier spaces of the eighteenth century. They were a hybridized cultural form steeped in practicality, borrowing and blending the most useful components of native, European, and French-Canadian cultural traditions. Moccasins fitted the lives of nonnatives such as Montresor, who could obtain and otherwise wore European or European-style attire yet consciously chose to refashion Indian footwear for their own use. Although symbolic of life on the frontier, Montresor's moccasins equally embodied Detroit's ties to empire. They were derived from a native form, altered to reflect colonists' tastes, fabricated using European-style manufacturing processes, disseminated via imperial networks, and publicized with Atlantic-world promotional practices. The entire course of moccasins' production and distribution reflected Detroit's bifurcated gaze. By drawing on components of both east and west, Detroit secured for itself a limited degree of commercial autonomy.

The fashioning of moccasins therefore embodies an instance of transculturation—an instance in which the frontier influenced the core. Detroit, after all, had been founded and continued to flourish because of what Europe had deemed "fashionable." For generations Indians and colonists at Detroit collected beaver and other skins for entrepreneurs in Europe to make into stylish hats, gloves, and other articles. The local production of moccasins for an eastern clientele not only inverted but also subverted that relationship: it reversed production, distribution, consumption, and fashionability to flow from west to east. And it provided this interior port town with a little space in

---

[37] Rexford, "Perils of Choice," 138–45; Swann, *Shoes*, 32–38.
[38] Rexford, *Women's Shoes in America*, 99, 151, 344.

which to exert both its importance within and its independence from the empire through the commodification of its "frontier" character.[39]

Analyzing Journal Articles

1. What made moccasins different from other kinds of footwear typically worn by European colonists? Who were the first colonists in the Great Lakes region to adopt moccasins as footwear? How were the moccasins they wore similar to and different from moccasins worn by Indians?

2. Briefly describe how the manufacturing process of moccasins changed as it moved from Native American into European hands. At what point were moccasins more likely to be produced by specialized wage laborers rather than by the person using or selling them? What kind of industries developed in Detroit to make the mass production of moccasins possible?

3. When did moccasins become available for consumers in eastern markets? How did their sale there reflect changing fashion trends and political values in the United States? When and why did Detroit lose its advantage in the production of moccasins for these markets?

4. How did producers and retailers of moccasins use advertising to sell them? With what particular gender roles or activities did these advertisements associate moccasins?

5. Any piece of persuasive writing relies on the author's command of argument, evidence, and organization. How does the organization of this article reinforce its argument? How does Cangany's evidence shape the organization and presentation of her argument?

6. Using this article as a model, what object of everyday use in modern society would you consider a good candidate for a similar historical study? How has the production and consumption of this object changed over time, and what do those changes tell us about the meanings attached to it by its users?

The Rest of the Story

Moccasins were just one aspect of the intercultural borrowing and adaptation in clothing that went on between Indians and colonists in early America. Woven cloth was perhaps the most popular item that Indians traded for with Europeans. Indian women who had once worked with hides and pelts to clothe

---

[39] John J. McCusker and Russell R. Menard estimate that between two-thirds and three-fourths of all English exported beaver hats—made from furs collected at centers including Detroit—were sent back to the American colonies. McCusker and Menard, *The Economy of British America, 1607–1789* (Chapel Hill, N.C., 1985), 286.

their families now processed those items for European traders, from whom they also acquired copper and brass kettles, iron-edged tools, guns and ammunition, and alcohol. European observers generally described the Indians they met as being nearly naked or immodestly dressed. They expected that Indians who participated in the fur trade would learn to dress like Europeans and to adopt the gender roles and social values associated with that clothing.

Indians wanted European goods, but they did not want to dress or look like Europeans. Indian men and women liked linen shirts and woolen blankets that could be worn as mantles or skirts, but they did not like tight-fitting clothing like waistcoats, breeches, or petticoats, and both sexes left much more skin exposed than Europeans considered appropriate. Indians also altered and accessorized their clothing with bead and quill work, ribbons and lace, and brass and silver items. Despite the objections of missionaries, they continued to paint and tattoo their bodies, sometimes incorporating new European tools and materials into these traditional practices. For example, razors and brass wire acquired in the fur trade made it easier for Indian males to cut and elongate their earlobes in the manner displayed in West's portrait of Karonghyontye.

Europeans also adapted Indian dress in ways that went beyond moccasins. Fur traders and other travelers in the borderlands found plenty of practical reasons to adopt leather leggings, fur robes, and snowshoes. Also, by donning Indian-style jewelry or clothing, they signaled their desire for peaceful exchange and friendship. Colonial agents such as Guy Johnson sometimes dressed in the "Indian fashion" when they attended treaty councils with native peoples, using their appearance as a way of signaling their diplomatic expertise. The Indian fashion's blending of European goods with Native American aesthetics is something commonly associated with colonial borderlands, but Europeans far removed from the frontier also donned native dress, for reasons that had nothing to do with its utility. The participants in the Boston Tea Party in December 1773 dressed as Mohawk Indians. No one, of course, thought an actual band of Mohawks destroyed the East India Company's tea. Rather, this costume allowed the patriots to step temporarily outside of their identities as British subjects and to act independently as "native" Americans who answered to no authority higher than their own (thus, it would be more historically accurate if members of the modern Tea Party movement dressed as Indians at their rallies rather than in tricorn hats and knee breeches). During the nineteenth and twentieth centuries, members of fraternal organizations such as the Tammany Society and the Order of Red Men adopted Indian dress as part of their costumes and rituals, expressing their social bonds in a way that invoked nostalgia for a mythical American frontier.

Sometimes, a moccasin is just a moccasin. Although the fur trade disappeared a long time ago, this form of footwear is still with us today, now mass-produced in factories for global markets. Modern versions of the moccasin remain comfortable and inexpensive, the same attributes that made them popular in eighteenth-century Detroit. As with any object of material culture, the moccasin's technological production and use tell only part of its story. When studied as a historical source produced in a particular time and place, it can tell us much more about the people who created it than its humble appearance would suggest.

To Find Out More

Journal Article Databases

A reference librarian can show you any number of online databases that can help you research articles by author, title, subject, keyword, or a variety of other parameters.

America: History and Life

Humanities Abstracts

JSTOR

Secondary Sources on Borderlands and Early American Material Culture

Cangany, Catherine. *Frontier Seaport: Detroit's Transformation into an Atlantic Entrepôt*. Chicago: University of Chicago Press, 2014.

Deetz, James. *In Small Things Forgotten: An Archaeology of Early American Life*. Garden City, NY: Anchor Books, 1977.

Deloria, Philip. *Playing Indian*. New Haven, CT: Yale University Press, 1998.

Johnson, Laura. "'Goods to Clothe Themselves': Native Consumers and Native Images on the Pennsylvania Trading Frontier, 1712–1760," *Winterthur Portfolio* 43 (Spring 2009): 115–40.

Reinhardt, Leslie. "British and Indian Identities in a Picture by Benjamin West," *Eighteenth-Century Studies* 31 (Spring 1998): 283–305.

Shannon, Timothy J. "Dressing for Success on the Mohawk Frontier: Hendrick, William Johnson, and the Indian Fashion," *William and Mary Quarterly*, 3rd ser., 53 (January 1996): 13–42.

Shannon, Timothy J. "Queequeg's Tomahawk: A Cultural Biography," *Ethnohistory* 52 (Summer 2005): 589–633.

White, Richard. *The Middle Ground: Indians, Empires, and Republics in the Great Lakes Region, 1650–1815*. Cambridge: Cambridge University Press, 1991.

CHAPTER 5

The Sound of Rebellion

Songs in Revolutionary America

The residents of Boston, Massachusetts, were in a rebellious mood during the summer of 1769. The previous fall, two regiments of British soldiers had arrived and encamped on the city's Common, sent there by royal officials who wanted to make certain that the colonists complied with new customs regulations and taxes. Led by a group of patriots known as the Sons of Liberty, the people of Boston had responded with various protests, ranging from the harassment of customs officers and soldiers to the signing of nonimportation agreements, in which merchants pledged not to import goods being taxed by Parliament.

The Sons of Liberty also organized public gatherings to encourage solidarity among the patriots. John Adams attended one such event on August 14, 1769, a dinner with 350 guests at the Liberty Tree tavern. According to a passage in Adams's diary, the crowd was too large to be accommodated indoors, so the tavern's proprietor set up tables for them in an open field. Rain caused "some Abatement in our Pleasures," but the guests still managed to enjoy themselves despite the bad weather. After they had eaten, they drank toasts and sang songs, including "The Liberty Song," which had been published in a Massachusetts newspaper the previous year. It was written by Pennsylvanian John Dickinson, who was also well known as the author of *Letters from a Farmer in Pennsylvania*, a pamphlet that explained why parliamentary taxation of the colonies was unconstitutional.

Adams had no doubt read Dickinson's pamphlet, but on that August day in 1769, he was more impressed by the famous Pennsylvanian's songwriting. Adams thought that "The Liberty Song" stirred "the Sensations of Freedom" among the guests as they joined together in singing it, and he was pleased by how the dinner had rallied support for the patriot cause. He also noted with pride the decorum of the crowd: despite all the singing and toasting, "I did not see one Person intoxicated, or near it." Adams called such gatherings "politick" because "they tinge the Minds of the People, [and] they impregnate them with the sentiments of Liberty. They render the People fond of their Leaders in the Cause, and averse and bitter against all opposers." In other words, drinking and singing together simultaneously promoted unity among the patriots and antipathy for the British.

Adams's experiences on that August day illustrated important connections between music and celebration in eighteenth-century American life. As Adams noted, festive gatherings were a great way to inspire feelings of solidarity among the American patriots, and songs conveyed the spirit and meaning of their common cause. Patriot leaders gave speeches and wrote pamphlets explaining the colonists' rights and liberties, but songs affected audiences in ways that those other forms of communication did not. Consider, for example, "The Liberty Song," which so impressed Adams (see Source 2). It might be described as the first American pop hit. Dickinson was not a professional musician or composer; rather, he borrowed the tunes of two well-known songs of the time—"Heart of Oak," a march used in the British Navy, and "Here's a Health," a Scottish folk song about emigration—and added new lyrics about Americans uniting to defend their liberties. The song circulated widely and proved to be so popular that loyalists wrote a parody of it (see Source 3), which in turn inspired another patriot songwriter to publish a parody of the parody. History has remembered Dickinson chiefly as the author of *Letters from a Farmer in Pennsylvania*, but "The Liberty Song" arguably reached and influenced far more people than his pamphlet ever did.

Music and song were woven into the fabric of colonial life. Different ethnic groups from Europe brought their traditions of folk and religious music with them when they migrated, and in America these traditions mixed with African and Native American musical cultures. Workers engaged in communal labor—such as slaves working in tobacco fields or sailors onboard a ship—used songs to coordinate and regulate the tempo of their movements. Soldiers drilled and marched to the sound of fifes and drums. Large crowds gathered for public celebrations and civic holidays, often to the sound of bells ringing or military music playing. On those occasions, elites hosted banquets and balls and hired musicians to play for dancers. The lower ranks of society—servants, slaves, sailors, and laboring people—were more likely to do their celebrating out-of-doors, in streets and around bonfires, consuming food and drink and enjoying their own music and dancing.

Whether they gathered indoors or out, colonists liked to sing when they celebrated. Traditional drinking songs were a part of common memory, and anyone with a knack for rhyming might compose a new one by grafting their own lyrics onto a familiar tune. "Yankee Doodle," regarded by subsequent generations as the quintessential patriot song, actually originated in the British army and was sung by redcoats as they marched toward Lexington, Massachusetts, on the fateful morning of April 19, 1775. It became an American standard only after a parody of it appeared satirizing the British retreat from Lexington and Concord. Ballads were also a part of the colonists' musical heritage. Ballads were a kind of informal narrative verse that combined elements of poetry and song. They told a story about a person or event using verses and choruses, and could be sung or recited by an individual or a group. Many traditional ballads dated to the medieval era (for example, the stories of Robin Hood first appeared as ballads), but ballads were also a popular way to satirize or celebrate public figures or recent events.

For many eighteenth-century Americans, rituals of public celebration shaped and defined their experience of the Revolution. History books often tell the story of the coming of the Revolution as a series of violent public confrontations between raucous crowds and British soldiers or officials—the Stamp Act riots, the tarring and feathering of customs officials, the Boston Massacre, the Boston Tea Party—but much more common were crowds like the one described by Adams in his diary that assembled in a peaceful, celebratory fashion to support the patriot cause, and their participants were more likely to be found carrying wine glasses and punch bowls than clubs and torches. In the decade between the Stamp Act and the battle of Lexington and Concord, colonial Americans expressed their political opinions in songs that asserted their rights and loyalty as British subjects. After 1776, Americans made changes, some obvious and some subtle, in the way they wrote, sang, or recited these songs. Lyrics now emphasized their shared love and sacrifice for the new nation, but the cultural purpose and expression of these songs remained much the same. Public celebration, drink, and song served as means by which Americans expressed their transformation from loyal British subjects into citizens of the United States of America.

Using the Source: Songs

Oral tradition transmitted songs from one generation to the next, and both found their way into printed sources as well. Songs were printed in newspapers or sometimes on large single sheets of paper known as ballad sheets that could be posted on walls or shared by groups in taverns or coffeehouses. Often, the songwriter would identify a commonly known tune to which the lyrics were written, which enabled readers to sing the song without needing to read music or have musical accompaniment. Other songs were little more than poorly metered attempts at patriotic drum beating, published in newspapers as "curiosities" that reflected the spirit of the times.

Singing could divide people as well as bring them together. A drinker in a tavern or a participant in a meal who declined to join in a song or lift a glass in a toast called for by its lyrics broke the fellowship symbolized by the communal punch bowl. Onlookers might interpret this passive act of refusal as an aggressive challenge to the values and opinions expressed by the group. Songs could, therefore, also be an effective way of exerting pressure on a reluctant participant to show solidarity with the rest of the crowd. In his diary, Adams described the participants at the dinner he attended as "Sons of Liberty," but what if someone in that crowd did not share the same dedication to the cause as a prominent patriot like Adams? Not joining in the singing of "The Liberty Song" or in the toast called for in its final stanza would single out such an individual among his neighbors and friends and perhaps subject him to more forceful means of persuasion, like a threat against his property or personal safety. Adams liked such occasions because they could "impregnate" people with the "sentiments of Liberty." They could also exert a powerful peer pressure on those reluctant or undecided about the patriot cause.

What Can Songs Tell Us?

Songs tell us much about popular political culture in Revolutionary America. In an age before universal adult suffrage or organized political parties, most people expressed their political opinions in ways that did not involve casting votes or supporting particular candidates for office. Unlike the elite males who sat in council chambers and assembly halls to pass laws or draft petitions, most people practiced their politics out-of-doors, assembling in crowds to celebrate, commemorate, or protest specific events or policies. A crowd might burn a despised political figure in effigy or bury a hated law, such as the Stamp Act, in a mock funeral procession. A crowd's attendance at a public celebration also lent legitimacy to the political authority of the elites who sponsored it. The songs and music that accompanied public events were a part of the experiential nature of politics in Revolutionary America for a much wider cross section of the population than that represented in the official channels of government.

Songs celebrated ideal roles and virtues for different elements in society. By analyzing their lyrics, we can glimpse how patriots mobilized these different groups—women and men, soldiers and civilians—for their cause. Songs and ballads also offer insights into the origins and development of American nationalism. At the outbreak of the Revolution, regional and cultural differences separated the thirteen colonies. Somehow, the patriots overcame these differences to forge a single nation that withstood not only the war with Britain but also the divisive politics of the postwar period. Songs of the era allow us to see how the former colonists created a shared political identity in the wake of independence. They tell us much about how colonists formerly connected only by their common status as British subjects manufactured a new inventory of public heroes, symbols, and rituals to express their new identity as Americans.

The disadvantages of using songs to study the American Revolution arise from the formulaic and idealized nature of these forms of political expression. Songs seldom described the world as it was; rather, they described the world as

Figure 5.1. Sign for Gordon's Inn, c. 1790–1830 *Tavern and inn signs in early America announced their businesses to potential customers on busy streets and offered visual cues to what went on inside their doors. This sign, from an inn of unknown location, reveals much about the social significance of drinking in Revolutionary America. The verses read:*

> *Gentlemen you are welcome*
> *sit down at your ease*
> *Pay what you call for &*
> *drink what you please*

The bowl and glass suggest plenty of good drink and companionship, but the figure and verses limit that invitation to indulgence to only well-to-do males.

Source: The Connecticut Historical Society.

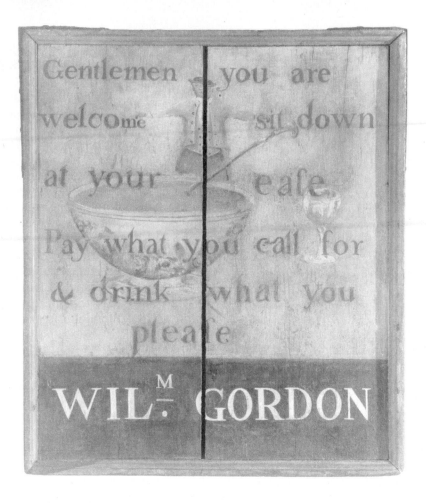

it ought to be, in the eyes of the people who composed them. In their lyrics, political unity and social harmony always prevailed; soldiers were always brave, women virtuous, and civilians self-sacrificing; and victory was always right around the corner. Patriots and loyalists wrote songs to rally support to their respective causes, but the songs themselves did not serve as avenues for debate or reflection on the nature of their divisions.

Another disadvantage to using songs has to do with the context in which they were made, sung, and printed. Public drinking in eighteenth-century America was a prerogative of free adult males (Figure 5.1). We know that women, slaves, and laboring peoples drank, but it is much harder to find descriptions of what political opinions they may have expressed during their consumption. Newspapers did not report songs associated with these groups. Society did not condone their public consumption of alcohol, associating it with disorder and violence rather than political solidarity and social cohesion. Although songs associated with the patriot movement claimed to state universally held sentiments, substantial elements of the social order were not invited to join in this form of expression, at least not in a public manner. If those left out did engage in such activity on their own, it was rarely recorded in a way historians can retrieve. The songs that have survived carry a distinct bias in favor of white, urban men from the middle and upper ranks of society.

Using songs as a source requires that you be attentive not only to the words used but also to the way in which they were arranged to express the singers' notions of solidarity, allegiance, and social order. Calls to resistance against the king or Parliament were inflammatory, and many eighteenth-century Americans defined political rebellion as a sin, a violation of the biblical commandment to honor your father and mother. Therefore, words and actions taken against Britain's controversial tax policies in the 1760s had to be distanced from outright rebellion by professions of loyalty to the Crown and empire. Notice how the lyrics in "The Liberty Song" engage in this balancing act.

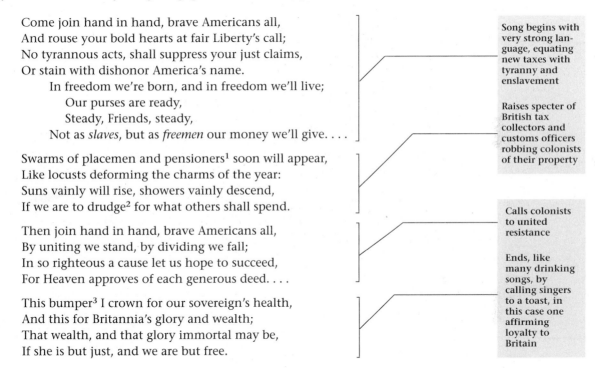

Come join hand in hand, brave Americans all,
And rouse your bold hearts at fair Liberty's call;
No tyrannous acts, shall suppress your just claims,
Or stain with dishonor America's name.
    In freedom we're born, and in freedom we'll live;
      Our purses are ready,
      Steady, Friends, steady,
    Not as *slaves*, but as *freemen* our money we'll give. . . .

Swarms of placemen and pensioners[1] soon will appear,
Like locusts deforming the charms of the year:
Suns vainly will rise, showers vainly descend,
If we are to drudge[2] for what others shall spend.

Then join hand in hand, brave Americans all,
By uniting we stand, by dividing we fall;
In so righteous a cause let us hope to succeed,
For Heaven approves of each generous deed. . . .

This bumper[3] I crown for our sovereign's health,
And this for Britannia's glory and wealth;
That wealth, and that glory immortal may be,
If she is but just, and we are but free.

Song begins with very strong language, equating new taxes with tyranny and enslavement

Raises specter of British tax collectors and customs officers robbing colonists of their property

Calls colonists to united resistance

Ends, like many drinking songs, by calling singers to a toast, in this case one affirming loyalty to Britain

Source: Boston Gazette, July 18, 1768 (in Frank Moore, ed., Songs and Ballads of the American Revolution [1856; repr., New York: Arno Press, 1969], 36–40).

As you work with the sources that follow, keep in mind the social and political contexts in which they were produced; the Checklist questions below will help you in this regard.

[1] "Placemen" and "pensioners" were derogatory terms for customs officials, military officers, and other officeholders who profited from royal appointments in the colonies.
[2] Labor.
[3] A type of toast in which all drinkers were expected to empty their glasses.

CHECKLIST: Interrogating Songs

- ☐ To what historical period does the song belong? For what specific occasion was the song likely to be sung?
- ☐ Who is singing the song? What do you know about the social class, gender, and ethnicity of this person or group?
- ☐ What beliefs, practices, or events is this song addressing? What sort of belief or action is the song trying to inspire among its listeners?
- ☐ How would you describe the tone of the song: patriotic, satirical, celebratory, angry?

Source Analysis Table

The following table will help you keep track of your notes regarding the individual songs reprinted in this chapter. Once you have addressed the questions for each song, you can then compare them and look for evidence of changing political attitudes or social identities over time.

Songs	Topic	What Group(s) Are Addressed in the Lyrics?	What Values or Ideas Are the Lyrics Promoting?
1. "To the Ladies"			
2. "The Liberty Song"			
3. "The Parody"			
4. "The Rebels"			
5. "The New Recruit/Fare Thee Well, Ye Sweethearts"			
6. "How Stands the Glass Around"			
7. "The Epilogue"			
8. "Volunteer Boys"			
9. "To the Traitor Arnold"			
10. "The Dance"			

The Source: Songs in Revolutionary America, 1767–1781

1   *To the Ladies*

This song appeared in several New England newspapers between 1767 and 1769. It rallied support for the nonimportation movement aimed at overturning the Townshend Duties, a series of taxes imposed by Parliament on colonial imports in 1767. Its tune was borrowed from "Advice to the Ladies," a popular comic song offering advice on what kinds of men women should avoid marrying.

Young ladies in our town, and those that live round,
Let a friend at this season advise you;
Since money's so scarce, and times are growing worse,
Strange things may soon hap and surprise you.
First, then, throw aside your topknots[1] of pride;
Wear none but your own country linen;
Of economy boast, let your pride be the most
To show clothes of your own make and spinning.
What if homespun they say is not quite so gay
As brocades, yet be not in a passion,
For when once it is known this is much worn in town,
One and all will cry out—'Tis the fashion!
And, as one, all agree, that you'll not married be
To such as will wear London factory,
But at first sight refuse, tell 'em such you will choose
As encourage our own manufactory.
No more ribbons wear, nor in rich silks appear;
Love your country much better than fine things;
Begin without passion, 'twill soon be the fashion
To grace your smooth lock with a twine of string.
Throw aside your Bohea, and your Green Hyson[2] tea,
And all things with a new-fashion duty;
Procure a good store of the choice Labrador,[3]
For there'll soon be enough here to suit you.
These do without fear, and to all you'll appear,
Fair, charming, true, lovely and clever;
Though the times remain darkish; young men may be sparkish,
And love you much stronger than ever.

[1] Fancy headdresses worn by women of fashion.

[2] Bohea and Green Hyson were types of tea imported into the colonies.

[3] An alternative to foreign tea, made from the red-root bush native to New England.

Source: Arthur F. Schrader, *American Revolutionary War Songs to Cultivate the Sensations of Freedom*, audio recording (New York: Smithsonian Folkways No. FH 5279, 1976).

2   *The Liberty Song*

Written by John Dickinson, this song appeared in colonial newspapers in 1768. Like "To the Ladies," it was meant to rally patriot support for opposition to the Townshend Duties.

Come join hand in hand, brave Americans all,
And rouse your bold hearts at fair Liberty's call;
No tyrannous acts, shall suppress your just claim,
Or stain with dishonor America's name.
    In freedom we're born, and in freedom we'll live;
      Our purses are ready,
      Steady, Friends, steady,
    Not as *slaves*, but as *freemen* our money we'll give.

Our worthy forefathers—let's give them a cheer—
To climates unknown did courageously steer;
Thro' oceans to deserts, for freedom they came,
And, dying, bequeath'd us their freedom and fame.

. . .

The Tree, their own hands had to Liberty rear'd,
They lived to behold growing strong and rever'd;
With transport then cried,—"Now our wishes we gain,
For our children shall gather the fruits of our pain."

How sweet are the labors that freemen endure,
That they shall enjoy all the profit, secure,—
No more such sweet labor Americans know,
If Britons shall reap what Americans sow.

Swarms of placemen and pensioners[1] soon will appear,
Like locusts deforming the charms of the year:
Suns vainly will rise, showers vainly descend,
If we are to drudge[2] for what others shall spend.

Then join hand in hand brave Americans all,
By uniting we stand, by dividing we fall;
In so righteous a cause let us hope to succeed,
For Heaven approves of each generous deed.

All ages shall speak with amaze and applause,
Of the courage we'll show in support of our laws;

---

[1] "Placemen" and "pensioners" were derogatory terms for customs officials, military officers, and other officeholders who profited from royal appointments in the colonies.
[2] Labor.

To die we can bear,—but to serve we disdain,
For shame is to freemen more dreadful than pain.

This bumper[3] I crown for our sovereign's health,
And this for Britannia's glory and wealth;
That wealth, and that glory immortal may be,
If she is but just, and we are but free.
    In freedom we're born, &c.

[3] A type of toast in which all drinkers were expected to empty their glasses.

Source: Frank Moore, ed., *Songs and Ballads of the American Revolution* [1856; repr., New York: Arno Press, 1969], 37–39.

3   *The Parody*

The unknown author of this song intended for it to be a parody of "The Liberty Song" (Source 2). It was published in Boston in 1768. No author was identified, but it was described as having originated at "Castle William," the fortification in Boston Harbor that housed British soldiers. As such, it gives us a view on the crisis in Boston from the perspective of the British soldiers who were garrisoned there. Song parodies like this one used humor to make a point, much like a political cartoon does today.

Come shake your dull noddles,[1] ye pumpkins, and bawl,
And own that you're mad at fair Liberty's call;
No scandalous conduct can add to your shame,
Condemn'd to dishonor, inherit the fame.
    In folly you're born, and in folly you'll live,
        To madness still ready,
        And stupidly steady,
    Not as men, but as monkeys, the tokens you give.

Your grandsire, old Satan, now give him a cheer,
Would act like yourselves, and as wildly would steer:
So great an example in prospect still keep,
Whilst you are alive, Old Belza[2] may sleep.

Such villains, such rascals, all dangers despise,
And stick not at mobbing when mischief's the prize;
They burst thro' all barriers, and piously keep
Such chattels and goods the vile rascals can sweep.

. . .

[1] Heads.
[2] The devil.

When in your own cellars you've quaff'd a regale,[3]
Then drive, tug and—, the next house to assail;
For short is your harvest, nor long shall you know
The pleasure of reaping what other men sow.

Then plunder, my lads, for when red coats appear,
You'll melt like the locust when winter is near;
Gold vainly will glow, silver vainly will shine,
But, faith, you must skulk, you no more shall purloin.

Then nod your poor numskulls, ye pumpkins, and bawl,
The de'il take such rascals, fools, whoresons[4] and all;
Your cursed old trade of purloining must cease,
The dread and the curse of all order and peace.

All ages shall speak with contempt and amaze,
Of the vilest banditti[5] that swarm'd in these days;
In defiance of halters,[6] of whips and of chains,
The rogues would run riot.—fools for their pains.

Gulp down your last dram,[7] for the gallows now groans,
And, over depress'd, her lost empire bemoans;
While we quite transported and happy shall be,
From mobs, knaves and villains, protected and free.

[3] Drunk a toast.

[4] Sons of whores.

[5] Bandits.

[6] Nooses.

[7] Alcoholic drink.

Source: Frank Moore, ed., *Songs and Ballads of the American Revolution* [1856; repr., New York: Arno Press, 1969], 41–43.

4   *The Rebels*

Authorship of this song is attributed to an officer in the Queen's Rangers, a loyalist unit raised at the outset of the Revolution. Published in Philadelphia in 1778, when the city was occupied by British troops, it borrowed its tune from "Black Joke," a bawdy drinking song that originated in London during the 1730s. The repeating reference to "hunting-shirts, and rifle-guns" in the lyrics illustrates the loyalists' view of the Continental Army as nothing more than an armed mob of frontier vigilantes.

Ye brave, honest subjects, who dare to be loyal,
And have stood the brunt of every trial,
    Of hunting-shirts, and rifle-guns:

Come listen awhile, and I'll sing you a song;
I'll show you, those Yankees are all in the wrong,
Who, with blustering look and most awkward gait,
'Gainst their lawful sovereign dare for to prate.[1]
   With their hunting-shirts, and rifle-guns.

The arch-rebels, barefooted tatterdemalions,[2]
In baseness exceed all other rebellions,
   With their hunting-shirts, and rifle-guns.
To rend the empire, the most infamous lies,
Their mock-patriot Congress, do always devise;
Independence, like the first of rebels, they claim,
But their plots will be damn'd in the annals of fame,
   With their hunting-shirts, and rifle-guns.

Forgetting the mercies of Great Britain's king,
Who saved their forefathers' necks from the string;
   With their hunting-shirts, and rifle-guns.
They renounce allegiance and take up their arms,
Assemble together like hornets in swarms,
So dirty their backs, and so wretched their show,
That carrion-crow follows wherever they go,
   With their hunting-shirts, and rifle-guns.

With load peals of laughter, your sides, sirs, would crack,
To see General Convict and Colonel Shoe-black,[3]
   With their hunting-shirts, and rifle-guns.
See cobblers and quacks, rebel priests and the like,
Pettifoggers[4] and barbers with sword and with pike,
All strutting, the standard of Satan beside,
And honest names using, their black deeds to hide.
   With their hunting-shirts, and rifle-guns.

. . .

For one lawful ruler, many tyrants we've got,
Who force young and old to their wars, to be shot,
   With their hunting-shirts, and rifle-guns.
Our good king, God speed him! never used men so,
We then could speak, act, and like freemen could go;
But committees enslave us, our Liberty's gone,

[1] Babble annoyingly.

[2] Poor folks dressed in rags.

[3] Satirical invented names for Continental Army officers, meant to imply that the patriots were led by criminals and poor laborers.

[4] Small-time lawyers of questionable ethics.

Our trade and church murder'd; our country's undone,
　By hunting-shirts, and rifle-guns.

Come take up your glasses, each true loyal heart,
And may every rebel meet his due desert,
　With his hunting-shirt, and rifle-gun.
May Congress, Conventions, those damn'd inquisitions,
Be fed with hot sulphur, from Lucifer's kitchens,
May commerce and peace again be restored,
And Americans own their true sovereign lord.
　Then oblivion to shirts, and rife-guns.
　　God save the King.

Source: Frank Moore, ed., *Songs and Ballads of the American Revolution* [1856; repr., New York: Arno Press, 1969], 196–99.

5   *The New Recruit / Fare Thee Well, Ye Sweethearts*

Recruitment was a constant problem for the Continental Army after the disastrous campaign of 1776. Drink and song helped facilitate the process, especially when recruiters appeared at taverns or other public places. It is easy to imagine this song being sung on such an occasion. Like other popular songs, recruitment songs appeared in countless variations. The lyrics below were printed under the title "The New Recruit, or the Gallant Volunteer, A New Song" in a colonial newspaper; the recorded version uses the title "Fare Thee Well, Ye Sweethearts" and has fewer stanzas.

Come on my hearts of tempered steel,
And leave your girls and farms,
Your sports and plays and holidays,
And hark, away to arms!
And to conquest we will go, will go, will go,
And to conquest we will go.
A Soldier is a gentleman,
His honour is his life,
And he that won't stand to his post,
Will never stand by his wife,
And to conquest we will go, &c.
For love and honour are the same,
Or else so near an ally,
That neither can exist alone,
But flourish side by side.
And to conquest we will go, &c.
So fare you well sweethearts a while,

You smiling girls adieu;
And when we drub the dogs away,[1]
We kiss it out with you.
And to conquest we will go, &c.
The spring is up, the winter flies,
The hills are green and gay,
And all inviting honour calls,
Away, my boys, away.
And to conquest we will go, &c.
In shady tents, by cooling streams,
With hearts all firm and free,
We chase the cares of life away,
In songs of liberty.
And to conquest we will go, &c.
No foreign slaves shall give us law,
No British tyrants reign;
'Tis Independence made us free;
And freedom we maintain.
And to conquest we will go, &c.
We charge the foe from post to post,
Attack their works and lines,
Or by some well laid stratagem,
We make them all Burgoynes.[2]
And to conquest we will go, &c.
And when the war is over, boys,
Then down we sit at ease,
And plow and sow and reap and mow,
And live just as we please.
When from conquest we shall go, &c.
Each hearty lad shall take his lass,
And beaming like a star,
And in her softer arms forget,
The dangers of the war.
When to conquest we did go, &c.
The rising world shall sing of us,
A thousand years to come,
And to their children's children tell,
The Wonders we have done.
When to conquest we did go, &c.
So my honest fellows here's my hand,
My heart, my very soul,

[1] Send the redcoats retreating.
[2] British general John Burgoyne suffered a humiliating defeat at the Battle of Saratoga in 1777.

With all the joys of Liberty,
Good fortune and a bowl.[3]
And to conquest we will go, &c.

[3] A punch bowl.

Source: Pennsylvania Packet, April 8, 1778, and The Committee of Correspondence, *Songs and Ballads of Colonial and Revolutionary America,* audio recording (New York: Smithsonian Folkways No. FH 5274, 1976).

 6   *How Stands the Glass Around*

This soldiers' drinking song first appeared in print in 1729 and was popular among British and American soldiers during the French and Indian and Revolutionary wars. It presents a much different view of military life than the recruiting songs sung at the time of enlistment.

How stands the glass around,
For shame ye take no care, my boys,
How stands the glass around,
Let mirth and wine abound,
The trumpets sound,
The colors they are flying, boys.
To fight, kill, or wound,
May we still be found,
Content with our hard fate, my boys,
On the cold ground.
Why, soldiers, why,
Should we be melancholy, boys?
Why, soldiers, why,
Whose business 'tis to die!
What, sighing, fie![1]
Damn fear, drink on, be jolly, boys,
'Tis he, you, or I!
Cold, hot, wet, or dry,
We're always bound to follow, boys,
And scorn to fly!
'Tis but in vain,
I mean not to upbraid you, boys,
'Tis but in vain,
For soldiers to complain.
Should next campaign,
Send us to him who made us, boys,
We're free from pain!

[1] An exclamation of disgust.

but if we remain,
A bottle and a kind landlady
Cure all again.

Source: The Committee of Correspondence, *Songs and Ballads of Colonial and Revolutionary America*, audio recording (New York: Smithsonian Folkways No. FH 5274, 1976).

7 | *The Epilogue*

This loyalist song appeared in October 1778 on ballad sheets published in British-occupied Philadelphia and New York. Its title suggests that the songwriter thought the war almost over and decided in the British favor. The tune is borrowed from the popular British song "Derry Down."

The farce is now finish'd, your sport's at an end,
But ere you depart, let the voice of a friend
By way of a chorus, the evening crown
With a song to the tune of a hey derry down.
CHORUS: Derry down, down, hey derry down . . .

Old Shakespeare, a poet who should not be spit on,
Although he was born in the island called Britain,
Hath said that mankind are all players at best,
A truth we'll admit of, for the sake of the jest.
CHORUS

On this puny stage, we have strutted our hour,
And acted our parts to the best of our power,
That the farce hath concluded not perfectly well,
Was surely the fault of the devil in Hell.
CHORUS

The devil, you know, out of spleen[1] for the church,
Will often abandon his friends in the lurch,
And turn them adrift in the midst of their joy,
'Tis a difficult matter to cheat the old boy.
CHORUS

Our great Independence we give to the wind,
And pray that Great Britain may once more be kind.
In this jovial song all hostility ends,
And Britons and we will for ever be friends.

[1] Ill temper.

Once more, here's a health[2] to the King and the Queen!
Confusion to him, who on rancor and spleen,
Refuses to drink with an English good friend,
Immutable amity to the world's end.

[2] A toast.

Source: Dorothy Messney, *Patchwork and Powder Horn: Songs of the American Revolution,* audio recording (New York: Smithsonian Folkways No. FH 5278, 1975).

8 | *Volunteer Boys*

By 1780, it had become difficult for the patriots to raise the troops and taxes necessary to support the Continental Army. The volunteer soldiers of 1775 and 1776 had for the most part been replaced by long-term enlistees and substitutes hired by draftees trying to avoid military service. This song, written by an Englishman who had recently immigrated to America and embraced the cause of independence, presented a very different picture of the social makeup of the Continental Army.

. . .

Nobles and beauties and such common toasts,
    Those who admire may drink, sir;
Fill up the glass to the volunteer hosts,
    Who never from danger will shrink, sir.
        Let mirth appear,
        Every heart cheer,
The toast that I give is the brave volunteer.

Here's to the squire who goes to parade
    Here's to the citizen soldier;
Here's to the merchant who fights for his trade,
    Whom danger increasing make bolder.
        Let mirth appear,
        Union is here,
The toast that I give is the brave volunteer.

Here's to the lawyer, who, leaving the bar,
    Hastens where honor doth lead, sir,
Changing the gown for the ensigns of war,
    The cause of his country to plead, sir.
        Freedom appears,
        Every heart cheers,
And calls for the health of the law volunteers.

Here's to the soldier, though batter'd in wars,
   And safe to his farm-house retir'd;
When called by his country, ne'er thinks of his scars,
   With ardor to join us inspir'd
     Bright flame appears,
     Trophies uprear,
To veteran chiefs who became volunteers.

Here's to the farmer who dares to advance
   To harvest of honor with pleasure;
Who with a slave the most skillful in France
   A sword for his country would measure.
     Hence with cold fear,
     Heroes rise here;
The ploughman is chang'd to the stout volunteer.

Here's to the peer,[1] first in senate and field,
   Whose actions to titles add grace, sir;
Whose spirit undaunted would never yet yield
   To a foe, to a pension or place, sir.
     Gratitude here,
     Toasts to the peer,
Who adds to his titles, "the brave volunteer."

Thus the bold bands for old Jersey's defence,[2]
   The muse hath with rapture review'd, sir;
With our volunteer boys, as our verses commence,
   With our volunteer boys they conclude, sir.
     Discord or noise,
     Ne'er damp our joys,
But health and success to the volunteer boys.

[1] Aristocrat.

[2] A reference to the Continental Army's success at the battles of Trenton (December 1776) and Princeton (January 1777).

Source: Frank Moore, ed., *Songs and Ballads of the American Revolution* [1856; repr., New York: Arno Press, 1969], 285–88.

9   *To the Traitor Arnold*

This song appeared in a Philadelphia newspaper in October 1780, about a month after the discovery of Benedict Arnold's treasonous plan to surrender West Point to the British. Since the anonymous author did not identify a tune to match with it, it was more likely to be recited than sung. It is a good

example of how songs could be used to demonize enemies as well as to celebrate heroes.

Arnold! thy name, as heretofore,
Shall now be Benedict no more;
Since, instigated by the devil,
Thy ways are turn'd from good to evil.

'Tis fit we brand thee with a name,
To suit thy infamy and shame;
And since of treason thou'rt convicted,
Thy name should now be maledicted.[1]

Unless by way of contradiction,
We style thee Britain's Benediction;
Such blessings she, with liberal hand,
Confers on this devoted land.

For instance, only let us mention,
Some proofs of her benign intention;
The slaves she sends us o'er the deep,
The bribes to cut our throats in sleep.
To take our lives and scalps away,
The savage Indians keeps in pay,
And Tories worse, by half, than they.

Then in this class of Britain's heroes,
The Tories, savage Indians, Negroes,
Recorded, Arnold's name shall stand,
While Freedom's blessings crown our land.
And odious for the blackest crimes,
Arnold shall stink to latest times.

[1] Cursed.

Source: Frank Moore, ed., *Songs and Ballads of the American Revolution* [1856; repr., New York: Arno Press, 1969], 333–34.

10   *The Dance*

This song from 1781 celebrates the American victory at Yorktown, Virginia, the last major battle of the war. Like many songs celebrating military victories, it incorporates the names of each army's commanding officers, lionizing the victors and lampooning the defeated. It is set to the tune of "Yankee Doodle," a popular British song that the patriots adapted to their cause.

Cornwallis[1] led a country dance,
The like was never seen, sir,
Much retrograde and much advance,
And all with General Greene,[2] sir.
They rambled up and rambled down,
Join'd hands, then off they run, sir,
Our General Greene to Charlestown,[3]
The Earl[4] to Wilmington,[5] sir.
Greene, in the South, then danc'd a set,
And got a mighty name, sir.
Cornwallis jigg'd with young Fayette,[6]
But suffer'd in his fame, sir.
Then down he figur'd to the shore,
Most like a lordly dancer,
And on his courtly honor swore,
He would no more advance, sir.
Quoth he, "my guards are weary grown
With footing country dances,
They never at St. James's[7] shone,
At capers, kick or prances."
Though men so gallant ne'er were seen,
While sauntering on parade, sir,
Or wriggling o'er the park's smooth green,
Or at a masquerade, sir.
Yet are red heels and long-lac'd skirts,
For stumps and briars meet, sir?
Or stand they chance with hunting-shirts,
Or hardy veteran feet, sir?
Now housed in York,[8]
he challenged all to minuets so sprightly,
And lessons for a courtly ball,
his soldiers studied nightly.
His challenge heard, full soon there came,
a set who knew the dance, sir,

[1] The British commander at Yorktown.

[2] The commander of the Continental troops who lured Cornwallis into Virginia from the Carolinas.

[3] Charleston, South Carolina.

[4] Cornwallis.

[5] North Carolina.

[6] The Marquis de Lafayette.

[7] St. James's Palace in Britain; that is, they were never skilled dancers at home.

[8] Yorktown, Virginia.

De Grasse and Rochambeau,[9]
whose fame proved certain to advance, sir.
And Washington, Columbia's son,
Who's easy nature taught, sir,
That grace which can't by pains be won,
Nor monarch's gold be bought, sir.
Now hand in hand they circle round,
This ever-dancing peer, sir;
Their gentle movements, soon confound
The Earl, as they draw near, sir.
His music he soon forgets to play—
His feet can no more move, sir,
And all his soldiers curse the day,
They jigged to our shore, sir.
Now Tories all, what can ye say?
Come—is not this a griper,[10]
That while your hopes are danc'd away,
'Tis you must pay the piper.

[9] French officers whose forces aided the Continental Army at the Battle of Yorktown.
[10] A cause for complaint.
Source: Dorothy Messney, *Patchwork and Powder Horn: Songs of the American Revolution,* audio recording (New York: Smithsonian Folkways No. FH 5278, 1975).

Analyzing Songs

1. Which of these songs were likely to have appealed to patriots and which to loyalists? How were songs that supported the patriot cause likely to depict those who supported and fought for the British cause? How were loyalist songs likely to depict patriot soldiers and civilians?

2. Which of the songs reproduced here invoke social drinking (both alcoholic and nonalcoholic) in their lyrics? How is that drinking defined by gender or occupation, and what political significance is attached to it in these songs?

3. How did references to King George III and other symbols of British power change over time or according to audience in these songs? Who or what replaced the king as the new focal points of American patriotism?

4. Using your notes from the table on page 101, what do these songs tell you about this society's definitions of male and female roles in public life? How did these songs attempt to mobilize men and women for the patriot cause, and did their messages challenge or reinforce traditional gender roles?

5. Eighteenth-century Americans used songs to describe who they were as well as who they were not. What individuals or groups were marked as outsiders or exiles from the body politic in these sources? Do you see any evidence here of

how these songs might have been used by those who wrote, published, and sung them to intimidate or coerce the reluctant or neutral into supporting a particular cause?

6. Do you think these songs describe mostly change or mostly stability in American society during the Revolutionary era? How does your answer to that question differ when you look at specific social groups referred to in these sources, such as women, soldiers, farmers, or political leaders?

The Rest of the Story

The necessity of mobilizing support for the patriot cause during the American Revolution did much to politicize drinking culture in the new nation. During the 1760s and 1770s, patriot leaders were quite liberal with the punch bowl and strong beer during public festivities meant to draw support to their cause. Once the war was over, the Fourth of July and George Washington's birthday became new public holidays that called for parades, bonfires, fireworks, and, of course, drink and song. (For more on the way early Americans celebrated Independence Day, see the Capstone chapter, "Coming Together and Pulling Apart: Nineteenth-Century Fourth of July Observations.") The rivalry between the Federalists and Democratic Republicans during the 1790s intensified the political partisanship associated with such events, as each side scrambled to use the new symbols and rituals of American civic culture to its own advantage. As the 1790s gave way to the nineteenth century, marginalized groups such as free blacks and women asserted their places in the new nation's political and social order by appropriating the rites of public celebration for their own purposes. In 1796, a group of women in York, Pennsylvania, attending an outdoor tea party made eight toasts honoring President Washington and the federal government, but ended with one to "The Rights of Women." In 1810, free blacks in Boston celebrating the American ban on the transatlantic slave trade made nine toasts to individuals, groups, and nations who supported the abolitionist cause.

Songs remained fixtures of nineteenth-century American political culture. As American politics grew more democratic and participatory, music became a vital part of how political parties and reform groups broadcast their messages and rallied supporters. Despite having declared their political independence in 1776, Americans still relied on their cultural inheritance from Britain to make their music. During the 1790s, a New York woman set lyrics titled "The Rights of Women" to the patriotic British anthem "God Save the King." In 1831, Samuel Francis Smith also borrowed the tune from "God Save the King" for his patriotic song "America." We still sing it today, only by its more familiar title "My Country, 'Tis of Thee." Of course, the most famous song written by a nineteenth-century American is "The Star-Spangled Banner," which Francis Scott Key composed after witnessing the bombardment of Baltimore's Fort McHenry by British warships during the War of 1812. It first appeared in newspapers and ballad sheets under the title "Defence of Fort M'Henry," and readers were instructed to sing it to the tune of "To Anacreon in Heaven," a popular English drinking song that had found its way to America during the 1770s, most likely carried there by British officers and soldiers sent to fight the American rebels. Officially adopted as the national anthem of the United States in 1931, "The Star-Spangled Banner" owes a debt to the Revolutionary generation that few of its singers ever realize.

To Find Out More

Songs from the Revolutionary Era

Library of Congress. "An American Time Capsule: Three Centuries of Broadsides and Other Political Ephemera" *American Memory.* http://memory.loc.gov/ammem /rbpehtml.

Moore, Frank, ed. *Songs and Ballads of the American Revolution.* 1856; repr., New York: Arno Press, 1969.

Secondary Sources on Early American Music and Drinking Culture

Conroy, David W. *In Public Houses: Drink and the Revolution of Authority in Colonial Massachusetts.* Chapel Hill: University of North Carolina Press, 1995.

Hooker, Richard J. "The American Revolution Seen through a Wine Glass." *William and Mary Quarterly*, 3rd ser., 11 (1954): 52–77.

Leepson, Marc. *What So Proudly We Hailed: Francis Scott Key, A Life.* New York: Palgrave Macmillan, 2014.

Newman, Simon P. *Parades and Politics of the Streets: Festive Culture in the Early American Republic.* Philadelphia: University of Pennsylvania Press, 1997.

Salinger, Sharon V. *Taverns and Drinking in Early America.* Baltimore: Johns Hopkins University Press, 2002.

Schlesinger, Arthur M. "A Note on Songs as Patriot Propaganda, 1765–1776." *William and Mary Quarterly*, 3rd ser., 11 (1954): 78–88.

Thompson, Peter. *Rum Punch and Revolution: Tavern-Going and Public Life in Eighteenth-Century Philadelphia.* Philadelphia: University of Pennsylvania Press, 1999.

Tick, Judith, ed. *Music in the USA: A Documentary Companion.* New York: Oxford University Press, 2008.

Waldstreicher, David. *In the Midst of Perpetual Fetes: The Making of American Nationalism, 1776–1820.* Chapel Hill: University of North Carolina Press, 1997.

CHAPTER 6

Debating the Constitution

Speeches from the New York Ratification Convention

The delegates who attended the Federal Convention in Philadelphia in the summer of 1787 knew that the result of their meeting would be controversial. During the months that followed, as the states organized special conventions to ratify or reject the new plan for a federal government, supporters of the Constitution watched anxiously, like bettors trying to handicap a horse race (Figure 6.1). One such observer was George Washington, who had come out of his retirement at Mount Vernon to preside over the Federal Convention. Writing to his friend and fellow Federalist Henry Knox in January 1788, Washington noted that of all the states, "the determinations of new York . . . seem the most problematical."

Washington had a gift for understatement. New York had sent three delegates to the Federal Convention, but when it became clear that the convention intended to replace rather than revise the Articles of Confederation, two of them—Robert Yates and John Lansing—left a few weeks into the proceedings. Yates and Lansing reported their misgivings to New York governor George Clinton, who shared their displeasure with what was happening in Philadelphia. A New York City newspaper, the *Daily Advertiser*, printed the first copy of the Constitution in the state on September 21. Other printers quickly followed, even printing the Constitution in translation so that Dutch-speaking inhabitants could read it in their native language. The Constitution's rapid dissemination throughout the state ensured that it would be the subject of a spirited public debate.

By the time Washington wrote his letter to Knox in early 1788, New York had become a ratification battleground, with well-organized factions on each side raising money and calling in outside support to make their case. Supporters of ratification were known as Federalists. As was the case in other states,

Figure 6.1 George Washington Presiding at the Federal Convention, 1787 *This 1799 illustration imagines the delegates at work at the Federal Convention twelve years earlier. No such images appeared at the time of the convention, in part because the delegates conducted their work behind closed doors and refused to discuss it in public until they were finished. The air of secrecy that surrounded the drafting of the Constitution aroused the opposition of some critics, who believed a privileged few were trying to impose a new and less democratic form of government on the many.* Source: Hulton Archive/Getty Images

they came chiefly from urban and commercial backgrounds and favored the Constitution because they believed it would create a more centralized and stable union between the states. They wanted a stronger federal government, one capable of acting independently of the states so that the United States could pursue its economic and diplomatic interests more effectively with foreign powers and Indian nations. They also wanted the federal government to have its own taxation power so that it could be financially independent of the states and pay off its debts at home and abroad. The most famous published commentary on the Constitution, a series of eighty-five editorials in New York's newspapers known collectively as *The Federalist*, was a product of their propaganda campaign on behalf of ratification in New York.

The Antifederalists, or opponents of the Constitution, met fire with fire, churning out their own editorials and pamphlets. As in other states, New York's Antifederalists tended to come from backgrounds more rural and less wealthy than Federalists. They were more likely than Federalists to be debtors instead of creditors and to be engaged in subsistence agriculture rather than commercial food or craft production. They opposed the Constitution because a strong central government reminded them too much of the government they had rebelled against in 1776. The proposed federal government looked too much like the British Crown and Parliament, distant from and unrepresentative of the common people. They feared that the rich and well-connected could easily monopolize power in such a government, shifting the burden of taxation to the lower and middle classes. Worst of all, the proposed Constitution did not even have a bill of rights, a common feature of the state constitutions, that guaranteed the civil liberties such as freedom of speech and freedom of religion that Americans had fought and died for during the Revolution.

When New York's ratification convention finally met in the Hudson River town of Poughkeepsie on June 17, 1788, the Constitution appeared dead on arrival. Governor Clinton, whose Antifederalist sympathies were already well known, chaired the proceedings. More important, of the sixty-five delegates in attendance, forty-six were Antifederalists, a better than two-to-one margin over the Constitution's supporters. The only counties to send Federalist delegations to Poughkeepsie were centered around New York City; every county north of the lower Hudson Valley was represented by Antifederalists. This geographic distribution reflected a division of interests within the state. Even though lawyers, merchants, and large landowners could be found on each side of the ratification debate, they made up a much larger proportion of the Federalist delegates at the convention (79 percent to 50 percent). From the outset, the New York ratification convention pitted a minority of wealthy, urban Federalists against a majority of Antifederalists from rural counties and more middling social backgrounds.

New York's vote on the Constitution had profound implications for the rest of the United States. When New York's convention opened, eight states had already ratified the Constitution, but contests too close to call were being fought in New Hampshire and Virginia. The Constitution stated that nine of the thirteen states had to ratify it before the new federal government could be formed. Regardless of how the votes in New Hampshire and Virginia turned out, the new federal government would not fare well if New York stood apart from the union. New York City had the best harbor in the country for overseas trade, and the Hudson and Mohawk rivers provided the nation with its most important route into the continent's interior. New York was also a vital geographic link for trade and communication between New England and the South. Without New York, no one expected the new federal government to prosper or endure.

Despite their numerical superiority at the convention, New York's Antifederalists could not afford to reject the Constitution out of hand. Eight states had already ratified, and the Antifederalist delegates were no more interested in seeing their state stand apart from the union than their opponents were. There was even some talk among the Federalists of splitting the state in two so that the lower Hudson Valley, New York City, and Long Island could join the new federal union if the delegations from the northern counties refused to budge. When news arrived in Poughkeepsie on June 25 of New Hampshire's positive vote for ratification, it became apparent to all concerned that some version of the Constitution would go into effect, regardless of what the New Yorkers decided. At that point, the chief goal of the Antifederalist leadership became securing a conditional ratification, contingent upon the acceptance of amendments to the Constitution before it went into effect. The Federalists opposed this strategy, because conditional ratification would require convening another interstate convention, thereby delaying and perhaps jeopardizing the installation of the new government. Worse yet, the new federal government might form without the New Yorkers on board, locking them out of key decisions on such matters as the location of the new federal capital.

Once deliberations got under way in Poughkeepsie, leaders emerged on both sides of the debate. As presiding officer, Governor Clinton needed to maintain an air of impartiality, so he spoke rarely. Instead, the Antifederalists' most effective speaker was Melancton Smith, a self-educated merchant and lawyer who lived mostly in New York City but who attended the convention as a delegate from upstate Dutchess County, where he owned a large estate. Smith's wealth did not make him a typical Antifederalist, but his unpolished manner and firm commitment to democratic principles made him suspicious of privilege and power and naturally sympathetic to the Antifederalist cause. His chief opponent was Alexander Hamilton, a former aide-de-camp to George Washington who had married into one of the state's wealthiest families. Hamilton had been New York's third delegate to the Federal Convention the previous year, but unlike Yates and Lansing, he supported the convention's designs and signed the Constitution when it was finished. With James Madison and John Jay, he coauthored the *Federalist* newspaper editorials in 1787–1788.

Observers at the ratification convention recognized the talents and energy of both Smith and Hamilton. Poughkeepsie lawyer James Kent called Smith "the most prominent and responsible speaker on the party of the anti-federalist majority . . . Hamilton's most persevering and formidable antagonist." Smith himself described Hamilton as the "champion" of the Federalists: "he speaks frequently, very long and very vehemently." The fate of the Constitution in New York and the nation hinged on the standoff between these two men and their political allies in a Hudson River courthouse.

Using the Source: The Ratification Debates

The Federal Convention that drafted the Constitution took place in secrecy. The delegates cloistered themselves behind closed doors and did not speak a word to anyone about their proceedings until they finished their business several months later. The process of ratification was different. Each state called a special convention solely for the purpose of passing judgment on the Constitution. These conventions were as open and public as the Federal Convention had been closed and secret. New York's ratification convention was no exception: the

Poughkeepsie courthouse accommodated two hundred spectators in addition to the sixty-five delegates. For the first two weeks of the convention, the *Daily Advertiser* printed each day's debates in full; after July 2 (when news of Virginia's ratification arrived), it printed summaries of each day's proceedings. Like the other state ratification conventions, New York left a substantial public record that has captivated historians ever since.

Each state determined the time and place of its ratification convention and the means by which delegates would be selected for it. Most states held special elections for delegates to their conventions, using the same eligibility requirements for voting that they did for elections to the state legislature. New York differed from this practice by temporarily expanding its franchise, allowing all free adult males to vote for delegates to the ratification convention. This move actually had little effect on the number of votes cast, because the state's 1777 constitution had already significantly lowered the amount of property a man had to own to be eligible to vote. It did, however, indicate the pervasive belief among Federalists and Antifederalists alike that the power of the proposed federal government would derive directly from the people, and, therefore, they would have to be the ultimate arbiters on ratification. Of course, this definition also reflected their consensus that the "people" did not include women, slaves, or other groups traditionally excluded from the political process.

What Can the Ratification Debates Tell Us?

The great advantage to studying the proceedings of the ratification conventions is that they provide the fullest record available of how Americans interpreted the Constitution at the time it was adopted. In other words, this source speaks directly to one of the guiding principles of constitutional interpretation: what was the original intent of the framers of the Constitution? Strict constructionists, those scholars and judges who believe that the power of the federal government should extend no further than is explicitly stated in the Constitution, place great emphasis on original intent and argue that the purposes and ideas of those men who adopted the Constitution should guide our interpretation of the document. Loose constructionists, on the other hand, believe that the Constitution is a "living document" that needs to be reinterpreted by each generation if it is to meet the needs of a changing society. They place less importance on original intent but still argue with strict constructionists about what the framers had in mind when they wrote and ratified the Constitution. Some of the most hotly debated constitutional issues of today, such as gay rights and affirmative action, testify to how far removed our modern society is from the world of Alexander Hamilton and Melancton Smith, yet the words they spoke in Poughkeepsie in 1788 are an important part of the textual record lawyers and judges use to interpret the Constitution in our courtrooms.

In arguing over original intent, strict constructionists and loose constructionists invariably refer to the same set of sources: the notes kept by James Madison during the Federal Convention, editorials and pamphlets published during the ratification process in 1787–1788, and the proceedings of the state ratification conventions. Madison's notes are important because he was the primary author of the Constitution, and he left the most complete account of what occurred during the Federal Convention in Philadelphia. The political tracts published during 1787–1788 convey the visceral intensity of the debate over ratification. Neither of these sources, however, compares to the proceedings of the state ratification conventions in presenting the range and depth of the Federalist and Antifederalist positions. Even a cursory review of the state convention records reveals that the debate over original intent should really be one over "original intents," because there was such a variety of opinions expressed among the delegates who decided the ratification issue.

The proceedings of the ratification conventions also illustrate the nature of political expression and ideology in post-Revolutionary America. In our age of modern media politics, in which politicians speak in sound bites that are measured in seconds, we may find it strange that convention delegates gave speeches that lasted for hours and commanded the rapt attention of their audiences. As indicated by the following excerpt from a June 21, 1788, speech by Alexander Hamilton, the delegates sprinkled their debates liberally with references to the republics of ancient Greece and Rome.

It was remarked yesterday, that a numerous representation was necessary to obtain the confidence of the people. This is not generally true. The confidence of the people will easily be gained by a good administration. This is the true touchstone. I could illustrate the position by a variety of historical examples, both ancient and modern. In Sparta, the ephori were a body of magistrates, instituted as a check upon the senate, and representing the people. They consisted of only five men; but they were able to protect their rights, and therefore enjoyed their confidence and attachment. In Rome, the people were represented by three tribunes, who were afterwards increased to ten. Every one acquainted with the history of that republic will recollect how powerful a check to the senatorial encroachments this small body proved; how unlimited a confidence was placed in them by the people, whose guardians they were; and to what a conspicuous station in the government their influence at length elevated the plebeians.

One of the city-states of ancient Greece

Representatives of the common people in the Roman republic, who possessed a veto power over other magistrates

The common people of ancient Rome

Elected annually as overseers of Sparta's kings, whom they could impeach and depose if the kings acted contrary to the law

What assumption is Hamilton making here about the education of his audience?

Refers to the Roman Senate, which represented the aristocracy

Source: Bernard Bailyn, ed., *The Debate on the Constitution: Federalist and Anti-Federalist Speeches, Articles, and Letters during the Struggle over Ratification* (New York: Library of America, 1993), 2:768.

These references may strike us now as haughty and obscure, but this political language resonated among Hamilton's listeners. By reading these speeches and trying to unlock their persuasive power, we can gain insight into the political culture and ideology that generated the Constitution.

A disadvantage arising from the use of this source is the difficulty of measuring how much effect public speeches and debates had on the votes cast at the ratification conventions. Delegates got elected to the New York ratification convention in part because their constituents already knew how they would vote. Then, as now, political debate made for good public theater, but did the eloquence of Alexander Hamilton or Melancton Smith actually convince any of the delegates to change their minds? We know from the final vote tally that some of the Antifederalist delegates ended up voting for ratification, but we do not know if they did so because of the persuasive power of the speeches they heard or because of some other motivation.

Certainly, factors external to New York influenced the proceedings. After news of Virginia's ratification reached Poughkeepsie on July 2, the proceedings changed markedly. Delegates gave fewer speeches and spent most of their time negotiating the wording of proposed amendments and ratification resolutions. How should historians weigh this change in circumstances when trying to determine the effect of the speeches made before July 2? In fathoming the motivations behind the final vote, we must also consider the possibility that some delegates voted for unstated reasons of personal interest, such as the desire for public office in the new federal government, or because of compromises struck with their rivals behind closed doors.

In other words, the ratification debates are a great source for reconstructing the public arguments Federalists and Antifederalists made for and against the Constitution, but we cannot rely on them solely if we wish to reconstruct the thoughts behind the votes cast in the ratification conventions. That is why historians usually supplement their work on the debates with research into the backgrounds and personal writings of the convention delegates. In private letters or recollections, the men who decided the fate of the Constitution were often more plainspoken about the delicate balancing of ideology and interests that determined their votes than they were in their public speech. Also, research into the economic and social background of the delegates helps uncover patterns in the voting on ratification that may confirm or contradict the delegates' public statements about the Constitution.

When examining the speeches from any political debate, you will want to ask some questions about the speaker, the ideas being expressed, and the interests being represented; the Checklist on page 125 will help you in this regard.

CHECKLIST: Interrogating Political Debates

☐ Who is the person delivering the speech? What do you know about the speaker's social and economic background?

☐ Which side of the debate does the speaker represent?

☐ What are the main points of the speaker's argument? What principles does the speaker defend or attack?

☐ What sort of terms or language does the speaker use to make his or her argument? How does it compare with the terms and language used by the opposing side?

☐ Can you discern any hidden bias or motives behind the rhetoric used by the speaker?

Source Analysis Table

As you read through the source, use the table on page 126 to help organize your notes and summarize the Federalist and Antifederalist positions on the issues of representation in Congress, sources of corruption, and the Constitution's effect on the states.

	Federalists	Antifederalists
Representation in Congress		
Sources of Corruption		
Constitution's Effect on the States		

The Source: Speeches Debating the Constitution from the New York Ratification Convention, June 21–28, 1788

The passages that follow are from debates that occurred between June 21 and June 28, when delegates on both sides gave long speeches detailing their contrasting opinions on the Constitution. You will notice that the style of presentation varies from one speech to the next. Some read like verbatim transcriptions, whereas others read like an editor's narrative summary of the speech's content. These differences resulted from day-to-day variances in how the proceedings were recorded by a newspaper editor who published them in the Daily Advertiser, *a New York newspaper.*

REPRESENTATION IN CONGRESS

One of the Antifederalists' chief objections to the Constitution was that the House of Representatives was not representative enough. The House would be limited in size to no more than one representative for every 30,000 people (today, it is about one representative for every 650,000 people). Antifederalists believed this limitation would lead to electoral districts much too large to represent the people adequately and that election would be out of the reach of any candidate not rich or famous enough to command reputation over such a wide area. Federalists responded to this argument by questioning whether more representatives actually meant better representation.

1   *Melancton Smith,* June 21, 1788

To determine whether the number of representatives proposed by this Constitution is sufficient, it is proper to examine the qualifications which this house[1] ought to possess, in order to exercise their power discreetly for the happiness of the people. The idea that naturally suggests itself to our minds, when we speak of representatives, is, that they resemble those they represent. They should be a true picture of the people, possess a knowledge of their circumstances and their wants, sympathize in all their distresses, and be disposed to seek their true interests. The knowledge necessary for the representative of a free people not only comprehends extensive political and commercial information, such as is acquired by men of refined education, who have leisure to attain to high degrees

---

[1] The House of Representatives.

Source: All debate passages reprinted in this chapter are excerpted from Bernard Bailyn, ed., *The Debate on the Constitution: Federalist and Anti-Federalist Speeches, Articles, and Letters during the Struggle over Ratification* (New York: Library of America, 1993), 2:759–835.

of improvement, but it should also comprehend that kind of acquaintance with the common concerns and occupations of the people, which men of the middling class of life are, in general, more competent to, than those of a superior class. To understand the true commercial interests of a country, not only requires just ideas of the general commerce of the world, but also, and principally, a knowledge of the productions of your own country, and their value, what your soil is capable of producing, the nature of your manufactures, and the capacity of the country to increase both. To exercise the power of laying taxes, duties, and excises, with discretion, requires something more than an acquaintance with the abstruse[2] parts of the system of finance. It calls for a knowledge of the circumstances and ability of the people in general—a discernment how the burdens imposed will bear upon the different classes.

From these observations results this conclusion—that the number of representatives should be so large, as that, while it embraces the men of the first class, it should admit those of the middling class of life. I am convinced that this government[3] is so constituted that the representatives will generally be composed of the first class in the community, which I shall distinguish by the name of the natural aristocracy of the country. I do not mean to give offence by using this term. I am sensible this idea is treated by many gentlemen as chimerical.[4] I shall be asked what is meant by the natural aristocracy, and told that no such distinction of classes of men exists among us. It is true, it is our singular felicity that we have no legal or hereditary distinctions of this kind; but still there are real differences. Every society naturally divides itself into classes. The Author of nature[5] has bestowed on some greater capacities than others; birth, education, talents, and wealth, create distinctions among men as visible, and of as much influence, as titles, stars, and garters. In every society, men of this class will command a superior degree of respect; and if the government is so constituted as to admit but few to exercise the powers of it, it will, according to the natural course of things, be in their hands. Men in the middling class, who are qualified as representatives, will not be so anxious to be chosen as those of the first. When the number is so small, the office will be highly elevated and distinguished; the style in which the members live will probably be high; circumstances of this kind will render the place of a representative not a desirable one to sensible, substantial men, who have been used to walk in the plain and frugal paths of life.

. . . A substantial yeoman,[6] of sense and discernment, will hardly ever be chosen. From these remarks, it appears that the government will fall into the hands of the few and the great. This will be a government of oppression. I do not mean to declaim against the great, and charge them indiscriminately with want of principle and honesty. The same passions and prejudices govern all men.

[2] Difficult to comprehend.

[3] The new federal government proposed by the Constitution.

[4] Imaginary.

[5] God.

[6] A middle-class farmer.

The circumstances in which men are placed in a great measure give a cast to the human character. Those in middling circumstances have less temptation; they are inclined by habit, and the company with whom they associate, to set bounds to their passions and appetites. If this is not sufficient, the want of means to gratify them will be a restraint: they are obliged to employ their time in their respective callings; hence the substantial yeomanry of the country are more temperate, of better morals, and less ambition, than the great. The latter do not feel for the poor and middling class; the reasons are obvious—they are not obliged to use the same pains and labor to procure property as the other. They feel not the inconveniences arising from the payment of small sums. The great consider themselves above the common people, entitled to more respect, do not associate with them; they fancy themselves to have a right of preeminence in every thing. In short, they possess the same feelings, and are under the influence of the same motives, as an hereditary nobility. I know the idea that such a distinction exists in this country is ridiculed by some; but I am not the less apprehensive of danger from their influence on this account. . . .

2   *Alexander Hamilton*, June 21, 1788

Mr. *Hamilton* then reassumed his argument. . . .

It has been observed, by an honorable gentleman,[1] that a pure democracy, if it were practicable, would be the most perfect government. Experience has proved that no position in politics is more false than this. The ancient democracies, in which the people themselves deliberated, never possessed one feature of good government. Their very character was tyranny; their figure, deformity. When they assembled, the field of debate presented an ungovernable mob, not only incapable of deliberation, but prepared for every enormity.[2] In these assemblies, the enemies of the people brought forward their plans of ambition systematically. They were opposed by their enemies of another party; and it became a matter of contingency, whether the people subjected themselves to be led blindly by one tyrant or by another.

It was remarked yesterday, that a numerous representation was necessary to obtain the confidence of the people. This is not generally true. The confidence of the people will easily be gained by a good administration. This is the true touchstone. I could illustrate the position by a variety of historical examples, both ancient and modern. In Sparta, the ephori were a body of magistrates, instituted as a check upon the senate, and representing the people. They consisted of only five men; but they were able to protect their rights, and therefore enjoyed their confidence and attachment. In Rome, the people were represented

---

[1] Melancton Smith.

[2] Outrage.

by three tribunes, who were afterwards increased to ten. Every one acquainted with the history of that republic will recollect how powerful a check to the senatorial encroachments this small body proved; how unlimited a confidence was placed in them by the people, whose guardians they were; and to what a conspicuous station in the government their influence at length elevated the plebeians. Massachusetts has three hundred representatives; New York has sixty-five. Have the people in this state less confidence in their representation than the people of that? Delaware has twenty-one. Do the inhabitants of New York feel a higher confidence than those of Delaware? I have stated these examples to prove that the gentleman's principle is not just. The popular confidence depends on circumstances very distinct from considerations of number. Probably the public attachment is more strongly secured by a train of prosperous events, which are the result of wise deliberation and vigorous execution, and to which large bodies are much less competent than small ones. . . .

It has been further, by the gentlemen in the opposition,[3] observed, that a large representation is necessary to understand the interests of the people. This principle is by no means true in the extent to which the gentlemen seem to carry it. I would ask, Why may not a man understand the interests of thirty as well as of twenty? The position appears to be made upon the unfounded presumption that all the interests of all parts of the community must be represented. No idea is more erroneous than this. Only such interests are proper to be represented as are involved in the powers of the general[4] government. These interests come completely under the observation of one or a few men; and the requisite information is by no means augmented in proportion to the increase of number. . . .

Sir, we hear constantly a great deal which is rather calculated to awake our passions, and create prejudices, than to conduct us to the truth, and teach us our real interests. I do not suppose this to be the design of the gentlemen. Why, then, are we told so often of an aristocracy? For my part, I hardly know the meaning of this word, as it is applied. If all we hear be true, this government is really a very bad one. But who are the aristocracy among us? Where do we find men elevated to a perpetual rank above their fellow-citizens, and possessing powers entirely independent of them? The arguments of the gentlemen only go to prove that there are men who are rich, men who are poor, some who are wise, and others who are not; that, indeed, every distinguished man is an aristocrat. This reminds me of a description of the aristocrats I have seen in a late publication styled the *Federal Farmer*.[5] The author reckons in the aristocracy all governors of states, members of Congress, chief magistrates, and all officers of the militia. This description, I presume to say, is ridiculous. The image is a

[3] The Antifederalists.

[4] Federal.

[5] A widely circulated Antifederalist pamphlet.

phantom. Does the new government render a rich man more eligible than a poor one? No. It requires no such qualification. . . .

It is a harsh doctrine that men grow wicked in proportion as they improve and enlighten their minds. Experience has by no means justified us in the supposition that there is more virtue in one class of men than in another. Look through the rich and the poor of the community, the learned and the ignorant. Where does virtue predominate? The difference indeed consists, not in the quantity, but kind, of vices which are incident to various classes; and here the advantage of character belongs to the wealthy. Their vices are probably more favorable to the prosperity of the state than those of the indigent, and partake less of moral depravity. . . .

3   *Melancton Smith,* June 21, 1788

The honorable *Melancton Smith* rose, and observed, that the gentleman[1] might have spared many of his remarks in answer to the ideas he had advanced. The only way to remedy and correct the faults in the proposed Constitution was, he imagined, to increase the representation and limit the powers. He admitted that no precise number could be fixed upon. His object only was to augment the number in such a degree as to render the government more favorable to liberty. . . .

The honorable member[2] had observed, that the confidence of the people was not necessarily connected with the number of their rulers, and had cited the ephori of Sparta, and the tribunes in Rome, as examples. But it ought to be considered, that, in those places, the people were to contend with a body of hereditary nobles; they would, therefore, naturally have confidence in a few men who were their leaders in the constant struggle for liberty. The comparison between the representations of several states did not better apply. New York had but sixty-five representatives in Assembly. But because sixty-five was a proper representation of two hundred and forty thousand, did it follow that it was also sufficient for three millions? The state legislatures had not the powers of the general government, and were not competent to those important regulations which might endanger liberty.

The gentleman, continued Mr. *Smith,* had ridiculed his idea of an aristocracy, and had entered into a definition of the word. He himself agreed to this definition, but the dispute was not of words, but things. He was convinced that in every society there were certain men exalted above the rest. These men he did not consider as destitute of morality or virtue. He only insisted that they could not feel sympathetically the wants of the people.

[1] Alexander Hamilton.
[2] Hamilton.

SOURCES OF CORRUPTION

Both the Federalists and the Antifederalists believed corruption in government resulted from the pursuit of individual ambitions for wealth, fame, and power. They disagreed over who was more or less likely to fall prey to such ambitions. The Antifederalists believed the Constitution gave free rein to the ambitions of the rich and powerful. The Federalists believed that under the Constitution those seeking office in the federal government were more likely to do so out of a sense of public-spiritedness than personal gain.

4   *Robert R. Livingston,* June 23, 1788

Robert R. Livingston was a Federalist delegate and chancellor of the New York State Supreme Court. He came from one of New York's wealthiest and most distinguished families.

The honorable gentleman from Dutchess,[1] who has so copiously declaimed against all declamation,[2] has pointed his artillery against the rich and the great. I am not interested in defending rich men: but what does he mean by telling us that the rich are vicious and intemperate?[3] Will he presume to point out to us the class of men in which intemperance is not to be found? Is there less intemperance in feeding on beef than on turtle?[4] or in drinking rum than wine? I think the gentleman does not reason from facts. If he will look round among the rich men of his acquaintance, I fancy he will find them as honest and virtuous as any class in the community. He says the rich are unfeeling; I believe they are less so than the poor; for it seems to me probable that those who are most occupied by their own cares and distresses have the least sympathy with the distresses of others. The sympathy of the poor is generally selfish, that of the rich a more disinterested[5] emotion.

The gentleman further observes, that ambition is peculiarly the vice of the wealthy. But have not all classes of men their objects of ambition? Will not a poor man contend for a constable's staff with as much assiduity and eagerness as a man of rank will aspire to the chief magistracy? The great offices in the state are beyond the view of the poor and ignorant man: he will therefore contemplate an humbler office as the highest alluring object of ambition; he will look with equal envy on a successful competitor, and will equally sacrifice to the attainment of his wishes the duty he owes to his friends or to the public. But, says the gentleman, the rich will be always brought forward; they will

[1] Melancton Smith.

[2] Spoken pompously against pompous speech.

[3] Prone to excess, especially in drink.

[4] Turtle was considered a delicacy of the rich.

[5] Concerned for the well-being of others.

exclusively enjoy the suffrages of the people. For my own part, I believe that, if two men of equal abilities set out together in life, one rich, the other of small fortune, the latter will generally take the lead in your government. The rich are ever objects of envy; and this, more or less, operates as a bar to their advancement. What is the fact? Let us look around us: I might mention gentlemen in office who have not been advanced for their wealth; I might instance, in particular, the honorable gentleman who presides over this state,[6] who was not promoted to the chief magistracy[7] for his riches, but his virtue.

. . . We are told that, in every country, there is a natural aristocracy, and that this aristocracy consists of the rich and the great: nay, the gentleman goes further, and ranks in this class of men the wise, the learned, and those eminent for their talents or great virtues. Does a man possess the confidence of his fellow-citizens for having done them important services? He is an aristocrat. Has he great integrity? Such a man will be greatly trusted: he is an aristocrat. Indeed, to determine that one is an aristocrat, we need only be assured he is a man of merit. But I hope we have many such. I hope, sir, we are all aristocrats. So sensible am I of that gentleman's[8] talents, integrity, and virtue, that we might at once hail him the first of the nobles, the very prince of the Senate. But whom, in the name of common sense, will we have to represent us? Not the rich, for they are sheer aristocrats. Not the learned, the wise, the virtuous, for they are all aristocrats. Whom then? Why, those who are not virtuous; those who are not wise; those who are not learned: these are the men to whom alone we can trust our liberties. He says further, we ought not to choose these aristocrats, because the people will not have confidence in them; that is, the people will not have confidence in those who best deserve and most possess their confidence. He would have his government composed of other classes of men: where will we find them? Why, he must go out into the highways, and pick up the rogue and the robber; he must go to the hedges and ditches, and bring in the poor, the blind, and the lame. As the gentleman has thus settled the definition of aristocracy, I trust that no man will think it a term of reproach; for who among us would not be wise? Who would not be virtuous? Who would not be above want? How, again, would he have us to guard against aristocracy? Clearly by doubling the representation, and sending twelve aristocrats instead of six. The truth is, in these republican governments, we know no such ideal distinctions. We are all equally aristocrats. Offices, emoluments,[9] honors, are open to all.

[6] Governor George Clinton, chair of the ratification convention.

[7] Governorship.

[8] Smith's.

[9] The profits of office.

5   *Melancton Smith,* June 23, 1788

The gentleman[1] wishes me to describe what I meant by representing the feelings of the people. If I recollect right, I said the representative ought to understand and govern his conduct by the true interest of the people. I believe I stated this idea precisely. When he attempts to explain my ideas, he explains them away to nothing; and, instead of answering, he distorts, and then sports with them. But he may rest assured that, in the present spirit of the Convention, to irritate is not the way to conciliate. The gentleman, by the false gloss[2] he has given to my argument, makes me an enemy to the rich: this is not true. All I said was, that mankind were influenced, in a great degree, by interests and prejudices; that men, in different ranks of life, were exposed to different temptations, and that ambition was more peculiarly the passion of the rich and great. The gentleman supposes the poor have less sympathy with the sufferings of their fellow-creatures, for that those who feel most distress themselves, have the least regard to the misfortunes of others. Whether this be reasoning or declamation, let all who hear us determine. I observed, that the rich were more exposed to those temptations which rank and power hold out to view; that they were more luxurious and intemperate, because they had more fully the means of enjoyment; that they were more ambitious, because more in the hope of success. The gentleman says my principle is not true, for that a poor man will be as ambitious to be a constable as a rich man to be a governor; but he will not injure his country so much by the party he creates to support his ambition.

The next object of the gentleman's ridicule is my idea of an aristocracy; and, indeed, he has done me the honor to rank me in the order. If, then, I am an aristocrat, and yet publicly caution my countrymen against the encroachments of the aristocrats, they will surely consider me as one of their most disinterested friends.

[1] Robert R. Livingston.
[2] Explanation.

THE CONSTITUTION'S EFFECT ON THE STATES

Another topic of debate at the New York ratification convention was the effect the Constitution would have on the powers of the state governments. The Federalists believed the Constitution would elevate the federal government above the state governments, allowing it to operate independently in such realms as international relations, interstate commerce, and taxation. Antifederalists balked at reducing the influence of the state governments within the federal union, because they believed those governments were more democratic and less prone to corruption than the federal one proposed by the Constitution.

6   *Melancton Smith,* June 27, 1788

Sir, I contemplate the abolition of the state constitutions as an event fatal to the liberties of America. These liberties will not be violently wrested from the people; they will be undermined and gradually consumed. On subjects of the kind we cannot be too critical. The investigation is difficult, because we have no examples to serve as guides. The world has never seen such a government over such a country. If we consult authorities in this matter, they will declare the impracticability of governing a free people on such an extensive plan. In a country where a portion of the people live more than twelve hundred miles from the centre, I think that one body cannot possibly legislate for the whole. Can the legislature frame a system of taxation that will operate with uniform advantages? Can they carry any system into execution? Will it not give occasion for an innumerable swarm of officers, to infest our country and consume our substance? People will be subject to impositions[1] which they cannot support, and of which their complaints can never reach the government.

Another idea is in my mind, which I think conclusive against a simple government for the United States. It is not possible to collect a set of representatives who are acquainted with all parts of the continent. Can you find men in Georgia who are acquainted with the situation of New Hampshire, who know what taxes will best suit the inhabitants, and how much they are able to bear? Can the best men make laws for the people of whom they are entirely ignorant? Sir, we have no reason to hold our state governments in contempt, or to suppose them incapable of acting wisely. I believe they have operated more beneficially than most people expected, who considered that those governments were erected in a time of war and confusion, when they were very liable to errors in their structure. It will be a matter of astonishment to all unprejudiced men hereafter, who shall reflect upon our situation, to observe to what a great degree good government has prevailed. It is true some bad laws have been passed in most of the states; but they arose from the difficulty of the times rather than from any want of honesty or wisdom. Perhaps there never was a government which, in the course of ten years, did not do something to be repented of. . . . We all agree that a general government is necessary; but it ought not to go so far as to destroy the authority of the members. We shall be unwise to make a new experiment, in so important a matter, without some known and sure grounds to go upon. The state constitutions should be the guardians of our domestic rights and interests, and should be both the support and the check of the federal government.

---

[1] Taxes.

7   *Alexander Hamilton,* June 28, 1788

The gentleman[1] has made a declaration of his wishes for a strong federal government. I hope this is the wish of all. But why has he not given us his ideas of the nature of this government, which is the object of his wishes? Why does he not describe it? We have proposed a system which we supposed would answer the purposes of strength and safety.—The gentleman objects to it, without pointing out the grounds, on which his objections are founded, or shewing[2] us a better form. These general surmises never lead to the discovery of truth. It is to be desired, that the gentleman would explain particularly the errors in this system, and furnish us with their proper remedies. . . .

The gentleman says, that the operation of the taxes[3] will exclude the states, on this ground, that the demands of the community are always equal to its resources; that Congress will find a use for all the money the people can pay. This observation, if designed as a general rule, is in every view unjust. Does he suppose the general government will want all the money the people can furnish; and also that the state governments will want all the money the people can furnish? What contradiction is this? But if this maxim be true, how does the wealth of a country ever increase? How are the people enabled to accumulate fortunes? Do the burthens regularly augment,[4] as its inhabitants grow prosperous and happy? But if indeed all the resources are required for the protection of the people, it follows that the protecting power should have access to them. The only difficulty lies in the want of resources: If they are adequate, the operation will be easy. If they are not, taxation must be restrained: Will this be the fate of the state tax alone? Certainly not. The people will say no. What will be the conduct of the national rulers? The consideration will not be, that our imposing the tax will destroy the states, for this cannot be effected; but that it will distress the people, whom we represent, and whose protectors we are. It is unjust to suppose that they[5] will be altogether destitute of virtue and prudence. It is unfair to presume that the representatives of the people will be disposed to tyrannize, in one government more than in another. If we are convinced that the national legislature will pursue a system of measures unfavorable to the interests of the people, we ought to have no general government at all. But if we unite, it will be for the accomplishment of great purposes. . . .

I shall conclude with a few remarks by way of apology. I am apprehensive, sir, that, in the warmth of my feelings, I may have uttered expressions which were too vehement. If such has been my language, it was from the habit of using strong phrases to express my ideas; and, above all, from the interesting nature of the subject. I have ever condemned those cold, unfeeling hearts, which no

[1] Melancton Smith.
[2] Showing.
[3] Taxes levied by the new federal government.
[4] Burdens regularly increase.
[5] Federal officeholders.

object can animate. I condemn those indifferent mortals, who either never form opinions, or never make them known. I confess, sir, that on no subject has my breast been filled with stronger emotions, or more anxious concern. If any thing has escaped me, which may be construed into a personal reflection, I beg the gentlemen,[6] once for all, to be assured that I have no design to wound the feelings of any one who is opposed to me.

While I am making these observations, I cannot but take notice of some expressions which have fallen in the course of the debate. It has been said that ingenious men may say ingenious things, and that those who are interested in raising the few upon the ruins of the many, may give to every cause an appearance of justice. I know not whether these insinuations allude to the characters of any who are present, or to any of the reasonings in this house. I presume that the gentlemen would not ungenerously impute such motives to those who differ from themselves. I declare I know not any set of men who are to derive peculiar advantages from this Constitution. Were any permanent honors or emoluments[7] to be secured to the families of those who have been active in this cause, there might be some grounds for suspicion. But what reasonable man, for the precarious enjoyment of rank and power, would establish a system which would reduce his nearest friends and his posterity to slavery and ruin? If the gentlemen reckon me amongst the obnoxious few, if they imagine that I contemplate with ambitious eye the immediate honors of the government, yet let them consider that I have my friends, my family; my children, to whom ties of nature and of habit have attached me. If, to-day, I am among the favored few, my children, tomorrow, may be among the oppressed; these dear pledges of my patriotism may, at a future day, be suffering the severe distresses to which my ambition has reduced them. The changes in the human condition are uncertain and frequent: many, on whom Fortune has bestowed her favors, may trace their family to a more unprosperous station; and many, who are now in obscurity, may look back upon the affluence and exalted rank of their ancestors. But I will no longer trespass on your indulgence. I have troubled the committee with these observations, to show that it cannot be the wish of any reasonable man to establish a government unfriendly to the liberties of the people. Gentlemen ought not, then, to presume that the advocates of this Constitution are influenced by ambitious views. The suspicion, sir, is unjust; the charge is uncharitable.

[6] His fellow convention delegates.
[7] Advantages.

Analyzing the Ratification Debates

1. Using your notes from the table on page 126, briefly explain the principles upon which Antifederalists objected to the Constitution. How did Federalists answer those objections? How did Antifederalists envision the future of the nation if the Constitution was ratified?

2. In Sources 1 through 5 (pp. 127–34), what meanings did the delegates attach to the following words and phrases: *natural aristocracy*, *ambition*, *passions*, and *interests*? Did the meanings of these words change depending on whether a Federalist or an Antifederalist uttered them?

3. What, if anything, do these passages tell you about the delegates who remained silent during the proceedings? What sort of evidence would you want to see before assuming that they shared the views expressed by their leaders on the floor?

4. Some historians describe the clash between Federalists and Antifederalists as a struggle between economic classes; others emphasize differences in political ideology. Having read these excerpts from the ratification debates, what do you think was the most distinguishing characteristic of the divide between Federalists and Antifederalists? Was the struggle over ratification ultimately about differences in economic interests, or was it about differences in political ideas?

5. How should scholars and judges trying to interpret original intent make use of the ratification convention proceedings? Antifederalists were present at the creation of the Constitution and yet spoke — and sometimes voted — against it. How, then, should modern scholars regard the opinions of Antifederalists when trying to reconstruct original intent?

6. Having read Federalist and Antifederalist predictions of how the Constitution would work, who do you think was right? Have any of the Antifederalists' fears come true? If you had attended the New York ratification convention, which side do you think you would have taken? Explain your choice.

The Rest of the Story

New York ratified the Constitution by a vote of 30 to 27, the narrowest margin of victory in any of the state ratification conventions that met in 1787–1788. (Rhode Island, which initially refused to call a ratification convention, finally did so in the spring of 1790 and ratified the Constitution by an even closer vote of 32 to 30.) If we consider New York along with two other key states, we can see a clearer picture of how narrowly the Constitution passed through the ratification process. Convention delegates in New York, Virginia, and Massachusetts cast a total of 580 votes, and the margin of victory in those states was 3, 10, and 19 votes, respectively. In other words, 32 of the 580 votes cast tilted the balance in favor of ratification, a margin of only 5.5 percent.

It might be said that New York's Antifederalists lost the battle but won the war. None of them ever seriously considered making New York an independent republic; after news of ratification in New Hampshire and Virginia reached them, they pegged their hopes on amending the Constitution. As was the case in several other states, the New York Antifederalists believed the Constitution needed to have a bill of rights that would protect the people's liberties from the power of the new federal government. Alexander Hamilton answered on behalf of the Federalists, calling a federal bill of rights unnecessary because the Constitution did not grant the federal government powers over the rights in question and the state constitutions already guaranteed such rights to their citizens.

The delegates at the New York convention broke their impasse by drafting a resolution that voted for ratification "in full confidence" that the new government would give "early and mature Consideration" to amendments recommended by the Antifederalists. James Madison introduced to the first United States Congress a list of twelve amendments to the Constitution that distilled many of the recommendations made by Antifederalists at the state ratification conventions, including New York's. Madison's proposed amendments dealt chiefly with the civil liberties the Antifederalists were so concerned about protecting: freedom of religion and freedom of the press; the rights to assembly, to bear arms, and to trial by jury; and prohibitions on excessive bail, cruel and unusual punishments, and unreasonable search and seizures. The states ratified ten of those amendments in 1791, and they became known collectively as the Bill of Rights. It is ironic that today the part of the Constitution with which Americans are most familiar—the Bill of Right's protection of freedom of religion, freedom of the press, and other civil liberties—would not be there had the Antifederalists not been so persistent in their demands for a more perfect union.

To Find Out More

The Ratification Debates and Federalist and Antifederalist Writings

Bailyn, Bernard, ed. *The Debate on the Constitution: Federalist and Anti-Federalist Speeches, Articles, and Letters during the Struggle over Ratification.* 2 vols. New York: Library of America, 1993.

Elliot, Jonathan. *The Debates in the Several State Conventions on the Adoption of the Federal Constitution.* 5 vols. New York: B. Franklin, 1968.

Jensen, Merrill, John P. Kaminski, Gaspare J. Saladino, and Charles H. Schoenleber, eds. *The Documentary History of the Ratification of the Constitution.* 23 vols. Madison: Wisconsin Historical Society Press, 1976.

Secondary Sources on the Constitution and Ratification

Beeman, Richard R. *Plain, Honest Men: The Making of the American Constitution.* New York: Random House, 2009.

Cornell, Saul. *The Other Founders: Anti-Federalism and the Dissenting Tradition in America, 1788–1828.* Chapel Hill: University of North Carolina Press, 1999.

De Pauw, Linda Grant. *The Eleventh Pillar: New York State and the Federal Constitution.* Ithaca, NY: Cornell University Press, 1966.

Holton, Woody. *Unruly Americans and the Origins of the Constitution.* New York: Hill and Wang, 2007.

Maier, Pauline. *Ratification: Americans Debate the Constitution, 1787–1788.* New York: Simon and Schuster, 2010.

Main, Jackson Turner. *The Anti-Federalists: Critics of the Constitution, 1781–1788.* Chapel Hill: University of North Carolina Press, 1961.

Rakove, Jack N. *Original Meanings: Politics and Ideas in the Making of the Constitution.* New York: Vintage Books, 1996.

CHAPTER 7

The Question of Female Citizenship

Court Records from the New Nation

William and Anna Martin left home in a hurry. William was an artillery officer in the British army, and when the army evacuated Boston in early 1776, he and Anna went with it. They left behind a substantial amount of property. Most of the family's wealth came from Anna, the daughter of a prosperous Boston merchant. When her father died in 1770, she had inherited a house with a wharf and stables in Boston, a farm in the nearby town of Braintree, and more than 800 acres of land in Massachusetts and New Hampshire.

The Martins were just two of the thousands of Americans who went into exile in Britain, Canada, or the West Indies as a result of the Revolution. Many loyalists tried to sit out the war by avoiding public life or military service, but the patriots did not make that easy to do. Local and state governments demanded loyalty oaths from people they considered suspect and required male adults to serve in the militia. Many loyalists left home for what they hoped would be temporary stays abroad until the rebellion ended. Others were forced out by neighbors and enemies anxious to seize their property. By the war's end, about 80,000 loyalists had left the United States. They ranged from some of the wealthiest families in British North America to slaves who did not even own the clothes on their backs.

We do not know whether William and Anna Martin intended their exile to be permanent, but they never returned to Boston. They first followed the British army to Nova Scotia and then to New York City, where they stayed until the army evacuated in 1783. From there, the Martins resettled in England. In the eyes of the revolutionary government of Massachusetts, the Martins were "absentees," people who had expressed their political allegiance with their feet by leaving the state after the War for Independence broke out on April 19, 1775.

Under a law passed in 1779, Massachusetts confiscated the property left behind by such absentees, and two years later the state sold the Martins' land and buildings to raise money for its treasury.

In 1801, James Martin, the son and heir of William and Anna (both of whom had since died), sued the state of Massachusetts for restoration of the confiscated property. After losing his case in a lower court, he appealed it to the Supreme Judicial Court of Massachusetts, which heard the case in 1805. Such legal cases were not uncommon in the aftermath of the Revolution. The peace treaty that ended the war recommended that the states allow loyalists to recover lost property. The novelty of *Martin v. Massachusetts* rested in its focus on the political and legal status of Anna Martin. Both sides agreed that the property in question had belonged to Anna by right of her inheritance from her father. James Martin's attorneys argued that because Anna was a wife, she had no

Figure 7.1 A Female Patriot *This woodcut of a woman wearing a tricornered hat and holding a powder horn and a musket appeared in a number of different contexts during the Revolutionary era, usually as testimony to the confusion of the times. The need to choose sides between patriots and loyalists raised many questions about the nature of female citizenship and a woman's right to hold and act on her political opinions. Could a married woman legally express political loyalties contrary to her husband's? What kind of duties, if any, did she owe to the state?*

Source: Granger, NYC—All rights reserved.

choice but to follow her husband into exile and, therefore, she was not subject to the state's confiscation law. The state's attorneys argued that the law's wording explicitly extended its authority over women as well as men and, therefore, the confiscation was legal and binding. Each side also argued other points about legal jurisdiction and due process, but the case ultimately hinged on the question of Anna Martin's status as a wife and citizen: did she voluntarily renounce her allegiance to Massachusetts when she left the state, or was she, as a woman and wife, a person who could exercise no option other than to obey her husband's wishes?

Martin v. Massachusetts tells us much about the limits and possibilities of change in women's legal status during the Revolutionary era. In a famous exchange of letters in 1776, Abigail and John Adams debated the extent to which political independence from Great Britain should affect gender relations in the new nation. Abigail urged her husband and his fellow delegates at the Second Continental Congress to "remember the Ladies" in the "new code of laws" they would pass after declaring independence, and she warned him that women would not "hold ourselves bound by any laws in which we have no voice, or Representation." John dismissed Abigail's request, noting that the patriots' cause against Britain had "loosened the bands of government everywhere" so that children, apprentices, students, slaves, Indians, and now even wives challenged the authority of their rightful masters. Historians have long used this exchange to illustrate dissension within American society over the meaning of independence. Many Americans previously excluded from the political process hoped the Revolution would make possible an expansion in their rights and liberties, but many patriot leaders worked to limit the effect that independence from Britain had on the people over whom they claimed authority.

The legal dispute over Anna Martin's property illustrates questions the Revolution raised about female citizenship. Before the Revolution, the colonists were subjects of the British Crown. A person became a subject to the Crown upon birth, and subjecthood, as the word implies, entailed obligations of submission, obedience, and loyalty. When the American patriots declared independence, they disavowed their status as subjects and redefined themselves as citizens of a republic. Then, as now, citizenship implied choice and equality: a person became a citizen by entering into a social contract with others and voluntarily assenting to the laws their government created. This social contract equated property ownership with citizenship: only those individuals who held property had the economic and political independence necessary to enter into the social contract. People without property—children, servants, slaves, the laboring poor—were by definition too dependent on others to live and act independently as fully enfranchised citizens. Under the old system of monarchy, subjecthood was hierarchical and authoritarian, but also inclusive; the British Crown claimed all sorts of people as its subjects, regardless of their race, gender, or ethnic origin. Citizenship in the new nation was egalitarian and contractual, but also exclusive; some people possessed the attributes necessary to become citizens, but others lacked them entirely.

In *Martin v. Massachusetts*, attorneys and judges debated the nature of female citizenship. The case raised all sorts of nettlesome questions about the intersection of property, gender, and a woman's allegiance to her husband and country. That the property in question had belonged to Anna Martin suggested that she had had the means to act independently when she had chosen to give her allegiance to Britain. On the other hand, she was also a wife, bound by personal vows, religious principles, and the law to submit to the will of her husband. The lawyers' arguments and judges' opinions in *Martin v. Massachusetts* raised a host of questions about citizenship in the new nation. Could a woman's obligations as a citizen take precedence over her obligations as a wife? Did independence turn *all* the former British subjects in the thirteen colonies into citizens of the new nation, or only some of them? And if only some subjects became citizens, how did gender figure into that equation?

Using the Source: Court Records

Court cases can be difficult to read because lawyers and judges speak and write in their own specialized language. This problem is compounded when a researcher confronts historical court cases that deal with legal principles and terms no longer in common use. Thus, the best place to start when analyzing a source such as *Martin v. Massachusetts* is to make sure you understand the legal concepts and language involved in the case.

A married woman in eighteenth-century Anglo-American law was known as a *feme-covert* (the plural *femes-covert* is often used in the excerpt on p. 145). This term meant that a wife was completely covered by her husband: she could not buy, sell, or own property independently of him; she could not write her own will or enter into contracts; she could not sue or be sued in a court of law; and she could not vote, serve on juries, or hold public office. In short, in Anna Martin's day, a *feme-covert* had no recognized legal identity because the law assumed that her husband spoke and acted for her.

A married woman's status as a *feme-covert* severely restricted her access to property, yet Anglo-American legal custom did provide certain protections to women in this regard. A woman such as Anna Martin who inherited real estate surrendered its management to her husband upon marriage but retained an interest in it. In legal terms, a husband acquired only a "life estate" in such property: he could lease or rent it and enjoy the profits it generated, but he did not own the property in "fee simple," that is, with no restrictions on transfer of ownership. He could not permanently sell or bequeath the property in question to someone else without his wife's consent. When he died, the management of the property reverted to his wife or her heirs. This legal custom ensured that property the wife brought to the marriage would remain in her family line; her husband could not divert it to the children of a previous or subsequent marriage.

Another important custom that governed female access to property was a woman's "dower right." Anglo-American probate courts, which settled estates when a property owner died without a will, set aside one third of the estate (both real estate and personal property) to support the widow of the deceased. This reservation was known as a "dower right" or "widow's thirds." Its purpose was to provide for a woman's subsistence during her widowhood. It did not grant her full possession of that property, only the right to the revenues it produced. Upon her remarriage or death, full possession of the property in question reverted to the heirs of her deceased husband.

During the Revolution, most of the states recognized a woman's dower right when they confiscated loyalist estates, preserving one third of the property to support the dependent women and children of absentees. The Massachusetts Confiscation Act specifically preserved the dower right of loyalist wives who stayed in America, but what about a woman such as Anna Martin who followed her husband into exile? Was she eligible to have her property seized by the state?

In debating this question, the lawyers and judges involved in *Martin v. Massachusetts* had two choices. Were the court to uphold the confiscation of Anna Martin's property, it would be endorsing the idea that a married woman could choose her political allegiance and be held accountable for it independently of her husband, and such a decision would seriously undermine the legal notion of a *feme-covert*. Were the court to overturn the confiscation, however, it would be upholding the more traditional view of married women as *femes-covert*, but it would also be giving land back to loyalists (or in this case, their heirs), which would undoubtedly prove a politically unpopular decision.

What Can Court Records Tell Us?

Popular images of the law present it as something divinely ordained, neutral, and unchanging, literally carved in stone like the commandments Moses carried down from a mountaintop. The architecture of many American courthouses, built in the style of ancient Greek temples and adorned with statues of blindfolded figures holding the scales of justice, certainly encourage such associations. Legal historians, however, emphasize the social and political context within which laws are made and enforced. Just as Abigail Adams recognized that declaring independence would make necessary a "new code of laws," legal historians find in the law a way of examining how society responds to changing political or social conditions. Legal decisions, from landmark United States Supreme Court cases such as *Roe v. Wade* to more obscure cases heard in local and state courts, mirror the critical issues of their day.

Examining court cases also helps historians see how legal abstractions get put into practice. Consider, for example, the republican rhetoric of the American Revolution. The patriots enshrined liberty, equality, and independence as the founding principles of the new nation, but how did these ideas actually affect social relations within the United States, and how did people react when these principles conflicted with traditional ideas about how society should work? In

Martin v. Massachusetts, the court had to reconsider the meaning of citizenship in light of a clash between a Revolutionary commitment to equality on the one hand and traditional gender roles on the other.

In the following excerpt from the case, Massachusetts solicitor general Daniel Davis argues that the court should uphold the confiscation because the Confiscation Act applied to absentee women as well as to absentee men. His argument hinges on how the traditional legal definitions of a *feme-covert* and dower right applied to this law.

> The question then is: whether a *feme-covert* is capable of committing the offences, or any *one* of the offences specified in the statute?[1] For if a *feme-covert* could commit any one of the offences mentioned, and that offence be well laid in the information, the judgment ought to be affirmed.[2] That a *feme-covert* could perform *one*, at least, of the acts described, that of withdrawing herself from the State into parts and places under the dominion of the King of *Great Britain*, &c. is proved by the *seventh section*—which provides, "that when the *wife* or widow of any of the persons aforedescribed, *shall have remained* within the jurisdiction of any of the said United States &c. she shall be entitled to the improvements and income of one third part of her husband's real and personal estate, after payment of debts, during her life *and continuance within* the said United States; and her dower therein shall be set off to her by the judge of probate in like manner as it might have been if her husband had *died intestate*,[3] within the jurisdiction of this State." The exception proves the rule. *Wives* who *remained here* are mentioned as an exception—the statute therefore embraced all persons who did not remain—who withdrew. The very supposition that *some* persons of this description, some *femes-covert* might remain, implies that all had the *power* of remaining or withdrawing as they pleased—and if *femes-covert* had not been *intended* to be included under the previous *general words* of the statute there could have been no necessity of making the exception in favour of those who remained behind.

> Asks whether a wife can commit any of the offenses that the law identifies as causes for confiscation

> Wording of the Confiscation Act that protects the dower right of women who remained in the United States after their loyalist husbands left the country

> Argues that the Confiscation Act subjects to confiscation all property held by women who chose to follow their husbands into exile

Source: Reports of Cases Argued and Determined in the Supreme Judicial Court of the State of Massachusetts from September 1804 to June 1805—Both Inclusive, vol. 1 (Boston: S. and E. Butler, 1805), 369–70.

Court cases and legal documents have their own narrative structure. Each court case tells a story with a clear beginning, middle, and end. Anglo-American legal culture emphasizes precedent and logic; lawyers build cases and judges render decisions based on what previous cases have said and the evidence before them. Anyone who has ever watched a film or television show based on

[1] The Massachusetts Confiscation Act of 1779.

[2] The judgment of the lower court upholding the confiscation should stand.

[3] Without a will.

a court trial is familiar with the adversarial nature of the American legal process; each side gets to present its case, countering the evidence and arguments presented by the other. Once you comprehend the vocabulary and procedure used in such court cases, you will find that they often render complex ideas in a concise, concrete manner.

Of course, the logic and order evident in a court case can also be a disadvantage if you do not approach the source with a critical eye. It is always important to remember the historical context under which the law was created as well as the circumstances of the legal case under examination. Legal decisions do not take place in a vacuum; all sorts of external factors influence how lawyers, witnesses, juries, and judges present and interpret evidence. Racism, prejudice, or outright bribery can and do corrupt the legal process. Legal historians must also be aware of more subtle biases that affect the administration of the law.

In *Martin v. Massachusetts*, for example, the political affiliations of those persons involved in the case may have been relevant to the verdict. All four judges who rendered written opinions in this case belonged to the Federalist Party, which generally attracted social and political conservatives. As a group, these judges were probably not particularly interested in using this case to rewrite the law on women's rights. James Sullivan, the attorney general of Massachusetts and chief spokesman for the state's case, belonged to the Democratic-Republican Party, which advocated more radical ideas about social and political equality. His argument makes a case for redefining female citizenship in light of the Revolution's commitment to contractual government. At the time of the trial, he was also Massachusetts's Democratic-Republican candidate for governor. How likely do you think it was that the judges listened to Sullivan's arguments without being prejudiced by their opposition to his politics? One does not have to accuse the judges of corruption to recognize that their decision may have been influenced by factors other than the evidence and arguments before them.

Gender bias may also have influenced the decision in the *Martin v. Massachusetts* case. This case was initiated, argued, and decided entirely by men, as was consistent with legal practices at that time. Anna Martin, the central figure in the legal arguments presented, remains mute throughout the entire proceedings. She was, of course, dead at the time, but neither side in the case seemed particularly interested in trying to retrieve what she thought about her loyalism, property, or status as a wife. Even if she had been alive, the legal system as it was then constructed would have offered her little opportunity to speak for herself in court. You must take into consideration the obvious gender bias built into the legal system that decided this case when determining its usefulness as a source.

Much like historians, lawyers and judges build arguments around their interpretation of facts. You can read documents from a court case in much the same way you read a journal article or book by a historian, by first familiarizing yourself with the basic facts and the principal figures involved in the case. The Checklist questions on page 147 will help you approach even the most complicated of historical court cases in a way that will render them comprehensible and meaningful to your research.

CHECKLIST: Interrogating Court Records

☐ When was the document produced, and what was the nature of the case being heard?

☐ Who is the author or speaker of the record being examined? What do you know about this person from other sources? Does the person have a political or personal agenda that may be influencing his or her statements?

☐ What is the main argument presented in the document? What evidence is used to support that argument?

☐ Who was the audience for this court document? How was the document meant to affect that audience?

☐ What appear to be objective facts in this document, and what appear to be subjective opinions? What bias is inherent in the document?

Source Analysis Table

As you read the *Martin v. Massachusetts* case, use the tables on page 148 to organize your notes on the lawyers' and judges' interpretations of the Massachusetts Confiscation Act of 1779.

	The Lawyers' Arguments and Evidence
Representing the Plaintiff, James Martin *George Blake*	
Theophilus Parsons	
Representing the Defendant (Commonwealth of Massachusetts) *Daniel Davis*	
James Sullivan	

	The Justices' Opinions
Justice Sedgwick	
Justice Strong	
Chief Justice Dana	

The Source: *James Martin (Plaintiff in Error) v. The Commonwealth and William Bosson and Other Ter-tenants*, 1805

James Martin is identified in the case's name as the "plaintiff in error," because he was arguing that he was wronged by an error in the lower court's decision. "The Commonwealth" identifies the state of Massachusetts as a codefendant in the suit. William Bosson and the other "ter-tenants" were the owners or occupants of the property at the time James Martin filed suit. "Ter" means three; thus, Bosson and three other owners or occupants were named as codefendants in the suit.

THE LAWYERS' ARGUMENTS

James Martin's lawsuit began in 1801 in a lower court, which upheld the confiscation of his mother's property. He appealed that decision to the Supreme Judicial Court of Massachusetts, which heard the case in 1805. His attorneys argued that the lower court had made four errors in its judgment. These "errors" were the points on which Martin made his case to the state's highest court. The first three dealt with issues of the original right of ownership in the land, due process, and the lower court's jurisdiction. The fourth (referred to in the source text as the "fourth error") concerned whether Anna Martin's status as a feme-covert *made her property liable for confiscation under the Massachusetts Confiscation Act of 1779. These excerpts follow the arguments of both sides on this point.*

 1   *The Fourth Error Identified by James Martin's Attorneys in Their Appeal*

Fourthly. Because, by the information and complaint aforesaid, it doth appear that the said *William Martin* was owner of the estates aforesaid during his natural life only, and that the fee-simple[1] thereof belonged to the said *Anna Martin*, the said *William's* wife, who by the act or law aforesaid, referred to in said information, was not liable to have her estates confiscated as aforesaid, and against whom the process and judgment aforesaid could not by law extend.

---

[1] Right of ownership.

Source: The arguments and opinions reprinted in this chapter are excerpted from *Reports of Cases Argued and Determined in the Supreme Judicial Court of the State of Massachusetts from September 1804 to June 1805—Both Inclusive*, vol. 1 (Boston: S. and E. Butler, 1805), 347–99.

2   *George Blake, Attorney for James Martin*

As to the *fourth* error assigned. *Femes-covert* are not within the statute.[1] They are not within the *letter* of the act—almost all the provisions of the act are masculine—nothing is said about females, excepting where provision is made for their dower. It is admitted that there are cases where statutes will extend to females, where the expressions are similar to those used in this act. But it is manifest from the act itself that women were not *intended* to be included under the general description of persons mentioned.

The first *section* of the act says "that every inhabitant and member of the State who &c." Upon the strict principles of law a *feme-covert* is not a member—[she] has no *political* relation to the State any more than an alien—upon the most rigid and illiberal construction of the words she cannot be a member within the meaning of the statute.... The legislation[2] *intended* to exclude *femes-covert* and infants from the operation of the act—otherwise the word *inhabitant* would have been used alone, and not coupled with the word *member*. This construction is strengthened by the provision in the same (*the first*) section of the act respecting an oath of allegiance. A *feme-covert* was never holden to take an oath of allegiance. The statute is highly penal—the court therefore will not extend it beyond the express words, or obvious meaning, by an equitable construction. The preamble is a key to unlock the meaning. What says the preamble?

> "Whereas every government has a right to command the personal services of all its members, whenever the exigencies of the State shall require it, especially in times of an impending or actual invasion, no member thereof can then withdraw himself from the jurisdiction of the government, and thereby deprive it of *his personal service*,[3] without justly incurring the forfeiture of all *his* property, rights and liberties holden under and derived from that conclusion of government, to the support of which *he* hath refused to afford *his* aid and assistance: and whereas the King of *Great Britain* did cause &c. &c. whereupon it became the indispensable duty of all the *people* of said States forthwith to *unite in defence* of their common freedom, and *by arms* to oppose the fleets and armies of the said King; yet, nevertheless, divers[4] of the *members* of this and the other United States of America, evilly disposed, or regardless of their duty towards their country, did withdraw themselves &c. &c. *aiding* or giving encouragement and countenance to the operations of the fleets and armies of the said King against the United States aforesaid."

It is impossible to read the preamble to the statute without seeing the object and intention of the act. The object was not to punish, but to retain the

---

[1] The Massachusetts Confiscation Act of 1779.

[2] The Confiscation Act.

[3] Military service.

[4] Many.

physical force of the state, as is evident from the expressions, *personal services in times of actual invasion*—opposing *by arms*—*aiding* the enemy, &c. How much physical force is retained by retaining married women? What are the *personal services* they are to render in opposing by *force* an actual invasion? What *aid* can they give to an enemy? So far are women from being of service in the defence of a country against the attacks of an enemy that it is frequently thought expedient to send them out of the way, lest they impede the operations of their own party.

In construing statutes[5] no rule is better established than that *general* expressions shall be *restrained* by the manifest intent of the legislature to be collected from the whole act taken together.

. . . And can it be supposed, in the case before the court, that the legislature contemplated the case of a wife withdrawing with her husband? It ought not to be, and surely was not, intended that she should be exposed to the loss of all her property for withdrawing from the government with her husband. If he commanded it she was bound to obey him, by a law paramount to all other laws—the law of God.

[5] In interpreting laws.

3 | *Daniel Davis, Solicitor General for Massachusetts*

As to the *fourth original* error. It is contended by the counsel for the plaintiff in error, that the statute does not extend to *femes-covert*, that women are not named, are not mentioned in the statute. The *first section* says, *every* inhabitant and member. *Anna Martin* was an inhabitant, and appears by the record to have been so. She is therefore within the statute. The *third section* says, any *person*—this is certainly sufficiently comprehensive to include all persons who could commit any of the offences mentioned in the act. The question then is: whether a *feme-covert* is capable of committing the offences, or any *one* of the offences specified in the statute? For if a *feme-covert* could commit any one of the offences mentioned, and that offence be well laid in the information, the judgment ought to be affirmed. That a *feme-covert* could perform *one*, at least, of the acts described, that of withdrawing herself from the State into parts and places under the dominion of the King of *Great Britain*, &c. is proved by the *seventh section*—which provides, "that when the *wife* or widow of any of the persons afore-described, *shall have remained* within the jurisdiction of any of the said United States &c. she shall be entitled to the improvements and income of one third part of her husband's real and personal estate, after payment of debts, during her life *and continuance within* the said United States; and her dower therein shall be set off to her by the judge of probate in like manner as it might have been if her husband had *died intestate*,[1] within the jurisdiction of this

[1] Without a will.

State." The exception proves the rule. *Wives* who *remained here* are mentioned as an exception—the statute therefore embraced all persons who did not remain—who withdrew. The very supposition that *some* persons of this description, some *femes-covert* might remain, implies that all had the *power* of remaining or withdrawing as they pleased—and if *femes-covert* had not been *intended* to be included under the previous *general words* of the statute there could have been no necessity of making the exception in favour of those who remained behind. If this be not so, still there is another reason. Where the husband has abjured[2] the realm the relation is dissolved between the husband and wife. This act of the husband, *William Martin*, amounts to an abjuration of the realm—and the consequence is that she became sole seized.[3] If this consequence is not liked, then they may both be considered as having abjured, which is in itself treason—which a *feme-covert* can certainly commit, and by which she forfeits her estate—and this process is sufficient to confiscate her estate for her act of treason.

[2] Renounced his allegiance.
[3] Sole owner of the property.

 ## 4   *James Sullivan, Attorney General for Massachusetts*

Under the *fourth* error *originally* assigned it has been contended by the counsel for the plaintiff that the statute did not extend to *femes-covert*. And it is said that the *words* of the act do not include them because the words are in the masculine gender—that they are *him*, *his*, &c. The same reasoning would go to prove that the *Constitution* of the Commonwealth[1] does not extend to women—secures to them no rights, no privileges—for it has no words in the feminine gender: it would prove that a great variety of crimes, made so by statute, could not be committed by women, because the statutes had used only the words *him* and *his*. It is also said that a *feme-covert* is not an *inhabitant* and *member* of the State. Surely a *feme-covert* can be an inhabitant, in every sense of the word. Who are members of the body-politic? Are not all the *citizens*, members; infants, idiots, insane or whatever may be their *relative* situations in society? Cannot a *feme-covert* levy war and conspire to levy war? She certainly can commit treason—and if so, there is no one act mentioned in the statute which she is not capable of performing. In the case before the court she was defaulted[2]—this, as in common civil actions, which may be brought against a *feme-covert*, confesses the facts alleged.

[1] Massachusetts.
[2] Failed to appear in court to contest the original confiscation.

5 *Theophilus Parsons, Attorney for James Martin*

The real question is whether the statute was intended to include persons who have, by law, no wills of their own. The statute extends to persons who have *freely* renounced their relation to the State. Infants, insane, *femes-covert*, all of whom the law considers as having no will, cannot act *freely*. Can they freely renounce? The statute meant such, and such only, as could. Is the State entitled to the *personal* services of a *feme-covert* to defend it in war? Can she render any? What aid and comfort can she give to an invading enemy? Has she the control of property? Is she ever required to take the oath of allegiance? — As to the provision in the statute for dower; that has no relation to *her* property — it is merely the donation of the State, giving to her a part of that which was absolutely its own. . . . It has been said that the husband abjured the realm, and that this dissolved the marriage contract — this is a strange consequence, and one till now unheard of.

THE JUSTICES' OPINIONS

Like the Supreme Court of the United States, the Supreme Judicial Court of Massachusetts did not use a jury. Rather, it was made up of five justices who heard each case and rendered a decision by vote. The justices then issued written opinions explaining their votes. Five justices heard Martin v. Massachusetts, *and four of those wrote opinions. In his opinion, Justice George Thacher called for reversing the confiscation because of a procedural error in the lower court, but he did not address the issue of Anna Martin's status as a* feme-covert. *The three remaining written opinions all addressed the "fourth error" concerning Anna Martin's status as a* feme-covert, *and they are excerpted below.*

6 *Justice Theodore Sedgwick*

. . . By the record before us it appears that *William Martin* and *Anna Martin*, the father and mother of the plaintiff in error, are *jointly* charged with the several acts which are alleged in the libel[1] of the Attorney-General as incurring the forfeiture for which he sued — that, since the 19th day of *April* 1775, they had levied war and conspired to levy war against the provinces, or colonies, or United States: that they had, adhered[2] to the king of *Great Britain* his fleets and armies and had given to them aid and comfort; that since that time they had, without permission of the legislative or executive authority of any of the United States, withdrawn themselves therefrom into parts and places under the

[1] Statement of charges against the Martins.
[2] Pledged their allegiance.

acknowledged authority of the king of *Great Britain*—all these charged as done jointly by the husband and wife—and we are called upon, by matter apparent on the record and by one of the errors expressly assigned, to say whether a *feme-covert* for *any* of these acts, *performed with her husband*, is within the intention of the statute: and I think that she is not.

In construing statutes the great object is to discover from the words, the subject-matter, the mischiefs contemplated and the remedies proposed, what was the true meaning and design of the legislature. In the relation of husband and wife the law makes, in her behalf, such an allowance for the authority of the husband and her duty of obedience, that guilt is not imputed to *her* for actions performed jointly by them, unless of the most heinous and aggravated nature. For instance—the law says, whoever steals shall be punished, and yet if the wife participates in a theft with her husband she is not punishable. Innumerable other instances might be given. She is exempted from punishment, not because she is within the letter of the law if she had sufficient will to be considered as acting voluntarily and as moral agent but, because she is viewed in such a state of subjection and so under the control of her husband that she acts merely as his instrument, and that no guilt is imputable[3] to her.

Compare this with the case under consideration. In a case of great political interest, in which men of great powers and equal integrity, as said by the Attorney-General, divided; and where a *feme-covert* is not expressly included, shall we suppose her to be so by general words? Can we believe that a wife for so respecting the understanding of her husband as to submit her own opinions to his, on a subject so all-important as this, should lose her own property and forfeit the inheritance of her children? Was she to be considered as criminal because she permitted her husband to elect his own and her place of residence? Because she did not, in violation of her marriage vows, rebel against the will of her husband? So hard and cruel a construction, against the general and known principles of law on this subject, could be justified by none but strong and unequivocal expressions. So far is this from being the case in this statute, that it seems to me understood that such was the intention of the legislature—but the contrary. The preamble of the statute has described the persons whom it intended to bring within it. It is that member who "withdraws himself from the jurisdiction of the government and thereby deprives it of the benefit of his personal services." A *wife* who left the country in the company of her husband did not *withdraw* herself—but was, if I may so express it, withdrawn by him. She did not deprive the government of the benefit of her personal services—she had none to render—none were exacted of her. "The member who so withdraws, incurs," says the preamble, "the forfeiture of all his property, right and liberties holden under and delivered from that constitution of government, to the support of which he has refused to afford his aid and assistance." Can any one believe it was the intention of the legislature to demand of *femes-covert* their *aid and assistance* in the support of their constitution and government? The preamble then goes on to particularize the violation of our rights by our

---

[3] Assignable.

former sovereign, and proceeds to declare that it thereupon "became the indispensable duty of all the *people* of said states forthwith to unite in defense of their common freedom, and *by arms* to oppose the fleets and armies of the said King; yet, nevertheless, divers of the *members* of this, and of the other United States of *America*, evilly disposed or regardless of their duty towards their country did withdraw themselves, &c." Now it is unquestionably true that the *members* here spoken of as "evilly disposed" are included in the *people* abovementioned. What then was the duty of these evilly disposed persons, for a violation of which they were to be cut off from the community to which they had belonged, and rendered aliens to it? It was "to unite in defense of their common freedom and *by arms* to oppose" an invading enemy. And can it be supposed to have been the intention of the legislature to exact the performance of this duty from *wives* in opposition to the will and command of their husbands? Can it be believed that an humane and just legislature ever intended that wives should be subjected to the horrid alternative of, either on the one hand, separating from their husbands and disobeying them, or, on the other, of sacrificing their property? It is impossible for me to suppose that such was ever their intention.

The conclusion of the preamble speaks of those who withdrew as thereby "aiding or giving encouragement and countenance to the operations" of the enemy. Were *femes-covert*, accompanying their husbands, thus considered by the legislature? I believe not. So far from believing that *wives* are within the statute, for any acts by them done jointly with their husbands, that a fair construction of the whole *act* together does, to my judgment, clearly exclude them. And I do not discern that the 7th *section* which has been cited to prove that *femes-covert*, for withdrawing with their husbands, were within the act, has the least tendency to that purpose. — This *section* does not contemplate those who withdrew with their husbands, but those who staid behind. The provision which it makes for them is not from their own estates, but from those of their husbands. And I cannot perceive that any inference is to be drawn from the one case which tends to illustrate the other. On the whole I am clearly of opinion that for this error the judgment must be reversed.

7   *Justice Simeon Strong*

. . . Upon the question whether the estates of *femes-covert* were, by this statute, liable to confiscation, I am of opinion that they were not. The *act* was intended to take the estates of those persons who had voluntarily withdrawn themselves from the country and joined the fleets and armies of *Great Britain* with whom we were then at war. Could a *feme-covert* in any reasonable sense of the words of the *act* do this? I think not. The law considers a *feme-covert* as having no will — she is under the direction and control of her husband — is bound to obey his commands — and in many cases which might be mentioned, indeed in all cases except perhaps treason and murder cannot jointly with her husband act at all — or at least so as to make herself liable to punishment. She could not even have conveyed this very estate during the coverture[1]—her husband could not have conveyed it so as to have bound her—and therefore I think that she could not forfeit it by any thing which she did or could do against the statute—and that no act of her husband could incur the forfeiture of *her* estate.—I am clearly of opinion that the statute does not extend to *femes-covert*. As to the other points in the cause I give no opinion—it not being necessary for the decision of the case now before us—but for the reasons already given I think that the judgment of the inferior[2] court ought to be reversed.

[1] Time of her marriage.
[2] Lower.

8   *Chief Justice Francis Dana*

. . . Another objection is, that "the statute does not extend to a *feme-covert* leaving the country with her husband." In a former stage of the cause I gave an opinion on this point, (a) and I see no reason to alter it. The words of the statute are general—*femes-covert* are not named—if the statute extends to them it must be by implication.—The statute does not charge a crime—every person had a right to take which side he pleased, in the contest in which we were then engaged. The statute rests on another principle. It is this—that every subject held his lands mediately[1] or immediately[2] from the *Crown*. Then it became a question whether all the *real* property[3] in the country was not holden under the authority of the states. And it was here adopted as a principle of the law that it was so holden. The consequence was that those persons who withdrew themselves from the country, for the purposes mentioned in the statute, lost the right of holding in the manner they would have been entitled to hold if the empire had not been divided. It was not thought fit and right that they should continue to possess and enjoy their property let the issue be what it might. The language of this statute was—go if you please—but if you withdraw we will not protect your property—we will take it. This was fair—they were not to be punished as criminal—but their property was considered as abandoned; and of course, that it belonged to the State. This was a consequence resulting from division of the empire.

. . . I am clearly of opinion that the judgment ought to be reversed . . . because *femes-covert*, having no will, could not incur the forfeiture. And that the statute never was intended to include them—and oblige them either to lose their property or to be guilty of a breach of the duties which by the laws of their country and the law of God they owed to their husbands.

JUDGMENT REVERSED.

[1] Through an intermediary landholder.
[2] Directly.
[3] Real estate.

[Justice] *Sewall* absent—but the Chief Justice said that he perfectly concurred with the rest of the court, on the ground that the statute did not extend to *femes-covert*.

Analyzing Court Records

1. Using your notes from the tables on page 148, summarize the arguments on each side of the case. On what principles or evidence do Martin's attorneys make their case, and how do the attorneys for the state of Massachusetts counter those points? Do the same for the justices' opinions.

2. The lawyers in this case argued about the purposes and uses of the Massachusetts Confiscation Act, but they agreed on certain ideas about the nature of citizenship. According to them, what were the duties of a citizen, and which members of society were fit or unfit to perform them?

3. What are some of the contradictions or tensions between a woman's status as a *feme-covert* and her role as a citizen that are made evident in this case? How did the justices resolve these contradictions in their decision? Had the justices decided in the state's favor, how would that resolution have differed?

4. At several points in this case, lawyers and justices referred to marriage as a relationship governed by law. Which law? How could a woman's adherence to the laws of marriage conflict with her adherence to the laws of the state? Which of the two did these lawyers and justices recognize as the higher law?

5. What implicit or explicit comparisons did the lawyers and justices in this case make between the British king's relationship to his subjects and a husband's relationship to his wife? What does their reasoning in this regard tell you about the effect the patriots' declaration of political independence from Britain had on other patriarchal relationships in American society?

The Rest of the Story

In rendering its decision in *Martin v. Massachusetts*, the Supreme Judicial Court of Massachusetts failed to challenge or reinterpret a woman's legal status as a *feme-covert* in post-Revolutionary America. By reversing the confiscation of Anna Martin's property, the justices endorsed the notion that a married woman could not act independently of her husband in political or economic matters. In the court's view, Anna Martin was bound by her marriage vows to obey her husband and follow him into exile. She could not, therefore, be subject to the state's confiscation law because she could exercise no choice in her political allegiance independently of her husband.

As this case illustrates, gender and citizenship intersected over the issue of property. In the Declaration of Independence, Thomas Jefferson had changed John Locke's enumeration of natural rights from "life, liberty, and property" to "life, liberty, and the pursuit of happiness." In the nation that Jefferson and his contemporaries created, a person's freedom to pursue happiness depended in a large part on that person's access to property. Adult male property holders could vote, hold office, and dispose of their labor as they wished. All others—women, children, slaves, servants—were defined legally as dependents ruled over by husbands, parents, or masters.

Some changes occurred in marriage and property laws after the Revolution, but the effect of such changes on women were limited as long as they remained *femes-covert*. In the 1780s and 1790s, many states liberalized their divorce laws, making it easier for women to divorce husbands who abused or deserted them. State legislatures also abolished primogeniture laws, which favored firstborn sons over daughters and younger sons in settling probate cases. These changes did not substantially alter a married woman's ability to own property, however.

Significant changes did not occur in laws governing female property ownership until the Jacksonian era. In the 1830s and 1840s, states passed laws that allowed married women to own and dispose of property independently of their husbands. These new laws reflected circumstances in the nation's rapidly expanding and highly volatile economy. As more husbands found themselves entangled in debt, they warmed to the idea of transferring property to their wives, where it would be shielded from creditors in the event of bankruptcy or default. The expansion of industrial wage earning in the early nineteenth century also eroded the economic significance of a woman's dower right by creating potential sources of income for her other than her husband's estate, and some states reduced or eliminated the dower right altogether. In the face of such economic uncertainty, married women sought greater access and control over a family's real estate and personal property to provide financial stability for themselves and their children. Women's rights advocates supported such legal reforms, because they regarded female property rights as one of the foundations of gender equality.

The American Revolution, in short, did not alter women's status as citizens or property holders as dramatically as Abigail Adams had hoped for in 1776. Despite the "new code of laws" drafted by her husband and his peers, the principles and practices behind the *feme-covert* remained embedded in the legal system. In the American republic, property was fundamental to defining citizenship, and the law defined both in masculine terms.

To Find Out More

Resources on Women and the Law

Dublin, Thomas, and Kathryn Kish Sklar. "Women and Social Movements in the United States, 1600–2000." Alexander Street Press. http://womhist.alexanderstreet .com.

Konig, David Thomas, and William Edward Nelson, eds. *Plymouth Court Records, 1686–1859.* 16 vols. Wilmington, DE: M. Glazier, 1978–1981.

Middleton, Ken. "American Women's History: A Research Guide." Middle Tennessee State University. http://mtsu.edu/~kmiddlet/history/women/wh-revol.html.

Secondary Sources on Gender and American Legal History

Basch, Norma. *In the Eyes of the Law: Women, Marriage, and Property in Nineteenth-Century New York.* Ithaca, NY: Cornell University Press, 1982.

Dayton, Cornelia Hughes. *Women before the Bar: Gender, Law, and Society in Connecticut, 1639–1789.* Chapel Hill: University of North Carolina Press, 1995.

Hoffman, Ronald, and Peter J. Albert, eds. *Women in the Age of the American Revolution.* Charlottesville: United States Capitol Historical Society and the University Press of Virginia, 1989.

Kerber, Linda K. *No Constitutional Right to Be Ladies: Women and the Obligations of Citizenship.* New York: Hill and Wang, 1998.

Salmon, Marylynn. *Women and the Law of Property in Early America.* Chapel Hill: University of North Carolina Press, 1986.

Secondary Sources on Women and Loyalism

Bodle, Wayne. "Jane Bartram's 'Application': Her Struggle for Survival, Stability, and Self-Determination in Revolutionary Pennsylvania." *Pennsylvania Magazine of History and Biography* 115 (1991): 185–220.

Kerber, Linda K. "The Paradox of Women's Citizenship in the Early Republic: The Case of *Martin v. Massachusetts*, 1805." *American Historical Review* 97 (1992): 349–78.

Norton, Mary Beth. "Eighteenth-Century American Women in Peace and War: The Case of the Loyalists." *William and Mary Quarterly*, 3rd ser., 33 (1976): 386–409.

CHAPTER 8

Family Values

Advice Literature for Parents and Children in the Early Republic

I n Philadelphia in 1783, twenty-year-old Nancy Shippen took time out of her busy day to record how she wanted to raise her seventeen-month-old daughter Peggy. The child was her first, and Shippen, like many new parents, wanted to have some purposeful design behind her parenting. Starting from the premise that her daughter's upbringing should in "some particulars . . . differ from mine," Shippen recorded in her journal a list of points "Concerning a Daughter's Education":

1st. Study well her constitution and genius.
2nd. Follow nature and proceed patiently.
3rd. Suffer not servants to terrify her with stories of ghosts and goblins.
4th. Give her a fine pleasing idea of good, and an ugly frightful one of evil.
5th. Keep her to a good and natural regimen of diet.
6th. Observe strictly the little seeds of reason in her, and cultivate the first appearance of it diligently.

Shippen listed thirty-five points in all. She ended her list with this thought: "When wisdom enters into her heart, and knowledge is made pleasant to her soul, 'discretion shall preserve her, and understanding shall keep her.'"

Almost fifty years later, in 1831, another parent paused to record his thoughts about child rearing. The Reverend Francis Wayland was a New England minister and the father of a fifteen-month-old son named Heman. One Friday morning, Heman began to cry. Francis took from the child a piece of bread, "intending to give it to him again after he became quiet." Heman quieted down, but when his father offered him the bread, the child threw it away in anger. Displeased by this fit of temper, Francis decided it was time to teach his son a lesson. He left the child alone in a room and gave orders that no one was to speak to Heman or give him food or drink until further notice. Every hour or two throughout the day, Francis visited his son, "offering him the bread and putting out my arms to take him," but the child refused to take any food or drink or to embrace him. Heman went to bed that night without having had anything to eat since the previous day. The next morning, the test of wills continued. At 10:00 a.m., Heman took some bread and milk from his father but still refused to embrace him, so Francis continued the child's confinement. Finally, around 3:00 p.m., Heman capitulated and came to his father, "completely subdued." Francis Wayland was so proud of his method of disciplining Heman, which had rendered the child so much more "mild and obedient," that he published a summary of the episode to serve as a model for other parents.

Between 1780 and 1830, middle-class Americans made child rearing a national project, devoting an enormous amount of time and energy to raising the first generation born after independence. Parents of all times and places have contemplated the best way to raise their children, and every culture produces a set of rules for doing so. Shippen and Wayland, however, were representatives of a conscious effort by American parents in the wake of the Revolution to reexamine and experiment with child-rearing practices. Parents such as Shippen and Wayland became self-consciously reflective about their child rearing, often writing about their experiences with an air of scientific observation and detachment. They also felt the urge to share their thoughts on child rearing with others, to read books by self-appointed experts, or even (as in Wayland's case) to publicize their own expertise. Along with this advice literature for parents came a steady flow of books and magazines aimed at children. By 1830, a homegrown genre of children's literature had emerged in the United States, offering not only instruction in reading and writing but also stories meant to instill habits and values in their young readers appropriate to the gender roles they would assume as adults.

This focus on child rearing and childhood in the early republic had its roots in several important cultural trends associated with American independence. First, the political ideology of the American Revolution, grounded in the scientific and intellectual movement known as the Enlightenment, challenged patriarchal power in all forms, whether it was held by kings or fathers. As a model of family government, patriarchy equated the father's power over the family with a king's power over his subjects: both were absolute and ordained by God. When the colonies disavowed their allegiance to the British Crown, they also dealt a blow to the unlimited power of the father within the family. A significant figure in this regard was the Enlightenment philosopher John Locke, whose *Second Treatise of Government* had inspired Thomas Jefferson's language in the Declaration of Independence. Locke also authored two works, *Essay Concerning Human Understanding* (1690) and *Some Thoughts Concerning Education* (1693), that influenced American attitudes about child rearing. Locke posited that an infant's mind was a tabula rasa, or blank slate, and that children learned and developed personalities according to the circumstances in which they were raised. Locke's ideas challenged long-held beliefs about original sin and the inherent depravity of children. Their popularity among many parents in eighteenth-century America is evident in Shippen's desire to control her daughter's environment and to nurture her reason.

Evangelical Protestantism also encouraged a reexamination of child rearing in the new nation, although often on principles much different from those associated with Locke. When Wayland waged battle with fifteen-month-old Heman, he was following a time-honored practice among many Anglo-American Protestants: "breaking the will" of the child. The Calvinist theology of many Protestant denominations (especially Congregationalists, Presbyterians, and Baptists) taught that original sin corrupted human nature. Left to their own devices, children would follow their natural inclination to do evil rather than good. A parent's job was to break the child of this predisposition early in life so that a temperament more submissive and obedient to parental and godly authority could be molded in its place. Wayland's episode with his son perfectly illustrates this process. During the early nineteenth century, a wave of religious revivals known as the Second Great Awakening reinvigorated evangelical religion in the United States, adding to the old Calvinist emphasis on original sin a new message of spiritual perfectionism made possible by God's grace. The evangelists' metaphor of being "born again" into salvation in Christ drew a parallel between spiritual redemption and childhood, inspiring many parents like Wayland to redouble their efforts to raise children who would be fit to respond to God's call when it came.

Economic change and political ideas also influenced family roles and child rearing in the early republic, especially in the Northeast, where urbanization and industrialization were separating the home from the workplace. As fathers took jobs outside the home, the mother's role in child rearing became more pronounced and the family's domestic life came increasingly under her authority. Middle- and upper-class women redefined their role in society as "republican mothers," charged with the task of raising children capable of governing themselves as productive citizens of the new nation. The notion of Republican Motherhood encouraged female education because mothers had to be capable of instructing their children not only in reading, writing, and arithmetic but also in the moral habits and virtues of a free citizenry: industry, frugality, trustworthiness, public duty, and piety. The "Cult of Domesticity," a phrase used by historians to describe nineteenth-century America's celebration of the home as a refuge from the cold, impersonal world outside, elevated mothers as the central figure in the household. Society praised them for the loving nurture and wise counsel they dispensed to their children. Unlike the patriarchal family model so evident in Wayland's disciplining of his son, Republican Motherhood and the Cult of Domesticity made affection and sentiment, not duty and obedience, the primary bonds of family life. In the South, where slavery persisted after the American Revolution and industrialization occurred much more slowly, patriarchy remained the defining principle behind family roles in white society.

The transformation of child rearing and childhood in the early republic had important ramifications for family and gender roles in American society. Many ideas and images associated with our modern debates over family values—the nuclear family, the stay-at-home mother, the breadwinner father—have their origins in the world of Nancy Shippen and Francis Wayland. In the half-century after the American Revolution, parents made a purposeful effort to redefine the meaning and purpose of family in a democratic society, and their efforts left a lasting imprint on our culture.

Using the Source: Advice Literature for Parents and Children

Before 1800, Anglo-Americans imported their advice on child rearing from Great Britain or wrote their own imitations of popular English works. Rising literacy rates in eighteenth-century Britain produced a consumer market for children's books in which colonial Americans participated as well. The market for these English works decreased during the Revolutionary era, when Americans rejected much of their cultural patrimony from Britain. Just as many artists thought it important for the new nation to create its own art rather than slavishly imitate Europe's, so too did prominent intellectuals such as Noah Webster, author of the first American dictionary, urge Americans to reinvent their methods of raising and educating children. By 1830, this impulse had led to a significant surge in magazines and books published by American authors for American parents and children.

What Can Advice Literature Tell Us?

Reading advice literature for parents and children is one of the best ways to reconstruct cultural expectations about roles within the family. All advice literature tells its readers how things ought to be, and parenting literature is no exception. Consider, for example, this excerpt from a popular parenting book, in which the author uses the occasion of a boy's question about a pot of boiling coffee to advise parents on how to deal with a child's curiosity:

> "Mother," says the little boy, "what makes the coffee bubble up so?"
> Here the motive is good, and the occasion is proper.[1] And one of the parents explains to the child the chemical process which we call the boiling. The parents have reason to be gratified at the observation of the child, and the

Note the scientific, experimental tone of author's language

[1] For the child to ask a question.

The author states a rule of child rearing

Note which parent intercedes

The rule is expressed to the child

explanation communicates to him valuable knowledge. But perhaps a stranger is present, with whom the father is engaged in interesting conversation. Under these circumstances, the child asks the same question. It is, however, now unseasonable.[2] He ought to be silent when company is present. The mother accordingly replies, "My son, you should not interrupt your father. You must be perfectly silent and listen to what he is saying."

Source: The Mother at Home, or, the Principles of Maternal Duty Familiarly Illustrated by John S. C. Abbott (1833; repr., New York: Harper and Brothers, 1852), 126–27.

This passage calls to mind the adage that "children should be seen and not heard," but closer reading also reveals assumptions the author is making about gender and the division of power within the family. The father is present in this scene, but the mother intercedes when the child speaks before company. What does this vignette tell you about the author's notion of how authority ought to be ordered within a family?

Even children's literature, which at first glance might seem formulaic and transparent in its purposes, reflects wider cultural currents. Consider the famous illustrated alphabet from *The New-England Primer* (see Figure 8.1), the most commonly used book for teaching spelling and reading to American children before 1850. The images and rhyming couplets that accompany the letters are meant to focus the children's attention as they memorize their ABCs, much in the same way the "Alphabet Song" is used today. These images and couplets also convey messages that teach moral lessons and proper behavior.

Another advantage to using advice literature to study the family and childhood in the early republic is its inclusion of both male and female voices. Before 1800, advice literature on child rearing was written overwhelmingly by men, usually ministers concerned with the moral instruction of youth. The notion of Republican Motherhood, however, gave women the social authority to write and publish their own opinions on the family and domestic life. Indeed, several of nineteenth-century America's most prominent female public figures first gained recognition for their advice literature on the home and child rearing. By comparing male and female authorship of such works, historians can get a sense of how women reshaped their private and public lives during the early nineteenth century.

When working with these sources, it is also important to bear in mind their shortcomings. First, advice literature on child rearing is prescriptive: its purpose is to tell people what to do, and if they need to be told, then they probably are not doing what the literature recommends. No one should assume, for example, from the glut of diet books available in modern American bookstores that we are a society in which everyone eats right. Likewise, nineteenth-century advice literature on parenting does not necessarily reflect how people raised their children, only what certain authors thought about the way people should raise their children. Historians always approach prescriptive literature with skepticism, assuming that

[2] Untimely.

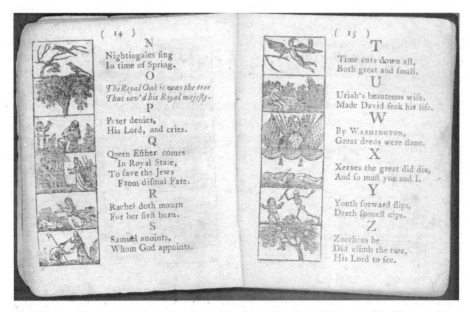

Figure 8.1 Illustrated Alphabet from **The New-England Primer** *This illustrated alphabet from an early nineteenth-century edition of* The New-England Primer *shows how children learned lessons about morality and proper behavior as they learned to read and write. The letters B, H, I, and S teach submission to the authority of God and parents. A, F, and P warn of the punishments that follow bad behavior. G, R, T, X, and Y remind children of their own mortality: death can come at any time, to the old or young, weak or strong. Source:* Courtesy of Special Collections/Musselman Library, Gettysburg College.

if everyone acted according to the instructions contained in such books, then their authors would not have been compelled to write them in the first place.

Second, regional, class, or racial biases may be evident in these sources. The authors often presume to speak for everyone, but who actually read these books? Obviously, the authors wrote for a literate audience, but literacy rates varied widely in the United States in early nineteenth century. Men were more likely to be literate than women, although this gap closed considerably in the Northeast, the center of the nation's publishing industry. Protestants were more likely to be literate than Catholics, many of whom were poor Irish immigrants working in urban centers, and African American slaves suffered from legal prohibitions against teaching them to read. Literacy also reflected a person's social class, and works on childhood and child rearing enshrined an ideal image of the family that was distinctively middle class, in which fathers were breadwinners, mothers were homemakers, and the nuclear family (parents and children living together under one roof) was the norm. Such an image held little meaning to many working-class, immigrant, and African American families.

This last point brings to mind another caveat about using these sources. Change in family roles and child-rearing practices was hardly uniform in the early republic, even for people living in the same region or in similar material circumstances. If you observe parents and their children at a playground today, you will not have to wait long to witness sharply different models of child rearing practiced by people who in many respects seem alike. The same is true for people of the past. Nancy Shippen and Francis Wayland both lived in northern cities and came from privileged backgrounds, yet each took a very different approach to raising children. As you read these sources, rather than thinking in terms of one type of family or approach to child rearing replacing another, try to identify the different types and approaches that coexisted and influenced one another. The Checklist questions on page 167 will help you examine advice literature, and the table on page 168 will help you organize your notes.

CHECKLIST: Interrogating Advice Literature

☐ Who is the author of this advice, and on what basis does he or she claim expertise on the subject?

☐ What do you know about the publication in which this advice appeared? When and where was it published?

☐ What kind of audience is the author trying to reach with this advice?

☐ What kind of role models does the advice literature establish for its readers to imitate?

☐ What sort of conduct or behavior is being criticized or condemned?

☐ What wider social values or prejudices are evident in the advice being given?

Source Analysis Table

Use the first three columns in the following table to organize your notes on how each of the sources establishes expectations and role models for its intended audience. In the far right column, note the values or biases that you think underlie the author's advice.

Source	Intended Audience	Characteristics of Ideal Father, Mother, Daughter, Son	Objectionable Practices or Conduct	Values or Biases Evident in Author's Advice
1. John S. C. Abbott, *The Mother at Home*				
2. Lydia Maria Child, *The Mother's Book*				
3. *The New-England Primer*				
4. *The Busy Bee*				
5. *The Life of George Washington*				

The Source: Advice Literature on Child Rearing and Children's Literature, 1807–1833

ADVICE LITERATURE ON CHILD REARING

1   *The Mother at Home* by John S. C. Abbott, 1833

John S. C. Abbott was a New England minister who published two of the most widely read books on child rearing in early nineteenth-century America, *The Child at Home* and *The Mother at Home*. These excerpts, from the latter book, concern a topic commonly addressed in such literature: the proper method of disciplining children.

Never Give a Command Which You Do Not Intend Shall Be Obeyed.

There is no more effectual way of teaching a child disobedience, than by giving commands which you have no intention of enforcing. A child is thus habituated to disregard its mother; and in a short time the habit becomes so strong, and the child's contempt for the mother so confirmed, that entreaties and threats are alike unheeded. . . .

Sometimes a child gets its passions excited and its will determined, and it can not be subdued but by a very great effort. Almost every faithful mother is acquainted with such contests, and she knows that they often form a *crisis* in the character of the child. If the child then obtain the victory, it is almost impossible for the mother afterward to regain her authority. . . . When once entered upon, they[1] must be continued till the child is subdued. It is not safe, on *any account*, for the parent to give up and retire vanquished.

The following instance of such a contest is one which really occurred. A gentleman, sitting by his fireside one evening, with his family around him, took the spelling-book and called upon one of his little sons to come and read. John was about four years old. He knew all the letters of the alphabet perfectly, but happened at that moment to be in a rather sullen humor, and was not at all disposed to gratify his father. Very reluctantly he came as he was bid, but when his father pointed with his pencil to the first letter of the alphabet, and said, "What letter is that, John?" he could get no answer. John looked upon the book, sulky and silent.

"My son," said the father pleasantly, "you know the letter *A*."

[1] Such contests.

Source: John S. C. Abbott, *The Mother at Home, or, the Principles of Maternal Duty Familiarly Illustrated* (1833; repr., New York: Harper and Brothers, 1852), 47, 60–66.

"I can not say *A*," said John.

"You must," said the father, in a serious and decided tone. "What letter is that?"

John refused to answer. The contest was now fairly commenced. John was willful, and determined that he would not read. His father knew that it would be ruinous to his son to allow him to conquer. He felt that he must, at all hazards, subdue him. He took him into another room, and punished him. He then returned, and again showed John the letter. But John still refused to name it. The father again retired with his son, and punished him more severely. But it was unavailing; the stubborn child still refused to name the letter, and when told that it was *A*, declared that he could not say *A*. Again the father inflicted punishment as severely as he dared to do it, and still the child, with his whole frame in agitation, refused to yield. The father was suffering from the most intense solicitude. He regretted exceedingly that he had been drawn into the contest. He had already punished his child with a severity which he feared to exceed. And yet the willful sufferer stood before him, sobbing and trembling, but apparently as unyielding as a rock. I have often heard that parent mention the acuteness of his feelings at that moment. His heart was bleeding at the pain which he had been compelled to inflict upon his son. He knew that the question was now to be settled, who should be master. And after his son had withstood so long and so much, he greatly feared the result. The mother sat by, suffering, of course, most acutely, but perfectly satisfied that it was their duty to subdue the child, and that in such a trying hour a mother's feelings must not interfere. With a heavy heart the father again took the hand of his son to lead him out of the room for farther punishment. But, to his inconceivable joy, the child shrunk from enduring any more suffering, and cried, "Father, I'll tell the letter." The father, with feelings not easily conceived, took the book and pointed to the letter.

"*A*," said John, distinctly and fully.

"And what is that?" said the father, pointing to the next letter.

"*B*," said John.

"And what is that?"

"*C*," he continued.

"And what is that?" pointing again to the first letter.

"*A*," said the now humble child.

"Now carry the book to your mother, and tell her what the letter is."

"What letter is that, my son?" said the mother.

"*A*," said John. He was evidently perfectly subdued. The rest of the children were sitting by, and they saw the contest, and they saw where was the victory. And John learnt a lesson which he never forgot—that his father had an arm too strong for him. He learned never again to wage such an unequal warfare. He learnt that it was the safest and happiest course for him to obey.

But perhaps some one says it was cruel to punish the child so severely. Cruel! It was mercy and love. It would indeed have been cruel had the father, in that hour, been unfaithful, and shrunk from his painful duty. The passions which he was then, with so much self-sacrifice, striving to subdue, if left unchecked, would, in all probability, have been a curse to their possessor, and have made him a curse to his friends. It is by no means improbable that upon the decisions of that hour depended the character and happiness of that child for life, and even for eternity. It is far from improbable that, had he then conquered, all future efforts to subdue him would have been in vain, and that he would have broken away from all restraint, and have been miserable in life, and lost in death. Cruelty! The Lord preserve children from the *tender mercies* of those who so regard such self-denying kindness.

2 | *The Mother's Book* by Lydia Maria Child, 1831

Lydia Maria Child was one of the most distinguished female authors of nineteenth-century America and was an outspoken advocate for the rights of women, Indians, and African Americans. Early in her career, she edited a successful children's magazine called *Juvenile Miscellany* and published *The Mother's Book*, a best-selling volume of child-rearing advice literature. The excerpts below are from Child's recommendations for dealing with teenage daughters.

The period of twelve to sixteen years of age is extremely critical in the formation of character, particularly with regard to daughters. The imagination is then all alive, and the affections in full vigor, while the judgment is un-strengthened by observation, and enthusiasm has never learned moderation of experience. During this important period, a mother cannot be too watchful. As much as possible, she should keep her daughter *under her own eye*; and above all things she should encourage *entire confidence towards herself*. This can be done by a ready sympathy with youthful feelings, and by avoiding all unnecessary restraint and harshness. I believe it is extremely natural to choose a mother in preference to all other friends and confidants; but if a daughter, by harshness, indifference, or unwillingness to make allowance for youthful feeling, is driven from the holy resting place, which nature has provided for her security, the greatest danger is to be apprehended. Nevertheless, I would not have mothers too indulgent, for fear of weaning the affections of children. This is not the way to gain the perfect love of young people; a judicious parent is always better loved, and more respected, than a foolishly indulgent one. The real secret is, for a mother never to sanction the slightest error, or imprudence, but at the same time to keep her heart warm and fresh, ready to sympathize with all the innocent gayety and enthusiasm of youth. . . .

Source: Mrs. [Lydia Maria] Child, *The Mother's Book* (Boston: Carter, Hendee, and Babcock, 1831), 129–30, 136–40, 145–47, 150–53.

I would make it an object so to educate children that they could in case of necessity support themselves respectably. For this reason, if a child discovered a decided talent for any accomplishment, I would cultivate it, if my income would possibly allow it. Everything we add to our knowledge, adds to our means of usefulness. If a girl has a decided taste for drawing, for example, and it is encouraged, it is a pleasant resource which will make her home agreeable, and lessen the desire for company and amusements; if she marries, it will enable her to teach her children without the expense of a master; if she lives unmarried, she may gain a livelihood by teaching the art she at first learned as a mere gratification of taste. The same thing may be said of music, and a variety of other things, not generally deemed *necessary* in education. In all cases it is best that what is learned should be learned well. In order to do this, good masters should be preferred to cheap ones. Bad habits once learned, are not easily corrected. It is far better that children should learn one thing thoroughly, than many things superficially. . . .

My idea is this—First, be sure that children are familiar with all the duties of their present situation; at the same time, by schools, by reading, by conversation, give them as much *solid* knowledge as you can, no matter how much, or of what kind; it will come in use some time or other; and lastly, if your circumstances are easy, and you can afford to indulge your children in any matter of taste, do it fearlessly, without any idea that it will unfit them for more important duties. Neither learning nor accomplishments do any harm to man or woman if the *motive* for acquiring them be a proper one. . . . I believe a variety of knowledge (acquired from such views as I have stated) would make a man a better servant, as well as a better president; and make a woman a better wife, as well as a better teacher. . . .

It is certainly very desirable to fit children for the station they are likely to fill, as far as a parent can judge what that station will be. In this country, it is a difficult point to decide; for half our people are in a totally different situation from what might have been expected in their childhood. However, one maxim is as safe, as it is true: A well-informed mind is the happiest and the most useful in all situations. Every new acquirement is something added to a solid capital. . . .

A knowledge of domestic duties is beyond all price to a woman. Every one ought to know how to sew, and knit, and mend, and cook, and superintend a household. In every situation of life, high or low, this sort of knowledge is a great advantage. There is no necessity that the gaining of such information should interfere with intellectual acquirement, or even with elegant accomplishments. A well regulated mind can find time to attend to all. When a girl is nine or ten years old, she should be accustomed to take some regular share in household duties, and to feel responsible for the manner in which it is done, such as doing her own mending and making, washing the cups and putting them in place, cleaning the silver, dusting the parlor, etc. This should not be done occasionally, and neglected whenever she finds it convenient; she should consider it her department. When they are older than twelve, girls should begin to take turns in superintending the household, keeping an account of weekly expenses, cooking puddings and pies, etc. To learn anything effectually, they should actually do these things themselves, not stand by and see others do them. It is a great mistake in mothers to make such slaves of themselves, rather than divide their cares with daughters. A variety of employment, and a feeling of trust and responsibility add very much to the real happiness of young people. . . .

There is one subject on which I am very anxious to say a great deal; but on which, for obvious reasons, I can say very little. Judging by my own observation, I believe it to be the greatest evil now existing in education. I mean the want of confidence between mothers and daughters on delicate subjects.[1] Children from books, and from their own observation, soon have their curiosity excited on such subjects; this is perfectly natural and innocent, and if frankly met by a mother, it would never do harm. But on these occasions it is customary to either put young people off with lies, or still further to excite their curiosity by mystery and embarrassment. Information being refused them at the only proper source, they immediately have recourse to domestics,[2] or immodest school-companions; and very often their young minds are polluted with filthy anecdotes of vice and vulgarity. This ought not to be. Mothers are the only proper persons to convey such knowledge to a child's mind. They can do it without throwing the slightest stain upon youthful purity; and it is an imperious duty that they should do it. A girl who receives her first ideas on these subjects from the shameless stories and indecent jokes of vulgar associates, has in fact prostituted her mind by familiarity with vice. A diseased curiosity is excited, and undue importance given to subjects, which those she has been taught to respect think it necessary to envelope in so much mystery; she learns to think a great deal about them, and to ask a great many questions. This does not spring from any natural impurity; the same restless curiosity would be excited by any subject treated in the same manner. On the contrary, a well-educated girl of twelve years old would be perfectly satisfied with a frank, rational explanation from a mother. It would set her mind at rest upon the subject; and instinctive modesty would prevent her recurring to it unnecessarily, or making it a theme of conversation with others. . . .

It is a bad plan for young girls to sleep with nursery maids, unless you have the utmost confidence in the good principles and modesty of your domestics. There is a strong love among vulgar people of telling secrets, and talking on forbidden subjects. From a large proportion of domestics this danger is so great, that I apprehend a prudent mother will very rarely, under any circumstances, place her daughter in the same sleeping apartment with a domestic, until her character is so much formed, that her own dignity will lead her to reject all improper conversation.

[1] Sexuality.
[2] Household servants.

CHILDREN'S LITERATURE

| 3 |

The New-England Primer, 1807

> *The New-England Primer* was first published in the late seventeenth century, but it remained the most common textbook for teaching children basic lessons in reading, writing, and religion throughout the first half of the nineteenth century. No author was ascribed to it, but the first editions were published by Boston printer Benjamin Harris in the 1690s. Over the next 150 years, many other printers published versions of it, varying the content little from one edition to the next. These excerpts illustrate *The New-England Primer's* moral instructions to boys and girls. Note how the material addressed to boys is rendered in prose form, whereas that to girls is in verse.

Description of a Good Boy

A Good boy is dutiful to his father and mother, obedient to his master, and loving to all his play fellows. He is diligent in learning his book, and takes a pleasure in improving his mind in every thing which is worthy of praise: he rises early in the morning, makes himself clean and decent, and says his prayers. If he has done a fault, he confesses, and is sorry for it, and scorns to tell a lie, though he might by that means conceal it. He never swears, nor calls names, nor uses any ill words to his companions. He is never peevish nor fretful, but always cheerful and good-humoured; he scorns to steal or pilfer any thing from his companions, and would rather suffer wrong, than to do wrong to any of them. He is always ready to answer when a question is asked of him—to do what he is bidden, and to mind what is said to him. He is not a wrangler nor quarrelsome, and refrains from all sorts of mischief into which other boys run. By this means he becomes, as he grows up, a man of sense and virtue, he is beloved and respected by all who know him; he lives in the world with credit and reputation, and when he dies, is lamented by all his acquaintances.

Description of a Bad Boy

A Bad boy is undutiful to his father and mother, disobedient and stubborn to his master, and ill natured to all his play fellows. He hates his book, and takes no pleasure in improving in any thing. He is sleepy and slothful in the morning, too idle to clean himself, and too wicked to say his prayers. He is always in mischief, and when he has done a fault, will tell twenty lies, in hopes to conceal it. He hates that any body should give him good advice, and when they are out of his sight, will laugh at them. He swears, wrangles, and quarrels with his companions. He will steal whatever comes his way, and if he is not caught, thinks it no crime, not considering that God sees what he does. He is frequently

Source: The New-England Primer Improved, Being an Easy Method to Teach Young Children the English Language (New York: Daniel D. Smith, 1807), 17–20.

out of humour, sullen and obstinate, so he will neither do what he is bid, nor answer any question which is asked him. In short, he neglects every thing which he should learn, and minds nothing but play or mischief, by which means he becomes as he grows up, a confirmed blockhead, incapable of any thing but wickedness or folly, despised by all men, and generally dies a beggar.

The Good Girl

So pretty Miss Prudence,
You've come to the Fair;
And a very good girl
They tell me you are:
Here take this fine Orange,
This Watch and this Knot;
You're welcome my dear,
To all we have got:
For a girl who is good,
And so pretty as you,
May have what she pleases,
Your servant, Miss Prue.

The Naughty Girls

So pert misses, prate-apace,[1] how came you here?
There's nobody wants to see you at the fair;
No Oranges, Apples, Cakes, or Nuts,
Will any one give to such saucy sluts.
For such naughty girls, we here have no room,
You're proud and ill-natur'd—Go hussies, go home.

[1] Chat or babble with no purpose.

4   *The Busy Bee,* 1831

The American Sunday School Union, a voluntary association formed by several Protestant denominations in 1824 to promote children's religious education, published thousands of short stories for children aimed at teaching proper values and habits. Like *The New-England Primer*, these stories usually appeared without any attribution to authorship. This typical story features the characters of Fanny and Jane, two eight-year-old orphans who live with a pious old woman, referred to in the story as their mother.

Source: The Busy Bee (Philadelphia: American Sunday School Union, 1831), 11–13, 15–17, 19–24.

The kind lady took the same pains with Fanny as she did with Jane, and taught both these little girls all those things which she thought necessary for children in their station. She endeavoured to teach them to read and write well, to cipher, and to do neatly all kinds of plain work, as well as to understand household business: but though, as I before said, she bestowed the same labour on both children, yet there was great difference in their improvement. Little Jane took every opportunity of profiting, not only by the instructions of her mother, as she called the lady, but like the busy bee, who gathers honey from every flower which comes her way, she strove to gain some good thing, some useful piece of knowledge, from every person she became acquainted with.

Her mother kept only one servant, whose name was Nanny. Nanny was a clever servant, and understood many useful things, though she was often rude and ill-tempered, and spoke in a vulgar manner. But little Jane had sense to know, that although she was not to imitate the manners of Nanny, and her improper way of speaking, yet she might learn many useful things from her: therefore, when she went into the kitchen with the lady, she shut her ears against Nanny's disagreeable way of speaking, and gave her whole mind to learn how to iron, or to make pies and puddings, or whatever useful thing she might be doing.

When any ladies came to drink tea with her mother, Jane would take notice what work they were doing; and if it was pretty or useful, she would try to do something like it for her doll: and thus she taught herself many useful works. . . .

But while Jane was thus daily learning all that is good, Fanny, in the mean time, was gathering all that is evil. Into whatever company she might chance to fall, she always first took notice of what each person was saying or doing wrong, and afterwards tried to do the same. Whenever she went into the kitchen with her mother, instead of learning to do any thing which might be useful from Nanny, she noticed her way of talking or moving, and then tried to do like her. . . .

But I can scarcely tell you (and indeed it would only give you pain if I could) how many naughty things Fanny learned from the young people she met with, when she went with her mother to pay a visit in the town. She came home, I am sorry to say, much worse than she went, and that indeed was bad enough. . . .

One afternoon, at tea, she[1] said to the little girls, "To-morrow will be my birth day, and I mean to give you a feast, in which I intend to consult the taste of each of you."

The little girls said they were very glad to hear it, and the lady told them to come the next evening into her dressing room, where she said the feast would be set out.

When Fanny and Jane came, at the hour which the lady had fixed upon, to the dressing room, they found their mother sitting reading by the fire, and two little round tables were placed in the middle of the room. One of these tables was covered with a neat white napkin and a little dessert set out upon it in

[1] The old woman.

doll's dishes, made of white china with blue edges. There were four little dishes on this table: one contained an orange, another a few yellow apples, another a roasted apple, and a fourth a few biscuits; and in the middle was a little covered china cup, made in the shape of a bee-hive, which contained honey in the honey-comb.

The little girls had scarcely time to examine this table, so neatly laid out, before their eyes were caught by the other table, which was set out in a manner so strange, that they stood still with surprise, and were not able to move. This second table was covered with straw instead of a table cloth, and instead of dishes, there was a great empty wooden bowl.

The lady got up when the little girls came in, and, drawing her chair between the two tables, she said, "Come, Fanny, come Jane; come and enjoy yourselves. I have been trying to make a feast suitable to the tastes of each of you." She then pointed to the table neatly set out with china and fine linen, and invited Jane to seat herself at it, and directed Fanny to place herself by the other table. . . .

"And now," said the lady, as soon as they were seated, "I will divide the feast." So saying, she began to peel the oranges, pare the apples, take the roasted apple out of its skin, and pour the honey from the comb. And, as she went on doing these things, she threw the rind of the orange, the parings of the apple, and the other refuse of the feast, into the wooden bowl, while she placed the best parts on the dishes before Jane. When all this was done, she invited the children to begin to eat. . . . Fanny looked very red, and at last, broke into a violent fit of crying.

"What do you cry for?" said the lady. "I know that you heartily love, and have for a long time sought after every thing that is hateful, filthy, and bad; and like a pig, you have delighted in wallowing in mire. I therefore am resolved to indulge you. As you love what is filthy, you shall enjoy it, and shall be treated like a pig."

Fanny looked very much ashamed; and throwing herself on her knees before her mother, begged her to forgive her, and promised that she would never again seek after wickedness, and delight in it, as she had done.

"Fanny," said the lady, "it is very easy for little girls to make fine promises, and to say, 'I will be good,' and 'I am sorry I have behaved ill.' But I am not a person who will be satisfied with words, any more than you can be with orange-peel and skins of apples. I must have deeds, not words. Turn away from your sins, and call upon your God to help you to repent your past evil life. If you do not wish to partake of the portion of dogs and swine and unclean creatures in the world to come, you must learn to hate sin in the present world." . . .

I am happy to say, that this day was the beginning of better things to Fanny: for she at once forsook her evil habits, and, with God's blessing upon her endeavours, and the care of the good old lady, she so far overcame her faults, as to be allowed, by the next birth-day, to feast with little Jane.

<table><tr><td>5</td></tr></table>

The Life of George Washington, 1832

George Washington was a fixture in nineteenth-century children's literature, and his life was used to teach moral lessons about honesty and piety as well as civic lessons about patriotism and citizenship. In children's biographies of Washington, his mother also played a prominent role and served as an exemplar of motherhood for the new nation.

Mrs. Washington was an affectionate parent; but she did not encourage in herself that imprudent tenderness, which so often causes a mother to foster the passions of her children by foolish indulgences, and which seldom fails to destroy the respect which every child should feel for a parent. George was early made to understand that he must obey his mother, and therefore he respected as well as loved her. She was kind to his young companions, but they thought her stern, because they always felt that they must behave correctly in her presence. The character of the mother, as well as that of the son, are shown in the following incident.

Mrs. Washington owned a remarkably fine colt, which she valued very much; but which though old enough for use, had never been mounted; no one would venture to ride it, or attempt to break its wild and vicious spirit. George proposed to some of his young companions, that they should assist him to secure the colt until he could mount it, as he had determined that he would try to tame it. Soon after sunrise one morning, they drove the wild animal into an enclosure, and with great difficulty succeeded in placing a bridle on it. George then sprang upon its back, and the vexed colt bounded over the open fields, prancing and plunging to get rid of its burden. The bold rider kept his seat firmly, and the struggle between them became alarming to his companions, who were watching him. The speed of the colt increased, until at length, in making a furious effort to throw his conqueror, he burst a large blood-vessel, and instantly died.

George was unhurt, but was much troubled by the unexpected result of his exploit. His companions soon joined him, and when they saw the beautiful colt lifeless, the first words they spoke were: "What will your mother say—who can tell her?" They were called to breakfast, and soon after they were seated at the table, Mrs. Washington said, "Well, young gentlemen, have you seen my fine sorrel colt in your rambles?" No answer was given, and the question was repeated; her son George then replied, "Your sorrel colt is dead, mother." He gave her an exact account of the event. The flush of displeasure which first rose on her cheek, soon passed away; and she said calmly, "While I regret the loss of my favourite, *I rejoice in my son, who always speaks the truth.*"

Source: The Life of George Washington (Philadelphia: American Sunday School Union, 1832), 21–23.

Analyzing Advice Literature

1. Using your notes from the table on page 168, compare and contrast the different types of ideal fathers, mothers, sons, and daughters depicted in these sources. How do these ideals complement or contradict one another? How do the parenting philosophies depicted in these sources compare with those of Nancy Shippen and Francis Wayland?

2. How do these sources depict parental discipline? How do the methods of discipline differ between fathers and mothers? What do those differences tell you about assumptions these sources make about the distribution of power and authority within the family?

3. What sorts of positive and negative examples do these sources present for the behavior of boys and girls? Compare and contrast the language and plots of *The Busy Bee* (Source 4) and *The Life of George Washington* (Source 5): How do they define virtue and character differently for girls and for boys? In what ways are the shortcomings of bad boys and bad girls gender specific? For example, compare Child's discussion of sexuality in *The Mother's Book* (Source 2) with *The New-England Primer's* descriptions of bad behavior (Source 3).

4. What clues do these sources offer about the economic class of their intended audience? How do they depict members of the household who are not biologically related to the parents or children? Where in these sources do you perceive any biases or assumptions that would limit their usefulness for studying the domestic life and family roles of immigrants, slaves, or the urban working class?

5. How do *The New-England Primer* (Source 3), *The Busy Bee* (Source 4), and *The Life of George Washington* (Source 5) compare with the books and stories you read as a child? What does this comparison tell you about the cultural construction of childhood in the United States in the early nineteenth century versus today? What role has television taken in the moral and civic education of present-day American children, and how does it compare in that respect to the efforts of the American Sunday School Union?

The Rest of the Story

In the two decades after 1830, the changes that Republican Motherhood and the Cult of Domesticity wrought in the middle-class American family came into full bloom. Capitalizing on the influence and moral authority that society ascribed to them as mothers and household managers, women stepped into public roles, forming female benevolent societies and maternal associations that embraced such causes as Christian missionary work and temperance reform. Lydia Maria Child was on the vanguard of this transformation, giving up her writing on domestic and family topics in the 1830s to promote abolitionism. Men continued to publish advice literature on family government and child rearing, but the tone of this literature gradually shifted from its roots in evangelical

Protestantism to a more scientific concern for controlling the early childhood environment and promoting public education. Horace Bushnell's influential *Christian Nurture* (1847) attacked the practice of breaking the child's will and recommended instead "bending the will" through loving and mild nurture. Bushnell's approach assigned even greater importance to the role of the mother as a teacher and disciplinarian, because it discounted the effect of grand confrontations between parent and child, such as that between Francis and Heman Wayland, in favor of a mother's constant surveillance of children in their earliest years.

As the nineteenth century progressed, American children's literature diverged into gender-specific themes that reflected the boundary between the female world of the household and the male world beyond it. Although the exemplary lessons in honesty and manly virtue from George Washington's boyhood remained a mainstay of schoolbooks, boys in the mid-nineteenth century also read the tales of a fictional world traveler named Peter Parley and the rags-to-riches stories of Horatio Alger. Girls were expected to read books that celebrated the roles they would assume as wives and mothers. Female fiction writers dominated the genre of the domestic novel, which featured female characters and mother-child relationships at the center of the plot. Perhaps the most enduring work in this genre is Louisa May Alcott's *Little Women* (1868), the tale of a temporarily fatherless family of four girls and their mother during the Civil War. Harriet Beecher Stowe's *Uncle Tom's Cabin* (1852) was not originally published for young readers, but it did appear in storybook editions for children. Its remarkable influence on its mostly female readership rested in a large part on its sympathetic portrayal of a slave family and its condemnation of slaveholders for violating middle-class domestic values.

The model of family that emerged in middle-class American culture in the early nineteenth century perpetuated itself in future generations through literature that prepared children to assume gender-specific roles as adults. Boys' adventure stories anticipated the ups and downs and geographic mobility they would experience in the competitive marketplace of industrial America, and girls learned the joys and duties of domestic life from idealized fictional versions of themselves. As the careers of Lydia Maria Child and Harriett Beecher Stowe suggest, however, society's elevation of women as mothers also gave them an entrée into the public sphere as writers, reformers, and advocates for the political and social causes they embraced.

To Find Out More

Resources on Early American Childhood

Bremner, Robert H., ed. *Children and Youth in America: A Documentary History*. Vol. 1, *1600–1865*. Cambridge, MA: Harvard University Press, 1970.

Fass, Paula S., and Mary Ann Mason, eds. *Childhood in America*. New York: New York University Press, 2000.

Greven, Philip J., Jr., ed. *Child-Rearing Concepts, 1628–1861: Historical Sources*. Itasca, IL: F. E. Peacock, 1973.

The New-England Primer. 1805, 1807. Scanned images of primer pages available at http://public.gettysburg.edu/~tshannon/courses/341/colonialamer.htm.

Pflieger, Pat. *Nineteenth-Century American Children and What They Read*. http://merrycoz.org/kids.htm.

Secondary Sources on Gender, Family, and Childhood in Nineteenth-Century America

Avery, Gillian. *Behold the Child: American Children and Their Books, 1621–1922*. Baltimore: Johns Hopkins University Press, 1994.

Cott, Nancy F. *The Bonds of Womanhood: "Woman's Sphere" in New England, 1780–1835*. New Haven, CT: Yale University Press, 1977.

Greven, Philip J., Jr. *The Protestant Temperament: Patterns of Child-Rearing, Religious Experience, and the Self in Early America*. New York: Knopf, 1977.

Hulbert, Ann. *Raising America: Experts, Parents, and a Century of Advice about Children*. New York: Knopf, 2003.

Illick, Joseph E. *American Childhoods*. Philadelphia: University of Pennsylvania Press, 2002.

Lewis, Jan. *The Pursuit of Happiness: Family and Values in Jefferson's Virginia*. Cambridge: Cambridge University Press, 1983.

Rotundo, E. Anthony. *American Manhood: Transformations in Masculinity from the Revolution to the Modern Era*. New York: Basic Books, 1993.

Ryan, Mary P. *Cradle of the Middle Class: The Family in Oneida County, New York, 1790–1865*. Cambridge: Cambridge University Press, 1981.

CHAPTER 9

The Meaning of Cherokee Civilization

Newspaper Editorials about Indian Removal

As a potential in-law, Elias Boudinot had much to recommend him. He was the product of a boarding school education in Cornwall, Connecticut, where he had met his fiancée, Harriet Gold. A committed Christian, he counted ministers and missionaries among his closest friends and associates. Although not wealthy himself, he was well connected to the social and political elites of his community back home in the South. By any measure, Boudinot had a bright future ahead of him. What more could his fiancée's family and neighbors have wanted for her?

They most definitely did not want Boudinot to be an Indian. The residents of Cornwall supported missionaries working among Indians in the South and allowed them to open a boarding school in their town. But when two of the most promising students, Boudinot and his cousin John Ridge, fell in love with local girls, the townsfolk drew the line. There was a public outcry when Ridge married Sarah Bird Northrup in 1824. When it became known that Boudinot and Gold intended to follow suit, Harriet's own brother helped burn her in effigy. Boudinot and Gold went ahead with their plans anyway, but local officials closed the school permanently to prevent any more such unions.

Boudinot and Ridge had grown up in what is now northwestern Georgia. Their lives illustrated the remarkable changes that the Cherokee people had undergone after the American Revolution. In the colonial era, the Cherokees were the most powerful Indians in the American South. Their homelands stretched along the southern Appalachians, covering territory in the present-day states of Virginia, North Carolina, South Carolina, Tennessee, Georgia, and Alabama. As epidemic disease and warfare decimated coastal Indians, the Cherokees emerged as the dominant native participants in the southern deerskin trade. American independence, however, dealt them a serious blow. The Cherokees allied with the British, and after the war the victorious Americans regarded them as a conquered enemy who had forfeited their right to the land.

In response to that crisis, the Cherokees undertook a cultural and political transformation. Adopting the language used by the federal government in its Indian relations, they decided to embrace "civilization" rather than resist it. To survive in the United States, they would learn to live and work as their non-Indian neighbors did. The federal government's Indian policy was designed by Henry Knox, President George Washington's Secretary of War. Knox rejected the notion that the United States had a right of conquest that allowed it to dispossess Indians at will. Such high-handed tactics, tried by the federal and state governments during the 1780s, only caused hostilities that the new nation was ill-equipped to handle. Knox wanted to create an Indian policy that would be more peaceful and less costly, while at the same time asserting the federal government's power over the states. His approach was twofold. First, he revived the colonial era practice of conducting treaties with Indian nations, regarding them as separate, sovereign powers who controlled their own borders and internal affairs. Treaties conducted by federal officials became the means by which the U.S. government exercised its exclusive power under the Constitution to purchase western land from its native inhabitants.

The second part of Knox's plan was the so-called civilization policy: the federal government would encourage Indians to adopt the habits and customs of white society by providing them with plows, livestock, spinning wheels, and teachers to instruct them in their use. Ever since the arrival of the first colonists, European missionaries had been trying to "civilize" Indians in such a manner, but with little success. Even those Indians who embraced Christianity were reluctant to engage in such full-scale abandonment of their traditional cultures. Knox and his contemporaries, however, believed that Indians could be assimilated into American society if they simply learned to conduct themselves as white Americans did. Thomas Jefferson thought that teaching Indians to farm on the European model would inculcate in them the values—industry, independence, a respect for private property—that were the bedrock of the American republic. Indians who grew crops or bred animals for commercial markets would no longer need vast hunting grounds. They would fix themselves on the landscape and cede their excess territory to the federal government. In Jefferson's vision, these Indians would ultimately become indistinguishable from other U.S. citizens. As president, he told a delegation of Indian chiefs, "In time you will be as we are: you will become one people with us; your blood will flow and mix with ours, and will spread with ours over this great island."

Although the federal government pursued this civilization policy with all Indians, it became most associated with Indians in the Southeast, particularly the Cherokees. The Cherokees had historically lived in towns dispersed along the river valleys of the southern Appalachians. Power was localized, and clanship provided the most important social and political ties between these communities. Clan matrons selected the chiefs who represented their lineages in councils, and warriors enforced the code of blood vengeance intended to protect clan members from violence perpetrated by outsiders. During the Jeffersonian era, however, a new generation of Cherokee leaders emerged who were committed to centralizing power in a way that would make it easier to defend the Cherokee borders and prevent Cherokee land from being sold away piecemeal. These leaders embraced the civilization policy for a number of reasons. Some of the leaders were the children of British traders and Cherokee women and so were already comfortable living in two worlds. Others were entrepreneurs who had acquired land and slaves and saw in the civilization policy a way to cement their wealth and power in Cherokee society. Elias Boudinot and John Ridge were members of this new elite, raised as Cherokees but also acclimated to white society and savvy in the ways of its business and politics.

Boudinot and Ridge also represented a new spirit of Cherokee nationalism. The violent reaction to their marriages they experienced in Connecticut convinced them that no matter how much Indians learned to live like whites, they would never be accepted as equals among them. They believed that the Cherokees' future rested instead in defending their territorial and political autonomy from the outside world. Cherokee leaders decided in 1822 not to give up another inch of their territory in treaty negotiations. They also worked to unify the Cherokee people by creating a more powerful national government led by the Cherokee National Council, a legislative body based on male voting and representation. In 1827, the Cherokees adopted a written constitution modeled after the United States Constitution. Cherokee nationalism also found expression in the promotion of literacy. A silversmith named Sequoyah developed a syllabary for rendering Cherokee into a written language, and in 1828, the *Cherokee Phoenix* became the first newspaper published by and for Native Americans.

The chief opposition to the Cherokees' new nationalism came from neighboring states, particularly Georgia, which claimed sovereignty over Cherokee territory. State governments insisted that Indian lands within their borders fell under their civil jurisdiction. In many states, Indian populations had already been confined to small reservations on marginal lands, but the Cherokees were different. They occupied a large and fertile chunk of northwestern Georgia that state officials were anxious to seize and distribute to their constituents. Furthermore, when Georgia ceded its western land claims to the United States in 1802, the federal government promised to extinguish all Indian title to land within Georgia's borders. By 1820, the Georgians' patience had worn thin; they wanted the Cherokee out. The Georgia legislature challenged the independence of the Cherokee government by passing laws asserting its sovereignty over all land and people within the state. Subsequent acts extended the jurisdiction of Georgia's courts over the Cherokees while at the same time denying them the right to testify in legal cases against whites. Such discriminatory measures made it increasingly difficult for the Cherokees to defend their property, individual liberties, and political autonomy.

As a presidential candidate in 1828, Andrew Jackson made clear that his sympathies rested with the state governments rather than the Indians. He called making treaties with Indians an "absurdity," a relic of an earlier time when Indians had been much more powerful. Jackson believed that living near

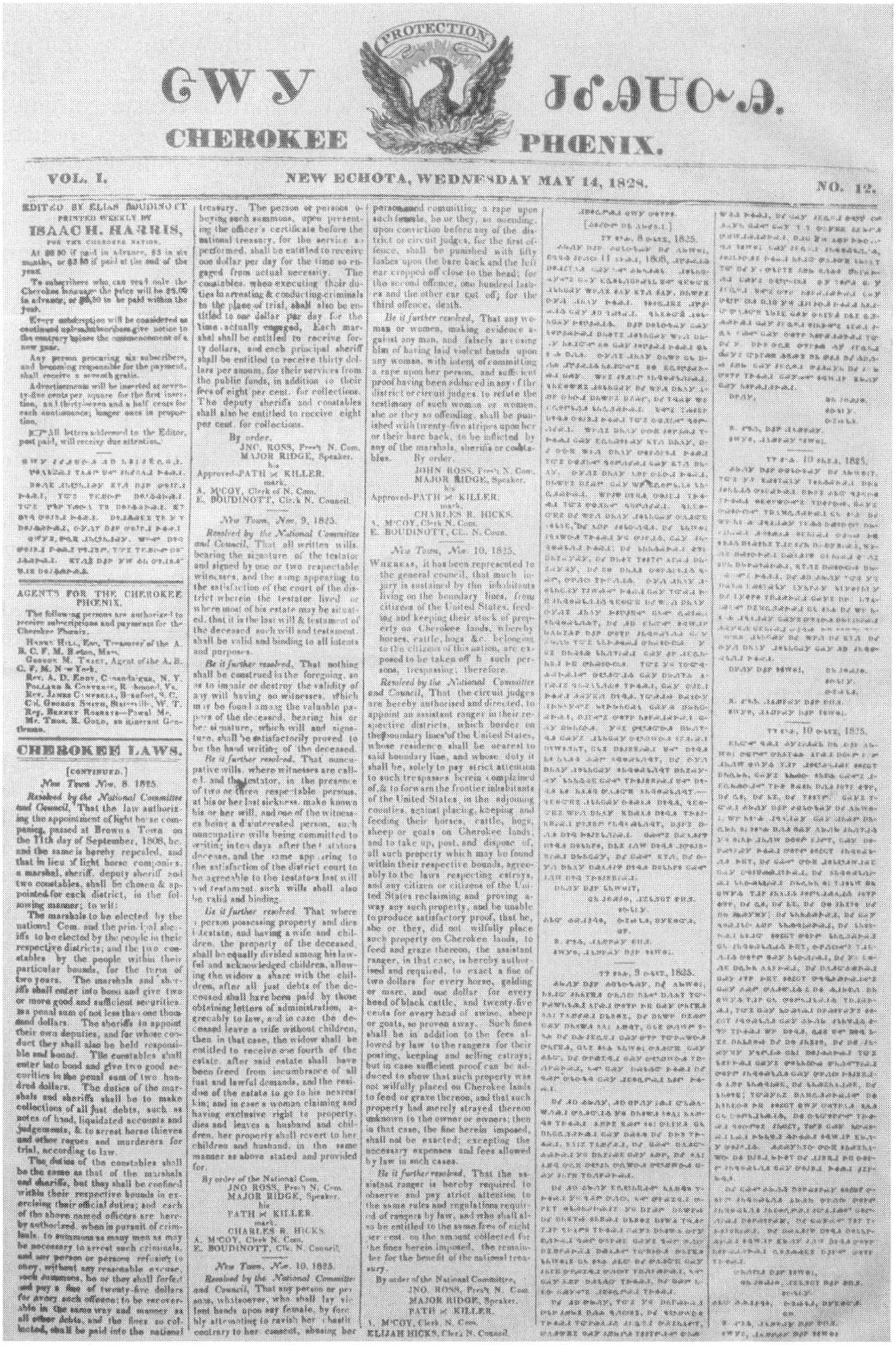

PROTECTION.

ᏣᎳᎩ ᏧᎴᎯᏌᏅᎯ.

CHEROKEE PHŒNIX.

VOL. I. NEW ECHOTA, WEDNESDAY MAY 14, 1828. NO. 12.

EDITED BY ELIAS BOUDINOTT
PRINTED WEEKLY BY
ISAAC H. HARRIS,
FOR THE CHEROKEE NATION.

AGENTS FOR THE CHEROKEE PHŒNIX.

CHEROKEE LAWS.

[CONTINUED.]

New Town Nov. 8. 1825.

Resolved by the National Committee and Council, That the law authorizing the appointment of light horse companies, passed at Browns Town on the 11th day of September, 1808, be, and the same is hereby repealed, and that in lieu of light horse companies, a marshal, sheriff, deputy sheriff and two constables, shall be chosen & appointed for each district, in the following manner; to wit:

By order.
JNO. ROSS, Pres't N. Com.
MAJOR RIDGE, Speaker.
Approved—PATH ⋈ KILLER.
A. M'COY, Clerk of N. Com.
E. BOUDINOTT, Clerk N. Council.

New Town, Nov. 9, 1825.

New Town, Nov. 10, 1825.

By order of the National Committee,
JNO. ROSS, Pres't N. Com.
MAJOR RIDGE, Speaker.
PATH ⋈ KILLER.
A. M'COY, Clerk, N. Com.
ELIJAH HICKS, Clerk N. Council.

***Figure 9.1 The Cherokee Phoenix** The first Native American newspaper published in the United States, the* Cherokee Phoenix *printed content in both English and the Cherokee syllabary developed by Sequoyah in the 1820s.*

Source: © Photri/Topham/The Image Works.

whites invariably spelled doom for native populations; he described resettlement west of the Mississippi as the only humane alternative to the extinction Indians faced if they remained in the East. Jackson did not invent the idea of Indian removal; U.S. presidents since Jefferson had endorsed granting federal assistance to Indians willing to move voluntarily to new homes in the West. Jackson, though, was the first president to condone actions taken by state governments to evict unwilling Indians from their homelands. This position contributed to his popularity among southern voters, who expected that his election would break the resistance to removal offered by the Cherokees and several other southeastern Indian nations: the Creek, Choctaw, Chickasaw, and Seminole.

Using the Source: Newspaper Editorials

Many Americans did not share Jackson's view on Indian removal, and it became one of the most contentious issues in national politics during the Jacksonian era. Missionaries who had been working among the Cherokees and other southern Indians defended their right to stay put. Other opponents of Jackson thought it a matter of national honor that the federal government uphold treaties in which it had guaranteed Indians security in their homelands. Congress hotly debated the issue before narrowly passing the Indian Removal Act of 1830, which gave the president the power to create new homelands for eastern Indians west of the Mississippi and to provide federal assistance to them in removing there.

The debate over Indian removal spilled into newspapers as well. Alexis de Tocqueville, a French visitor to the United States in 1831, described newspapers as the lifeblood of American democracy, the means by which citizens communicated with one another and pushed their interests forward. "Nothing but a newspaper can drop the same thought into a thousand minds at the same moment," Tocqueville wrote. "A newspaper is an adviser that . . . comes of its own accord and talks to you briefly every day of the common weal [the public good], without distracting you from your private affairs." That the Cherokee National Council made the publication of a newspaper one of its priorities during the 1820s testifies to how thoroughly Cherokee elites had adopted the practices and values of American politics.

The *Cherokee Phoenix* printed its first issue in February 1828 in the Cherokee town of New Echota, and Elias Boudinot served as its editor. The National Council subsidized the paper by paying for its printing and Boudinot's salary. The newspaper's content included laws passed by the National Council and other local news, items Boudinot reprinted from other sources, and editorials he wrote about Cherokee affairs. Boudinot sent copies to subscribers elsewhere in the United States, and other newspapers occasionally reprinted items from the *Cherokee Phoenix* in their pages. In each issue of the *Cherokee Phoenix*, about 30 percent of the content was printed in parallel columns of English and Cherokee, using Sequoyah's syllabary. Although never published daily, the *Cherokee Phoenix* functioned in the way Tocqueville described: it enabled the National

Council to "drop the same thought into a thousand minds," whether Indian or white, and it helped unite resistance to Indian removal.

Other newspapers served a similar purpose. The most widely read white advocate for the Cherokees was Jeremiah Evarts, a New England attorney and secretary for a missionary organization that worked with southern Indians. In 1829, he published a series of antiremoval editorials in Washington, D.C.'s *National Intelligencer* using the pseudonym "William Penn." (The Quaker founder of Pennsylvania, William Penn, had been well known as an advocate for fair treatment of Indians, although he had died more than a century earlier.) Boudinot's editorials and Evarts's "William Penn Letters" offered the most sustained critique in the nation's press of President Jackson's and Georgia's treatment of the Cherokees.

What Can Newspaper Editorials Tell Us?

Historians can approach a great political issue such as Indian removal from any number of angles. They can read the legislative acts, speeches, and debates of the politicians who put this policy in place; they might look at the personal correspondence or journals of people involved in the issue; they might even analyze census reports and other data to get a sense of population and economic growth among white and Indian communities. Newspapers, however, provide a perspective on what is often referred to as "public opinion": what did the common folk, the proverbial "person on the street," think about this issue? As Tocqueville noted, Jacksonian America was awash in newspapers; they were the preferred means by which people publicly expressed their opinions and tried to rally others to their cause.

Determining what constitutes public opinion has its own challenges. Newspapers of the Jacksonian era made no attempt to be objective in their news coverage or editorial policy. They were usually affiliated with political parties or reform organizations that published the newspaper to advance their agendas. The Cherokee National Council expected the *Cherokee Phoenix* to toe the party line in this regard. The *National Intelligencer*, in which Evarts published the "William Penn Letters," was critical of Jackson and eventually became a mouthpiece for the Whig Party, the rival to Jackson's Democrats. So, although newspaper editorials were both opinionated and public, they cannot be construed as representing a single, uniform public opinion. If anything, newspapers encouraged the expression of multiple public opinions.

Nevertheless, newspaper editorials do offer certain advantages for studying the debate over Indian removal. Boudinot and Evarts gave voice to the opposition. Their editorials help historians recover the argument made on behalf of the Cherokees and other Indians, to see more clearly the alternatives to removal that appeared viable to at least some Americans at this critical point in U.S.-Indian relations. Furthermore, by reading Boudinot and Evarts alongside each other, it is possible to compare how Indian and non-Indian opponents of removal made their cases. Consider, for example, how Boudinot and Evarts invoked the idea of nationhood:

FROM BOUDINOT IN THE *CHEROKEE PHOENIX*

Boudinot's language emphasizes the national identity of the Cherokees independent from other Indian nations

While he possesses a national character, there is hope for the Indian. But take his rights away, divest him of the last spark of national pride, and introduce him to a new order of things, invest him with oppressive laws, grevious to be borne, he droops like the fading flower before the noon day sun. Most of the Northern tribes have fallen prey to such causes, & the Catawbas[1] of South Carolina, are a striking instance of the truth of what we say. There is hope for the Cherokees as long as they continue in their present situation, but disorganize them, either by removing them beyond the Mississippi, or by imposing on them "heavy burdens,"[2] you cut a vital string in their national existence.

Source: Elias Boudinot, *Cherokee Editor: The Writings of Elias Boudinot*, ed. Theda Perdue (Knoxville: University of Tennessee Press, 1983), 105.

FROM EVARTS IN THE "WILLIAM PENN LETTERS"

Evarts invokes historical examples and God-given rights to defend Cherokee nationhood

It has been said, indeed, that the Indians, being an uncivilized people, are not to be ranked among nations. But this is said gratuitously, and without the least shadow of proof. How many treaties did Julius Caesar make with savage tribes, who were greatly inferior, in every intellectual and moral respect, to the Cherokees of the present day? There is as little reason as truth in the objection. Has not God endowed every community with some rights? and are not these rights to be regarded by every honest man and by every fair-minded and honorable ruler?

Source: Jeremiah Evarts, *Cherokee Removal: The "William Penn" Essays and Other Writings by Jeremiah Evarts*, ed. Francis Paul Prucha (Knoxville: University of Tennessee Press, 1981), 73.

In these passages, Boudinot and Evarts both argue that the Cherokees are a sovereign nation. Evarts does so by invoking historical comparisons and God-given rights. Boudinot, on the other hand, uses abstractions like "character" and "pride" to describe the Cherokees. Evarts rests his case on generalization and precedent; his language is legalistic and formal. Boudinot's language is more emotional, making a case for a distinctive and communal Cherokee identity.

Working with newspaper editorials has some disadvantages to keep in mind when you read these sources. Editorials are the voice of the newspaper's publisher, not necessarily its readers. Although it is reasonable to assume that the editors and readers of a partisan newspaper such as the *National Intelligencer* had much in common, it is important to bear in mind that a newspaper's content is ultimately determined by the people who print it. That was certainly the

---

[1] A once powerful southern Indian nation reduced to a small, impoverished population by the 1820s.

[2] The discriminatory laws Georgia passed against the Cherokees.

case with the National Council and the *Cherokee Phoenix*. Initially, Boudinot and the council saw eye to eye in their opposition to removal. As it became clear that Jackson would not help protect Cherokee land from seizure by Georgia, Boudinot's opinion changed and he decided that moving west was the best option for preserving Cherokee nationhood. When he tried to express such opinions in the pages of the *Cherokee Phoenix*, the National Council relieved him of his duties as editor and suspended publication of the newspaper. It is also important to remember that the *Cherokee Phoenix* was the voice of those Cherokees who had most thoroughly immersed themselves in the federal government's civilization policy. They were wealthy and politically influential, but they were a minority of the approximately 16,000 Cherokees living in the East at that time. We cannot presume that the *Cherokee Phoenix* spoke for all Cherokees any more than we can assume that the *National Intelligencer* spoke for all non-Indians.

American newspapers have changed substantially since the Jacksonian era, but they remain an important part of how our democracy works. Most newspapers today strive to be more objective in their news coverage than their Jacksonian predecessors for the sake of attracting a wide readership, but most still have partisan political orientations that are evident on their editorial pages, from the liberal *New York Times* to the conservative *Wall Street Journal*. The Checklist questions below will help you make use of any editorial as a historical source, regardless of when it was published or the issue it addressed.

CHECKLIST: Interrogating Newspaper Editorials

☐ Who is the author of the editorial? What do you know about that person?

☐ When did the editorial appear, and in what historical context did it appear?

☐ In what newspaper did the editorial appear? Was the paper associated with any particular parties or organizations?

☐ Who was the newspaper's primary audience?

☐ What issue is the editorial addressing? What position is it taking on that issue?

☐ What sort of evidence does the editorial present to make its case? Can you detect any bias in the author's language or tone?

☐ How do you think readers reacted to this editorial? Does it recommend that they take any particular action concerning the issue it addresses?

Source Analysis Table

Use this table to take notes on the arguments Boudinot and Evarts make on behalf of the Cherokees and against Indian removal.

	Elias Boudinot, *Cherokee Phoenix* (1828–1831)	Jeremiah Evarts, "William Penn Letters" (1829)
Why should the federal government oppose Indian removal?		
What are the motives and character of the supporters of Indian removal?		
What will be the consequences of removal for the Cherokees and the United States?		

The Source: Newspaper Editorials about Indian Removal

ELIAS BOUDINOT, EDITORIALS FROM THE *CHEROKEE PHOENIX* (1828–1831)

1 | *February 21, 1828*

> Boudinot wrote this editorial for the first issue of the *Cherokee Phoenix*.

In regard to the controversy with Georgia, and the present policy of the General Government, in removing, and concentrating the Indians, out of the limits of any state, which, by the way, appears to be gaining strength, we will invariably and faithfully state the feelings of the majority of the people. Our views, as a people, on this subject, have been sadly misrepresented. These views we do not wish to conceal, but are willing that the public should know what we think of this policy, which, in our opinion, if carried into effect, will prove pernicious to us. . . .

How far we shall be successful in advancing the improvement of our people, is not now for us to decide. We hope, however, our efforts will not be altogether in vain. Now is the moment when mere speculation on the practicability of civilizing us is out of the question. Sufficient and repeated evidence has been given, that Indians can be reclaimed from a savage state, and that with proper advantages, they are as capable of improvement in mind as any other people; and let it be remembered, notwithstanding the assertions of those who talk to the contrary, that this improvement can be made, not only by the Cherokees, but by all the Indians, *in their present location.* We are rendered bold in making this assertion, by considering the history of our people within the last fifteen years. There was a time within our remembrance, when darkness was sadly prevalent, and ignorance abounded amongst us—when strong and deep rooted prejudices were directed against many things relating to civilized life—and when it was thought a disgrace, for a Cherokee to appear in the costume of a white man. We mention these things not by way of boasting, but to shew our readers that it is not a visionary thing to attempt to civilize and christianize all the Indians, but highly practicable. . . .

We would now commit our feeble efforts to the good will and indulgence of the public, praying that God will attend them with his blessings, and hoping for that happy period, when all the Indian tribes of America shall arise, Phoenix like, from their ashes, and when the terms, "Indian depredation,"

Source: All editorials presented in this section are excerpted from Elias Boudinot, *Cherokee Editor: The Writings of Elias Boudinot*, ed. Theda Perdue (Knoxville: University of Tennessee Press, 1983), 93–143.

"war-whoop," "scalping knife" and the like, shall become obsolete, and for ever be "buried deep under ground."

2   *January 21, 1829*

"Vigil" might reasonably entertain one cheering consideration, and that is, the gradual diminution of such practices as described by him in his communication.[1] If he had visited this Nation *thirty years* ago, and witnessed the practices of the inhabitants in their full extent, his tears would have flowed more freely, and the consideration of their wretchedness would have been without a redeeming thought. At that period the Cherokees resided in villages, in each of which was a "Townhouse," the head quarter of frivolity. Here were assembled almost every night (we are told, we speak from hearsay for we were born under an era of reformation,) men and women, old and young, to dance their *bear dance, buffalo dance, eagle dance, green-corn dance* &c. &c. &c. and when the day appeared, instead of going to their farms, and laboring for the support of their families, the young and middle aged of the males were seen to leave their houses, their faces fantastically painted, and their heads decorated with feathers, and step off with a merry whoop, which indicated that they were *real men*, to a ball play,[2] or a meeting of a similar nature. Such in a word was the life of a Cherokee in those days during spring & summer seasons. In the fall and winter seasons they were gone to follow the chase,[3] which occupation enabled them to purchase of the traders a few items of clothing, sufficient to last perhaps until the next hunting time. From the soil they derived a scanty supply of corn, barely enough to furnish them with gah-no-ha-nah[4] and this was obtained by the labor of women and grey headed men, for custom would have it that it was disgraceful for a young man to be seen with a hoe in his hand, except on particular occasions.

In those days of ignorance and heathenism, prejudices against the customs of whites were inveterate, so much so that white men, who came along the Cherokees, had to throw away their costume and adopt the *leggings*.[5] In a moral and intellectual point of view the scenery was dark & gloomy, nevertheless it has not been impenetrable. The introduction of light and intelligence has struck a mortal blow to the superstitious practices of the Cherokees, and by the aid of that light, a new order of things is introduced, and it is to be hoped will now eradicate the vestiges of older days.

---

[1] Boudinot is replying to an item in an earlier edition of the *Cherokee Phoenix*, from a correspondent describing a Native American dance.

[2] A Native American athletic game, criticized by missionaries and other whites for encouraging gambling and excessive leisure among the Cherokees.

[3] To hunt deer.

[4] Hominy, a corn-based staple of the Cherokee diet.

[5] Colonial traders had to dress in Cherokee buckskin to be accepted among them.

3   *January 28, 1829*

The causes which have operated to exterminate the Indian tribes that are produced as instances of the certain doom of the whole Aboriginal family appear plain to us. These causes did not exist in the Indians themselves, nor in the will of heaven, nor simply in the intercourse of Indians with civilized man, but they were precisely such causes as are now attempted by the state of Georgia—by infringing upon their rights, by disorganizing them, and circumscribing their limits. While he possesses a national character, there is hope for the Indian. But take his rights away, divest him of the last spark of national pride, and introduce him to a new order of things, invest him with oppressive laws, grevious to be borne, he droops like the fading flower before the noon day sun. Most of the Northern tribes have fallen prey to such causes, & the Catawbas[1] of South Carolina, are a striking instance of the truth of what we say. There is hope for the Cherokees as long as they continue in their present situation, but disorganize them, either by removing them beyond the Mississippi, or by imposing on them "heavy burdens," you cut a vital string in their national existence.

 Things will no doubt come to a final issue before long in regard to the Indians, and for our part, we care not how soon. The State of Georgia has taken a strong stand against us, and the United States must either defend us in our rights, or leave us to our foe. In the former case the General Government[2] will redeem her pledge solemnly given in treaties.—In the latter, she will violate her promise of protection, and we cannot, in future, depend consistently, upon any guarantee made by her to us, either here or beyond the Mississippi.

[1] A once powerful southern Indian nation reduced to a small, impoverished population by the 1820s.

[2] The federal government of the United States.

4   *February 18, 1829*

Most of our readers probably know what is meant by Indian clans. It is no more than a division of an Indian tribe into large families. We believe this custom is universal with the North American Indians. Among the Cherokees are seven clans such as Wolf, Deer, Paint, &c. This simple division of the Cherokees formed the grand work by which marriages were regulated, and murder punished. A Cherokee could marry into any of the clans except two, that to which his father belongs, for all of that clan are his fathers and aunts and that to which his mother belongs, for all of that clan are his brothers and sisters, a child invariably inheriting the clan of his mother. . . .

 But it was the mutual law of clans as connected with murder, which rendered this custom savage and barbarous. We speak of what it was once, not as it is now, for the Cherokees, after experiencing sad effects from it, determined to, and did about twenty years ago in a solemn council, abolish it. From that time, murder has been considered a governmental crime.—Previous to that, the following were too palpably true, viz:

The Cherokees as a nation, had nothing to do with murder.

Murder was punished upon the principle of retaliation.

It belonged to the clan of the murdered to revenge his death.

If the murderer fled, his brother or nearest relative was liable to suffer in his stead.

If a man killed his brother, he was answerable to no law or clan.

If the murderer (this however is known only by tradition) was not as respectable as the murdered, his relative, or a man of his clan of a more respectable standing was liable to suffer.

To kill, under any circumstance whatever, was considered murder, and punished accordingly.

Our readers will say, "those were savage laws indeed." They were, and the Cherokees were then pitied, for the above were not mere inoperative laws, but were rigorously executed. But we can now say with pleasure, that they are all repealed, and are remembered only as vestiges of ignorance and barbarism.

5 *April 21, 1830*

In this editorial, Boudinot responded to a congressional committee that recommended removal west of the Mississippi as the best option for preserving eastern Indian nations from extinction.

The Committee of Indian Affairs in the House of Representatives, in page 21 of their report say:

> That the greatest portion, even of the poorest class of the Southern Indian, may, for some years yet, find the means of sustaining life, is probable; but, when the game is all going, as it soon must be, and their physical as well as moral energies shall have undergone the farther decline, which the entire failure of the resources of the chase has never failed to mark in their downward career, the hideous features in their prospects will become more manifest.

Whoever really believes that the Cherokees subsist on game, is most wretchedly deceived, and is grossly ignorant of existing facts. *The Cherokees do not live upon the chase*, but upon the fruits of the earth produced by their labour. We should like to see any person point to a single family in this nation who obtain their clothing and provisions by hunting. *We* know of no one. We do not wish to be understood as saying that they do not hunt—they do hunt some, probably, about as much as white people do in new counties, but they no more depend upon this occupation for living than new settlers do. Game has been nearly extinct for the last thirty years, and even previous to that, when the

Cherokees depended upon the chase for subsistence, they were obliged to obtain their full supply of meat and skins out of what is now the limits of this nation. Cut off the last vestige of game in these woods, and you cannot starve the Cherokees—they have plenty of corn and domestic animals, and they raise their own cotton, and manufacture their own clothing. . . .

The maxim of our enemies, "that an Indian cannot work," the committee suppose "well established," and it would most certainly be well established if they could but prove their naked assertions. We know of many Indians who not only *work*, but work *hard*. Who labors for the Cherokee and builds his house, clears his farm, makes his fences, attends to his hogs, cattle and horses; who raises his corn, his cotton and manufactures his clothing? Can the committee tell? Yes, they have an answer at hand. He has no house, no farm, no hogs, cattle, no corn to save him from starvation, and clothing to cover him from nakedness. We know not what to say to such assertions. The above maxim has been received by many as truth, but not by the intelligent observers of their character, but by their enemies and such as have not had the means of knowing facts. But suppose it was once well founded and correctly applied, it has long since lost its universality. We invite any person who may be hesitating on this point to come and see and judge for himself—we are not afraid that the truth, the whole truth, should be known—we desire it—we invite "the most rigid scrutiny."

"That an Indian has an inherent thirst for spirituous liquor," is another maxim which the committee think is well applied to the Cherokees. On the charge of intemperance, we are very far from this crying sin. But if the charge is, that the Cherokees have greater thirst for spirits than whitemen, we unhesitatingly deny it. It is not so—we speak from personal observation. Facts form the only proper criterion in this case, and what is the actual state of things? We know, most certainly know, that among the whites of the surrounding counties intemperance and brutal intoxication (at which humanity may well shudder,) may be witnessed in every neighborhood. Go to their elections and courts and number those who are under the indulgence of inebriating drink and then come into the nation, and visit the Indian elections, courts and the General Council and make a disinterested comparison, and we pledge ourselves that there is less intemperance here on these occasions than among the whites. It is an incontrovertible fact, for the truth of which we appeal to all honest eyewitnesses, that on those public occasions, particularly at the General Council, which continues four weeks, a drunken Indian is seldom to be seen. We are sorry that intemperance does exist, but is it not universal? There has been of late considerable reformation among the Cherokees in common with other parts of the country.

6   *November 12, 1831*

We have on more than one occasion remarked upon the difficulties which lie in the way of civilizing the Indians. Those difficulties have been fully developed in the history of the Cherokees within the last two years. They are such as no one can now mistake—their nature is fully revealed, and the source from whence they rise can no longer be a matter of doubt. They are not to be found in the "nature" of the Indians, which a man in high authority once said was as difficult to change as the Leopard his spots. It is not because they are, of all others, the most degraded and ignorant that they have not been brought to enjoy the blessings of a civilized life. But it is because they have to contend with obstacles as numerous as they are peculiar.

With accommendable zeal the first Chief magistrate of the United States[1] undertook to bring the Cherokees into the pale of civilization, by establishing friendly relations with them by treaties, and introducing the mechanic arts[2] among them. He was indeed a "father" to them—They regarded him as such—They placed confidence in what he said, and well they might, for he was true to his promises. Of course the foundation for the improvement which the Cherokees have since made was laid under the patronage of that illustrious man. His successors followed his example and treated their "red children" as human beings, capable of improvement, and possessing rights derived from the source of all good, and guarantied by compacts as solemn as a great Republic could make. The attempts of those good men were attended with success, because they believed those attempts were feasible and acted accordingly. . . .

But alas! no sooner was it made manifest that the Cherokees were becoming strongly attached to the ways and usages of civilized life, than was aroused the opposition of those from whom better things ought to have been expected. No sooner was it known that they had learned the proper use of the earth, and that they were now less likely to dispose of their lands for a mess of pottage,[3] that they came in conflict with the cupidity and self-interest of those who ought to have been their benefactors. Then commenced a series of obstacles hard to overcome, and difficulties intended as a stumbling block, and unthought of before. The "Great Father" of the "red man" has lent his influence to encourage those difficulties.[4] The *guardian* has deprived his *wards* of their rights—The sacred obligations of treaties and laws have been disregarded—The promises of Washington and Jefferson have not been fulfilled. The policy of the United States on Indian affairs has taken a different direction, for no other reason than that the Cherokees have so far become civilized as to appreciate a regular form of Government. They are now deprived of rights they once enjoyed—A

---

[1] President George Washington.

[2] Farming, animal breeding, and weaving, for example.

[3] A trifling compensation.

[4] Boudinot is now referring to President Andrew Jackson.

neighboring power[5] is now permitted to extend its withering hand over them—Their own laws, intended to regulate their society, to encourage virtue and to suppress vice, must now be abolished, and civilized acts, passed for the purpose of expelling them, must be substituted.—Their intelligent citizens who have been instructed through means employed by former administrations, and through the efforts of benevolent societies, must be abused and insulted, represented as avaricious, feeding upon the poverty of the common Indians—the hostility of all those who want the Indian lands must be directed against them. . . .

Is not here an array of *difficulties*?—The truth is, while a portion of the community have been, in the most laudable manner, engaged in using efforts to civilize and Christianize the Indian, another portion of the same community have been busy in counteracting those efforts. Cupidity and self-interest are at the bottom of all these difficulties—A desire to possess the Indian land is paramount to a desire to see him *established* on the soil as a *civilized* man.

[5] Georgia.

JEREMIAH EVARTS, "WILLIAM PENN LETTERS" (1829)

7   *From Letter I*

It may be truly said, that the character which a nation sustains, in its intercourse with the great community of nations, is of more value than any other of its public possessions. Our diplomatic agents have uniformly declared, during the whole period of our national history, in their discussions with the agents of foreign powers, that we offer to others the same justice which we ask from them. And though, in times of national animosity, or when the interests of different communities clash with each other, there will be mutual reproaches and recriminations, and every nation will, in its turn, be charged with unfairness or injustice, still, among nations, as among individuals, there is a difference between *the precious and the vile*; and that nation will undoubtedly, in the long course of years, be most prosperous and most respected, which most sedulously cherishes a character for fair dealing, and even generosity, in all its transactions.

There is a higher consideration still. The Great Arbiter of Nations[1] never fails to take cognizance of national delinquencies. No sophistry can elude his scrutiny; no array of plausible arguments, or of smooth but hollow professions, can bias his judgment; and he has at his disposal most abundant means of

[1] God.

All editorials presented in this section are excerpted from Jeremiah Evarts, *Cherokee Removal: The "William Penn" Essays and Other Writings by Jeremiah Evarts*, ed. Francis Paul Prucha (Knoxville: University of Tennessee Press, 1981), 50–195.

executing his decisions. In many forms, and with awful solemnity, he has declared his abhorrence of oppression in every shape; and especially of injustice perpetrated against the weak by the strong, *when strength is in fact made the only rule of action*. The people of the United States are not altogether guiltless, in regard to their treatment of the aborigines of this continent; but they cannot as yet be charged with any *systematic legislation* on this subject, inconsistent with the plainest principles of moral honesty. At least, I am not aware of any proof, by which such a charge could be sustained.

Nor do I, in these preliminary remarks, attempt to characterize measures now in contemplation. But it is very clear, that our government and our people should be extremely cautious, lest in judging between ourselves and the Indians, and carrying our own judgment into execution with a strong hand, we incur the displeasure of the Most High.

8   *From Letter II*

In my first number I prepared the way to inquire, *What right have the Cherokees to the lands which they occupy?* This is a plain question, and easily answered.

The Cherokees are human beings, endowed by their Creator with the same natural rights as other men. They are in peaceable possession of a territory which they have always regarded as their own. This territory was in possession of their ancestors, through an unknown series of generations, and has come down to them with a title *absolutely unencumbered in every respect*. It is not pretended, that the Cherokees have ever alienated[1] their country, or that the whites have ever been in possession of it.

If the Cherokees are interrogated as to their title, they can truly say, "God gave this country to our ancestors. We have never been in bondage to any man. Though we have sold much land to our white neighbors, we have never bought any from them. We own the land which we now occupy, by the right of the original possessors; a right which is allowed in all countries to be of incontestable validity. We assert, therefore, that no human power can lawfully compel us to leave our lands."

If the Cherokees are correct in their statement of facts, who can resist their conclusion? We might as well ask the Chinese, what right *they* have to the territory which they occupy. To such a question they would answer, "God gave this land to our ancestors. Our nation has *always* been in possession of it, so far as history and tradition go back. The nations of Europe are comparatively of recent origin; the commencement of ours is lost in remote antiquity."

What can be said to such a statement as this: Who can argue so plain a case?

It has been alleged, that the savage of the wilderness can acquire no title to the forests, through which he pursues his game. Without admitting this doctrine, it is sufficient to reply here, that it has no application to the case of the

---

[1] Sold.

Cherokees. They are at present neither savages nor hunters. It does not appear that they ever were mere wanderers, without a stationary residence. At the earliest period of our becoming acquainted with their condition, they had fixed habitations, and were in undisputed possession of a widely extended country. They were then in the habit of cultivating some land near their houses, where they planted Indian corn, and other vegetables. From about the commencement of the present century, they have addicted themselves more and more to agriculture, till they now derive their support from the soil, as truly and entirely as do the inhabitants of Pennsylvania or Virginia. For many years they have had their herds, and their large cultivated fields. They now have, in addition, their schools, a regular civil government, and places of regular Christian worship. They earn their bread by the labor of their own hands, applied to the tillage of their own farms; and they clothe themselves with fabrics made at their own looms, from cotton grown in their own fields.

9   *From Letter V*

The Cherokees then are a *nation*; and the best definition of a nation is, that it is *a community living under its own laws*.

A nation may be a power of the first, second, third, or tenth rate. It may be very feeble, and totally incompetent to defend its own rights. But so long as it has distinct rights and interests, and manages its own concerns, it is a substantive power; and should be respected as such. Any other rule of interpretation would make force the only arbiter. St. Marino, in Italy, is described in our best gazetteers as "a small but independent republic;" and yet it has not half so many people, nor the three hundredth part so much land, as the Cherokee nation now has.

It has been said, indeed, that the Indians, being an uncivilized people, are not to be ranked among nations. But this is said gratuitously, and without the least shadow of proof. How many treaties did Julius Caesar make with savage tribes, who were greatly inferior, in every intellectual and moral respect, to the Cherokees of the present day? There is as little reason as truth in the objection. Has not God endowed every community with some rights? and are not these rights to be regarded by every honest man and by every fair-minded and honorable ruler?

10   *From Letter XV*

The Georgians say to the Cherokees: "We are a civilized people; you are a vagrant, hunting and savage people. By virtue of this distinction, the lands which you occupy, and which your fathers called their hunting grounds, belong in reality to us; and we must take possession. The writers on the law of nations bear us out in the demand."

To such a statement the Cherokees might justly reply: "We are not about to dispute as to your being a civilized people, though the manner of urging this demand of the houses and lands of your poor neighbors, argues neither great modesty nor benevolence. We do not profess to be learned in the law of nations; but we read the Bible, and have learned there some plain principles of right and wrong. The Governor of the world gave us this country. We are in peaceable possession. We have never acknowledged any earthly lord, or sovereign. If our Creator has taken away our land and given it to you, we should like to see some proof of it, beside your own assertion. We have read in the book, which we understand you to acknowledge as the word of God, that *'to oppress a stranger wrongfully'* is a mark of a great national wickedness.

"But we are not the sort of people that you take us to be. We are not vagrants, like some tribes of which we have heard; nor were our fathers. They always had a fixed place of residence. And as to *our* wandering about, we have not the time. We are busy with our crops and many of us do not go so far as our nearest county court once a year, unless called out as jurymen. We do not hunt. Not a family within our bounds derives its subsistence from the chase. As to our being savages, we appeal to the white men, who travel on our turnpike roads, whether they receive any ill treatment. We have a legislature and a judiciary, and the judges of our supreme court are very rigid in punishing immorality. We have herds of cattle, farms and houses, mills and looms, clothing and furniture. We are not rich; but we contrive, by our industry, to provide against hunger and nakedness; and to lay up something comfortable for winter. Besides these things, we have schools and places of public worship. Judge ye, whether we are such a sort of people, as the writers on the laws of nations and in their minds, when they talked of vagrants, hunters, and savages."

To this the Georgians rejoin: "But you had no business to betake yourselves to an agricultural life. It is a downright imposition upon us. This is the very thing that we complain of. The more you work on land, the more unwilling you are to leave it. Just so it is with your schools; they only serve to attach you the more strongly to your country. It is all designed to keep us, the people of a sovereign and independent State, from the enjoyment of our just rights. We must refer you to the law of nations again, which declares that populous countries, whose inhabitants live by agriculture, have a right to take the lands of hunters and apply them to a better use."

11   *From Letter XXIV*

It is now proposed *to remove the landmarks*, in every sense;—to disregard territorial boundaries, definitely fixed, and for many years respected;—to disregard a most obvious principle of natural justice, in accordance with which the possessor of property is to hold it, till some one claims it, who has a better right;—to forget the doctrine of the law of nations, that engagements with dependent allies are as rigidly to be observed, as stipulations between communities of equal power and sovereignty;—to shut our ears to the voice of our own sages of the law, who say, that Indians have a right *to retain possession of their land and to use it according to their discretion*, antecedently to any positive compacts; and, finally, to dishonor Washington, the Father of his country,—to stultify the Senate of the United Sates during a period of thirty-seven years,—to burn 150 documents, as yet preserved in the archives of State, under the denomination of treaties with Indians, and to tear out sheets from every volume of our national statute-book and scatter them to the winds.[1]

Nothing of this kind has ever yet been done, certainly not on a large scale, by Anglo-Americans. To us, as a nation, it will be a new thing under the sun. We have never yet acted upon the principle of seizing the lands of peaceable Indians, and compelling them to remove. We have never yet declared treaties with them to be mere waste paper.

[1] To overturn the treaties with Indian nations that the Senate has ratified since the creation of the federal government.

Analyzing Newspaper Editorials about Indian Removal

1. According to Boudinot and Evarts, what makes the Cherokees civilized? What aspects of traditional Cherokee culture does Boudinot use to illustrate the progress the Cherokees have made toward civilization?

2. Compare and contrast the reasons Boudinot and Evarts give for why the federal government should side with the Cherokees rather than Georgia on the removal issue. What concerns does Evarts raise about the international reputation of the United States in this regard?

3. How do Boudinot and Evarts challenge the reasons and evidence given in support of Indian removal by state and federal officials (see especially Sources 5 and 10)? What stereotypes about Indians are Boudinot and Evarts trying to overturn, and in what ways are they questioning the "civilization" of their opponents?

4. Compare how Boudinot and Evarts write about nations and nationhood. Do they share a common definition of these terms, or are their views on what constitutes a nation fundamentally different? Why do you suppose Boudinot focuses so intently on Cherokee nationhood, whereas Evarts concentrates on American nationhood?

5. Both Boudinot's and Evarts's editorials were widely reprinted and circulated, yet they failed to stop either the federal government or the state of Georgia from proceeding with the dispossession of the Cherokees. Why do you think the advocates of Indian removal ultimately won on this issue? How has reading Boudinot's and Evarts's editorials influenced your answer to that question?

6. All eastern Indians faced pressure during the 1830s to remove westward, but the so-called civilized nations of the Southeast, such as the Cherokees, endured the most severe consequences of this policy. Why do you think that is? Do you think Boudinot and Evarts would have written so positively about the Cherokees' success with the civilization policy had they been able to foresee the outcome of their struggle against removal?

The Rest of the Story

Although they were widely circulated, neither Boudinot's nor Evarts's editorials were enough to reverse the push for Indian removal in either Georgia or the Congress. With the president's tacit approval, Georgia officials began surveying Cherokee land and dividing it for distribution to white settlers via lottery. The Cherokees countered by taking their case all the way to the Supreme Court. In *Cherokee Nation v. Georgia* (1831) and *Worcester v. Georgia* (1832), Chief Justice John Marshall wrote opinions sympathetic to the Cherokees, defining them and other Indians as "domestic dependent nations" with sovereign rights independent of the states within which they resided. Jackson, however, disagreed with the Court's verdicts, and the president refused to intercede on the Cherokees' behalf.

The Cherokees' inability to find recourse in the courts or federal government convinced Boudinot that the only way to preserve the political and territorial integrity of the Cherokee nation was to move west. Along with John Ridge and Major Ridge—who was John's father and Boudinot's uncle—Boudinot formed a faction that believed dispossession was now inevitable and, therefore, it was better to negotiate a removal treaty than face continued abuse in Georgia. The Treaty Party, as it became known, broke from the National Council and its principal leader John Ross. At New Echota, Georgia, in 1835, Boudinot and his compatriots negotiated a removal treaty with U.S. agents. Although never endorsed by the Cherokee National Council, the Treaty of New Echota was ratified by the Senate in 1836, providing the cover necessary for Georgia and the federal government to proceed with the full-scale removal of the Cherokees. Boudinot, the Ridges, and several hundred of their supporters moved west shortly thereafter. The vast majority of Cherokees stayed behind until armed forces evicted them in 1838. Approximately four thousand Cherokees, one fourth of the nation's population, died on their exodus to the Oklahoma Territory in what became known as the Trail of Tears.

Jeremiah Evarts did not live to see any of these events. He died in 1831 after a long illness. Elias Boudinot, John Ridge, and Major Ridge met a different fate. All three of them were murdered in the Oklahoma Territory on June 22, 1839, by assassins working on behalf of John Ross. According to Cherokee law, selling Cherokee land without National Council approval was a capital offense; many Cherokees saw the murder of the Ridges and Boudinot as fitting revenge for their complicity in the Treaty of New Echota.

In the story of the Cherokees' removal, Boudinot is a tragic figure, a leader of his people who in trying to defend their interests was ultimately condemned as a traitor by them. His troubled legacy does have other facets. Not long after the Cherokees established themselves in Oklahoma, they resumed publishing their newspaper. True to its namesake, the *Cherokee Phoenix* rose from the ashes. Today, it is published by the Cherokee nation in Oklahoma (now numbering about 240,000 persons), dropping "the same thought into a thousand minds" and continuing to serve as a voice for the Cherokee people to the outside world.

To Find Out More

Online Resources for the Cherokee Phoenix *and Other Newspapers*

Cherokee Phoenix. 1828–1834. Western Carolina University. http://www.wcu.edu/library/CherokeePhoenix.

Cherokee Phoenix. 2008–present. http://www.cherokeephoenix.org.

National Digital Newspaper Program (NDNP). National Endowment for the Humanities. http://neh.gov/projects/ndnp.html. Digitizes "historically significant" U.S. newspapers published between 1836 and 1922.

United States Newspaper Program (USNP). National Endowment for the Humanities. http://neh.gov/projects/usnp.html. A publicly funded project designed to "locate, catalog, and preserve on microfilm newspapers published in the United States from the eighteenth century to the present."

Writings of Elias Boudinot and Jeremiah Evarts

Boudinot, Elias. *Cherokee Editor: The Writings of Elias Boudinot.* Edited by Theda Perdue. Knoxville: University of Tennessee Press, 1983.

Evarts, Jeremiah. *Cherokee Removal: The "William Penn" Essays and Other Writings by Jeremiah Evarts.* Edited by Francis Paul Prucha. Knoxville: University of Tennessee Press, 1981.

Other Sources on the Cherokees and Indian Removal

McLoughlin, William G. *Cherokee Renascence in the New Republic.* Princeton, NJ: Princeton University Press, 1986.

Perdue, Theda, and Michael D. Green. *The Cherokee Nation and the Trail of Tears.* New York: Penguin, 2007.

Perdue, Theda, and Michael D. Green, eds. *The Cherokee Removal: A Brief History with Documents.* 2nd ed. Boston: Bedford/St. Martin's, 2004.

Young, Mary E. "The Exercise of Sovereignty in Cherokee Georgia." *Journal of the Early Republic* 10 (1990): 43–63.

CHAPTER 10

Challenging the "Peculiar Institution"

Slave Narratives from the Antebellum South

Solomon Northup thought twice before going to Washington, D.C., in 1841, but he needed the work. At home in Saratoga Springs, New York, he had a wife and three children to support. He made his living by driving carriages and playing the violin for tourists who came to bathe in Saratoga's hot springs. Although not poor, his family was not prospering in Saratoga, especially during the slow season. So Northup listened intently when two men who were visiting town offered him high-paying work as a musician for a traveling circus based in Washington. He agreed to go with them, but along the way, he stopped in New York City to secure his "free papers" from the Custom House. As a free African American who would be traveling in the slaveholding South, he needed these documents to serve as his passport and protection.

They did not work well enough. Not long after arriving in Washington, Northup suddenly fell ill and slipped into unconsciousness. "How long I remained in that condition—whether only that night, or many days and nights—I do not know," he later wrote, "but when consciousness returned, I found myself alone, in utter darkness, and in chains." Northup had been kidnapped and his money and free papers stolen. Whether his companions had poisoned him, he did not know for certain, but they were gone and he was now in the hands of a slave dealer named James Burch. Northup insisted he was a free man and demanded his release, but Burch told him he was a runaway slave from Georgia and beat him with a whip and paddle for denying it. "Even now the flesh crawls upon my bones, as I recall the scene," Northup wrote. "My sufferings I can compare to nothing else than the burning agonies of hell!"

Burch took Northup overland to Richmond, Virginia, and then by ship to New Orleans, where he was sold in that city's slave market to a planter who lived on the Red River in Louisiana. Over the next several years, Northup worked for a succession of masters and came to know the daily life of plantation slaves intimately. He labored alongside them in cotton and sugarcane fields, ate their food, wore their clothes, slept in their quarters, and endured their discipline. In the face of repeated beatings, he stopped asserting his free status before his masters and overseers, but with the aid of a sympathetic stranger, he did manage to send a letter home. An attorney hired by his wife worked with government officials in New York and Louisiana to track him down. In 1853, after finally proving his identity in a Louisiana court, Northup regained his freedom.

He returned to his family in New York, where newspapers circulated his remarkable story. A local attorney helped Northup publish a book, *Twelve Years a Slave*, which sold more than thirty thousand copies over the next three years. Reviewers praised its searing, firsthand description of slave life in the Deep South, and many compared it to Harriet Beecher Stowe's wildly popular novel *Uncle Tom's Cabin*, which had been published a year earlier. Frederick Douglass, the nation's most prominent African American and himself the author of a slave narrative, wrote of Northup's book that "its truth is stranger than fiction."

The circumstances by which Northup became a slave were extraordinary, but the life he lived as a slave in the American South was typical in many ways. In 1840, slavery was the bedrock of the South's economy and social order. The number of slaves counted, 700,000, in the first U.S. census in 1790 had increased to almost three million in the 1840 census. From its origins along the southeastern Atlantic coast, slavery had expanded west of the Appalachian Mountains, along the Gulf Coast, and across the Mississippi River. As Northup's own experience testifies, a thriving domestic slave trade moved slaves from eastern states such as Virginia to southwestern ones such as Louisiana. Quite unwillingly, Northup had been caught up in a tide of human migration that breathed new vitality into American slavery.

Several factors accounted for slavery's rise as the South's "peculiar institution." First, unlike most New World slave populations, North American slaves achieved a positive rate of natural reproduction by 1750. So even though Congress ended U.S. participation in the Atlantic slave trade in 1808, the number of slaves in the United States continued to grow during the first half of the nineteenth century. Second, the acquisition of new western territories allowed slavery to spread beyond its colonial-era strongholds. Congress banned slavery north of the Ohio River in 1787, but it did not interfere with the expansion of slavery south of that border in new states such as Kentucky, Tennessee, Alabama, and Mississippi. In 1803, the Louisiana Purchase opened the door to slavery west of the Mississippi River. Of course, white settlers of these new territories would not have taken slaves with them were it not profitable to do so. They found those profits by shifting their production away from tobacco and rice, the cash crops of the eastern seaboard, to cotton and sugarcane. The invention of the cotton gin increased the productivity of slave labor by reducing the hours necessary to process cotton for market. By the 1830s, cotton accounted for more than 50 percent of U.S. exports, and Great Britain, the world's leading

Figure 10.1 Male and Female Field Laborers in the Cotton South *The invention of the cotton gin in the 1790s revolutionized the processing of cotton for sale to textile mills and ignited the rapid expansion of slavery in the American South. Technological change, however, had little effect on planting and reaping cotton, which was still done by male and female slaves toiling for long hours in hot fields.* Source: Courtesy North Carolina Collection, Wilson Special Collections Library, UNC-Chapel Hill.

industrial nation, imported more than 70 percent of the cotton used in its textile mills from the United States.

The expansion of slavery in the South did not go unnoticed in the northern states. During the 1830s, an abolitionist movement emerged in the North that called for the immediate emancipation of American slaves. Inspired by the evangelical fervor of the Second Great Awakening, abolitionists defined slavery as a sin weighing on the soul of the nation, and they used the same fiery rhetoric as revivalist preachers to condemn it. They offered assistance and protection to runaway slaves and publicized their stories in antislavery newspapers, pamphlets, and magazines. Working together in this manner, runaway slaves and abolitionists also produced autobiographical slave narratives that provided some of the most important and controversial eyewitness testimonies about slavery in the antebellum South.

Using the Source: Slave Narratives

Autobiographical slave narratives were an early and significant part of American literature. The first wave of slave autobiographies was published during the second half of the eighteenth century, and they commonly told the story of Africans who had been enslaved in their native country, carried across the Atlantic in the slave trade, and by perseverance and fortunate circumstance gained their freedom. Many of these earliest African American autobiographies were published in London because in the 1780s and 1790s it was the center of a movement to ban the Atlantic slave trade. In their plots and themes, these books had much in common with colonial-era Indian captivity narratives (see Chapter 2). They featured heroes violently torn away from home and family and forced to endure captivity among strangers in distant lands. Their stories emphasized physical trials and dangers, but also spiritual rebirth and redemption when they gained their freedom. Several of these early slave narratives were written by sailors who had spent time in Africa, Europe, and the Americas and reflected an international perspective on slavery, condemning the Atlantic slave trade and defending the equality of Africans with the rest of humankind.

The next wave of slave narratives was published during the antebellum period, the thirty years before the American Civil War. Like the narratives of the first wave, they were a product of the antislavery movement, but now their heroes were much more likely to have been born in the United States rather than Africa and less likely to have traveled, willingly or unwillingly, across the Atlantic. Having not experienced the Atlantic slave trade, they focused their antislavery sentiments on the abuses and horrors of the plantation system. The authors of these narratives were also far more likely to have gained their freedom by running away rather than by self-purchase or their master's voluntary manumission, as had been the case with the first wave of slave autobiographers. Slave narratives from antebellum America, in other words, had a distinctive style that reflected the historical circumstances of the time in which they were written.

Slave narratives also appeared in many forms. Some were brief stories reported in abolitionist newspapers and magazines; others were privately printed tracts and pamphlets sold at rallies or from door to door to raise money for the abolitionist cause. Authors also wrote fictional slave narratives by creating composite characters out of tales they heard or read in other sources. Of these many types, the most intriguing to historians have been the sixty or so book-length slave autobiographies published during the antebellum era. Some of them were best sellers of their time, and even for present-day readers it is not hard to understand why. They featured direct first-person narration, graphic violence, heart-wrenching stories of family separation and loss, daring escapes, and exhilarating triumphs for their protagonists.

What Can Slave Narratives Tell Us?

The slave narrative was one of the most effective weapons in the propaganda war abolitionists launched against slavery. Abolitionists recognized the persuasive power that could be found in the stories of slaves who had run away to escape ill treatment, pursue freedom, or preserve or reunite a family torn apart on the slave auction block. Antebellum slave narratives were inseparable from the abolitionist movement. Today, they offer much insight into how the abolitionists made their case against slavery and how they packaged it for public consumption.

They also provide historians with a valuable source on American slavery from the slave's perspective. In the antebellum South, it was illegal to teach slaves to read or write, so slaves rarely left behind diaries, journals, letters, or similar written documents that historians can use to reconstruct plantation life from the perspective of the slaves themselves. Archaeological evidence, plantation account books, and census data can help us recover important information about the material and demographic circumstances of slaves' lives, such as what they ate, how they dressed, and how many children they had, but such evidence provides little to reconstruct the emotional and psychological dimensions of slavery found in day-to-day interactions between slaves and masters or among the members of a slave family. Aspects of slave life typically ignored by masters and overseers—such as spiritual beliefs and practices, community rituals and celebrations, or social relations within the slave community—were often described at length in slave narratives.

Consider, for example, this excerpt from Northup's narrative, in which he describes the end of a day spent picking cotton:

Building that housed raw cotton for processing

Note how Northup generalizes his experience as that of all slaves

The quota of picked cotton given to each slave

The end of the work day brings dread rather than comfort to the slave

The day's work over in the field, the baskets are "toted," or in other words, carried to the gin-house, where the cotton is weighed. No matter how fatigued and weary he may be—no matter how much he longs for sleep and rest—a slave never approaches the gin-house with his basket of cotton but with fear. If it falls short in weight—if he has not performed the full task appointed him, he knows that he must suffer. And if he has exceeded it by ten or twenty pounds, in all probability his master will measure the next day's task accordingly. So, whether he has too little or too much, his approach to the gin-house is always with fear and trembling. Most frequently they have too little, and therefore they are not anxious to leave the field.

Source: Solomon Northup, *Twelve Years a Slave: Narrative of Solomon Northup, a Citizen of New-York, Kidnapped in Washington City in 1841, and Rescued in 1853, from a Cotton Plantation Near the Red River, in Louisiana* (Auburn, NY: Derby and Miller, 1853), 126.

An overseer or master might have recorded in a daily account book how much cotton slaves picked, and a historian could use that information in conjunction with other data to figure out how much an average slave picked on an average day. Such quantitative information, however, cannot convey the psychological drama depicted in this brief passage as the slave approaches the scales in the gin-house. The slave's fear of having picked too much or too little cotton elicits the reader's sympathy for the "damned if you do, damned if you don't" nature of plantation work.

When working with a slave narrative, it is important to remember that the story it tells does not necessarily reflect the experience of the typical slave. Most slaves in the antebellum South worked as field hands on the plantations of the Cotton Belt, a broad region that stretched along the southern tier of the United States from the Carolinas and Georgia through Alabama and Mississippi into Louisiana, Arkansas, and Texas. These slaves were less likely to escape to the North because of their distance from free states and the surveillance involved in plantation life. Most antebellum slave narratives, on the other hand, were written by slaves from the border states of Maryland, Kentucky, and Missouri who worked as tradesmen, domestic servants, or maritime laborers—jobs that gave them the freedom of movement and familiarity with white society necessary for a successful run to freedom. Also, although the slave population of the antebellum South was evenly divided between men and women, the authors of antebellum slave narratives were overwhelmingly men, making it harder to recover the experience of slave women from this source.

Other disadvantages associated with slave narratives derive from the motives behind their production. Authors and editors hoping to profit from the sale of such narratives focused on sensationalistic tales of abuse and escape rather than the workaday lives of slaves. One such author was Henry "Box" Brown, who escaped from Virginia by shipping himself to Philadelphia in a box he designed for that purpose. Brown's unique method of escape made him a celebrity, and he toured the lecture circuit in the northern states and Great Britain displaying his eponymous box.

Practically all antebellum slave narratives were written with the aid of an amanuensis, usually an abolitionist who arranged the story into chapters and provided additional information in annotations and appendices that corroborated the slave's story. Not all runaway slaves wishing to publish their story needed an amanuensis. Some had managed to become literate despite their enslavement and proudly proclaimed in a preface that they had written their narrative themselves. In other instances, abolitionists who had served as amanuenses assured readers that they had done nothing to alter the story's content and truthfulness. Despite such assurances, one does not have to read many slave narratives to realize that they conform to a standard style. Common features include a summary of the slave's birth and parents, a description of a slave market or sale that breaks apart a slave family, an assessment of slavery's negative effect on whites as well as blacks, a dramatic confrontation between the narrator and an overseer or master, and an indictment of the religious hypocrisy of slave owners. Antebellum slave narratives also mirrored the sentimental language used in the popular novels of their day, appealing to the emotional sensibilities of their readers and inviting them to sympathize with their imperiled heroes and heroines. *Uncle Tom's Cabin*, the masterpiece of abolitionist fiction, borrowed heavily from slave narratives for its characters and plot and in turn left an indelible influence on the literary styling of slave narratives that appeared in its wake.

Critics of slave narratives note that their value as a source is compromised by the difficulty of separating the slave whose story is told in the narrative from the abolitionists who helped get it written and published, leading historians to devote considerable research to tracking down evidence that helps separate the fictional from nonfictional elements in such stories. This work has sometimes yielded remarkable conclusions, proving, as Frederick Douglass said of Solomon Northup's narrative, that truth can be stranger than fiction. The Checklist questions below will help you weigh the value of any slave narrative you read as a testimonial on slave life and as a piece of abolitionist propaganda.

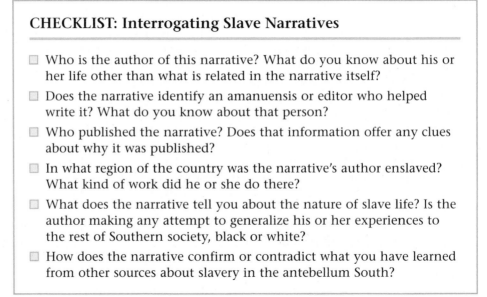

CHECKLIST: Interrogating Slave Narratives

- ☐ Who is the author of this narrative? What do you know about his or her life other than what is related in the narrative itself?
- ☐ Does the narrative identify an amanuensis or editor who helped write it? What do you know about that person?
- ☐ Who published the narrative? Does that information offer any clues about why it was published?
- ☐ In what region of the country was the narrative's author enslaved? What kind of work did he or she do there?
- ☐ What does the narrative tell you about the nature of slave life? Is the author making any attempt to generalize his or her experiences to the rest of Southern society, black or white?
- ☐ How does the narrative confirm or contradict what you have learned from other sources about slavery in the antebellum South?

Source Analysis Table

As you read the source selections, use the following table to take notes about the information they convey about slavery in the antebellum South. Not every category on the table will be relevant to each source.

Source	Identity of Amanuensis or Editor	Description of Slave Work, Family, and Culture	Description of Masters and White Society	Evidence of Slave Resistance	Your Reaction to the Selection
1. Henry Bibb (1849)					
2. Solomon Northup (1853)					
3. Harriet Jacobs (1861)					

The Source: Antebellum Slave Narratives

1   Henry Bibb, *Narrative of the Life and Adventures of Henry Bibb, An American Slave, Written by Himself,* 1849

Henry Bibb was born a slave in Kentucky and married another slave who lived on a nearby plantation. After multiple escape attempts, he and his family were sold to a new master in Louisiana, who subsequently sold Bibb away from his wife and child. Bibb ran away for the last time in 1842 and settled in Detroit, where he became an abolitionist speaker. He published his narrative in 1849 with the assistance of Lucius C. Matlack, a minister and abolitionist author. Matlack stated in the book's introduction that his only alterations to Bibb's original manuscript were corrections in punctuation and spelling and the arrangement of the story into chapters.

I was born May 1815, of a slave mother, in Shelby County, Kentucky, and was claimed as the property of David White Esq. He came into possession of my mother long before I was born. I was brought up in the Counties of Shelby, Henry, Oldham, and Trimble. Or, more correctly speaking, in the above counties, I may safely say, I was *flogged up*; for where I should have received moral, mental, and religious instruction, I received stripes without number, the object of which was to degrade and keep me in subordination. I can truly say, that I drank deeply of the bitter cup of suffering and woe. I have been dragged down to the lowest depths of human degradation and wretchedness by Slaveholders.

My mother was known by the name of Milldred Jackson. She is the mother of seven slaves only, all being sons, of whom I am the eldest. She was also so fortunate or unfortunate, as to have some of what is called the slaveholding blood flowing through her veins. I know not how much; but not enough to prevent her children though fathered by slaveholders, from being bought and sold in the slave markets of the South. It is almost impossible for slaves to give a correct account of their male parentage. All that I know about it is, that my mother informed me that my father's name was JAMES BIBB. He was doubtless one of the present Bibb family of Kentucky[1]; but I have no personal knowledge of him at all, for he died before my recollection. . . .

The poor and loafering class of whites, are about on a par in point of morals with the slaves at the South. They are generally ignorant, intemperate,

---

[1] Bibb is implying here that his father was James Bibb, a prominent Kentucky politician who served in the U.S. Senate.

Source: Henry Bibb, *Narrative of the Life and Adventures of Henry Bibb, An American Slave, Written by Himself* (New York: Published by the Author, 1849), 13–14, 24–27, 42–44, 176–78.

The Source: Antebellum Slave Narratives

licentious, and profane. They associate much with the slaves; are often found gambling together on the Sabbath; encouraging slaves to steal from their owners, and sell to them, corn, wheat, sheep, chickens, or any thing of the kind which they can well conceal. For such offences there is no law to reach a slave but lynch law. But if both parties are caught in the act by a white person, the slave is punished with the lash, while the white man is often punished with both lynch and common law. But there is another class of poor white people in the South, who, I think would be glad to see slavery abolished in self defence; they despise the institution because it is impoverishing and degrading to them and their children.

The slave holders are generally rich, aristocratic, overbearing; and they look with utter contempt upon a poor laboring man, who earns his bread by the "sweat of his brow," whether he be moral or immoral, honest or dishonest. No matter whether he is white or black; if he performs manual labor for a livelihood, he is looked upon as being inferior to a slaveholder, and but little better off than the slave, who toils without wages under the lash. It is true, that the slaveholder, and non-slaveholder, are living under the same laws in the same State. But the one is rich, the other is poor; one is educated, the other is uneducated; one has houses, land and influence, the other has none. This being the case, that class of the non-slaveholders would be glad to see slavery abolished, but they dare not speak it aloud.

There is much superstition among slaves. Many of them believe in what they call "conjuration," tricking, and witchcraft; and some of them pretend to understand the art, and say that by it they can prevent their masters from exercising their will over slaves. Such are often applied to by others, to give them power to prevent their masters from flogging them. The remedy is most generally some kind of bitter root; they are directed to chew it and spit towards their masters when they are angry with their slaves. At other times they prepare certain kinds of powders, to sprinkle about their masters' dwellings. This is all done for the purpose of defending themselves in some peaceable manner, although I am satisfied there is no virtue at all in it. I have tried it to perfection when I was a slave at the South. I was then a young man, full of life and vigor, and was very fond of visiting our neighbors' slaves, but had no time to visit only Sundays, when I could get a permit to go, or after night, when I could slip off without being seen. If it was found out, the next morning I was called up to give an account of myself for going off without permission; and would very often get a flogging for it.

I got myself into a scrape at a certain time, by going off in this way, and I expected to be severely punished for it. I had a strong notion of running off, to escape being flogged, but was advised to go to one of those conjurers, who could prevent me from being flogged. I went and informed him of the difficulty. He said if I would pay him a small sum, he would prevent my being flogged. After I had paid him, he mixed up some alum, salt, and other stuff into a powder, and said I must sprinkle it about my master, if he should offer to strike me; this would prevent him. He also gave me some kind of bitter root to chew, and spit towards him, which would certainly prevent my being flogged. According to order I used this remedy, and for some cause I was let pass without being flogged that time.

I had then great faith in conjuration and witchcraft. I was led to believe that I could do almost as I pleased, without being flogged. So on the next Sabbath my conjuration was fully tested by my going off, and staying away until Monday morning, without permission. When I returned home, my master declared that he would punish me for going off; but I did not believe that he could do it while I had this root and dust; and as he approached me, I commenced talking saucy to him. But he soon convinced me that there was no virtue in them. He became so enraged at me for saucing him, that he grasped a handful of switches and punished me severely, in spite all of my roots and powders. . . .

[Bibb's first wife was Malinda, a slave on the nearby plantation of William Gatewood. According to Bibb, his master sold him to Gatewood because he realized Bibb would absent himself to be with Malinda anyway.—Eds.]

Not many months after I took up my residence on Wm. Gatewood's plantation, Malinda made me a father. The dear little daughter was called Mary Frances. She was nurtured and caressed by her mother and father, until she was large enough to creep over the floor after her parents, and climb up by a chair before I felt it my duty to leave my family and go into a foreign country for a season. Malinda's business was to labor out in the field the greater part of her time, and there was no one to take care of poor little Frances, while her mother was toiling in the field. She was left at the house to creep under the feet of an unmerciful old mistress, whom I have known to slap with her hand the face of little Frances, for crying after her mother, until her little face was left black and blue. I recollect that Malinda and myself came from the field one summer's day at noon, and poor little Frances came creeping to her mother smiling, but with large tear drops standing in her dear little eyes, sobbing and trying to tell her mother that she had been abused, but was not able to utter a word. Her little face was bruised black with the whole print of Mrs. Gatewood's hand. This print was plainly to be seen for eight days after it was done. But oh! this darling child was a slave; born of a slave mother. Who can imagine what could be the feelings of a father and mother, when looking upon their infant child whipped and tortured with impunity, and they placed in a situation where they could afford it no protection. But we were all claimed and held as property; the father and mother were slaves!

On this same plantation I was compelled to stand and see my wife shamelessly scourged and abused by her master; and the manner in which this was done, was so violently and inhumanly committed upon the person of a female, that I despair in finding decent language to describe the bloody act of cruelty. My happiness or pleasure was then all blasted; for it was sometimes a pleasure to be with my little family even in slavery. I loved them as my wife and child. Little Frances was a pretty child; she was quiet, playful, bright, and interesting. She had a keen black eye, and the very image of her mother was stamped upon her cheek; but I could never look upon the dear child without being filled with sorrow and fearful apprehensions, of being separated by slaveholders, because she was a slave, regarded as property. And unfortunately for me, I am the father of a slave, a word too obnoxious to be spoken by a fugitive slave. It calls fresh to my mind the separation of husband and wife; of stripping, tying up and flogging; of tearing children from their parents, and selling them on the auction block. It calls to mind female virtue trampled under foot with impunity. But oh! when I remember that my daughter, my only child, is still there, destined to share the fate of all these calamities, it is too much to bear. If ever there was any one act of my life while a slave, that I have to lament over, it is that of being a father and a husband of slaves. I have the satisfaction of knowing that I am only the father of one slave. She is bone of my bone, and flesh of my flesh; poor unfortunate child. She was the first and shall be the last slave that ever I will father, for chains and slavery on this earth. . . .

> [After running away for the last time, Bibb tried to locate and reunite with Malinda and Mary Frances. His efforts brought him back in touch with his former master William Gatewood. Although he was a runaway, Bibb did not fear contact with Gatewood at this point because Gatewood's claim to him had ceased when he had sold Bibb to a new master in 1839. In his narrative, Bibb included this letter from his correspondence with Gatewood. —Eds.]

DEAR SIR:—I am happy to inform you that you are not mistaken in the man whom you sold as property,[2] and received pay for as such. But I thank God that I am not property now, but am regarded as a man like yourself, and although I live far north, I am enjoying a comfortable living by my own industry. If you should ever chance to be traveling this way, and will call on me, I will use you better than you did me while you held me as a slave. Think not that I have any malice against you, for the cruel treatment which you inflicted on me while I was in your power. As it was the custom of your country, to treat fellow man as you did me and my little family, I can freely forgive you.

I wish to be remembered in love to my aged mother, and friends; please tell her that if we should never meet again in this life, my prayer shall be to God that we may meet in Heaven, where parting shall be no more.

You wish to be remembered to King and Jack.[3] I am pleased, sir, to inform you that they are both here, well, and doing well. They are both living in Canada West. They are now the owners of better farms than the men are who once owned them.

You may perhaps think hard of us for running away from slavery, but as to myself, I have but one apology to make for it, which is this: I have only one regret that I did not start at an earlier period. I might have been free long before I was. But you had it in your power to have kept me there much longer than you did. I think it is very probable that I should have been a toiling slave on your plantation to-day, if you had treated me differently. . . .

Henry Bibb

---

[2] Gatewood had written previously to Bibb, asking him to confirm that he was indeed the same Henry Bibb that Gatewood had owned as a slave.

[3] Two runaway slaves Bibb knew from his days on Gatewood's plantation.

| 2 | **Solomon Northup, *Twelve Years a Slave,* 1853** |

For Northup's background, see the introduction to this chapter (pages 204–06). Northup was assisted in publishing his narrative by David Wilson, a Hudson Valley attorney. Wilson was not an abolitionist, and he seems to have been drawn to Northup chiefly out of interest in his story and a desire to profit from it. In his preface, Wilson stated that his only purpose as editor was "to give a faithful history of Solomon Northup's life, as [I] received it from his lips."

Having been born a freeman, and for more than thirty years enjoyed the blessings of liberty in a free State—and having at the end of that time been kidnapped and sold into Slavery, where I remained, until happily rescued in the month of January, 1853, after a bondage of twelve years—it has been suggested that an account of my life and fortunes would not be uninteresting to the public.

Since my return to liberty, I have not failed to perceive the increasing interest throughout the Northern States, in regard to the subject of Slavery. Works of fiction, professing to portray its features in their more pleasing as well as more repugnant aspects, have been circulated to an extent unprecedented, and, as I understand, have created a fruitful topic of comment and discussion.

I can speak of Slavery only so far as it came under my own observation—only so far as I have known and experienced it in my own person. My object is, to give a candid and truthful statement of facts: to repeat the story of my life, without exaggeration, leaving it for others to determine, whether even the pages of fiction present a picture of more cruel wrong or a severer bondage. . . .

[In the passage below, Northup describes a confrontation he had with John M. Tibeats, who had purchased Northup from his first master, William Ford.—Eds.]

As the day began to open, Tibeats came out of the house to where I was, hard at work. He seemed to be that morning even more morose and disagreeable than usual. He was my master, entitled by law to my flesh and blood, and to exercise over me such tyrannical control as his mean nature prompted; but there was no law that could prevent my looking upon him with intense contempt. I despised both his disposition and his intellect. I had just come round to the keg for a further supply of nails, as he reached the weaving-house.

"I thought I told you to commence putting on weatherboards this morning," he remarked.

"Yes, master, and I am about it," I replied.

"Where?" he demanded.

"On the other side," was my answer.

Source: Solomon Northup, *Twelve Years a Slave: Narrative of Solomon Northup, A Citizen of New-York, Kidnapped in Washington City in 1841, and Rescued in 1853, from a Cotton Plantation Near the Red River, in Louisiana* (Auburn, NY: Derby and Miller, 1853), 17–18, 109–14, 165–71.

He walked round to the other side, examined my work for a while, muttering to himself in a fault-finding tone.

. . . I knew he intended to whip me, and it was the first time any one had attempted it since my arrival at Avoyelles.[1] I felt, moreover, that I had been faithful—that I was guilty of no wrong whatever, and deserved commendation rather than punishment. My fear changed to anger, and before he reached me I had made up my mind fully not to be whipped, let the result be life or death.

Winding the lash around his hand, and taking hold the small end of the stock, he walked up to me, and with a malignant look, ordered me to strip.

"Master Tibeats," said I, looking him boldly in the face, "I will *not*." I was about to say something further in justification, but with concentrated vengeance, he sprang upon me, seizing me by the throat with one hand, raising the whip with the other, in the act of striking. Before the blow descended, however, I had him by the collar of the coat and drawn him closely to me. Reaching down, I seized him by the ankle, and pushing him back with the other hand, he fell over on the ground. . . . I cannot tell how many times I struck him. Blow after blow fell fast and heavy upon his wriggling form. At length he screamed—cried murder—and at last the blasphemous tyrant called on God for mercy. But he who had never shown mercy did not receive it. The stiff stock of the whip warped his cringing body until my right arm ached. . . .

As I stood there, feelings of unutterable agony overwhelmed me. I was conscious that I had subjected myself to unimaginable punishment. The reaction that followed my ebullition of anger produced the most painful sensation of regret. An unfriended, helpless slave—what could I *do*, what could I *say*, to justify in the remotest manner, the heinous act I had committed, of resenting a *white* man's contumely and abuse. I tried to pray—I tried to beseech my Heavenly Father to sustain me in my sore extremity, but emotion choked my utterance, and I could only bow my head upon my hands and weep. For at least an hour I remained in this situation, finding relief only in tears, when, looking up, I beheld Tibeats, accompanied by two horsemen, coming down the bayou. They rode into the yard, jumped from their horses, and approached me with large whips, one of them also carrying a coil of rope. . . .

"Now, then," inquired one of Tibeats companions, "where shall we hang the nigger?" . . .

[Northup was saved from hanging when an overseer reminded Tibeats that he still owed money to Ford for Northup's purchase. Northup was eventually sold to another master, Edwin Epps, who put him to work on his cotton plantation.—Eds.]

In the latter part of August begins the cotton picking season. At this time each slave is presented with a sack. A strap is fastened to it, which goes over the neck, holding the mouth of the sack breast high, while the bottom reaches

---

[1] Avoyelles Parish, on the Red River in Louisiana.

nearly to the ground. Each one is also presented with a large basket that will hold about two barrels. This is to put the cotton in when the sack is filled. The baskets are carried to the field and placed at the beginning of the rows.

When a new hand, one unaccustomed to the business, is sent for the first time into the field, he is whipped up smartly, and made for that day to pick as fast as he can possibly. At night it is weighed, so that his capability in cotton picking is known. He must bring in the same weight each night following. If it falls short, it is considered evidence that he has been laggard, and a greater or less number of lashes is the penalty.

An ordinary day's work is considered two hundred pounds. A slave who is accustomed to picking, is punished, if he or she brings in a less quantity than that. There is a great difference among them as regards this kind of labor. Some of them seem to have a natural knack, or quickness, which enables them to pick with great celerity, and with both hands, while others, with whatever practice or industry, are utterly unable to come up to the ordinary standard. Such hands are taken from the cotton field and employed in other business. Patsey,[2] of whom I shall have more to say, was known as the most remarkable cotton picker on Bayou Boeuf.[3] She picked with both hands and with such surprising rapidity, that five hundred pounds a day was not unusual for her. Each one is tasked, therefore, according to his picking abilities, none, however, to come short of two hundred weight. I, being unskillful always in that business, would have satisfied my master by bringing in the latter quantity, while on the other hand, Patsey would surely have been beaten if she failed to produce twice as much. . . .

The hands are required to be in the cotton fields as soon as it is light in the morning, and, with the exception of ten or fifteen minutes, which is given them at noon to swallow their allowance of cold bacon, they are not permitted to be a moment idle until it is too dark to see, and when the moon is full, they often times labor till the middle of the night. They do not dare to stop even at dinner time, nor return to the quarters, however late it be, until the order to halt is given by the driver.

The day's work over in the field, the baskets are "toted," or in other words, carried to the gin-house, where the cotton is weighed. No matter how fatigued and weary he may be—no matter how much he longs for sleep and rest—a slave never approaches the gin-house with his basket of cotton but with fear. If it falls short in weight—if he has not performed the full task appointed him, he knows that he must suffer. And if he has exceeded it by ten or twenty pounds, in all probability his master will measure the next day's task accordingly. So, whether he has too little or too much, his approach to the gin-house is always with fear and trembling. Most frequently they have too little, and therefore they are not anxious to leave the field. After weighing, follow the whippings; and then the baskets are carried to the cotton house, and their contents stored away like hay, all hands being sent to tramp it down. . . .

[2] Another of Epps's slaves.
[3] The location of Epps's plantation in Avoyelles Parish.

This done, the labor of the day is not yet ended, by any means. Each one must then attend to his respective chores. One feeds the mules, another the swine—another cuts the wood, and so forth; besides, the packing is all done by candle light. Finally, at a late hour, they reach the quarters, sleepy and overcome with the long day's toil. Then a fire must be kindled in the cabin, the corn ground in the small hand-mill, and supper, and dinner for the next day in the field, prepared. All that is allowed them is corn and bacon, which is given out at the corncrib and smoke-house every Sunday morning. Each one receives, as his weekly allowance, three and a half pounds of bacon, and corn enough to make a peck of meal. This is all—no tea, coffee, sugar, and with the exception of a very scanty sprinkling now and then, no salt. I can say, from a ten years' residence with Master Epps, that no slave of his is ever likely to suffer from gout,[4] superinduced by excessive high living. . . .

An hour before day light the horn is blown. Then the slaves arouse, prepare their breakfast, fill a gourd with water, in another deposit their dinner of cold bacon and corn cake, and hurry to the field again. It is an offence invariably followed by a flogging, to be found at the quarters after daybreak. Then the fears and labors of another day begin; and until its close there is no such thing as rest. He fears he will be caught lagging through the day; he fears to approach the gin-house with his basket-load of cotton at night; he fears, when he lies down, that he will oversleep himself in the morning. Such is a true, faithful, unexaggerated picture and description of the slave's daily life, during the time of cotton-picking, on the shores of Bayou Boeuf.

[4] A disease that causes painful inflammation in the joints, often referred to in Northup's time as the "rich man's disease" because it was associated with excessive eating and drinking.

3   Harriet Jacobs, *Incidents in the Life of a Slave Girl. Written by Herself,* 1861

Harriet Jacobs was a slave from North Carolina who escaped to Philadelphia in 1842. She spent most of the next seventeen years working as a household servant in New York City. Her narrative, published in 1861, was not the first female slave narrative, but it is remarkable for its depiction of the psychological and sexual torments of slavery from a woman's perspective. Jacobs had editorial assistance from writer and abolitionist Lydia Maria Child (you read an excerpt from one of her child-rearing books in Chapter 8). Child described her contributions to the book as changes made only "for the purposes of condensation and orderly arrangement."

I was born a slave; but I never knew it till six years of happy childhood had passed away. My father was a carpenter, and considered so intelligent and skillful in his trade, that, when buildings out of the common line were to be erected, he was sent for from long distances, to be head workman. On condition of paying his mistress two hundred dollars a year, and supporting himself, he was allowed to work at his trade, and manage his own affairs. His strongest wish was to purchase his children; but, though he several times offered his hard earnings for that purpose, he never succeeded. In complexion my parents were a light shade of brownish yellow, and were termed mulattoes. They lived together in a comfortable home; and, though we were all slaves, I was so fondly shielded that I never dreamed I was a piece of merchandise, trusted to them for safe keeping, and liable to be demanded of them at any moment. . . .

> [Jacobs devotes much her narrative to her struggle to defend herself from the sexual advances of her master, Dr. Flint. In the passage below, she describes the vulnerability of a female slave to such abuse.—Eds.]

During the first years of my service in Dr. Flint's family, I was accustomed to share some indulgences with the children of my mistress. Though this seemed to me no more than right, I was grateful for it, and tried to merit the kindness by the faithful discharge of my duties. But now I entered on my fifteenth year—a sad epoch in the life of a slave girl. My master began to whisper foul words in my ear. Young as I was, I could not remain ignorant of their import. I tried to treat them with indifference or contempt. The master's age, my extreme youth, and the fear that his conduct would be reported to my grandmother,[1] made him bear this treatment for many months. He was a crafty man, and resorted to many means to accomplish his purposes. Sometimes he had stormy, terrific ways, that made his victims tremble; sometimes he assumed a gentleness that he thought must surely subdue. Of the two, I preferred his stormy moods, although they left me trembling. He tried his utmost to corrupt the pure principles my grandmother had instilled. He peopled my young mind with unclean images, such as only a vile monster could think of. I turned from him with disgust and hatred. But he was my master. I was compelled to live under the same roof with him—where I saw a man forty years my senior daily violating the most sacred of commandments of nature. He told me I was his property; that I must be subject to his will in all things. My soul revolted against the mean tyranny. But where could I turn for protection? No matter whether the slave girl be as black as ebony or as fair as her mistress. In either case, there is no shadow of law to protect her from insult, from violence, or even from death; all these are inflicted by fiends who bear the shape of men. The mistress, who ought to protect the helpless victim, has no other feelings towards her but those of jealousy and rage. The degradation, the wrongs, the vices, that grow out of slavery, are more than I can describe. They are greater than you would willingly believe. Surely, if you credited one half the truths that are told you concerning the helpless millions suffering in this cruel bondage,

[1] Jacobs's grandmother was a free black woman who lived nearby and served as a mother figure for her.

Source: Harriet Jacobs, *Incidents in the Life of a Slave Girl. Written by Herself,* ed. L. Maria Child (Boston: Published for the Author, 1861), 11–12, 44–47, 90–93, 302–3.

you at the north would not help to tighten the yoke. You surely would refuse to do for the master, on your own soil, the mean and cruel work which trained bloodhounds and the lowest class of whites do for him at the south.

Every where the years bring to all enough of sin and sorrow; but in slavery the very dawn of life is darkened by these shadows. Even the little child, who is accustomed to wait on her mistress and her children, will learn, before she is twelve years old, why it is that her mistress hates such and such a one among the slaves. Perhaps the child's own mother is among those hated ones. She listens to violent outbreaks of jealous passion, and cannot help understanding what is the cause. She will become prematurely knowing in evil things. Soon she will learn to tremble when she hears her master's footfall. She will be compelled to realize that she is no longer a child. If God has bestowed beauty upon her, it will prove her greatest curse. That which commands admiration in the white woman only hastens the degradation of the female slave. I know that some are too much brutalized by slavery to feel the humiliation of their position; but many slaves feel it most acutely, and shrink from the memory of it. I cannot tell how much I suffered in the presence of these wrongs, nor how I am still pained by the retrospect. My master met me at every turn, reminding me that I belonged to him, and swearing by heaven and earth that he would compel me to submit to him. If I went out for a breath of fresh air, after a day of unwearied toil, his footsteps dogged me. If I knelt by my mother's grave, his dark shadow fell on me even there. The light heart which nature had given me became heavy with sad forebodings. The other slaves in my master's house noticed the change. Many of them pitied me; but none dared to ask the cause. They had no need to inquire. They knew too well the guilty practices under the roof; and they were aware that to speak of them was an offense that never went unpunished. . . . .

O, what days and nights of fear and sorrow that man caused me! Reader, it is not to awaken sympathy for myself that I am telling you truthfully what I suffered in slavery. I do it to kindle a flame of compassion in your hearts for my sisters who are still in bondage, suffering as I once suffered. . . . .

> [Jacobs refused Flint's advances. Instead, she began a consensual sexual relationship with a local free white man and became pregnant. In the passage below, she describes a confrontation with Flint several days after she told him of her pregnancy. — Eds.]

I had not seen Dr. Flint for five days. I had never seen him since I made the avowal to him. He talked of the disgrace I had brought on myself; how I had sinned against my master, and mortified my old grandmother. He intimated that if I had accepted his proposals, he, as a physician, could have saved me from exposure. He even condescended to pity me. Could he have offered wormwood[2] more bitter? He, whose persecutions had been the cause of my sin!

---

[2] Wormwood was an herb used in the nineteenth century to end an unwanted pregnancy. Flint has implied that if he had impregnated Jacobs, he could have used his knowledge as a doctor to perform an abortion.

"Linda,"[3] said he, "though you have been criminal torwards me, I feel for you, and I can pardon you if you obey my wishes. Tell me whether the fellow you wanted to marry is the father of your child. If you deceive me, you shall feel the fires of hell."

I did not feel as proud as I had done. My strongest weapon with him was gone. I was lowered in my own estimation, and had resolved to bear his abuse in silence. But when he spoke contemptuously of the lover who had always treated me honorably; when I remembered that but for *him* I might have been a virtuous, free, and happy wife, I lost my patience. "I have sinned against God and myself," I replied; "but not against you."

He clinched his teeth, and muttered, "Curse you!" He came towards me, with ill-suppressed rage, and exclaimed, "You obstinate girl! I could grind your bones to powder! You have thrown yourself away on some worthless rascal. You are weak-minded, and have been easily persuaded by those who don't care a straw for you. The future will settle accounts between us. You are blinded now; but hereafter you will be convinced that your master was your best friend. My lenity towards you is a proof of it. I might have punished you in many ways. I might have had you whipped till you fell dead under the lash. But I wanted you to live; I would have bettered your condition. Others cannot do it. You are my slave. Your mistress, disgusted by your conduct, forbids you to return to the house; therefore I leave you here for the present; but I shall see you often. I will call tomorrow."

He came with frowning brows, that showed a dissatisfied state of mind. After asking about my health, he inquired whether my board was paid, and who visited me. He then went on to say that he had neglected his duty; that as a physician there were certain things that he ought to have explained to me. Then followed talk such as would have made the most shameless blush. He ordered me to stand before him. I obeyed. "I command you," said he, "to tell me whether the father of your child is white or black." I hesitated. "Answer me this instant!" he exclaimed. I did answer. He sprang upon me like a wolf, and grabbed my arm as if he would have broken it. "Do you love him?" said he, in a hissing tone.

"I am thankful that I do not despise him," I replied.

He raised his hand to strike me; but it fell again. I don't know what arrested the blow. He sat down, with lips tightly compressed. At last he spoke. "I came here," said he, "to make you a friendly proposition; but your ingratitude chafes me beyond endurance. You turn aside all my good intentions towards you. I don't know what it is that keeps me from killing you." Again he rose, as if he had a mind to strike me.

But he resumed. "On one condition I will forgive your insolence and crime. You must henceforth have no communication of any kind with the father of your child. You must not ask any thing from him, or receive any thing from him. I will take care of you and your child. You had better promise this at once,

---

[3] Because she feared being discovered and returned to her master, Jacobs used the pseudonym Linda Brent when she published her narrative. "Dr. Flint" was likewise an alias for her master's real name.

and not wait till you are deserted by him. This is the last act of mercy I shall show torwards you."

I said something about being unwilling to have my child supported by a man who had cursed it and me also. He rejoined, that a woman who had sunk to my level had not right to expect any thing else. He asked, for the last time, would I accept his kindness: I answered that I would not.

"Very well," said he; "then take the consequences of your wayward course. Never look to me for help. You are my slave, and shall always be my slave. I will never sell you, that you may depend upon."

Hope died in my heart as he closed the door after him. I had calculated that in his rage he would sell me to a slave-trader; and I knew that father of my child was on the watch to buy me. . . .

Reader, my story ends with freedom; not in the usual way, with marriage. I and my children are now free! We are as free from the power of slaveholders as are the white people of the north; and though that, according to my ideas, is not saying a great deal, it is a vast improvement in *my* condition. The dream of my life is not yet realized. I do not sit with my children in a home of my own. I still long for a hearthstone of my own, however humble. I wish it for my children's sake far more than for my own. But God so orders circumstances as to keep me with my friend Mrs. Bruce.[4] Love, duty, gratitude, also bind me to her side. It is a privilege to serve her who pities my oppressed people, and who has bestowed the inestimable boon of freedom on me and my children.

It has been painful to me, in many ways, to recall the dreary years I passed in bondage. I would gladly forget them if I could. Yet the retrospection is not altogether without solace; for with those gloomy recollections come tender memories of my good old grandmother, like light, fleecy clouds floating over a dark and troubled sea.

[4] The woman for whom Jacobs worked as a servant in New York.

Analyzing Slave Narratives

1. What insights does each of these sources offer into slave life in the antebellum South? Using your notes from the Source Analysis Table on page 211, summarize what they tell you about the nature of slave work, family, and culture.

2. Each source contains a passage describing a confrontation between slave and master. How do Bibbs's and Northup's accounts of their confrontations with their masters differ from Jacobs's confrontation with hers? What do these passages tell you about the different approaches slave men and slave women took to resisting their masters?

3. Slave narratives were written by African Americans, but were read overwhelmingly by white audiences. Where in these passages do you see evidence that Bibb, Northup, and Jacobs had their white audiences in mind as they crafted

their stories? What core ideas or impressions of slavery were they trying to convey to their readers? How do you think such narratives affected the North's perception of Southern slavery?

4. Where in these sources do you see evidence of a consistent style or structure followed by slave narratives? Despite such similarities, do you think that each of these narratives conveys a sense of its author as an individual? If so, how would you compare the personalities of Bibb, Northup, and Jacobs?

5. The author of each source selection had an amanuensis who claimed to contribute nothing more to the narrative than editorial corrections and organization. Do you see any evidence in these sources that would cause you to doubt such claims? How might the interests or objectives of an amanuensis have affected the composition and presentation of these narratives?

6. Which of these narratives would you like to read in its entirety? Why?

The Rest of the Story

The authors of antebellum slave narratives often became public figures, telling their stories on the abolitionist lecture circuit and raising money to purchase the freedom of relatives they had left behind. Passage of the Fugitive Slave Act in 1850, however, made living such a public life extremely risky for runaway slaves. Henry Bibb, who was never able to redeem his first wife and child out of slavery, emigrated to Ontario with his second wife in 1851. He started Canada's first newspaper for African Americans and remained active in the abolitionist cause until his death in 1854. Solomon Northup settled in Glens Falls, New York, supported abolitionism, and pursued an unsuccessful legal case against the men he believed responsible for his enslavement. He died sometime before 1863, but the circumstances of his death are unknown. During the Civil War, Harriet Jacobs worked in Washington, D.C., providing relief to runaway and refugee slaves. After the war, she became an advocate for African American education. She died in Cambridge, Massachusetts, in 1897.

The slave narrative continued to evolve in the wake of the Civil War. With the institution of slavery now dead, the purpose of such narratives shifted from securing emancipation to promoting black equality. Some authors of antebellum slave narratives, including Frederick Douglass and Sojourner Truth, became prominent voices for African American rights during Reconstruction and updated their narratives to reflect the struggle for the full enfranchisement of free blacks in American society. Other African American authors published memoirs of their lives to illustrate the achievements former slaves were capable of once they were free. Booker T. Washington's *Up from Slavery* (1901) became the most widely read example of this new wave of African American autobiographies. During the 1930s, the Federal Writers' Project (a New Deal employment program) recorded interviews with more than two thousand elderly ex-slaves. This ambitious project produced thousands of pages of testimony from the last generation to know slavery as a living memory. It is still used by historians today to reconstruct the experience of antebellum slavery from the slaves' perspective.

To Find Out More

Slave Narrative Anthologies and Online Resources

Andrews, William L., and Henry Louis Gates Jr., eds. *Slave Narratives*. New York: Library of America, 2000.

Gates, Henry Louis Jr., ed. *The Classic Slave Narratives*. New York: Penguin, 1987.

"North American Slave Narratives." *Documenting the American South*. University of North Carolina. http://docsouth.unc.edu/neh/chronautobio.html.

"Slave Narratives: A Folk History of Slavery in the United States from Interviews with Former Slaves, Typewritten Records Prepared by the Federal Writers' Project, 1936–1938." *American Memory*. Library of Congress. http://memory.loc .gov/ammem/snhtml/.

"Slave Narratives." Newberry Library. http://www.newberry.org/slave-narratives.

Other Sources on Slave Narratives and Antebellum Slavery

Andrews, William L. *To Tell a Free Story: The First Century of African-American Auto-biography, 1760–1865*. Urbana: University of Illinois Press, 1986.

Douglass, Frederick. *Narrative of the Life of Frederick Douglass, An American Slave, Written by Himself*. 2nd ed. Edited by David Blight. Boston: Bedford/St. Martin's, 2002.

Fisch, Audrey. *Cambridge Companion to the African American Slave Narrative*. Cambridge: Cambridge University Press, 2007.

Smith, Frances Foster. *Witnessing Slavery: Development of the Ante-Bellum Slave Narratives*. Westport, CT: Greenwood, 1994.

Starling, Marion Wilson. *The Slave Narrative: Its Place in American History*. 2nd ed. Washington, DC: Howard University Press, 1988.

White, Deborah Gray. *Ar'n't I a Woman? Female Slaves in the Plantation South*. New York: Norton, 1985.

Yellin, Jean Fagan. *Women and Sisters: The Anti-Slavery Feminists in American Culture*. New Haven, CT: Yale University Press, 1989.

CHAPTER 11

Martyr or Madman?

Biographies of John Brown

Late on the night of May 24, 1856, a small band of men led by abolitionist John Brown visited several homesteads along the Pottawatomie Creek in the Kansas Territory. Brown and his men pounded on the doors of men known in the area for their proslavery sympathies. Those unlucky enough to be home and unarmed were hurried outside, despite the protestations of crying wives and children. Brown asked each man a series of questions about his involvement in the proslavery cause in Kansas. Once Brown was convinced of their guilt, he ordered the men killed. Brown's party, which included four of his sons, shot some of their victims at point-blank range and cut others to pieces with broadswords. They left behind five mutilated corpses as a warning to any others who would try to bring slavery to Kansas.

Violence between proslavery and antislavery forces in Kansas was a fact of life in the 1850s. In 1854, Congress had passed the Kansas-Nebraska Act, establishing the doctrine of "popular sovereignty" in this newly organized territory. The brainchild of Illinois senator Stephen Douglas, popular sovereignty sought to sidestep the federal debate over the admission of free and slave states into the union by allowing the settlers within a territory to decide the question for themselves. Douglas may have hoped that the Kansas-Nebraska Act would cool sectional tensions, but it had the opposite effect. In New England and New York, abolitionists created emigrant aid societies to speed the territory's settlement by "free-soilers" opposed to slavery's expansion, while proslavery Missourians poured over their state's western border into Kansas to make sure the territory voted their way. Armed clashes between Missouri "border ruffians" and Northern free-soilers gave the territory a lawless character that earned it the nickname "Bleeding Kansas." Men on both sides formed voluntary brigades and armed themselves with Bowie knives, swords, guns, and even cannons. Brown, who had never served in a regular military force, earned the title of "Captain" for organizing some family and neighbors into a company of "Liberty Guards" to defend the free-soil town of Lawrence. They were unsuccessful. Just days before the Pottawatomie murders, a small army of proslavery men sacked Lawrence, putting free-soilers on the defensive. Nothing that had happened in Kansas matched the Pottawatomie murders for cold-blooded ruthlessness, however. The actions of Brown's band electrified the nation and raised the sectional conflict to a fever pitch.

As news of the Pottawatomie murders reached the national press, everyone was asking the same question: who was John Brown? He had arrived in Kansas just months earlier, in October 1855, to help his sons who were homesteading there and to advance the antislavery cause. Brown's family had deep New England roots, and he believed firmly in the same God—the divine, all-seeing judge of human affairs—that his Puritan ancestors had worshipped. He quoted the Bible at length in his verbal attacks on slavery. He did the same with the Declaration of Independence. "All men are created equal" was as much an article of faith for John Brown as the Ten Commandments. This fusion of religious and political principles had made him an abolitionist from an early age. He regarded African Americans as his brothers and sisters and slavery as a grave sin on the nation's conscience.

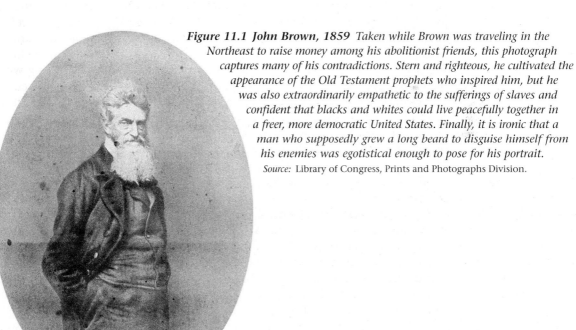

Figure 11.1 John Brown, 1859 Taken while Brown was traveling in the Northeast to raise money among his abolitionist friends, this photograph captures many of his contradictions. Stern and righteous, he cultivated the appearance of the Old Testament prophets who inspired him, but he was also extraordinarily empathetic to the sufferings of slaves and confident that blacks and whites could live peacefully together in a freer, more democratic United States. Finally, it is ironic that a man who supposedly grew a long beard to disguise himself from his enemies was egotistical enough to pose for his portrait.
Source: Library of Congress, Prints and Photographs Division.

Brown was a man of ambition as well as principle. Before gaining notoriety in Kansas in 1856, he had moved about frequently in New England, New York, Pennsylvania, and Ohio, seeking economic opportunity and stability for his ever-growing family. Born into humble circumstances in Connecticut in 1800, Brown spent most of his adult life in hardscrabble frontier communities, trying his hand at different businesses but often falling prey to debt, lawsuits, and misfortune. He was at various times a farmer, tanner, shepherd, wool merchant, and land speculator. He married twice and fathered twenty children, but only eleven of those survived to adulthood. In 1849, Brown moved his family to a farm in the Adirondack Mountains of northern New York, where they lived among escaped slaves and other free blacks who had been granted land by abolitionist Gerrit Smith. Brown's second wife and several of their children made a home there, but Brown himself remained constantly on the move, going where his business ventures and political convictions led him.

After the Pottawatomie murders, Brown stayed in Kansas and lived for a while as a guerrilla fighter, hiding in swamps and other remote areas with a group of dedicated followers. Territorial officials were unable to capture him, and to proslavery supporters, he became a symbol of "black Republicanism," a radical movement to foment slave rebellion and overthrow the South's racial and economic system. To free-soilers in Kansas, he became something of a folk hero, especially after his band of armed men put up a brave, albeit unsuccessful, defense of the free-soil town of Osawatomie against a much larger proslavery force in August 1856. One of Brown's sons was killed, and the town was burned to the ground, but many regarded "Osawatomie Brown," as he became known, as a freedom fighter whose bravery helped turn the tide against slavery in Kansas.

Brown took his newfound celebrity east in 1858, touring the drawing rooms of prominent abolitionists in Ohio, New York, and New England and soliciting funding for his battle against slavery. He also met with free blacks in Canada and the northern states to recruit their assistance in money, arms, and men. The famous black abolitionist Frederick Douglass was impressed by Brown's convictions but declined an offer to join him; a group of six prominent white abolitionists, however, opened their pocketbooks to Brown, despite their pacifist convictions.

Brown's militant abolitionism culminated in the raid on Harpers Ferry, Virginia (now West Virginia), in October 1859. Since the 1840s, Brown had considered Harpers Ferry, a town nestled in the hills of western Virginia along the eastern edge of the Appalachian Mountains, a logical site for starting a slave rebellion that could spread and ultimately engulf every slave state from there to Georgia. It was home to a rifle factory as well as a federal armory that could provide arms to runaway slaves, who could then form guerrilla bands in the nearby mountains. There was not a large slave population near Harpers Ferry, but Brown believed that plantation slaves in eastern Virginia and Maryland would flock to his cause once they knew a rebellion was under way.

In the summer and fall of 1859, Brown assembled a force of twenty-one men, about one fourth of whom were African Americans, for the raid on Harpers

Ferry. On the night of Sunday, October 16, they seized the armory and took many local citizens prisoner. The following morning, the local militia turned out to do battle with Brown's force. Several men were killed on each side, including two of Brown's sons, but Brown held out in a fire-engine house on the armory grounds, expecting assistance from runaway slaves who would help his men escape into the mountains. That night, U.S. Marines under the command of Colonel Robert E. Lee arrived and offered Brown a chance to surrender. Brown refused, and the next morning, Lee's men charged and quickly overcame Brown's defenses. More of Brown's men were killed, but Brown was only wounded and placed under arrest.

Brown's raid on Harpers Ferry was a military disaster. Half of his men were killed, and most of the survivors, including Brown himself, were quickly convicted of treason and executed. Not a single slave had been freed, despite the months of planning, and news of the raid failed to spark any slave rebellions. Brown had failed as an emancipator, but he had succeeded brilliantly as an incendiary. During the six weeks of his imprisonment and trial in Charlestown, Virginia (now Charles Town, West Virginia), the nation's attention was riveted on him. From his jail cell, Brown wrote letters and received visitors, sharing with many his belief that "the crimes of this guilty land will never be purged away but with blood." Southern newspapers depicted him as the homicidal madman who lurked at the heart of the abolitionist cause. Leaders of the Republican Party distanced themselves from him, but other Northerners embraced him as a Christian soldier and martyr. No one doubted that the events at Harpers Ferry had brought the nation one step closer to disunion. Years later, Frederick Douglass said it best: "If John Brown did not end the war that ended slavery, he did, at least, begin the war that ended slavery."

Using the Source: Biographies of John Brown

Who was John Brown? Was he a religious fanatic or a revolutionary? A military genius or a hopeless bungler? A man of conviction or an egomaniac? A visionary advocate of racial equality or a cold-blooded murderer? Was he the first terrorist to carry out an attack on U.S. soil? Like an anxious student facing a multiple-choice exam, historians have often found "all the above" the safest way to answer these questions.

Brown's contemporaries asked these questions about him in the wake of the Pottawatomie murders, and their debate over the meaning of his life and death only intensified after the events at Harpers Ferry in 1859. Most of what was written about Brown in the fifty years after his death was the work of people who eulogized him as an American hero. James Redpath, an antislavery journalist who had met Brown in Kansas, contributed much to this mythology, as did surviving family members and friends who wished to justify Brown and their association with him. These narratives of John Brown's life belong in the genre of hagiography, a type of historical writing that originated in the Middle Ages, when monks wrote lives of saints that blended fact and fiction and uncritically celebrated their subjects. Not until the early twentieth century, a half century after Brown's execution, did the first scholarly biographies of Brown appear, written by authors using historical methods and sources and claiming to take an even-handed approach to their subject. In the century since, enough biographies have been written about Brown to fill a bookshelf.

Standing in front of that bookshelf, you might wonder why anyone would want to write another biography of John Brown. It is a fair question. At the time of his execution, most of what makes up the standard narrative of his life was already known: his difficult beginnings, his intense spirituality, his failed business enterprises, his bloody career as a militant abolitionist. In the absence of any new evidence that challenges that story, why would anyone feel compelled to squeeze yet another Brown biography onto that crowded shelf?

Historians write biographies as much for themselves as they do for their subjects. A historical figure like John Brown is a sort of Rorschach test for historians, an inkblot spread out against an empty background that each viewer interprets differently according to his or her background, expertise, and biases. Moreover, contemporary issues constantly affect our view of the past, and each generation demands new interpretations of historical events. It is not surprising, then, that biographers continue to write about a figure as famous and controversial as Brown. Any biography of him will provide the basic facts of his life, but comparing several of them will also reveal how historians have altered their interpretations of Brown to suit their own sensibilities as well as the sensibilities of their audience.

What Can Biographies Tell Us?

Biography is perhaps the most popular form of historical writing. Most bookstores devote the bulk of their history sections to biographies, and each year, biographies top nonfiction best-seller lists. One reason for this popularity is the inherent narrative structure biographies provide to their writers and readers. A big part of history, after all, is *story*, and whether in the form of a play, film, or book, people like their stories to have clear beginnings, middles, and endings. The story of one person's life neatly fits that structure.

A good biography, however, will do more than merely recapitulate the events of a person's life; it will situate that person in a wider historical context, using the life story told in its pages to illuminate some greater aspect of the world in which its subject lived. How did the subject of a biography shape history, and how was he or she shaped by it? Biographies allow us to explore the role of the individual in society, the intersection of private and public life, and the ways in which personality can shape the broad tide of political and social change.

The disadvantages of working with biographies reflect the advantages in some ways. Biographers often inflate the importance of their subjects and overstate the ways in which their subjects shaped history rather than the ways in which they were shaped by it. Traditional biographies often subscribe to the "great men of history" approach to studying the past, asking, for example, who was the greatest general of World War II, who was the most indispensable Founding Father, or who was the greatest president? "Great women" occasionally get their due in these works, but women in general and other groups that have traditionally been excluded from the corridors of power are shortchanged by this kind of historical writing.

It is also important to remember that biographies are a secondary source. Like the journal articles discussed in Chapter 4, biographies are a product of someone else's interpretation of the facts, and despite their protestations otherwise, biographers are seldom neutral observers of their subjects' lives. After all, biographers are drawn to their subjects for very human reasons of love or hate. They may wish to sing the praises of their subject or damn that person with the judgment of history. No biographer responds to his or her subject with a shoulder shrug or wants the reader to do so. As with any other type of source, bias plays a role in how a biography gets made, and the attentive reader will take it into account when judging the quality of the work.

Even the most basic facts of a person's life are subject to interpretation and bias in a biography. Consider, for example, the description of John Brown's marriage to his second wife, Mary Day, found in biographies written by Robert Penn Warren and David S. Reynolds. Each relates the same basic facts. Brown's first wife, Dianthe, died from complications sustained in giving birth to a child who also died. Not long after, Brown became acquainted with the sixteen-year-old sister of his housekeeper and married her. Notice, however, how each author creates a strikingly different picture of Brown and his new bride from these facts.

FROM WARREN'S *JOHN BROWN: THE MAKING OF A MARTYR*

John Brown soon got used to this big-boned, reticent girl who did chores about the house or sat at the spinning wheel, manipulating the yarn with heavy, competent hands. One evening he gave her a letter. This restless, severe man, more than twice her age and looking even older, must have terrified her a little. In any case it was the next morning before she dared read the letter, nor did she dare, when she saw John Brown, to answer the question he had written her. Instead, she took the bucket and went about the customary work of bringing the morning water from the spring. He followed her to the spring and got his answer there. Mary Anne Day married John Brown in July, only a little less than a year after Dianthe and her unnamed son had been buried in the tanyard.[1]

Source: Robert Penn Warren, *John Brown: The Making of a Martyr* (1929; repr. Nashville: J. S. Sanders, 1993), 29.

Is this an attractive portrait of Mary Day?

How is John Brown portrayed?

[1] The grounds of Brown's family business, a tannery for processing animal hides into leather.

What is Warren predicting for the marriage here?

But the new wife had in her more of the stuff that made for survival; beneath a certain awkwardness was a great physical vigor, and the embarrassed silences covered a profound, unquestioning devotion to the hard responsibilities of her life. She was ignorant, but possessed a primitive stoicism which meant an efficient if sometimes uncomprehending adaptability to fact. It is doubtful if the grave by the tanyard lay much in her thoughts.

FROM REYNOLDS'S *JOHN BROWN, ABOLITIONIST*

Brown moved back into his own home and took on a housekeeper whose sixteen-year-old sister, Mary Day, came occasionally to spin cloth. Mary caught his eye as she sat at her spinning wheel. Tall and deep bosomed, she had striking black hair and a sturdy frame. The daughter of Charles Day, a blacksmith and farmer in nearby Troy Township, she had had little formal education but impressed Brown as a practical, hard-working woman.

Language suggesting playful romance

It wasn't long before Brown, too bashful to propose verbally, presented her with a written offer of marriage. The girl nervously put his note under her pillow and slept on it a night before opening it. After reading it, she grabbed a bucket and rushed off to a spring to fetch water. Brown followed her. By the time the two returned to the house, he had received the answer he wanted. They were married on June 14, 1833. Ten months later a baby girl, Sarah, arrived.

What is Reynolds predicting for the marriage?

Unlike the erratic Dianthe, Mary would prove to be a rock of stability for John Brown. Staunch and stoical, she set a tone of quiet courage that would influence the whole family.

Source: David S. Reynolds, *John Brown, Abolitionist: The Man Who Killed Slavery, Sparked the Civil War, and Seeded Civil Rights* (New York: Knopf, 2005), 49.

Warren's version of Brown's second marriage has all the gothic doom and gloom of an Edgar Allan Poe story: an older, overbearing man forces himself on a much younger, powerless woman, while the ghosts of his dead wife and child linger nearby in the family graveyard. Warren's Brown is forceful and bullying, and his Mary Day is a simpleminded stoic, already resigned to the fate of being a martyr's wife. Reynolds, on the other hand, paints a much rosier picture, one that might not be out of place on the cover of a romance novel. The grieving Brown falls hard for the raven-haired beauty at the spinning wheel. After a playful game of cat and mouse, he wins her over, and they get busy making babies. As these short passages indicate, no biography presents an entirely neutral view of its subject. Authors arrange and interpret facts to suit their purposes, nor are they above embellishing details (for example, the grave in the tanyard or Mary's striking black hair) to elicit an emotional response from their readers.

To get more than the simple facts of a person's life out of a biography, it is important to ask questions about the book's own life story. The Checklist questions below will help you get the most out of any biography you may read for research or pleasure. It is helpful to know something about the author of the book and his or her motives for writing it. In addition, be a critical reader of the book's evidence. Many authors of biographies merely repackage what previous biographers have written about their subject and end up repeating the same errors. A biography that relies extensively on original archival research promises to offer the reader something new in terms of evidence and interpretation.

CHECKLIST: Interrogating Biographies

- ☐ When was this biography written and by whom?
- ☐ What do you know about the author and the period in which he or she wrote the biography?
- ☐ How does the author describe the subject's historical legacy? Why does the author think people should still read and learn about this person today?
- ☐ Does the author appear to be in control of the facts? Has he or she completed original archival research to write this book or instead relied on previously published secondary sources for the book's material?
- ☐ What approach does the author take to the biography's subject? Does the author emphasize the subject's virtues or vices? What bias is evident in the author's choice of language and subject matter?

Source Analysis Table

Use the columns in the table on page 234 to take notes that will help you compare and contrast how each author depicts Brown, the characters in his life story, and his legacy.

Source	Description of John Brown, His Motives, and His Methods	Description of Brown's Accomplices, Supporters, and Enemies	Historical Significance of Brown
1. Du Bois (1909)			
2. Warren (1929)			
3. Reynolds (2005)			

The Source: Biographies of John Brown

1 | *John Brown* by W. E. B. Du Bois, 1909

W. E. B. Du Bois was one of the most influential American intellectuals and activists of the twentieth century. He established his reputation as a voice for African Americans with the publication of *The Souls of Black Folk* in 1903 and played a founding role in the National Association for the Advancement of Colored People (NAACP), a pathbreaking civil rights organization. *John Brown* was his second book. The passages below reflect Du Bois's interest in the history of American race relations.

So Kansas was free.[1] In vain did the sullen Senate in Washington fume and threaten and keep the young state knocking for admission; the game had been played and lost and Kansas was free. Free because the slave barons played for an imperial stake in defiance of modern humanity and economic development. Free because strong men had suffered and fought not against slavery but against slaves in Kansas. Above all, free because one man hated slavery and on a terrible night rode down with his sons among the shadows of the Swamp of the Swan—that long, low-winding and somber stream "fringed everywhere with woods" and dark with bloody memory.[2] Forty-eight hours they lingered there, and then on a pale May morning rode up to the world again. Behind them lay five twisted, red, and mangled corpses. Behind them rose the stifled wailing of widows and little children. Behind them the fearful driver gazed and shuddered. But before them rode a man, tall, dark, grim-faced and awful. His hands were red and his name was John Brown. Such was the cost of freedom.

Of all this development[3] John Brown knew far more than most white men and it was on this great knowledge that his great faith was based. To most Americans the inner striving of the Negro was a veiled and an unknown tale: they had heard of Douglass,[4] they knew of fugitive slaves, but of the living, organized, struggling group that had made both these phenomena possible they had no conception.

From his earliest interest in Negroes, John Brown sought to know individuals among them intimately and personally. He invited them to his home and he went to theirs. He talked to them, and listened to the history of their trials,

[1] Du Bois is referring here to the clinching of a free-soil government for Kansas in 1858.

[2] The site of the Pottawatomie murders.

[3] The growing spirit for rebellion among American slaves.

[4] Frederick Douglass, the leading African American abolitionist of the era.

Source: W. E. B. Du Bois, *John Brown* (Philadelphia: G. W. Jacobs and Company, 1909), 247–48, 143–44, 338, 340–41, 374–75.

advised them and took advice from them. His dream was to enlist the boldest and most daring spirits among them in his great plan.

When, therefore, John Brown came East[5] in January, 1858, his object was not simply to further his campaign for funds, but more especially definitely to organize the Negroes for his work. Already he had disclosed his intentions to Thomas Thomas[6] of Springfield and to Frederick Douglass. He now determined to enlist a larger number and he particularly had in mind the Negroes of New York and Philadelphia, and those in Canada. At no time, however, did John Brown plan to begin his foray with many Negroes. He knew that he must gain the confidence of black men first by a successful stroke, and that after initial success he could count on large numbers. His object then was to interest a few leaders like Douglass, organize societies with wide ramifications, and after the first raid to depend on these societies for aid and recruits.

The deed was done.[7] The next day the world knew and the world sat in puzzled amazement. It was ever so and ever will be. When a prophet like John Brown appears, how must we of the world receive him? Must we follow out of the drear, dread logic of surrounding facts, as did the South, even if they crucify a clean and pure soul, simply because consistent allegiance to our cherished, chosen ideal demands it? If we do, the shame will brand our latest history. Shall we hesitate and waver before his clear white logic, now helping, now fearing to help, now believing, now doubting? Yes, this we must do so long as the doubt and hesitation are genuine; but we must not lie. If we are human, we must thus hesitate until we know the right. How shall we know it? That is the Riddle of the Sphinx. We are but darkened groping souls, that know not light often because of its very blinding radiance. Only in time is truth revealed. To-day at last we know: John Brown was right. . . .

Such a light was the soul of John Brown. He was simple, exasperatingly simple; unlettered, plain, and homely. No casuistry of culture or of learning, or well-being or tradition moved him in the slightest degree: "Slavery is wrong," he said, "kill it." Destroy it—uproot it, stem, blossom, and branch; give it no quarter, exterminate it and do it now. Was he wrong? No. The forcible staying of human uplift by barriers of law, and might, and tradition is the most wicked thing on earth. It is wrong, eternally wrong. It is wrong, by whatever name it is called, or in whatever guise it lurks, and whenever it appears. But it is especially heinous, black, and cruel when it masquerades in the robes of law and justice and patriotism. So was American slavery clothed in 1859, and it had to die by revolution, not by milder means. And this men knew. They had known it for a hundred years. Yet they shrank and trembled. From round about the white and blinding path of this soul flew equivocations, lies, thievings and red murders. And yet all men instinctively felt that these things were

---

[5] From Kansas, to raise money for his cause among Northern abolitionists.

[6] A New England free black man with whom Brown had shared his plan for inciting slave rebellion.

[7] The raid on Harpers Ferry.

not of the light but of the surrounding darkness. It is at once surprising, baf-
fling, and pitiable to see the way in which men—honest American citizens—
faced this light.

Was John Brown simply an episode, or was he an eternal truth? And if a
truth, how speaks that truth today? John Brown loved his neighbor as himself. He could not endure therefore to see his neighbor, poor, unfortunate or
oppressed. This natural sympathy was strengthened by a saturation in Hebrew
religion[8] which stressed the personal responsibility of every human soul to a
just God. To this religion of equality and sympathy with misfortune, was added
the strong influence of the social doctrines of the French Revolution with its
emphasis on freedom and power in political life. And on all this was built John
Brown's own inchoate but growing belief in a more just and a more equal distribution of property. From this he concluded, and acted on that conclusion, that
all men are created free and equal, and that the cost of liberty is less than the
price of repression.

[8] Here Du Bois is referring to Brown's Calvinist faith, rooted in Old Testament notions of
God as a divine judge and controller of human affairs.

2 | *John Brown* by Robert Penn Warren, 1929

> Robert Penn Warren was a prominent twentieth-century American author
> whose work often focused on themes of Southern culture and history. In the
> 1930s, he associated with a group of like-minded writers, known as the
> Southern Agrarians, who criticized modern industrial society and defended
> the South as a region of traditional values. Although Warren is most famous
> for his poetry, literary criticism, and fiction, his first book, written while he
> was still a student, was a biography of John Brown.

A short while after dark John Brown gave the order to march.[1] The company
moved rapidly and quietly northward toward Mosquito Creek. They forded the
creek above the Doyle place and soon reached the first cabin. One of the men
knocked on the door, while the others stood by waiting. Everything was silent
for a moment and then they heard the sound of a gun being rammed through
the chinks of the cabin wall. The raiders scattered on the instant; they had not
come for a stand-up fight. If that was all they wanted they could have gotten it
quickly enough without leaving the militia. . . .

They next reached the Doyle cabin, which stood on Mosquito Creek, only
a mile or so from where it emptied into the Pottawatomie. As they cautiously

[1] Warren describes in this passage the Pottawatomie murders.
Source: Robert Penn Warren, *John Brown: The Making of a Martyr* (1929; repr. Nashville:
J. S. Sanders, 1993), 161–68, 314, 420–21.

approached, two large and savage watchdogs leaped up at them. Frederick[2] swung his short two-edged sword at one of the beasts and Townsley[3] stepped in to dispatch it with a blow of his saber. The first of the Bierce swords[4] was stained with blood. Townsley, Weiner,[5] and Frederick stopped a little way from the house, while John Brown, Thompson,[6] and three of the sons went up to the door and knocked. Doyle's voice answered. There was no saving sound of a rifle being rammed through the cabin chinks, and the gleam of a newly lighted candle shone within. "We want to know where Mr. Wilkinson[7] lives," one of the men said. Doyle replied that he would tell them the way and then opened the door. John Brown and his men pushed inside. "We are from the Northern army. You and your boys must surrender. You are our prisoners." Mahala Doyle cried out in protest; she saw the meaning of the business. Old Doyle must also have understood, but he only said, "Hush, mother, hush." The prisoners of the Northern army were marched out of the house — the father Doyle, the twenty-two-year-old William, and Drury who was only twenty. Mahala Doyle's tears prevailed a little, for the next son, John, was left in the cabin with her and the younger children.

The three victims were hurried a short distance down the road toward Dutch Henry's[8] and there the party halted. John Brown set the example. He presented a revolver to the forehead of old Doyle and fired. It had begun; there was no turning back now. The Brown sons fell on William and Drury Doyle and hacked them down. Drury tried to flee but they pursued and overtook him. In the young grass near a ravine they left his mangled body. The other two lay in a bloody heap by the roadside where they had fallen.

The killing at Doyle's was perforce one of principle, for the family's horses had been out on the prairie. The little group, with their stained swords, hurried forward on foot to Wilkinson's. It was not yet midnight; and the business was far from finished. . . .

Wilkinson was killed in the roadway, to the south of his house. The murderers dragged his body a short distance to one side and left it in some dry bush. It was over neatly and quickly; they proceeded in the direction of Dutch Henry's Crossing. They must have gone along more rapidly now. The saddles could not have been taken from the house for nothing, but at that most of the company had to ride bareback.[9] . . .

John Brown and his party returned to their camp between the two deep ravines. The old blades, stained with the blood of five men, were washed in the

---

[2] Frederick Brown, one of John Brown's sons who accompanied him on the Pottawatomie raid.

[3] One of Brown's men.

[4] Lucius Bierce was an Ohio abolitionist who supplied Brown with artillery sabers.

[5] One of Brown's men.

[6] One of Brown's men.

[7] One of the proslavery men Brown's party was after that night.

[8] Another proslavery supporter targeted by Brown.

[9] Warren is referring here to horses and saddles that Brown's party stole from their victims.

waters of Pottawatomie Creek. But there remained more important evidence of the crime to be effaced before the gang could confront the world again. Before dawn they were in possession, not of the murdered men's horses, but of fast running horses brought to them and exchanged by their confederates. The terms of the transaction will never be known. The sons who survived John Brown even denied for years his presence on the Pottawatomie on the night of May 25. When the truth was out at last and the world had prepared a motive—a motive which would fit the martyr—there were confessions from the sons. The world had justified the murderer; the Browns knew that it is a little more difficult to justify a horse thief. When daylight came the evidence was gone, for the stolen horses were well on their way north to be sold.

The stooped but still rigid old man[10] with his neat rural dress, his talk about bayonets and bullets and God's will, his immense awkward dignity, immense egotism, his white beard and hard grey-blue eyes which glittered, as one host put it, with a "little touch of insanity," moved impressively about the albums and pleasant china of those New England parlors. Most of the people who sat about him in those parlors, and gave their earnest attention to his words, found something peculiarly congenial to their own prejudices and beliefs. Captain Brown was a "higher law man." He was "superior to any legal tradition"—just as most of these people felt themselves to be—and if he claimed to have a divine commission, they could understand what he meant, for they too were privy to God. The Southerner pointed to the Constitution and said: "There is the law and the bargain; keep them and give us justice." Garrison[11] burned the Constitution and said it was a "covenant with Hell" and many other countrymen of his, if they were not ready to do this, could still call on conscience and the higher law. Unhappily, a corollary of this divine revelation was to make the South pay, and pay again. The disagreement might conceivably have been settled under terms of law, but when it was transposed into terms of theology there was no hope of settlement. There is only one way to conclude a theological argument: bayonets and bullets. And in that last appeal God's hand reached down to prove the "higher law men" perfectly right; as events demonstrated, God was, obviously, not on the side of the South. By the same logic, it may be added, God was not, personally, on the side of John Brown.

Certainly John Brown was not normal—whatever that may mean. His egotism, his enormous force of will, his power of endurance, his deliberate cruelties, his deliberate charities, his intolerance, his merciless ambition, and the element of religious fanaticism which worked regularly as a device of self-justification—all these things made up an intensity of nature which appeared,

[10] Warren is referring in this passage to John Brown's appearances in the homes of wealthy eastern supporters.

[11] Massachusetts's leading abolitionist, William Lloyd Garrison.

beyond doubt, as abnormal. The issue of responsibility remains, and, pragmatically, it is not begging the question to say that John Brown was as responsible for his actions as are the general run of criminals who have suffered similar penalties; that is another problem.

Wise[12] said that John Brown was more sane than his prompters and promoters; certainly he was more intelligent and stronger. If he were insane it is a grave criticism of Sanborn[13] and the other conspirators, and they must assume a horrible weight of responsibility for the whole affair. Sanborn's belief in divinely confirmed missions, especially in his own and John Brown's missions, his absolute certainty that he was right, his irrationality, and his peculiar romanticism give some color to the charge made by Governor Wise; the difference is that Sanborn lacked John Brown's courage and strength, and that difference made the sum total of his other qualities equivalent simply to a habit of rhetoric and a sort of snobbery. If Sanborn had acted out his professions he also might have been called a fanatic. Parker and Higginson were at the same time more rational, more courageous, more intelligent, and stronger than Sanborn, and they were never so well pleased with themselves. As for poor old Gerrit Smith,[14] he went to a lunatic asylum on November 7, 1859.

[12] Governor Henry A. Wise of Virginia, who oversaw Brown's trial and execution.

[13] One of the "Secret Six" abolitionists who funded Brown's attack on Harpers Ferry.

[14] Parker, Higginson, and Smith were all other members of the Secret Six.

3 | *John Brown, Abolitionist* by David S. Reynolds, 2005

David S. Reynolds, a professor at the City University of New York, is a leading scholar of American literature and history of the antebellum era. Before writing about John Brown, he published an award-winning biography of Walt Whitman, a nineteenth-century American poet. The selection below reflects a twenty-first-century perspective on Brown informed by the September 11, 2001, terrorist attacks on the United States.

A crucial question remains: How could John Brown square murder[1] with his religious faith? He was, after all, a Christian, and most Abolitionists of his day used Christianity to endorse pacifism, not violence. Even if we say that Kansas was in a state of war, how could he, as a Christian, commit what amounted to a war crime?

By mid-May 1856 the events in Kansas and on the national scene made the Old Testament God of Battles seem more relevant to him than the New

[1] Reynolds is discussing the Pottawatomie murders in this passage.

Source: David S. Reynolds, *John Brown, Abolitionist: The Man Who Killed Slavery, Sparked the Civil War, and Seeded Civil Rights* (New York: Knopf, 2005), 164–67, 502, 503.

Testament's Prince of Peace. In this sense he followed the example of his greatest hero among white Christians, Oliver Cromwell.[2]

... The most positive way to view Cromwell's and Brown's crimes is to regard them as what Doris Lessing[3] calls "good terrorism"—that is, terrorism justified by obvious social injustice. Terrorism is violence that avoids combat, is used against the defenseless (often civilians), and is intended to shock and horrify, with the aim of bringing about social change. Cromwell's massacres in Ireland and Brown's Pottawatomie murders may qualify as terrorism on these counts.

It might be argued that excessive force in each case challenged real social injustice: centuries of oppressive British royalty in Cromwell's case and the twin horrors of chattel slavery and Southern violence in Brown's. Just as the populists of late czarist Russia, to whom John Brown was compared in the nineteenth century, are sometimes called "good" terrorists because they envisioned a free, nonviolent society, so Brown is open to a sympathetic interpretation because he used violence in order to create a society devoid of slavery and racism.

Choice of victims is a consideration in gauging whether terrorism is "good." Wholesale slaughter of numerous innocents, as in the September 11, 2001, attack on the World Trade Center, resists this affirmative reading.

Was Brown justified in his choice of victims at Pottawatomie Creek? The most extreme statement he was known to have made on the topic was his declaration to the Free State settler James Hanway that he "proposed to sweep the creek . . . of all the proslavery men on it." If this statement accurately describes Brown's intentions, it avoids the stigma of indiscriminate killing, but just barely. It specifies its victims by politics ("proslavery") and by gender ("men"): but the phrase "sweep the creek" sounds arbitrary, as though he were out to kill any political enemy he could find in the area. If, however, Pottawatomie was a response to long- and short-term proslavery outrages waged against carefully selected targets, it becomes less random and thus more defensible.

Brown's sons Jason and John Jr. insisted that their father did not go on an unsystematic murder spree but instead chose his victims, who were active in proslavery politics and had challenged the Browns personally. As mentioned, three of the victims—James P. Doyle, his son William Doyle, and Allen Wilkinson—had served at the proslavery hearing of Judge Cato, who had issued warrants for the arrest of the Browns. Another victim, William Sherman, was part of the family whose tavern at Dutch Henry's Crossing was the local center for proslavery activities, including Cato's trial. William's brutish brother Henry Sherman had threatened to lynch a merchant who sold lead to Jason Brown.

---

[2] Leader of the English Civil Wars (1641–1649), responsible for the execution of King Charles I and many atrocities committed by his troops against his opponents in Ireland.

[3] A British writer best known for works sympathetic to the cause of Africans and other indigenous peoples suffering under colonial rule.

The idea that "one man's terrorist is another man's freedom fighter" is no less true now than it was in Brown's day. For some ardent foes of abortion, Paul Hill,[4] who claimed to follow Brown, was a hero. Others thought that Timothy McVeigh[5] carried out justice—Gore Vidal,[6] for instance, disgusted by what he saw as an oppressive American government, compared McVeigh not only to Brown but also to Paul Revere, spreading the alarm that "The Feds are coming, the Feds are coming." Some militant Muslims, appalled by what they regarded as the decadence and corrupt imperialism of the United States, applauded bin Laden's[7] destruction of the World Trade Center. In this sense, contemporary terrorists are no different from Brown, deified by some and demonized by others.

Still, it is misleading to identify Brown with modern terrorists. Actually, Brown would have disapproved of the use of violence by most of those who have proclaimed themselves as his heirs. It is important to recognize that many of the social ills that later bred radical violence plagued the nation in his time, but he went to war only over the issue of slavery. . . .

Why? Because slavery was a uniquely immoral institution that seemed cemented in place by law, custom, and prejudice. Bad economic times came and went. The status of women promised to change. Native Americans, although horribly mistreated, still had a measure of freedom. City conditions were improving as technology progressed. But slavery, the "sum of all evils," was there to stay, at least for the foreseeable future. And slavery was qualitatively different from all other social issues, since it deprived millions of their rights as Americans and their dignity as human beings. No other social phenomenon approached its wickedness. No other problem, Brown believed, called for the use of arms.

Brown had a breadth of vision that modern terrorists lack. He was an *American* terrorist in the amplest sense of the word. He was every bit as religious as Osama bin Laden—but was the Muslim bin Laden able to enlist Christians, atheists, or Jews among his followers? The Calvinistic Brown, reflecting the religious toleration of his nation, counted Jews, liberal Christians, spiritualists, and agnostics among his most devoted soldiers. Bin Laden's ultimate goal was the creation of a Muslim theocracy in which opposing views, especially Western ones, were banned. Brown's goal was a democratic society that assigned full rights to all, irrespective of religion, race, or gender.

[4] Paul Hill was convicted of murdering an abortion provider and was executed in 2003.

[5] Timothy McVeigh was convicted of the 1995 Oklahoma City bombing and was executed in 2001.

[6] American novelist and journalist.

[7] Osama bin Laden, leader of Al Qaeda, killed by U.S. forces in 2011.

Analyzing Biographies

1. Briefly summarize how each author describes Brown's motives and methods as an abolitionist. How does each describe Brown's accomplices, supporters, victims, and enemies?

2. Which authors are most similar in their interpretations of Brown? Which author differs the most from the others in his treatment of Brown? Considering what you know about the authors of these biographies and the times in which they wrote, what biases do you think they brought to their work, and where do you see evidence of those biases in these selections?

3. One of these selections refers to Brown as a "terrorist"; do you agree with that assessment? How does Reynolds, the author of that source, apply his distinction between bad terrorism and good terrorism to Brown's actions? Do you agree with Reynolds's conclusion in this regard?

4. The sources in this chapter are from much longer biographies of John Brown. On the basis of the excerpts you have read here, which of these works would you like to read in its entirety? Why?

5. In the concluding pages of his biography of John Brown, Du Bois wrote, "Was John Brown simply an episode, or was he an eternal truth? And if a truth, how speaks that truth today?" In light of what you have learned about Brown, how would you answer these questions? What was Brown's significance in 1859, and what is his significance to us today?

The Rest of the Story

John Brown remained as controversial in death as he had been in life. Even before his death at the gallows on the morning of December 2, 1859, he was being ushered into heaven by some and condemned to hell by others. Henry David Thoreau, the New England philosopher and writer who had strong anti-slavery convictions but usually found abolitionists a tiresome, sanctimonious lot, eulogized Brown while he was still among the living. In "A Plea for Captain John Brown," read before the citizens of Concord, Massachusetts, on October 30, Thoreau compared his subject to the crucified Christ, called him "the most American of us all," and concluded, "He is not Old Brown any longer; he is an angel of light." Other leading intellectuals and reformers of the North—Henry Ward Beecher, Ralph Waldo Emerson, William Lloyd Garrison—chimed in to praise Brown as a man of conviction and action, a martyr whose sacrifice had forced the nation to recognize the sin of slavery.

From the South came protests that Northerners were using their presses and pulpits to make a hero of a man who had committed treason and murder. On the floor of the Senate, Mississippi senator Jefferson Davis voiced the belief of many slaveholders when he accused his Republican colleagues of conspiring with Brown to "wage violent, irreconcilable, eternal warfare upon the institution of American slavery, with the view of its ultimate extinction throughout the land." On the campaign trail, Republican presidential candidate Abraham Lincoln believed it necessary to answer Davis's charge by stating blankly, "John Brown was no Republican," only a deluded man who "fancied himself commissioned by Heaven" to free the slaves.

Five years later, Lincoln might have reconsidered those words when he drafted his Second Inaugural Address. With more blood spilled in the act of ending slavery than Brown or anyone else could have imagined in 1859, Lincoln struggled to make sense of the war that had torn the country apart. He ended up using the same biblical language that Brown had used to explain his actions: God wills it. Lincoln told the people that God had given the war to North and South alike as punishment for their complicity in slavery. Everyone had hoped for a less destructive end to slavery, but if God willed it to continue until "every drop of blood drawn with the lash, shall be paid by another drawn with the sword, as was said three thousand years ago, so still it must be said, 'the judgments of the Lord, are true and righteous altogether.'" John Brown, if he could have heard these words, would have answered with a simple "Amen."

To Find Out More

Resources for John Brown and the Raid on Harpers Ferry

Earle, Jonathan Halperin. *John Brown's Raid on Harpers Ferry: A Brief History with Documents*. Boston: Bedford/St. Martin's, 2008.
"John Brown and the Valley of the Shadow." *The Institute for Advanced Technology in the Humanities*. The University of Virginia. http://www2.iath.virginia.edu /jbrown/master.html.

Secondary Sources on John Brown

Carton, Evan. *Patriotic Treason: John Brown and the Soul of America*. New York: Free Press, 2006.
Oates, Stephen. *To Purge This Land with Blood: A Biography of John Brown*. New York: Harper and Row, 1970.
Peterson, Merrill. *John Brown: The Legend Revisited*. Charlottesville: University Press of Virginia, 2002.
Russo, Peggy A., and Paul Finkelman, eds. *Terrible Swift Sword: The Legacy of John Brown*. Athens: Ohio University Press, 2005.
Villard, Oswald Garrison. *John Brown, A Biography, Fifty Years After*. Boston: Houghton Mifflin, 1910.
Wilson, Hill Peebles. *John Brown, Soldier of Fortune*. Lawrence, KS: H. P. Wilson, 1913.

CHAPTER 12

The Illustrated Civil War

Photography on the Battlefield

On September 17, 1862, Union and Confederate armies collided in the small western Maryland town of Sharpsburg. The ensuing Battle of Antietam, named after a nearby creek where much of the action took place, was the bloodiest single day of the Civil War. Seventy-five thousand Union troops, led by General George B. McClellan, suffered more than 12,000 casualties. The Confederate army of 52,000 men, led by General Robert E. Lee, suffered almost 14,000 casualties. Put another way, the combined armies of the Union and Confederacy experienced an astounding 20 percent casualty rate: one in five soldiers was killed, wounded, or missing in action by the end of the day.

The Battle of Antietam was nominally a victory for McClellan, because Lee's troops withdrew from the field first. In Washington, D.C., President Abraham Lincoln had been hoping for news of a decisive Union victory to prime public opinion for the Emancipation Proclamation and to improve Republican fortunes in the upcoming congressional election. Instead, Lincoln grew incensed when McClellan failed to pursue Lee's badly damaged army as it retreated into Virginia. His patience worn thin by McClellan's foot-dragging, Lincoln traveled to the Antietam battlefield to discuss the matter in person. Anticipating that meeting, Lincoln supposedly told his wife, "General McClellan and myself are to be photographed . . . if we can be still long enough. I feel General McClellan should have no problem." A few weeks later, Lincoln relieved McClellan of his command.

Lincoln and McClellan did indeed pose for a battlefield portrait (see Source 4 on p. 259), but their photographer took some other pictures as well. About one month after the battle, its horrible cost was brought home to the American public when Mathew Brady opened an exhibit at his New York City gallery of photographs taken at Sharpsburg. Brady and other photographers had been taking pictures related to the war since its start in early 1861, but those were mostly portraits of soldiers. What was different about Brady's Antietam exhibit was the inclusion of images of corpses, horribly twisted, mangled, and bloated from the summer sun, strewn across the fields of Sharpsburg. In a review published on October 20, 1862, the *New York Times* praised the photographs' realism:

> Mr. Brady has done something to bring home to us the terrible reality and earnestness of war. If he has not brought bodies and laid them in our dooryards and along the streets, he has done something very like it. At the door of his gallery hangs a little placard, "The Dead of Antietam." Crowds of people are constantly . . . bending over photographic views of that fearful battlefield, taken immediately after the action. . . . There is a terrible fascination about it that draws one near these pictures, and makes him lo[a]th to leave them. You will see hushed, reverend groups standing around these weird copies of carnage, bending down to look in the pale faces of the dead, chained by the strange spell that dwells in dead men's eyes.

Ironically, Brady had not taken any of the photographs that he exhibited in his gallery that October. Although his name had become synonymous with photography in the United States during the 1850s, his poor eyesight meant that he rarely operated the cameras that made him famous. Instead, Brady hired and trained others to do much of the photography published under his name. The Antietam images were taken by Alexander Gardner, who managed a gallery owned by Brady in Washington, D.C. A few months before the Battle of Antietam, Gardner had joined General McClellan's staff as its official photographer. This appointment enabled him to travel with the army and to photograph battlefields immediately before and after action took place. It was this sort of inside access that gave his Antietam photographs the stunning realism that entranced the crowds in Brady's gallery.

Gardner's Antietam photographs were a tremendous commercial success, but Gardner was not pleased that Brady published them without giving him credit. The two men parted ways a few months later and became commercial rivals for the rest of the war, with Gardner working out of his own gallery in Washington, D.C. (see Figure 12.1). Brady, who had made his name in the 1850s as the photographer of the nation's leading citizens, continued to publish photographs of the war's famous figures and landmarks. Meanwhile, Gardner led a new wave of photographers who focused their work on images of wartime destruction: battlefield dead, blasted buildings, and landscapes transformed by the hard hand of war.

Photographers such as Brady and Gardner produced a rich visual record of the Civil War. Previous wars had been photographed: military portraits and landscapes date to the Mexican-American War (1846–1848) and the British-Russian Crimean War (1854–1856). Both of those conflicts, however, occurred when the technology of photography was in its infancy, and their battlefields

Figure 12.1 Photographer Unknown, "Gardner's Gallery" *This undated photograph shows what the exterior of an urban photographer's gallery looked like. Notice the billboards advertising the different types of photographs and photographic services available, as well as the prominent advertisement for "Views of the War."* Source: Library of Congress, Prints and Photographs Division.

were far removed from the cities where photographers worked. The Civil War was different in two significant ways. First, the war's eastern theater of operations was close to urban centers such as Washington, D.C., that already had a commercial photography industry. Second, the consumer market for photographs in the United States had expanded exponentially during the 1850s because of technological improvements that made photographs affordable to just about everyone. Photographs had been a novelty of the well-to-do in the 1840s; by 1860, they were a part of American consumer culture, thanks in part to the relentless innovation and promotion of entrepreneurs such as Mathew Brady and Alexander Gardner.

Photography had a profound effect on how Americans experienced the Civil War. As the review of Brady's Antietam exhibit indicates, photography brought the violence and destruction of the battlefield to the doorsteps of the American public and elicited a strong emotional response, even from people far removed from the fighting. Photographers such as Brady and Gardner cultivated their reputations as the war's most accurate and impartial observers, describing their work as a visual record unvarnished by sentimentality or political bias. They also turned the war into a commodity available for purchase. Their claims to rendering the war in objective, unfiltered truth must be weighed against their efforts to market the war for public consumption in a way that suited their own commercial and artistic purposes.

Using the Source: Civil War Photographs

In 1860, there were more than three thousand photographers working in the United States. During the Civil War, they took tens of thousands of pictures of military subjects: individual and group portraits of soldiers, scenes of camp life and field hospitals, battlefield and city landscapes, railroad depots, fortifications, and shipyards. To use these images as a source, you must first familiarize yourself with the history, technology, and terminology of nineteenth-century photography.

The age of photography began with the invention of the daguerreotype in the late 1830s. Named for one of its inventors, Louis-Jacques-Mandé Daguerre, the daguerreotype was a fixed image produced on a silver-coated copper plate. Shortly after Daguerre introduced his invention in Europe, Samuel F. B. Morse brought the technology to the United States, where he taught the craft to several students, including Mathew Brady. During the 1840s, daguerreotypists opened studios in cities throughout the United States, drawing as their customers members of the urban middle and upper classes, who sat for their portraits individually, with their children, or as married couples. A successful daguerreotypist ran a kind of factory, keeping a public gallery and reception area where he displayed samples of his work to attract customers, a studio where he posed his subjects, and back rooms where workers prepared and developed his plates and fit them into frames for display at home. As one of many daguerreotypists in New York competing for business, Brady built his reputation by photographing famous politicians, authors, and actors, styling himself the "national historian," and publishing *The Gallery of Illustrious Americans*, a book based on his daguerreotypes, in 1850.

The next great leap in photography's development came in the mid-1850s with the invention of the wet-plate process. Unlike the daguerreotype, which was a one-time, nonreproducible image, the wet-plate process used glass plates immersed in a solution of photosensitive chemicals to produce negative images from which "positive" paper copies could be made. The wet-plate process expanded the market for photography, making possible mass-produced copies and enlargements suitable for exhibit or sale. Two important product innovations based on this improved technology—the stereograph and the *carte-de-visite*—occurred in the years just before the Civil War. The stereograph was a double image produced by fitting two lenses on a single camera. When viewed through a stereoscope, a handheld device that could be purchased from a photographer's studio, it produced a three-dimensional effect. Stereoscopes helped turn the viewing of photographs into a leisure activity that could occur in every home. The *carte-de-visite* was a small print made by fitting four lenses onto one camera, which produced four identical images on a single plate. Prints from such a negative, when cut into quarters, were used as calling cards. Brady led the way in marketing them as collector's cards (sometimes called album cards), selling *cartes-de-visite* of famous figures in numbered series much like baseball cards are sold and collected today.

Paper reproduction in such formats made photographs available to even working-class people. A portrait-size print might cost $1.50, a stereoscope 50 cents, and a *carte-de-visite* only 25 cents. When Union and Confederate armies mobilized in 1861, soldiers in uniform rushed to have their portraits taken as souvenirs of their service or as keepsakes for loved ones at home. The vast majority of the tens of thousands of Civil War photographs fall into this category. Once photographers realized the demand that the war was creating for their services, they expanded their work to include other subjects that they thought might turn a profit.

What Can Civil War Photographs Tell Us?

The most obvious advantage to using such photographs as a historical source was one immediately realized by the government and military. Photography made possible the recording and communication of visual information with much greater speed and detail than other media. Armies had long relied on sketch artists to record useful information about the scene of battle. During the Civil War, generals added photographers to their staffs so that they could make images of fortifications, bridges, railroads, and natural landmarks, not to mention portraits of the generals themselves as they sallied forth into history. Military photographers also aided in the reproduction of maps. Ever since, historians have used these images to reconstruct the military history of the war, from engagements on rural battlefields like Antietam to scorched-earth attacks on cities such as Richmond, Virginia, and Charleston, South Carolina.

Cultural and social historians find many advantages to working with these photographs as well. How people create visual images of war tells us much about the values and emotions they associate with it. Paintings, drawings, and photographs of battlefields are as much attempts to create meaning out of the violence and death of warfare as are letters home, diary entries, and memoirs. Before the invention of photography, the visual record of U.S. warfare was usually created by painters who worked long after the battle raged. John Trumbull was the most famous painter of the American Revolution, and the federal government commissioned his work for the new nation's Capitol in the early

George Washington leading the Continental Army forward

Compare Mercer's facial expression with that of the dead soldier in the foreground of O'Sullivan's image

Mercer dies in close proximity to the enemy, witnessing the tide of battle around him

Source: © Niday Picture Library/Alamy.

nineteenth century. Compare his *Death of General Mercer at the Battle of Princeton, New Jersey, 3 January 1777* (above) with the most famous photograph from the Gettysburg battlefield, Timothy O'Sullivan's "A Harvest of Death, Gettysburg, Pennsylvania" (on p. 251). Both depict battlefield carnage, but convey very different messages to their viewers.

Trumbull's painting, which he started ten years after the Battle of Princeton took place, makes Mercer's death heroic: he dies with sword in one hand, his other hand grasping the bayonet that will deliver his fatal wound. He literally stares death in the face, gazing directly into the eyes of his adversary. The worth of his sacrifice is evident by the action occurring behind him. While Mercer dies, General George Washington leads the Continental Army forward to victory.

Now consider O'Sullivan's 1863 photograph "A Harvest of Death," which he took two days after the fighting at Gettysburg. Corpses litter the battlefield to

The photo's title, "A Harvest of Death," calls to mind the fields on which the battle took place and invokes popular images of the Grim Reaper

Compare the shadowy figure on horseback to Washington's figure in Trumbull's painting

No evidence here that these dead soldiers ever saw the faces of their enemy

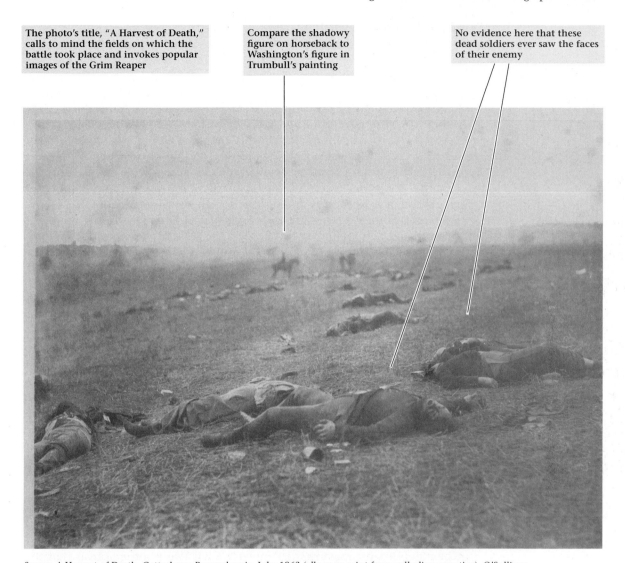

Source: A Harvest of Death, Gettysburg, Pennsylvania, July, 1863 (albumen print from collodion negative), O'Sullivan, Timothy (1840–82)/Dallas Museum of Art, Texas, USA/Foundation for the Arts Collection, Neiman-Marcus Foundation in memory of Alan Marcus Jacobus/Bridgeman Images.

the horizon. Their horrible disfiguration is most evident on the figure in the fore-ground, whose mouth gapes open and whose face, stomach, and hands have bloated in the process of decomposing. Off in the distance, a figure shrouded in mist appears on horseback, but this is not the confident commanding officer of Trumbull's painting. Rather, it is a ghostly presence surveying the battlefield, a Grim Reaper–like figure come to collect his harvest. Unlike Trumbull's painting, this photograph shows no evidence that these soldiers died heroic deaths or even saw the faces of their enemy. They are as anonymous as they are lifeless. This image, one of the most widely reproduced battlefield photographs of the Civil War, challenges the notions of military sacrifice and valor celebrated in

Trumbull's American Revolution painting. O'Sullivan's photograph testifies to the crisis that the massive casualties of the Civil War caused in the traditional values nineteenth-century Americans associated with military service.

Studying these photographs also reveals much about how civilians experienced the war. Photographers such as Brady and Gardner sold prints of their work almost as quickly as they made them, constructing a history of the war for public consumption while the conflict was still under way. Stereographs brought the war into the home for viewing the same way television does today, and *cartes-de-visite* made celebrities of political and military leaders of the war. By studying the arrangement of photographs in private collections or in the catalogs that advertised them for sale, historians can recover the civilian effort to make sense of the brutality and destruction the war unleashed.

One disadvantage of working with Civil War photographs is that there was no "blanket coverage" of the war by photographers. Their work favored the North and East at the expense of the South and West. The photography industry in the Confederacy all but collapsed after 1861 as the economic privations of the war increased. Also, the farther removed the scene of battle was from eastern urban centers, the less likely it was to be photographed. Antietam and Gettysburg were the most thoroughly photographed battlefields of the war. Not coincidentally, both were within ninety miles of Washington, D.C., where Brady and Gardner had galleries. By contrast, little to no photographic evidence exists of many campaigns west of the Appalachian Mountains.

Another disadvantage to bear in mind when looking at Civil War photographs is the technological limits on photographing battles as they occurred. Cameras had to be mounted on tripods and required exposure time measured in minutes rather than a fraction of a second. Because the glass plates had to be prepared, exposed, and developed in one continuous process, before their chemical coating dried and rendered them useless, photographers had to bring their darkrooms with them. As one historian of nineteenth-century photography has noted, these technical limitations meant that we have many "before" and "after" images of Civil War battlefields but no "during," because the photographers and their equipment were not mobile enough to capture the actual battles.

The chief disadvantage to working with Civil War photographs is that the photographers manipulated their subjects, dead as well as living, for commercial purposes. Brady, Gardner, and their peers were businessmen, and they took pictures that they thought would sell. If they could increase sales by posing their subjects in a particular manner, they did not hesitate to do so. Then and now, people invoked the phrase "the camera never lies" to emphasize the accuracy and impartiality of photography. Knowing something about how Civil War photographs were made, however, should dissuade you from taking that adage too literally when dealing with this source. When soldiers, officers, and civic leaders posed for their portraits, they assumed postures and carried props meant to broadcast their bravery, leadership, or virtue, but because of the long exposure time required for early photographs, even less formal scenes of camp life or field hospitals had to be carefully arranged by their photographers. One might assume that photographs of corpses on the battlefield were the least posed of the photographer's subjects, but Gardner and his associates moved bodies, added props, and altered backgrounds to achieve the effect they desired. If you remember that every Civil War photograph was posed in the sense that its creator and subjects went through a long, complicated process to produce it, then you will be less likely to assume that the camera presented an unfiltered representation of reality. The Checklist questions below will help you approach photographs like any other kind of historical source that needs to be analyzed and interpreted in light of the time and place it was produced.

CHECKLIST: Interrogating Photographs

- ☐ Who took the photograph? Is there a caption or credit line that identifies the photographer?
- ☐ Where and when was the photograph taken? If there is no caption or credit line to answer that, does the image itself offer any clues?
- ☐ Who or what is the subject of the photograph? If the photograph is of people, what relationship do they have to one another (for example, is it a family portrait, a group of friends)?
- ☐ What event is the photograph intended to document? What ideas, values, or emotions are the photographer and subject(s) trying to convey?
- ☐ Who is the intended audience for the photograph? What effect do you think the photograph had on its viewers?
- ☐ Can you detect any bias or agenda that the photographer may be promoting?

Source Analysis Table

The table on pages 254–55 will help you record your impressions of the photographs you will examine in the next section.

Photograph	What Is the Subject Matter of This Photograph?	What Information, Ideas, or Emotions Are the Photographer and Subjects Trying to Convey?	How Do You Think the Photograph Influenced Its Viewers' Experience of the War?
MILITARY PORTRAITS			
1. Lieut. Washington and Capt. Custer			
2. Gen. Potter and Staff			
3. Portrait of a Soldier Group			
4. Pres. Lincoln at Antietam			
BATTLEFIELD LANDSCAPES AND CITYSCAPES			
5. Gettysburg			
6. Ruins of Charleston			
AFRICAN AMERICANS IN MILITARY LIFE			
7. Brig. Gen. McLaughlin			
8. Culpeper "Contrabands"			
9. African American Soldiers and Officers			

Photograph	What Is the Subject Matter of This Photograph?	What Information, Ideas, or Emotions Are the Photographer and Subjects Trying to Convey?	How Do You Think the Photograph Influenced Its Viewers' Experience of the War?
BATTLEFIELD DEAD			
10. Antietam, Bodies for Burial			
11. A Contrast			
12. He Sleeps His Last Sleep			
13. Body of Soldier in the Wheat Field			
14. Field Where Gen. Reynolds Fell			
15. Fort Mahone, Petersburgh, Va.			
16. Cold Harbor, Va.			

The Source: Photographs of Civil War Battlefields and Military Life, 1861–1866

MILITARY PORTRAITS

Many soldiers posed in uniform for formal portraits before they left home. Photographers also brought their cameras to military camps near battlefields, to capture armies at work.

1   *Lieut. Washington, a Confederate Prisoner, and Capt. Custer, U.S.A.,* James F. Gibson, 1862

This photograph, published in one of Alexander Gardner's catalogs, has an interesting history. Lieutenant James Barroll Washington (left), a Confederate, was taken prisoner during McClellan's Peninsula Campaign in Virginia. Captain George Armstrong Custer (right), a Union officer who would achieve fame at Gettysburg a year later (and a different kind of notoriety at Little Big Horn in 1876), was an old friend of Washington's. Upon finding the two chatting amiably, James Gibson decided to photograph them. Washington called out for a young African American boy to join them. An illustration based on this image subsequently appeared in *Harper's Weekly* under the title *Both Sides, the Cause*.

Source: Library of Congress, Prints and Photographs Division.

2

Gen. Robert B. Potter and Staff of Seven, Recognized Capt. Gilbert H. McKibben, Capt. Wright, A.A.G. Also Mr. Brady, Photographer, Mathew Brady, c. 1863

Brady owed his reputation in the 1850s to photographing famous people, so it is not surprising that he devoted much of his work on the battlefield during the war to taking pictures of officers and their staffs. A relentless self-promoter, he also had a penchant for inserting himself into his own work. General Potter is the bareheaded figure at the center of this image. Brady, in civilian clothes, leans against a tree to the right.

Source: National Archives and Records Administration.

3   *Portrait of a Soldier Group,*
photographer unknown, c. 1861–1865

Soldiers often posed for portraits, either individually or in groups. Sometimes, as one soldier does here, they posed with weapons as well. Notice that two of the figures in this portrait are holding hands, a sign of intimacy that although rare in such photographs was not scandalous either.

Source: Library of Congress, Prints and Photographs Division.

4 | *President Lincoln on Battle-Field of Antietam*
Alexander Gardner, 1862

Gardner took this photograph when President Lincoln traveled to Antietam in October 1862 to confer with General McClellan. McClellan is to the left of Lincoln, standing in profile and facing the president. McClellan's staff forms an arc around the two figures.

Source: Photo Researchers/Getty Images.

BATTLEFIELD LANDSCAPES AND CITYSCAPES

Photographers often took pictures of battlefield landscapes and cityscapes, juxtaposing civilian and military life or depicting the destructive effects of the war.

5   *Pennsylvania, Gettysburg 07/1863*
Timothy O'Sullivan, 1863

O'Sullivan worked with Gardner in photographing the Gettysburg battlefield. This image, taken from a hill south of the town's center, shows the small remnant of a military camp after most of the Union and Confederate forces had withdrawn. During the Civil War, many small towns saw their farms and fields occupied by armies that dwarfed the local population.

Source: National Archives and Records Administration.

6   *Ruins of Charleston, S.C.,* George P. Barnard, 1866

Photographer George P. Barnard documented the devastating effect of war on the South. This image shows one of the South's greatest cities in ruins, with only two men in the scene, contemplating the destruction.

Source: George N. Barnard/George Eastman House/Getty Images.

AFRICAN AMERICANS IN MILITARY LIFE

African Americans, free and enslaved, worked on and near Civil War battlefields as soldiers and laborers. Slaves who ran away from their masters and sought refuge with the Union army were known as "contrabands." Before the Emancipation Proclamation, they occupied a limbo between freedom and slavery. Union officers did not have the legal authority to free them, but neither did they wish to return them to their masters, where their labor might benefit the Confederate war effort. Many contrabands ended up in battlefield and camp photographs.

7   ### Portrait of Brig. Gen. Napoleon B. McLaughlin, Officer of the Federal Army, and Staff, Vicinity of Washington, D.C., Mathew Brady, 1861

This photograph from early in the war is typical of Brady's portraits of Union officers and their staffs (see Source 2 on p. 257). Sometimes these portraits included African Americans, posed in subservient positions to indicate their status as servants.

Source: Library of Congress, Prints and Photographs Division.

8   *Culpeper, Va. "Contrabands,"* Timothy O'Sullivan, 1863

African American men worked for Union and Confederate armies in a number of capacities. These two men are pictured outside a cook's tent at a Union camp.

Source: Library of Congress, Prints and Photographs Division.

9 *African American Soldiers with Their Teachers and Officers,* photographer and date unknown

Many African American men, including contrabands, enlisted in the Union army and were photographed in uniform. These recruits posed with their white commanding officers and female teachers. Instead of bearing arms, the recruits hold books.

Source: Library of Congress, Prints and Photographs Division.

BATTLEFIELD DEAD

Battlefield dead made up only a tiny fraction of Civil War photographs, but they became some of the most enduring visual images of the war. To take such images, a photographer had to arrive on the battlefield before corpses were buried, usually within two days of the fighting. Gardner's and O'Sullivan's photographs from Antietam and Gettysburg are the most famous of this category, but equally powerful ones were taken after other battles in the war's eastern theater, including Cold Harbor and Petersburg, both in Virginia.

10 | ### *Antietam, Md. Bodies of Dead Gathered for Burial*
Alexander Gardner, 1862

This image, one of the Antietam series exhibited in Mathew Brady's New York gallery, presents a line of corpses arranged as if in formation. No single soldier is identified. The line running across the photograph is from a crack in the original glass plate.

Source: Library of Congress, Prints and Photographs Division.

11   *A Contrast. Federal Buried; Confederate Unburied, Where They Fell on the Battle Field of Antietam*
Alexander Gardner, 1862

This is a stereograph of one of Gardner's Antietam photographs. It juxtaposes the marked grave of Union officer John A. Clark with the unburied corpse of an anonymous Confederate soldier.

Source: Collection of the New-York Historical Society, id number ad18001.

Entered according to Act of Congress, in the year 1863, by Alex. Gardner, in the Clerk's Office of the District Court of the District of Columbia.

12 *He Sleeps His Last Sleep,* Alexander Gardner, 1862

As he did with the image shown in Source 11, Gardner sold stereographs and album cards of this Antietam photograph via his catalog. Unlike most of his other photographs of the dead from the Battle of Antietam, this one shows a single casualty far removed from any other fallen soldiers. Gardner's catalog caption for this image read: "A Confederate Soldier, who after being wounded, had evidently dragged himself to a little ravine on the hill-side, where he died."

Source: Collection of the New-York Historical Society, id number ad04002.

Entered according to Act of Congress, in the year 1864, by Alex. Gardner, in the Clerk's Office of the District Court of the District of Columbia.

13 *Battlefield of Gettysburg—Body of a Soldier in "the Wheat Field," Evidently Killed by the Explosion of a Shell,* James F. Gibson, 1863 (next page)

Photographers manipulated their subjects, even dead ones, to achieve the desired effect. Gibson accompanied Gardner to Gettysburg to take photographs after the battle. In his catalog, Gardner described this anonymous soldier as a sharpshooter, but a sharpshooter would not have affixed a bayonet to his weapon. Also, by the time photographers reached battlefield corpses, the soldiers' weapons had usually been collected by the victorious army or by scavengers. The weapon shown here is a "prop gun" placed there by Gibson or Gardner; it shows up in several of their Gettysburg photographs. The photographer also placed an unexploded shell near the corpse's right knee to suggest the source of the horrible wound in the abdomen. It is more likely that a pig fed on the body shortly after death. The dismembered hand and canteen in the right foreground are also likely props.

Source: Library of Congress, Prints and Photographs Division.

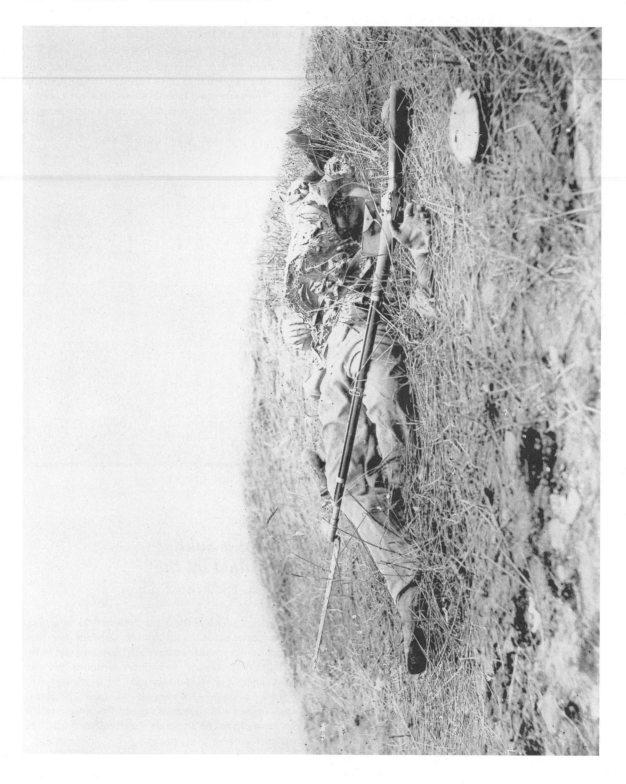

14   *Field Where General Reynolds Fell, Gettysburg*
Timothy O'Sullivan, 1863

This image from the Gettysburg battlefield stands in sharp contrast to the caption Gardner chose for it. Reynolds was the highest-ranking Union officer killed at Gettysburg and became in death one of the battle's heroes. This image offers no trace of Reynolds (in fact, he was killed in a wooded area), only anonymous, bloodied, and bloated corpses.

Source: Dead on the Field of Gettysburg, July 1863, American Photographer, (19th century)/Private Collection/Peter Newark American Pictures/Bridgeman Images.

15   *. . . View of the Covered Ways inside the Rebel Fort Mahone, Called by the Soldiers "Fort Damnation" . . . Taken the Morning after the Storming of Petersburgh, Va. 1865,* T. C. Roche, 1865

T. C. Roche, a former cameraman for Mathew Brady, documented the Union army's assault on Petersburg, a vital railroad junction in Virginia, in April 1865. This stereographic image of a solitary Confederate soldier lying dead in one of the trenches built to defend the city anticipates the photographs that would document trench warfare in World War I. The spiked device in the foreground is a cheval-de-frise, a type of movable fortification designed to slow an enemy advance.

Source: Collection of the New-York Historical Society, id number ad41018.

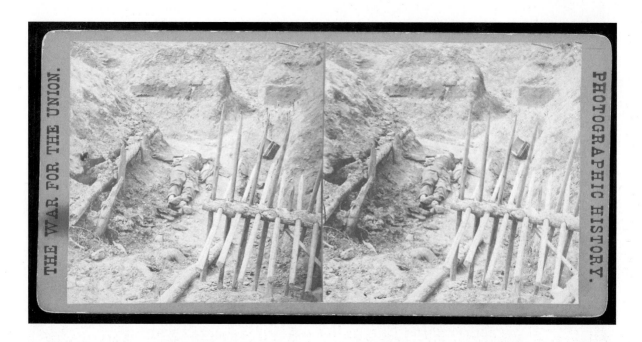

16 | *Cold Harbor, Va. African Americans Collecting Bones of Soldiers Killed in Battle,* John Reekie, 1865

John Reekie was a cameraman for Alexander Gardner and worked with him documenting the final weeks of the war in Virginia in 1865. In this photograph, a burial party made up of African American men is collecting and interring the skeletal remains of soldiers who had died on the Cold Harbor battlefield almost a year earlier. The figures working in the background suggest that Reekie has captured them "in action," but bear in mind that the exposure time required for such a photograph would have meant that they were posed. Likewise, the skull on the far left appears to have been posed to stare directly at the photograph's viewer. The glass plate used to make this image has been damaged, as evidenced by the crack across the photograph and the missing shard on the right-hand side.

Source: Library of Congress, Prints and Photographs Division.

Analyzing Civil War Photographs

1. Overall, would you describe these photographs as critical of the war or supportive of it? Does your answer to this question vary if you ask it of individual groups of photographs (for example, "Military Portraits" or "African Americans in Military Life") rather than of the entire lot?

2. How is death presented and interpreted in these photographs? How do the images challenge the notions of military glory and valor embodied in earlier military art such as Trumbull's *Death of General Mercer* (p. 250)? Compare the notes you took on Sources 10, 11, 14, and 16 with those you took on Sources 12, 13, and 15. What messages do you think photographers were trying to convey when they "posed" the dead either as individuals or in groups?

3. How do these photographs present African Americans and the role they played in the Civil War? Did the depiction of African Americans in these images change over time? How does that depiction compare with what you have learned about African Americans and slavery in earlier chapters?

4. Civil War photographers marketed their work to a civilian audience. What needs do you think these images fulfilled for the civilian population during and after the war? How might the visual record of the war have differed had the South been able to sustain a photography industry as productive as the North's during the war?

5. Compare these images with the visual records you have seen of warfare in the twentieth and twenty-first centuries (for example, photographs, films, documentaries, newscasts). In what ways did the Civil War establish precedents for the ways in which today's society uses visual images to transmit and document information from the battlefield for the civilian population?

The Rest of the Story

Some Civil War photographers collected the best of their work into albums for sale to the public. Gardner's two-volume *Gardner's Photographic Sketch Book of the Civil War* (first edition, 1865) offered a selection of one hundred of his most popular photographs, arranged to provide a chronological narrative of the war, but its $150 price tag put it far beyond the reach of most American consumers. Such collections had a limited audience because of their expense. For most people, their visual record of the Civil War remained a portrait of a soldier in uniform or a few stereographs or *cartes-de-visite* purchased from a catalog or at a photographer's gallery.

After the war, Gardner took his camera west to photograph the Union Pacific Railroad expedition of 1867, landscapes, and American Indians. He also pioneered the use of what are now called "mug shots," taking photographs of criminals for the police department of Washington, D.C. He died in 1882, leaving behind a reputation as one of the most innovative photographers of the nineteenth century.

Mathew Brady spent much of his career after the Civil War trying to sell his collection of negatives so that he could pay off his debts. Always more of an impresario than an actual working photographer, he continued to live in a high style long after he could afford to do so. In 1872, Congress approved purchasing Brady's collection for $25,000. Despite this deal, he declared bankruptcy a few years later and spent much of his remaining life dodging his creditors. He died in 1896, regarded as the Civil War's greatest photographer, even though he took very few of the pictures published under his name.

The work of Civil War photographers like Brady and Gardner marked the birth of photojournalism. For the first time, photographers used their craft to convey news of the world around them to a waiting public. The Civil War forever wedded the camera to U.S. warfare. During the war, the popular press had to rely on images reproduced from engravings, although many of those were based on photographs. By World War I, printing technology allowed for photographic reproductions in newspapers and magazines. During World War II, newsreel footage of Pacific and European battlefields brought the war home to Americans, but these images were heavily edited by the government to limit the public's exposure to the sort of carnage depicted in Civil War battlefield photographs. The Vietnam War was America's first televised war, and much of the public's discontent with that conflict can be traced to the images broadcast into American living rooms every night by photojournalists working half a world away.

In 2003, in the early days of the Iraq War, the phrase "embedded journalist" entered the American lexicon, as reporters traveling with military personnel used digital technology to transmit war coverage to American televisions in real time. These reporters are the modern descendants of Alexander Gardner and other Civil War photographers who attached themselves to military units and traveled to battlefields. In many respects, however, Gardner and his contemporaries enjoyed greater freedom in deciding what to report and how to publish it than military journalists do today. The camera may never lie, but the constant improvement in photographic technology since the 1860s does not necessarily mean that images produced by it today are any more truthful or complete than those produced during the Civil War.

To Find Out More

Collections of Civil War Photographs

National Historical Society. *The Image of War.* 6 vols. Garden City, NY: Doubleday, 1981–1984.

"Pictures of the Civil War." National Archives. http://www.archives.gov/research/military/civil-war/photos/index.html.

"Selected Civil War Photographs." *American Memory*. Library of Congress. http://memory.loc.gov/ammem/cwphtml/cwphome.html.

Secondary Sources on Civil War Photographers and Photography

Frassanito, William. *Antietam: The Photographic Legacy of America's Bloodiest Day*. 1978; repr., New York: Simon and Schuster, 1995.

Frassanito, William. *Gettysburg: A Journey in Time*. New York: Charles Scribner's Sons, 1975.

Frassanito, William. *Grant and Lee: The Virginia Campaigns, 1864–65*. New York: Charles Scribner's Sons, 1983.

Katz, D. Mark. *Witness to an Era: The Life and Photographs of Alexander Gardner*. Nashville, TN: Rutledge Hill Press, 1991.

Panzer, Mary. *Mathew Brady and the Image of History*. Washington, DC: Smithsonian Institution Press, 1997.

Trachtenberg, Alan. *Reading American Photographs*. New York: Hill and Wang, 1989.

CHAPTER 13

Political Terrorism during Reconstruction

Congressional Hearings and Reports on the Ku Klux Klan

Elias Thomson was an old man in 1871. Born a slave in Spartanburg County, South Carolina, he had lived his entire life on the plantation of Dr. and Mrs. Vernon. When he gained his freedom in 1865, he continued to live there, farming land he rented from his former masters. Thomson's daily life after the war must have gone on much the same as it did before, but freedom did bring some opportunities he was anxious to seize, even at his advanced age. In particular, the ratification of the Fifteenth Amendment in March 1870 guaranteed him the right to vote. Thomson exercised that right in the fall of 1870, casting his ballot in the state and congressional elections for the Republican ticket.

Late one night the following May, a group of men disguised in hoods appeared on his doorstep. They dragged him from his home and told him to start praying, for "your time is short." When Thomson refused, they pointed pistols at his head and asked him, "Who did you vote for?" Thomson responded that he had voted for Claudius Turner, a neighbor whom he held in high esteem. The disguised men told him he had made the wrong choice and whipped him. They told Thomson to remain silent about what had happened and left him with a final warning: "We will have this country right before we get through."

Thomson was one of many Southern men and women to suffer at the hands of the Ku Klux Klan between 1867 and 1871. In fact, his hometown of Spartanburg, South Carolina, was at the center of one of the most violent and prolonged outbreaks of Klan activity during Reconstruction. The Klan had first appeared there in 1868, using intimidation, arson, whippings, sexual assault, and murder to keep potential Republican voters away from the polls in that year's election. Despite such efforts, the state government remained in the hands of the Republicans, and the Klan temporarily receded as a public threat in 1869.

Klan violence rose again, however, with the next election in 1870, and it became more intense as white and black Republicans tried to mobilize the vote. In addition to intimidation and physical assaults on potential black voters, Klansmen burned black churches, schools, and homes and murdered black men who had enrolled in the state militia. In several counties of the Carolina up-country, the inland piedmont region where white and black populations were roughly equal or whites held a slight majority, the Klan conducted these crimes without fear of prosecution. Local sheriffs failed to make arrests, and if they did, white juries refused to deliver guilty verdicts. In some up-country counties, such as Spartanburg, state Republican officials estimated that practically the entire white adult male population belonged to the Klan or sympathized with it.

The Ku Klux Klan was of very recent origins in 1871 but had spread quickly throughout the former Confederate states. It was founded in 1867 by a group of Confederate veterans in Pulaski, Tennessee, who initially intended for it to be nothing more than a social club, similar to the Freemasons and other secret fraternal orders popular with American men in the nineteenth century. Like the Freemasons, early Klan members created their own ritual, costume, and hierarchy from a mishmash of precedents in ancient mythology: the name "Ku Klux" was derived from the Greek word *kuklos*, meaning circle, and one of the titles in the organization was "Grand Cyclops," named after a figure in Greek mythology. As the Klan spread, however, it acquired a different purpose. In Tennessee and the Carolinas in 1868, local "dens" of the Klan began to act as vigilantes, calling themselves "regulators" or "night riders" who enforced law and order according to local custom rather than the dictates of the postwar state governments created by Congress and the Republican Party. Local Klansmen operated autonomously and rarely cooperated with one another beyond the county level. Regardless of that fragmentation, the primary targets of the Klan's terrorism remained the same: any blacks who challenged white supremacy by daring to vote, teach, or acquire land; and "carpetbaggers," white Northerners who came to the South seeking their fortunes or taking positions in the Reconstruction state governments.

The violence and intimidation the Klan visited upon freedmen, freedwomen, and white Republicans seriously challenged the federal government's plans for the postwar South. After passing the Civil Rights Act of 1866, congressional Republicans had pegged their hopes for Reconstruction on enfranchising the former slaves as full and equal U.S. citizens. In this manner, the freedmen would become a core constituency for the Republican Party in the South and prevent the defeated Confederates from reassuming control there. The ratification of the Fourteenth Amendment in 1868 made this plan part of the Constitution by granting former slaves U.S. citizenship and guaranteeing them equal protection under the law. When some Southern states failed to extend their franchise to the freedmen, Republicans in Congress responded with the Fifteenth Amendment, which prohibited states from denying the right to vote to any citizen because of "race, color, or previous condition of servitude."

Republicans had great success in passing their legislative agenda for Reconstruction in Washington, D.C., but the enforcement of those laws in the South remained very much in question. The twenty thousand federal troops stationed

Figure 13.1 Racial Violence in the Reconstruction South Political cartoonist Thomas
Nast condemns the Ku Klux Klan and other perpetrators of racial violence in this illustration
from the magazine Harper's Weekly. At the center, a black couple kneeling under the words
"Worse Than Slavery" cradle their dead child, while a schoolhouse burns and a lynched figure
hangs in the background. A hooded Klansman and "White League" supporter clasp hands over
their work. The federal government intervened by passing the Ku Klux Klan Act and launching
a congressional investigation of racial violence in the South. *Source:* Library of Congress, Prints and
Photograph Division.

in the South in 1867 were not nearly enough to pacify regions such as the Carolina up-country, where the Klan was at its greatest strength. Furthermore, military officers were reluctant to assume control over matters of law enforcement
without specific requests from civilian authorities to do so lest they alienate the
defeated Southern white population even further. As news of the Klan's expansion and pervasive influence in the South made its way to the nation's capital,
Republican leaders agreed that federal action against it was necessary.

In a special message to Congress in December 1870, President Ulysses S. Grant noted that the Klan and similar organizations were using violence to prevent citizens from voting in the Southern states. Acting on a request he had received from the governor of North Carolina, he asked Congress to investigate the matter. Congress formed a committee to review affairs in North Carolina and then, in April 1871, created another, much larger committee to expand the investigation into other states. This latter group, titled the Joint Select Committee to Inquire into the Condition of Affairs in the Late Insurrectionary States, had twenty-one members—seven senators and fourteen representatives—thirteen of whom were Republicans and eight of whom were Democrats.

At approximately the same time it formed the Joint Select Committee to investigate the Klan, Congress also passed the Ku Klux Klan Act. This law gave the president the power to use federal troops and courts to protect the lives, property, and rights of U.S. citizens in the South. For the first time, crimes committed by private persons against other citizens became eligible for prosecution under federal rather than state law. Provisions included in the Ku Klux Klan Act effectively gave the president the ability to declare martial law in any state or region he deemed under Klan influence. The most controversial of these provisions concerned suspension of the writ of habeas corpus, a cornerstone of civil liberties in the United States. The writ of habeas corpus protects citizens from unlawful imprisonment by requiring that any person placed under arrest be charged with a specific crime and placed on trial. By allowing the president to suspend this writ, Congress made it possible for suspected Klansmen to be jailed indefinitely. Many congressmen, even some Republicans, questioned the constitutionality of this provision and of the Ku Klux Klan Act in general, but the majority who supported the law believed that the Klan could not be defeated without such powerful measures.

Members of Congress formulated and debated this legislation in Washington while African Americans in the South confronted the Klan face-to-face. Casting a ballot or even expressing an interest in voting could put a former slave's life in jeopardy. Those who joined militias, held office, or tried to improve their economic circumstances faced similar reprisals, and the promise of assistance from Washington must have seemed far off indeed. In 1871, a showdown was brewing between the Ku Klux Klan and the federal government that placed people like Elias Thomson squarely in the middle of the battle to determine Reconstruction's fate.

Using the Source: Congressional Hearings and Reports

The Joint Select Committee undertook one of the most far-reaching congressional investigations ever conducted up to that time. During the summer and fall of 1871, it heard testimony from witnesses in Washington, D.C., and sent subcommittees to interview witnesses throughout the South. Most of its work was concentrated on North Carolina and South Carolina, where the activities and effect of the Klan were reported to be most severe, but committee members also visited Alabama, Florida, Georgia, Mississippi, and Tennessee, compiling thousands of pages of testimony. In February 1872, the Joint Select Committee submitted this testimony and its reports to Congress. The majority report, signed by every Republican on the committee, endorsed the Ku Klux Klan Act of 1871 and recommended continuing the president's powers to combat the Klan through the use of federal troops, courts, and suspension of the writ of habeas corpus. The minority report, signed by every Democrat on the committee, did not deny the existence of Klan-related violence but blamed it on misguided federal Reconstruction policy, which had left the Southern states in the hands of carpetbaggers and former slaves.

What Can Congressional Hearings and Reports Tell Us?

Since its publication in 1872, historians have found the thirteen volumes of the Joint Select Committee's report a remarkably detailed and comprehensive source for studying Reconstruction in the South. One of its chief advantages as a source is its sheer size. The committee conducted its work thoroughly, and the hundreds of witnesses who testified before it represented a broad spectrum of Southern society: white and black, rich and poor, male and female, Republican and Democrat. One historian has called their testimony "the richest single source" for understanding Southern society during the Reconstruction era. In the case of African Americans, testimony before the committee provides invaluable first-person narratives of what the transition from bondage to freedom was like.

Another advantage of working with this source has to do with the methods by which the Joint Select Committee collected its evidence. Its procedures resembled legal hearings: oaths were administered to witnesses, and witnesses were subjected to cross-examination, all in meetings open to the public. No witnesses appeared anonymously or gave secret testimony. Although those procedures may have prevented many from testifying for fear of reprisals, they nevertheless lent an air of authenticity to the witnesses' descriptions of the Klan that was not accorded to rumors or sensationalistic stories reported in the press. The Klan conducted its terrorism under cover of night and in disguise. By its very nature, it did not submit willingly to public scrutiny. For the most part, however, the witnesses who appeared before the committee in Southern towns and counties were eyewitnesses to the Klan's activities, making their testimony the most complete and reliable account of this secret organization's operations during Reconstruction.

The disadvantages associated with using the Joint Select Committee's report stem mostly from its inherent political biases. The Republicans who dominated the Joint Select Committee by a two-to-one margin were most interested in finding evidence that the Klan was a conspiratorial organization bent on depriving black and white Republicans of their civil and political liberties. Such evidence could be used to justify imposing martial law in those regions affected by the Klan. Democrats accused the Republicans of using the committee to drum up stories of Klan brutality and lawlessness that could be publicized to Republican advantage in the upcoming election of 1872. Although the Democrats on the committee could not deny the violence of the Klan, they used their questioning of witnesses to cast doubt on its political motives, depicting Klansmen instead as isolated, ill-advised characters pushed to extremes by desperation and offended honor. It is important to remember that Congress had already passed the Ku Klux Klan Act when the Joint Select Committee conducted its work. Given that the committee's majority was made up of the same Republicans who had passed that piece of legislation, how likely was it that the committee's findings would challenge its enforcement? By passing the Ku Klux Klan Act *before* its investigation of the Klan, Congress clearly anticipated the outcome of the Joint Select Committee's work.

As you read the testimony, you will quickly realize that neither the Republicans nor the Democrats on the Joint Select Committee resembled neutral fact finders; each side brought an agenda to the proceedings. Consider, for example, these excerpts from the testimony of D. H. Chamberlain, the Republican attorney general of South Carolina, given before the committee in Washington, D.C., on June 10, 1871. A good historian quickly learns to read between the lines of such evidence, looking carefully at the questions as well as the answers to determine what biases and ulterior motives are contained in this source.

D. H. Chamberlain, sworn and examined.

By the Chairman:

> *Question:* How long have you been a resident of the State?
>
> *Answer:* I have been a resident there since December, 1865.
>
> *Question:* Please go on and state to the committee the knowledge you have acquired, from your official position, as to the efficiency with which the laws are executed throughout the State of South Carolina, and the protection afforded to life and property in the State. Make your statement in general terms.
>
> *Answer:* The enforcement of the law has, from time to time, been very much interrupted and disturbed from special causes; lately by what are popularly known as Ku-Klux operations. . . .

An oath to tell the truth similar to that given in a court of law

Republican senator John Scott of Pennsylvania chaired the committee and typically initiated the questioning

Invites Chamberlain to speak freely about law enforcement

By Mr. Van Trump: ——————————————————————

Philadelph Van Trump, a Democratic representative from Ohio, typically led the cross-examination

Returns to the subject of Chamberlain's background, seeking to discredit him as a carpetbagger

Question: You say you went to South Carolina in 1865?

Answer: Yes, sir.

Question: How long after the termination of the war; what part of the year?

Answer: I went in December, 1865.

Question: From where did you go?

Answer: From Massachusetts. I had been in the Union army during the war. I settled at Charleston in December, 1865, and remained there, and my residence is there now, although I have to be at the capital of the State most of the time.

Source: United States Congress, *Report of the Joint Select Committee to Inquire into the Condition of Affairs in the Late Insurrectionary States*, vol. 2, *South Carolina, Part 1* (Washington, DC: Government Printing Office, 1872), 48–51.

One other disadvantage to bear in mind about the Joint Select Committee's report is that even though the committee's hearings had the appearance of legal proceedings, the committee did not work with the same standards of evidence as a court of law. In particular, the Republican majority of the committee was willing to accept hearsay, what someone had heard but not personally witnessed, as evidence. Democrats on the committee objected, likening it to accepting rumors and gossip as facts. They accused local Republican officials of coaching witnesses, and they equated the $2-a-day allowance the committee paid to witnesses with bribery. In the thousands of pages of testimony in the Joint Select Committee's report, some witnesses do appear more reliable than others.

Congressional hearings have remained a part of our national politics, and today they are often televised. They serve an important role in the legislative process by acting as fact-finding investigations for members of Congress. They also provide an opportunity for congressional leaders to push their own political agendas before large audiences, regardless of the testimony they are hearing from witnesses. The Checklist questions on page 282 will help you read congressional hearings and reports with a critical eye that takes into account the politics as well as the issues involved in such sources.

CHECKLIST: Interrogating Congressional Hearings and Reports

☐ What issue or legislation is the hearing investigating?

☐ Who is the witness providing the testimony? Where is the witness from, and why is he or she testifying?

☐ What does the witness say in his or her testimony?

☐ Who are the members of Congress conducting the hearings? What do you know about their backgrounds and political affiliations?

☐ How reliable does the testimony appear to be? Is it based on first-hand experience, personal opinion, or hearsay?

☐ What bias is evident in the questions being asked of the witness?

☐ What measures do the congressional investigators recommend in their report on the testimony they have heard? If there is a minority report, how does it differ in its interpretation of the testimony and its recommendations for action from the majority report?

Source Analysis Table

As you read the witness testimonies and committee reports, use the following table to organize your notes on the descriptions of the Klan, the reliability of the evidence provided, and your assessment of the majority and minority reports.

Source	Personal Information	Description of the Klan's Activities and Motives	Reliability of Evidence Provided
WITNESS TESTIMONY			
1. Samuel T. Poinier			
2. D. H. Chamberlain			
3. Elias Thomson			
4. Lucy McMillan			
5. Mervin Givens			

(continued)

Source	Description of the Klan	Assessment of Federal Response to the Klan
COMMITTEE REPORTS		
6. Majority Report		
7. Minority Report		

The Source: Testimony and Reports from the Joint Select Committee to Inquire into the Condition of Affairs in the Late Insurrectionary States

The testimony that follows is taken from the Joint Select Committee's investigation of the Ku Klux Klan in South Carolina. Sources 1 and 2 come from testimony heard in Washington, D.C., whereas Sources 3, 4, and 5 are from testimony heard in Spartanburg, South Carolina. Sources 6 and 7 are excerpts from the committee's majority and minority reports, respectively, which were completed after the investigation was over.

WITNESS TESTIMONY

1. *Testimony of Samuel T. Poinier,*
Washington, D.C., June 7, 1871

Poinier was a Republican newspaper editor and a federal tax collector in South Carolina at the time of his testimony.

Samuel T. Poinier sworn and examined.

By the Chairman:[1]

>*Question:* Please state in what part of South Carolina you reside.
>*Answer:* In Spartanburg County, the most northern county in the State.
>*Question:* How long have you resided there?
>*Answer:* Since February, 1866; a little over five years.
>*Question:* From what part of the United States did you go to South Carolina?
>*Answer:* I went there from Louisville, Kentucky. . . . I went there in 1866 with
no intention whatever of remaining. I went entirely for social reasons, to marry, and I was persuaded to stay there. My wife was a native of Charleston, and I found her up in Spartanburg after the war, where a large number of Charleston people went during the bombardment of the city. . . .
>*Question:* Were you in the Union Army?
>*Answer:* Yes, sir: I went out from Kentucky.

[1] Republican senator John Scott from Pennsylvania.

Source: United States Congress, *Report of the Joint Select Committee to Inquire into the Condition of Affairs in the Late Insurrectionary States*, vol. 2, *South Carolina, Part I* (Washington, DC: Government Printing Office, 1872), 25–28, 33–34.

Question: Proceed with your statement.

Answer: Just before our last campaign,[2] it was May a year ago, I . . . identified myself publicly with the republican party. I made my paper a republican paper. I did everything I could in the last State election for the reelection of Governor Scott[3] and our other State officers. From that time I have been in very deep water. . . . I was ordered away last fall, immediately after our last election, in November. It was soon after the first appearance of this Ku-Klux organization, or whatever it is. Soon after these outrages occurred in our county I received a note ordering me away from there, stating that I must leave the county; that all the soldiers of the United States Army could not enable me to live in Spartanburg. . . . Two days prior to our election, a party of disguised men went, at night, and took out two white men and three negroes, one of them a colored woman, and whipped them most brutally. Two of them were managers of the box[4] at that election; and the men told them that if they dared to hold an election at that box they would return and kill them. That was the first appearance of any trouble in the State. . . .

Question: Were those people of whom you spoke in disguise?

Answer: They were all in disguise. One of the colored men who were whipped swore positively as to the identity of some of them, and the parties were arrested, but nothing could ever be done with them; they proved an *alibi*, and some of them have since gone to Texas. . . .

Question: Go on and state any similar occurrences in that county since that time. . . .

Answer: Since that time outrages of that nature have occurred every week. Parties of disguised men have ridden through the county almost nightly. They go to a colored man's house, take him out and whip him. They tell him that he must not give any information that he has been whipped. They tell him, moreover, that he must make a public renunciation of his republican principles or they will return and kill him. . . .

Question: Do the facts that have transpired and the manner in which they have occurred satisfy you of the existence of the organization in that portion of South Carolina?

Answer: Yes, sir; I have no doubt of it in the world. I have received anonymous communications signed by the order of "K.K.K.," directing me to leave the county, stating that I could not live there; that I was a carpet-bagger. But personally I have never met with any trouble.

By Mr. Van Trump:[5]

Question: You have a connection with the partisan press there?

Answer: Yes, sir. I am editing a republican paper.

---

[2] The election of 1870.

[3] Robert K. Scott was the Republican governor of South Carolina.

[4] Ballot box.

[5] Democratic representative Philadelph Van Trump from Ohio.

Question: Do you advocate the cause of the negro in your paper?

Answer: Not the negro especially. I advocate the general principles of republicanism.

Question: You support the whole republican doctrine in your paper?

Answer: So far as general principles go, I do. I do not approve or uphold the State government in many of its acts; but, so far as the general principles of republicanism are concerned, I uphold it very strongly. I advocate the right of the colored people to vote and to exercise their civil and political privileges. . . .

Question: These men who assert that their object is to put down the negro and get possession of the Government are prominent men, are they not?

Answer: Yes, sir.

Question: Can you name a single man?

Answer: Well, I cannot name anybody specially who has made such a remark, but I hear it in the hotels.

Question: Have you yourself heard them make the remark?

Answer: I have heard the remark made; it is a common thing.

Question: Is it not rather an uncommon remark?

Answer: It is not, there.

Question: You cannot recollect the name of a single person who has made that declaration?

Answer: No sir, I cannot recall any now.

2   *Testimony of D. H. Chamberlain,*
Washington, D.C., June 10, 1871

Chamberlain was a Republican and the attorney general of South Carolina.

D. H. Chamberlain, sworn and examined.

By the Chairman:

Question: How long have you been a resident of the State?

Answer: I have been a resident there since December, 1865.

Question: Please go on and state to the committee the knowledge you have acquired, from your official position, as to the efficiency with which the laws are executed throughout the State of South Carolina, and the protection afforded to life and property in the State. Make your statement in general terms.

Answer: The enforcement of the law has, from time to time, been very much interrupted and disturbed from special causes; lately by what are popularly known as Ku-Klux operations. There have been a great many outrages committed, and

Source: Report of the Joint Select Committee, vol. 2, South Carolina, Part I, 48–51.

a great many homicides, and a great many whippings. I speak now, of course, of what I have heard; I have never seen any outrages committed myself; I am simply stating what I believe to be fact. . . .

Question: In what part of the State are these offenses committed which you attribute to the influence of this organization?

Answer: Notably in Spartanburg, Newberry, Union, and York Counties; those are the principal counties that have been the scenes of these disturbances. But they have extended into Laurens, Chester, and Lancaster Counties.[1] . . .

Question: Have there been any convictions for these offenses in the State, so far as your information goes; offenses committed by these organized bands?

Answer: No sir, no convictions, and no arrests, except in the case of this wounded Ku-Klux.[2] . . .

By Mr. Van Trump:

Question: You say you went to South Carolina in 1865?

Answer: Yes, sir.

Question: How long after the termination of the war; what part of the year?

Answer: I went in December, 1865.

Question: From where did you go?

Answer: From Massachusetts. I had been in the Union army during the war. I settled at Charleston in December, 1865, and remained there, and my residence is there now, although I have to be at the capital of the State most of the time.

By Mr. Stevenson:[3]

Question: When did it first come to your knowledge that this organization existed in the State of South Carolina?

Answer: It would be difficult to say. My conviction that there is such an organization has grown up very gradually. . . . I cannot fix the date exactly.

Question: Had you any knowledge of the fact that there were acts of violence and disorders in that State about the time of the election in 1868?

Answer: Yes, sir.

Question: Had you any information of the sending of arms at that time into that State?

Answer: O, I remember that a great many arms were purchased by private individuals, if you refer to that. I know that at the time, during the canvass,[4] there was considerable excitement when it was understood that the democrats,

---

[1] All seven of these counties were in the piedmont, or up-country, region of South Carolina, where the black and white populations were roughly equal.

[2] Chamberlain is referring to a Klansman wounded during a raid on the Newberry County Courthouse. He was jailed and then released on bail and subsequently either died while in the care of a friend or was spirited away by friends to avoid prosecution.

[3] Republican representative Job Stevenson from Ohio.

[4] Campaigning for votes.

as we call them, were arming themselves with Winchester and Henry rifles, or something of the kind.

Question: Repeating rifles?

Answer: Yes, sir. . . .

By Mr. Blair:[5]

Question: Did you have any actual knowledge of the fact that the democrats were then arming?

Answer: No, sir.

Question: Then you make this statement as a rumor merely?

Answer: Well, yes, sir; I should use, perhaps, a little stronger term than rumor. I had heard it so often that it came to be a belief with me, but it was hearsay. . . .

Question: Was it a common report that those arms all went into the hands of democrats?

Answer: As I heard it, it was understood that those arms were imported into the State upon order of individuals. I do not know but a republican might have had his order filled, but the belief was that they were generally ordered by democrats.

By Mr. Stevenson:

Question: You have no knowledge of any general arming among the republicans at that time?

Answer: No, sir.

Question: You were a republican, then, were you not?

Answer: Yes, sir.

By Mr. Blair:

Question: Did not the republicans have arms?

Answer: O, yes.

By Mr. Van Trump:

Question: Did not the negroes have arms?

Answer: Yes, sir; it is very common for people to have their shot-guns, to have some kind of arms. I suppose that in this instance people thought that there was an unusually large number brought in at a particular time, and that they were not for sporting purposes. They were repeating rifles.

Question: Have you been a politician for any part of your life?

Answer: No, sir; I do not think I have ever been a politician.

Question: Have you never heard a thousand rumors during an election that had no foundation in fact?

Answer: Yes, sir; many of them.

Question: Got up for excitement merely?

Answer: Yes, sir.

[5] Democratic senator Frank Blair from Missouri.

3

Testimony of Elias Thomson,
Spartanburg, South Carolina, July 7, 1871

Elias Thomson (colored) sworn and examined.

By the Chairman:

> *Question:* Where do you live?
> *Answer:* Up on Tiger River, on Mrs. Vernon's plantation.[1]
> *Question:* What do you follow?
> *Answer:* Farming.
> *Question:* Do you live on rented land?
> *Answer:* Yes, sir.
> *Question:* How much have you rented?
> *Answer:* I think about fifty acres.
> *Question:* How long have you been living there?
> *Answer:* Ever since the surrender; I never left home.
> *Question:* Have you ever been disturbed any up there?
> *Answer:* Yes, sir.
> *Question:* How?

Answer: There came a parcel of gentlemen to my house one night—or men. They went up to the door and ran against it. My wife was sick. I was lying on a pallet, with my feet to the door. They ran against it and hallooed to me, "Open the door, quick, quick, quick." I threw the door open immediately, right wide open. Two little children were lying with me. I said, "Come in gentlemen." One of them says, "Do we look like gentlemen?" I says, "You look like men of some description; walk in." One says, "Come out here; are you ready to die?" I told him I was not prepared to die. "Well," said he, "Your time is short; commence praying." I told him I was not a praying man much, and hardly ever prayed; only a very few times; never did pray much. He says, "You ought to pray; your time is short, and now commence to pray." I told him I was not a praying man. One of them held a pistol to my head and said, "Get down and pray." I was on the steps, with one foot on the ground. They led me off to a pine tree. There was three or four of them behind me, it appeared, and one on each side, and one in front. The gentleman who questioned me was the only one I could see. All the time I could not see the others. Every time I could get a look around, they would touch me on the side of the head with a pistol, so I had to keep my head square in front. The next question was, "Who did you vote for?" I told him I voted for Mr. Turner—Claudius Turner, a gentleman in the neighborhood. They said, "What did you vote for him for?" I said, "I thought a good deal of him; he was my neighbor." I told them I disremembered who was on the ticket besides, but they had several, and I voted the ticket. "What did you do that for?" they said. Says I, "because I thought it was right." They said, "You thought it

[1] The Vernons were Thomson's former masters.

Source: Report of the Joint Select Committee, vol. 2, South Carolina, Part I, 410–15.

was right? It was right wrong." I said, "I never do anything hardly if I think it is wrong; if it was wrong, I did not know it. That was my opinion at the time and I thought every man ought to vote according to his notions." He said, "If you had taken the advice of your friends you would have been better off." I told him I had. Says I, "You may be a friend to me, but I can't tell who you are." Says he, "Can't you recognize anybody here?" I told him I could not. "In the condition you are in now, I can't tell who you are." One of them had a very large set of teeth; I suppose they were three-quarters of an inch long; they came right straight down. He came up to me and sort of nodded. He had on speckled horns and calico stuff, and had a face on. He said, "Have you got a chisel here I could get?" I told him I hadn't, but I reckoned I could knock one out, and I sort of laughed. He said, "What in hell are you laughing at? It is no laughing time." I told him it sort of tickled me, and I thought I would laugh. I did not say anything then for a good while. "Old man," says one, "have you got a rope here, or a plow-line, or something of the sort?" I told him, "Yes; I had one hanging on the crib." He said, "Let us have it." One of them says, "String him up to this pine tree, and we will get all out of him. Get up, one of you, and let us pull him up, and he will tell the truth." I says, "I can't tell you anything more than I have told. There is nothing that I can tell you but what I have told you and you have asked me." One man questioned me all this time. One would come up and say, "Let's hang him a while, and he will tell us the truth"; and another then came up and said, "Old man, we are just from hell; some of us have been dead ever since the revolutionary war." . . . I was not scared, and said, "You have been through a right smart experience." "Yes," he says, "we have been through a considerable experience." One of them says, "we have just come from hell." I said, "If I had been there, I would not want to go back." . . . Then they hit me thirteen of the hardest cuts I ever got. I never had such cuts. They hit me right around my waist and by my hip, and cut a piece about as wide as my two fingers in one place. I did not say a word while they were whipping, only sort of grunted a little. As quick as they got through they said, "Go to your bed. We will have this country right before we get through; go to your bed," and they started away. . . .

Question: Who is Claudius Turner?

Answer: He is a gentleman that run for the legislature here. He was on the ticket with Mr. Scott.

Question: The republican ticket?

Answer: Yes, sir; the radical[2] ticket. . . .

By Mr. Van Trump:

Question: Explain to me, if you can, if the object of this Ku-Klux organization is to intimidate the colored people, why they were so particular as to make you promise, under penalty of death, that you would never disclose the fact that you had been visited; do you understand why that is?

---

[2] Radical Republicans were known for their support of black suffrage and the disenfranchisement of former Confederate military and civilian officers.

Answer: I can explain this fact this far: You know when they said to me to not say anything about this matter, I asked them what I must say, and when I asked, "What must I say? I will have to say something," they said, "What are you going to say?" I said, "What must I say?" He said, "Are you going to tell it?" I told them, "I have to say something, of course, and what must I say; what can I say?" Then they said, looking straight at me—

Question: Why is it that so often in giving your testimony you have to get up and make gesticulations like an orator? Have you been an orator?

Answer: No, sir, but I was showing the way they did me, and what they said to me. They said, "You just let me hear of this thing again, and we will not leave a piece of you when we come back."

Question: To whom have you talked lately about this case, or consulted here in town?

Answer: I have not consulted much about it.

Question: How long have you been waiting to be examined?

Answer: Since Tuesday about 10 o'clock.

Question: Have any white republicans been to see you?

Answer: No, sir; nobody at all.

Question: Did you see them?

Answer: I don't know who the republicans are here. I may have seen some.

Question: Do you pretend to say that since Tuesday you have not talked with any white about your case?

Answer: With none about the Ku-Klux matter.

 ## 4   *Testimony of Lucy McMillan,*
Spartanburg, South Carolina, July 10, 1871

Lucy McMillan (colored) sworn and examined.

By the Chairman:

Question: Where do you live?

Answer: Up in the country. I live on McMillan's place, right at the foot of the road.

Question: How far is it?

Answer: Twelve miles.

Question: Are you married?

Answer: I am not married. I am single now. I was married. My husband was taken away from me and carried off twelve years ago.

Question: He was carried off before the war?

Answer: Yes, sir; the year before the war; twelve years ago this November coming.

Source: Report of the Joint Select Committee, vol. 3, South Carolina, Part II, 604–7.

Question: How old are you now?

Answer: I am called forty-six. I am forty-five or -six.

Question: Did the Ku-Klux come where you live at any time?

Answer: They came there once before they burned my house down. The way it happened was this: John Hunter's wife came to my house on Saturday morning, and told they were going to whip me. I was afraid of them; there was so much talk of Ku-Klux drowning people, and whipping people, and killing them. My house was only a little piece from the river, so I laid out at night in the woods. The Sunday evening after Isham McCrary[1] was whipped I went up, and a white man, John McMillan, came along and says to me, "Lucy, you had better stay at home, for they will whip you anyhow." I said if they have to, they might whip me in the woods, for I am afraid to stay there. Monday night they came in and burned my house down; I dodged out alongside of the road not far off and saw them. I was sitting right not far off, and as they came along the river I knew some of them. I knew John McMillan, and Kennedy McMillan, and Billy Bush, and John Hunter. They were all together. I was not far off, and I saw them. They went right on to my house. When they passed me I run further up on the hill to get out of the way of them. They went there and knocked down and beat my house a right smart while. And then they all got still, and directly I saw the fire rise.

Question: How many of these men were there?

Answer: A good many; I couldn't tell how many, but these I knew. The others I didn't. . . .

Question: What was the reason given for burning your house?

Answer: There was speaking down there last year and I came to it. They all kept at me to go. I went home and they quizzed me to hear what was said, and I told them as far as my senses allowed me.

Question: Where was this speaking?

Answer: Here in this town. I went on and told them, and then they all said I was making laws; or going to have the land, and the Ku-Klux were going to beat me for bragging that I would have land. John Hunter told them on me, I suppose, that I said I was going to have land. . . .

Question: Was that the only reason you know for your house being burned?

Answer: That is all the reason. All the Ku-Klux said all that they had against me was that I was bragging and boasting that I wanted the land. . . .

By Mr. Van Trump:

Question: Do you mean to say that they said they burned the house for that reason?

Answer: No sir; they burned the house because they could not catch me. I don't know any other reason. . . .

Question: Who was John Hunter?

Answer: He is a colored man. I worked for him all last summer. I worked with him hoeing his cotton and corn.

---

[1] Another freedman who testified before the committee in Spartanburg.

Question: What was he doing with these Ku-Klux?

Answer: I don't know. He was with them. . . .

Question: How did you come to be named Lucy McMillan?

Answer: I was a slave of Robert McMillan. I always belonged to him.

Question: You helped raise Kennedy and John?[2]

Answer: Not John, but Kennedy I did. When he was a little boy I was with him.

Question: Did he always like you?

Answer: Yes, sir. They always pretended to like us.

Question: That is while you were a slave?

Answer: Yes, sir, while I was a slave, but never afterward. They didn't care for us then.

---

[2] Sons of Robert McMillan.

5   *Testimony of Mervin Givens,*
Spartanburg, South Carolina, July 12, 1871

Mervin Givens (colored) sworn and examined.

By Mr. Stevenson:

Question: Your name in old times was Mery Moss?

Answer: Yes, sir; but since freedom I don't go by my master's name. My name now is Givens.

Question: What is your age?

Answer: About forty I expect. . . .

Question: Have you ever been visited by the Ku-Klux?

Answer: Yes, sir.

Question: When?

Answer: About the last of April.

Question: Tell what they said and did.

Answer: I was asleep when they came to my house, and did not know anything about them until they broke in on me.

Question: What time of night was it?

Answer: About twelve o'clock at night. They broke in on me and frightened me right smart, being asleep. They ordered me to get up and make a light. As quick as I could gather my senses I bounced up and made a light, but not quick enough. They jumped at me and struck me with a pistol, and made a knot[1] that you can see there now. By the time I made the light I catched the voice of them, and as soon as I could see by the light, I looked around and saw by the size of the men and voice so that I could judge right off who it was. By that time they

---

[1] Bump.

Source: Report of the Joint Select Committee, vol. 2, South Carolina, Part II, 698–700.

jerked the case off the pillow and jerked it over my head and ordered me out of doors. That was all I saw in the house. After they carried me out of doors I saw nothing more. They pulled the pillow-slip over my head and told me if I took off they would shoot me. They carried me out and whipped me powerful.

Question: With what?

Answer: With sticks and hickories. They whipped me powerful.

Question: How many lashes?

Answer: I can't tell. I have no knowledge at all about it. May be a hundred or two. Two men whipped me and both at once.

Question: Did they say anything to you?

Answer: They cursed me and told me I had voted the radical ticket, and they intended to beat me so I would not vote it again.

Question: Did you know any of them?

Answer: Yes, sir; I think I know them.

Question: What were their names?

Answer: One was named John Thomson and the other was John Zimmerman. Those are the two men I think it was.

Question: How many were there in all?

Answer: I didn't see but two. After they took me out, I was blindfolded; but I could judge from the horse tracks that there were more than two horses there. Some were horses and some were mules. It was a wet, rainy night; they whipped me stark naked. I had a brown undershirt on and they tore it clean off. . . .

By Mr. Van Trump:

Question: There were, then, two men who came to your house?

Answer: Yes, sir; that was all I could see.

Question: Were they disguised?

Answer: Yes, sir.

Question: How?

Answer: They had on some sort of gray-looking clothes, and much the same sort of thing over their face. One of them had a sort of high hat with tassel and sort of horns.

Question: How far did John Thomson live from there?

Answer: I think it is two or three miles.

Question: Were you acquainted with him?

Answer: Yes, sir.

Question: Where?

Answer: At my house. My wife did a good deal of washing for them both. I was very well-acquainted with their size and their voices. They were boys I was raised with. . . .

Question: Did you tell anybody else it was John Thomson?

Answer: I have never named it.

Question: Why?

Answer: I was afraid to.

Question: Are you afraid now?

Answer: I am not afraid to own the truth as nigh[2] as I can.

Question: Is there any difference in owning to the truth on the 12th of July and on the 1st of April?

Answer: The black people have injured themselves very much by talking, and I was afraid.

Question: Are you not afraid now?

Answer: No, sir; because I hope there will be a stop put to it. . . .

Question: Do you think we three gentlemen can stop it?

Answer: No, sir; but I think you can get some help.

Question: Has anybody been telling you that?

Answer: No, sir; nobody told me that. . . .

Question: Why did you not commence a prosecution against Thomson and Zimmerman?

Answer: I am like the rest, I reckon; I am too cowardly.

Question: Why do you not do it now; you are not cowardly now?

Answer: I shouldn't have done it now.

Question: I am talking about bringing suit for that abuse on that night. Why do you not have them arrested?

Answer: It ought to be done.

Question: Why do you not do it?

Answer: For fear they would shoot me. If I were to bring them up here and could not prove the thing exactly on them, and they were to get out of it, I would not expect to live much longer.

[2] Near.

COMMITTEE REPORTS

<table>
<tr><td>6</td><td>Majority Report of the Joint Select Committee to Inquire into the Condition of Affairs in the Late Insurrectionary States, February 19, 1872, Submitted by Luke P. Poland</td></tr>
</table>

Poland was a Republican representative from Vermont.

The proceedings and debates in Congress show that, whatever other causes were assigned for disorders in the late insurrectionary States, the execution of the laws and the security of life and property were alleged to be most seriously threatened

Source: Report of the Joint Select Committee, vol. 1, Reports of the Committee, 2–3, 98–99.

by the existence and acts of organized bands of armed and disguised men, known as Ku-Klux. . . .

The evidence is equally decisive that redress cannot be obtained against those who commit crimes in disguise and at night. The reasons assigned are that identification is difficult, almost impossible; that when this is attempted, the combinations and oaths of the order come in and release the culprit by perjury either upon the witness-stand or in the jury-box; and that the terror inspired by their acts, as well as the public sentiment in their favor in many localities, paralyzes the arm of civil power. . . .

The race so recently emancipated, against which banishment or serfdom is thus decreed, but which has been clothed by the Government with the rights and responsibilities of citizenship, ought not to be, and we feel assured will not be left hereafter without protection against the hostilities and sufferings it has endured in the past, as long as the legal and constitutional powers of the Government are adequate to afford it. Communities suffering such evils and influenced by such extreme feelings may be slow to learn that relief can come only from a ready obedience to and support of constituted authority, looking to the modes provided by law for redress of all grievances. That Southern communities do not seem to yield this ready obedience at once should not deter the friends of good government in both sections from hoping and working for that end. . . .

The law of 1871[1] has been effective in suppressing for the present, to a great extent, the operations of masked and disguised men in North and South Carolina. . . . The apparent cessation of operations should not lead to a conclusion that community would be safe if protective measures were withdrawn. These should be continued until there remains no further doubt of the actual suppression and disarming of this wide-spread and dangerous conspiracy.

The results of suspending the writ of *habeas corpus* in South Carolina show that where the membership, mysteries, and power of the organization have been kept concealed this is the most and perhaps only effective remedy for its suppression; and in review of its cessation and resumption of hostilities at different times, of its extent and power, and that in several of the States where it exists the courts have not yet held terms at which the cases can be tried, we recommend that the power conferred on the President by the fourth section of that act[2] be extended until the end of the next session of Congress.

For the Senate:	For the House of Representatives:
JOHN SCOTT, Chairman	LUKE P. POLAND, Chairman
Z. CHANDLER[3]	HORACE MAYNARD[4]

---

[1] The Ku Klux Klan Act.

[2] To suspend the writ of habeas corpus.

[3] Republican senator from Michigan.

[4] Republican representative from Tennessee.

BENJ. F. RICE[5]   GLENNI W. SCOFIELD[6]

JOHN POOL[7]   JOHN F. FARNSWORTH[8]

DANIEL D. PRATT[9]   JOHN COBURN[10]

                               JOB E. STEVENSON

                               BENJ. F. BUTLER[11]

                               WILLIAM E. LANSING[12]

[5] Republican senator from Arkansas.
[6] Republican representative from Pennsylvania.
[7] Republican senator from North Carolina.
[8] Republican representative from Illinois.
[9] Republican senator from Indiana.
[10] Republican representative from Indiana.
[11] Republican representative from Massachusetts.
[12] Republican representative from New York.

7 — Minority Report of the Joint Select Committee to Inquire into the Condition of Affairs in the Late Insurrectionary States, February 19, 1872, Submitted by James B. Beck

Beck was a Democratic representative from Kentucky.

The atrocious measures by which millions of white people have been put at the mercy of the semi-barbarous negroes of the South, and the vilest of the white people, both from the North and South, who have been constituted the leaders of this black horde, are now sought to be justified and defended by defaming the people upon whom this unspeakable outrage had been committed. . . .

There is no doubt about the fact that great outrages were committed by bands of disguised men during those years of lawlessness and oppression. The natural tendency of all such organizations is to violence and crime. . . . It is so everywhere; like causes produce like results. Sporadic cases of outrages occur in every community. . . . But, as a rule, the worst governments produce the most disorders. South Carolina is confessedly in the worst condition of any of the States. Why? Because her government is the worst, or what makes it still worse, her people see no hope in the future. . . . There never was a Ku-Klux in Virginia, nobody pretends there ever was. Why? Because Virginia escaped carpet-bag rule. . . .

Source: Report of the Joint Select Committee, vol. 1, Reports of the Committee, 289, 463–64, 514–16, 588.

The Constitution was trampled under foot in the passage of what is known as the Ku-Klux law; a power was delegated to the President which could be exercised by the legislative authority alone; whole communities of innocent people were put under the ban of executive vengeance by the suspension of the writ of *habeas corpus* at the mere whim and caprice of the President; and all for what? For the apprehension and conviction of a few poor, deluded, ignorant, and unhappy wretches, goaded to desperation by the insolence of the negroes, and who could, had the radical authorities of South Carolina done their duty, just as easily have been prosecuted in the State courts, and much more promptly and cheaply, than by all this imposing machinery of Federal power, through military and judicial departments. . . .

. . . The antagonism, therefore, which exists between these two classes of the population of South Carolina does not spring from any political cause, in the ordinary party sense of the term; but it grows out of that instinctive and irrepressible repugnance to compulsory affiliation with another race, planted by the God of nature in the breast of the white man, perhaps more strongly manifested in the uneducated portion of the people, and aggravated and intensified by the fact that the Negro has been placed as a *ruler* over him. . . .

We feel it would be a dereliction of duty on our part if, after what we have witnessed in South Carolina, we did not admonish the American people that the present condition of things in the South cannot last. It was an oft-quoted political apothegm, long prior to the war, that no government could exist "half slave and half free." The paraphrase of that proposition is equally true, that no government can long exist "half black and half white." If the republican party, or its all-powerful leaders in the North, cannot see this, if they are so absorbed in the idea of this newly discovered political divinity in the negro, that they cannot comprehend its social repugnance or its political dangers; or, knowing it, have the wanton, wicked, and criminal purpose of disregarding its consequences, whether in the present or in the future, and the great mass of American white citizens should still be so mad as to sustain them in their heedless career of forcing negro supremacy over white men, why then "farewell, a long farewell," to constitutional liberty on this continent, and the glorious form of government bequeathed to us by our fathers. . . .

The foregoing is a hurried, but, as we believe, a truthful statement of the political, moral, and financial condition of the State of South Carolina, under the joint rule of the Negro and the "reconstructive" policy of Congress.

Frank Blair

T. F. Bayard[1]

S. S. Cox[2]

James B. Beck

[1] Democratic senator from Delaware.

[2] Democratic representative from New York.

P. VAN TRUMP

A. M. WADDELL[3]

J. C. ROBINSON[4]

J. M. HANKS[5]

[3] Democratic representative from North Carolina.
[4] Democratic representative from Illinois.
[5] Democratic representative from Arkansas.

Analyzing Congressional Hearings and Reports

1. How did the descriptions of the Ku Klux Klan differ between witnesses examined in Washington, D.C. (Sources 1 and 2), and those examined in South Carolina (Sources 3, 4, and 5)? How would you explain those differences?

2. Briefly compare the nature of evidence presented in the testimony. How did it differ between black and white witnesses? In what ways did the Klan's attacks on blacks differ from those on white Republicans? What do you think accounts for such differences?

3. What patterns did you find in the cross-examination of witnesses? How did Van Trump and other Democrats on the committee seek to discredit or shape the testimony they heard, and do you think they succeeded in any instances? Which witnesses do you think were most successful in answering their cross-examinations? Did any of the witnesses contradict themselves?

4. Consider whether the majority and minority reports (Sources 6 and 7) could have been written before the committee heard any witnesses. Using your notes from the second portion of the table on page 284, do you think any of the congressmen sitting on the committee had their minds changed about the Ku Klux Klan or the federal government's response to it by the testimony they heard? What specific examples or passages from the reports support your answer?

5. What does this source tell you about the limits of federal power during Reconstruction? According to the testimony and reports, what accounted for the breakdown of law and order in South Carolina, and how was it most likely to be restored? How did Republicans and Democrats differ in this regard?

6. Using the testimony you have read here, describe the social and economic conditions faced by African American men and women in the South during Reconstruction. What evidence do Thomson, McMillan, and Givens (Sources 3, 4, and 5) provide of the ways in which African American men and women valued and acted on their freedom after 1865 and of the limits whites tried to impose on that freedom?

The Rest of the Story

As noted in the Joint Select Committee's majority report, the Ku Klux Klan Act of 1871 did succeed in suppressing the Klan's activities in those regions where it was enforced. In October 1871, while the Joint Select Committee was still at work, President Grant suspended the writ of habeas corpus in nine South Carolina counties, including Spartanburg, and sent in federal troops to arrest approximately fifteen hundred suspected Klansmen. Even more Klansmen fled the region to avoid prosecution. In a series of trials managed by Amos Akerman, attorney general of the United States, in late 1871 and in 1872, approximately ninety Klansmen were sentenced to prison terms ranging from three months to ten years. Most of those given long sentences were released within a year or two, under amnesty offered by Grant. Overall, very few Klansmen were ever brought to meaningful justice for their crimes, but by the election of 1872, reports of Klan terrorism had declined considerably, and the organization's ability to intimidate black voters appeared to have been broken.

During the 1920s, the Ku Klux Klan was revived by whites who felt threatened by Catholic and Jewish immigrants as well as by African Americans. At its peak, this version of the Klan included three million members and spilled beyond the South into western and northern states. After ebbing in the 1940s, the Klan surged again during the civil rights movement of the 1950s and 1960s. This incarnation was much smaller than its predecessor in the 1920s but more violent in its resistance to racial equality. Today, a number of white supremacist organizations continue to call themselves the Ku Klux Klan, but they are poorly organized and constantly at odds with one another and with similar hate groups on the far right of American politics.

In the larger story of Reconstruction, the Ku Klux Klan Act and the congressional investigation of the Klan appeared to be shining examples of how the federal government and African Americans in the South acted in partnership to advance the cause of racial justice and equality in the United States. Unfortunately, these successes were short-lived. During his second term, Grant reduced the number of federal troops in the South, and the Republicans split between a liberal faction still committed to racial equality and a more conservative faction willing to jettison Reconstruction policies and black voters in return for political compromises with Democrats on other issues.

The third branch of the federal government did not help African Americans in their pursuit of equality either. In two cases from the 1870s, the Supreme Court interpreted the Fourteenth Amendment in such a way that it severely restricted the federal government's ability to intervene on behalf of private citizens when their civil and political rights were violated. In the *Slaughterhouse Cases* (1873), the Court ruled that the Fourteenth Amendment protected only those rights that were derived directly from the federal government, most of which dealt with matters of interstate or foreign travel or business; the civil rights of most concern to blacks in the South still fell under the jurisdiction of state courts and law enforcement. In *United States v. Cruikshank* (1876), the Court ruled that the Fourteenth Amendment empowered the federal government only to prosecute violations of civil rights by the states, not by individual persons (violations in that category still fell under state jurisdiction). The combined effect of these two decisions was to place responsibility for protecting the rights of the South's African American population under the authority of the state governments, while making any federal intervention on their behalf similar to that pursued under the Ku Klux Klan Act unconstitutional.

After the last of the former Confederate states had fallen back into Democratic hands in 1877, Southern whites found new ways to confine blacks to second-class citizenship. Insulated from federal intervention by the Supreme Court's decisions and congressional indifference, Southern states passed laws that disenfranchised blacks by imposing poll taxes and literacy tests. They also erected a system of social segregation known as Jim Crow laws that limited blacks' access to education and economic opportunity. When blacks challenged this system, mobs and night riders responded with the same methods used by the Klan, most notably lynching and arson, to prevent any sustained resistance to white rule. Not until the civil rights movement of the 1950s would the federal government again embrace the cause of racial justice in the South with the same vigor it had shown during its battle against the Klan in 1871.

To Find Out More

Resources on Reconstruction

"America's Reconstruction: People and Politics after the Civil War." *Digital History*. University of Houston. http://www.digitalhistory.uh.edu/reconstruction/.

Miller, Stephen F. *The Freedmen and Southern Society Project*. University of Maryland. http://www.history.umd.edu/Freedmen.

Report of the Joint Select Committee to Inquire into the Condition of Affairs in the Late Insurrectionary States. 13 vols. Washington, DC: Government Printing Office, 1872.

Tourgée, Albion W. *The Invisible Empire*. 1880; repr., Baton Rouge: Louisiana State University Press, 1989.

Secondary Sources on Reconstruction and the Struggle for Racial Equality

Foner, Eric. *Reconstruction: America's Unfinished Revolution, 1863–1877*. New York: Harper and Row, 1988.

Hahn, Steven. *A Nation under Our Feet: Black Political Struggles in the Rural South from Slavery to the Great Migration*. Cambridge, MA: Belknap Press, 2003.

Rable, George C. *But There Was No Peace: The Role of Violence in the Politics of Reconstruction*. Athens: University of Georgia Press, 1984.

Trelease, Allen W. *White Terror: The Ku Klux Klan Conspiracy and Southern Reconstruction*. New York: Harper and Row, 1971.

Coming Together and Pulling Apart

Nineteenth-Century Fourth of July Observations

For six months in 1876, the United States gave itself a birthday party in Philadelphia's Fairmount Park. Officially called the International Exhibition of Arts, Manufactures and Products of the Soil and Mine, this celebration was more popularly known as the Centennial Exposition, and by the time it was over, more than ten million people had passed through its gates. Previous international exhibitions had been held in London, Paris, and Vienna, but this event was the first of its kind to convene outside of Europe, and it marked the rising importance of the United States in world affairs.

The Centennial Exposition celebrated the one hundredth anniversary of American independence, but its most significant attractions looked forward rather than backward. The Main Building featured exhibits on manufacturing, mining, and metallurgy. Machinery Hall displayed the latest technological advances in steam engines, locomotives, and other heavy industrial equipment. The Horticultural Hall showcased the natural bounty and agriculture of the United States. Memorial Hall housed exhibits on the fine arts. The Women's Pavilion, the first of its kind at such international expositions, was dedicated to manufactures, arts, and crafts designed and produced by women. Twenty-six states sponsored their own buildings, as did a host of foreign countries representing every inhabited continent on the globe. Visitors to the exposition saw the first public displays of such technological marvels as the telephone, typewriter, and elevator and tasted for the first time such culinary innovations as Hires root beer and Heinz ketchup. They also caught their first glimpse of what was destined to become an American icon: the raised arm and torch of Frédéric Bartholdi's *Liberty Enlightening the World*, which became known more familiarly as the Statue of Liberty after its completion in 1886.

Figure 1 Colossal Hand and Torch: "Liberty" *Visitors to the 1876 Centennial Exposition saw for the first time what was destined to become an icon of American freedom, the torch held by the Statue of Liberty. The statue was not completed for another ten years.*
Source: Library of Congress, Prints and Photograph Division.

Of all the exposition's exhibits, one in particular—the Corliss Engine in Machinery Hall—symbolized the dawn of a new era in the United States. It was forty-five feet tall—the largest steam engine in the world—and it powered all the other machinery featured in the exposition. On the Centennial Exposition's opening day, President Ulysses S. Grant and his guest, Dom Pedro II, emperor of Brazil, stood on a platform and turned the switches that brought this behemoth and the rest of the celebration to life.

The United States may have been coming together in Philadelphia in 1876, but everywhere else it seemed to be coming apart. Nearing the end of his two terms in office, Grant was a lame-duck president whose administration had been mired in serial corruption scandals. Since 1870, the Republican Party's support for black equality in the former Confederate states had waned, and without federal support or protection, African Americans faced a growing tide of discrimination, disenfranchisement, and violence in the South. In the nation's cities, industrialization was not nearly as clean and frictionless as suggested by the humming machines at the Centennial Exposition. The panic of 1873, a financial crisis that caused bankruptcies in the banking and railroad industries, reverberated throughout the economy, leading to unemployment and labor unrest. Striking workers were attacked by police, militias, and private security forces. Mobs attacked immigrants, whom they accused of subverting American democracy with communism, socialism, and Catholicism. Violence was also endemic on the frontier, where the U.S. Army was fighting a scorched-earth campaign against the Indian peoples of the Great Plains. Just days before the Fourth of July celebrations in 1876, General George Armstrong Custer blundered badly by attacking Sioux, Cheyenne, and Arapaho warriors encamped on the Little Bighorn River in Montana. The vainglorious Custer and more than 260 soldiers under his command were killed in a humiliating defeat for the U.S. Army.

Not surprisingly, the Fourth of July in 1876 found many Americans in less than celebratory moods. William Lloyd Garrison, a towering figure in the struggle for racial equality since the 1830s, published an essay titled "Centennial Reflections" that chastised his fellow citizens for their superficial approach to this historic occasion. "Our national career, from 1776 to the present Centennial period calls for deep humiliation before God," he wrote, "and penitent confession that we have been guilty of dissimulation, perfidy, and oppression on a frightful scale." Slavery, Indian removal, wars of conquest against Mexico and Native Americans, the abandonment of Reconstruction: all were evidence that the United States had repeatedly violated its founding ideals. Susan B. Anthony, a contemporary of Garrison's in the abolitionist and temperance movements, likewise regarded the centennial as a time to remind the nation of its unfinished business. A leading figure in the National Woman Suffrage Association, Anthony had requested that her organization be included in the speakers program for a Fourth of July celebration in Philadelphia. When the event's sponsors denied her request, Anthony and a few of her associates attended anyway and commandeered a musicians' platform outside Independence Hall to read to the crowd their "Declaration of Rights for Women," which included "articles of impeachment" against "our rulers" for denying female citizens their most basic civil rights and liberties.

The Fourth of July has been a day of celebration on the American calendar for as long as the United States has existed. Much about the way we mark it has remained consistent over the years. Since the eighteenth century, Americans have used parades, picnics, speeches, and fireworks to celebrate their independence from Britain, making it an annual rite of joyous, and often raucous, patriotism. During the nineteenth century, as waves of immigration transformed the nation and western expansion dispersed its population over great distances, celebrating the Fourth of July became an important means by which people asserted their citizenship and claimed their right to enjoy its benefits. Patriotic rites of celebration also helped unite Americans across political, ethnic, racial, class, and religious lines.

Like William Lloyd Garrison and Susan B. Anthony in 1876, however, many nineteenth-century Americans often chose to *observe* Independence Day rather than to *celebrate* it, using the holiday as an occasion to challenge the triumphal narrative about U.S. history, to offer alternative interpretations of the nation's founding, and to claim membership in it for people ignored or written out of the story. The Fourth of July has been a fixture in American life since 1776, but Americans have always contested its meaning. Sources that show us nineteenth-century observations of the Fourth tell us not only about the history of a holiday, but also about how Americans struggled to define themselves as a nation and as a people over a long and tumultuous century.

Using Multiple Source Types on Fourth of July Observations

Historians interested in studying Fourth of July observations can approach the topic from a number of different angles. A rich trove of material can be found in the Fourth of July orations that speakers delivered at civic celebrations. In the nineteenth century, no town's Fourth of July celebration was complete without a speech delivered by a local or visiting dignitary, and although most of these speeches offered little more than recycled platitudes about the genius of the Founding Fathers and glories of the Revolution, they occasionally addressed the issues of the day in a forthright and even controversial manner. When such orations focused on slavery, Indian removal, or some other pressing national matter, they illustrated how Americans defined the nation's founding ideals and tried to apply them to their own times.

Alternative declarations of independence are another rich source in this regard. During the War for Independence, American civilians and soldiers marked the Fourth of July with public readings of the Declaration of Independence, but the practice declined with the bitterly partisan politics of the 1790s and early 1800s, especially among conservative Federalists who disliked the document's associations with the democratic ideals of the French Revolution. After the deaths of Thomas Jefferson and John Adams on July 4, 1826, the Declaration of Independence acquired a scriptural, almost mystical, authority in American culture and its public reading once again became a central part of Fourth of July observations. During the antebellum era, it became common for groups asserting their right to partake in American liberty to publish their own declarations of independence, modeled after the language and organization of the original. These alternative declarations made by labor groups, women's rights advocates, temperance reformers, and abolitionists offer another way for historians to examine how nineteenth-century Americans reinvented the Fourth of July for their own purposes.

By their nature, Fourth of July orations and alternative declarations of independence were filled with high-minded rhetoric; they offer little insight into how everyday people actually experienced the Fourth. Diaries and memoirs offer a much more intimate look at this holiday. Diaries contain some of the most vibrant accounts of the sights, sounds, and smells associated with public and private Fourth of July observations and tell us about what went on beyond the speaker's platform on such occasions. Some of the most critical comments written about the Fourth of July in nineteenth-century America came from diarists distressed by what they perceived to be the unbridled revelry of the lower classes. Of course, to write a diary or memoir a person had to be literate, so it is harder to find examples of this source in which people from the lower rungs of society speak for themselves.

Fourth of July celebrations also left a rich visual record. American artists wishing to break away from the classical subjects of their European contemporaries made the Fourth of July a favorite subject of their work, painting portraits or historical scenes that venerated the Revolutionary generation and its successful struggle for independence from Britain. Visual representations of the Fourth of July were not always complimentary, however. Paintings and cartoons satirizing disorderly and drunken crowds offered a stark contrast to the self-congratulatory patriotism expressed in Independence Day orations and other civic events. Whether they wished to satirize or encourage the expression of American patriotism through their work, artists conveyed the ethnic, racial, and social prejudices of their day.

What Can Multiple Source Types Tell Us?

In previous chapters, we examined particular kinds of sources associated with particular events in U.S. history. You have learned about the European-Indian encounter by analyzing captivity narratives, about the Constitution by reading speeches from New York's ratification convention, and about the Civil War by examining photographs from its battlefields. In each of these chapters, the focus has been on the advantages and disadvantages associated with a particular kind of source. This capstone chapter is different because it includes a variety of source types generated over a long period. Your job is to compare and contrast a number of different sources to see how they fit together in explaining how American observations of the Fourth of July both changed and stayed the same during the nineteenth century.

Examining multiple sources from a specific time period is the sort of work that historians do all the time. No source is perfect. No source can provide a single, definitive perspective on the past free from bias or error. Historians compensate for that imperfection in their materials by identifying and working with a variety of sources that provide multiple viewpoints on their subject. In a sense, the historian's task is similar to completing a jigsaw puzzle, linking individual pieces together by comparing them with and contrasting them to one another. Historians often call this process "triangulating evidence," verifying the accuracy of one source by fitting it together with several others. Alone, no single piece of evidence is entirely reliable; only by putting it together with several others can an accurate and useful picture emerge. After examining the evidence they have gathered, historians arrange the results of their research into a coherent narrative—with a beginning, middle, and end—just as a jigsaw puzzle assumes its final shape when the sections formed by the individual pieces are brought together to reveal the whole.

Using multiple kinds of sources can produce rich insights into a historical period, but this type of work also requires considerable attention to detail. It is necessary to devise a system for recording notes and keeping track of where each source came from so that you can properly document the sources later on. Although it is important to ask some questions about each source—Who produced it? where and when? for what audience?—you also need to tailor different questions to different types of sources. A diary entry will offer an opportunity to examine how one person experienced or thought about the Fourth of July; an alternative declaration of independence, on the other hand, will reflect the opinions of a particular group of people joined together behind a common cause.

When working with any source from the past, bear in mind the effect that the passage of time has on how sources are created, used, and interpreted. Tastes and technologies change over time, altering the effect and meaning of a source from one era to another. For example, in an age before radio, television, or other telecommunications, an oration delivered in a town square might have had a much more significant place in a Fourth of July observation than it would today. The president of the United States still makes a speech every year on the Fourth, but how many Americans do you think actually see or read that speech? Use caution, then, and avoid applying the dominant beliefs or technological capabilities of one historical period to another.

Source Analysis Table

The sources included in this chapter—speeches, alternative declarations, images, diaries, and memoirs—represent public and private attitudes about the United States in the years between 1819 and 1903. This chapter is your opportunity to review the principles of source analysis that we have been developing throughout this book and to apply them to your own interpretation of the sources. The table on pages 309–310 operates as your checklist of questions to ask of each source. Completion of this table will help you sort out the array of sources; identify differences and similarities in the purposes, audiences, points of view, and biases in these sources; and work toward your own conclusions.

Source	Source Type	Source Purpose	Source Audience	Source Viewpoint	Source Bias	What does this source tell you about how Americans observed the Fourth of July?
1. John Trumbull, *Declaration of Independence* (1819)						
2. John Lewis Krimmel, *Independence Day in Center Square* (1819)						
3. Daniel Webster, "Adams and Jefferson" (1826)						
4. Trades' Union of Boston (1834)						
5. Frederick Marryat (1837)						
6. Declaration of Sentiments (1848)						
7. Frederick Douglass (1852)						
8. John Wannuaucon Quinney (1854)						

(continued)

Source	Source Type	Source Purpose	Source Audience	Source Viewpoint	Source Bias	What does this source tell you about how Americans observed the Fourth of July?
9. Sidney George Fisher (1864 and 1866)						
10. Jacob E. Yoder (1866)						
11. Winslow Homer, "Fireworks on the Night of the Fourth of July" (1868)						
12. Thomas Worth, "The Fourth of July in the Country" (1868)						
13. Fernando Miranda, *"The Freed Slave* in Memorial Hall" (1876)						
14. Mamie Garvin Fields (1890s)						
15. Amos Bad Heart Bull, "4. July. 1903" (1903)						

The Sources: Documents and Images Portraying Fourth of July Observations, 1819–1903

1. *Declaration of Independence, July 4, 1776*
Painting. John Trumbull, 1819

John Trumbull, renowned for his paintings of historical subjects, was commissioned by the federal government to complete several works for the rotunda of the Capitol building in Washington, D.C. This work depicts the presentation of the Declaration of Independence by the committee that drafted it—John Adams, Roger Sherman, Robert Livingston, Thomas Jefferson, and Benjamin Franklin—to the president of the Second Continental Congress, John Hancock. In creating this iconic scene, Trumbull compressed several distinct events into a single, more dramatic one. The committee actually presented its work on June 28, and members of the Congress signed a copy specially prepared for them several weeks later. What actually happened on July 4 was Congress's vote to approve the document, which led to its proclamation and publication the following day.

Source: Culture Club/Getty Images.

2 *Independence Day in Center Square*
Painting. John Lewis Krimmel, 1819

Unlike his contemporary John Trumbull, John Lewis Krimmel was a "genre painter," an artist who took as his subject scenes of everyday life rather than great historical events. In this popular work, he depicted an Independence Day celebration in Center Square, Philadelphia. At the center of the scene, an army officer and a naval officer draw each other's attention to the decorations on the tents to their left and right, depicting scenes of U.S. victories from the War of 1812, a portrait of George Washington, and the U.S. and Pennsylvania flags. Other revelers enjoy drink, food, music, and dancing while militiamen try to organize for a parade in the background. In the lower right corner, a woman does her best to distribute temperance pamphlets.

Source: Fourth of July celebration in centre square, Philadelphia in 1819 (engraving), Krimmel, Johann Ludwig (John Lewis) (1787–1821) (after)/New York Public Library, USA/Bridgeman Images.

3   *Adams and Jefferson*

Speech. Daniel Webster, August 2, 1826

Thomas Jefferson and John Adams both died on July 4, 1826, the fiftieth anniversary of American independence. News of their deaths traveled quickly and had a profound effect on the national mood as people celebrated the jubilee year. The prominent New England politician Daniel Webster delivered the most famous eulogy to Adams and Jefferson. Although not technically a Fourth of July oration (it was delivered about one month after their deaths), the speech was written in that style, and Webster's reputation as a gifted speaker was based in part on his experience in delivering Fourth of July orations.

ADAMS and JEFFERSON are no more. On our fiftieth anniversary, the great day of national jubilee, in the very hour of public rejoicing, in the midst of echoing and reechoing voices of thanksgiving, while their own names were on all tongues, they took their flight together to the world of spirits.

If it be true that no one can safely be pronounced happy while he lives, if that event which terminates life can alone crown its honors and its glory, what felicity is here! The great epic of their lives, how happily concluded! Poetry itself has hardly terminated illustrious lives, and finished the career of earthly renown, by such a consummation. If we had the power, we could not wish to reverse this dispensation of the Divine Providence. The great objects of life were accomplished, the drama was ready to be closed. It has closed; our patriots have fallen; but so fallen, at such age, with such coincidence, on such a day, that we cannot rationally lament that the end has come, which we knew could not be long deferred.

Neither of these great men, fellow-citizens, could have died, at any time, without leaving an immense void in our American society. They have been so intimately, and for so long a time, blended with the history of the country, and especially so united, in our thoughts and recollections, with the events of the Revolution, that the death of either of them would have touched the chords of public sympathy. We should have felt that one great link, connecting us with former times, was broken; that we had lost something more, as it were, of the presence of the Revolution itself, and of the act of independence, and were driven on, by another great remove from the days of our country's early distinction, to meet posterity and to mix with the future. Like the mariner, whom the currents of the ocean and the winds carry along until he sees the stars which have directed his course and lighted his pathless way descend one by one, beneath the rising horizon, we should have felt that the stream of time had borne us onward till another great luminary, whose light had cheered us and whose guidance we had followed, had sunk away from our sight.

Source: Rev. B. F. Tefft, ed., *The Speeches of Daniel Webster and His Master-Pieces* (Philadelphia: Porter and Coates, 1854), 183–224.

But the concurrence of their death on the anniversary of Independence has naturally awakened stronger emotions. Both had been President, both had lived to great age, both were early patriots, and both were distinguished and ever honored by their immediate agency in the act of independence. It cannot but seem striking and extraordinary, that these two should live to see the fiftieth year from the date of that act, that they should complete that year, and that then, on the day which had fast linked for ever their own fame with their country's glory, the heavens should open to receive them both at once. As their lives themselves were the gifts of Providence, who is not willing to recognize in their happy termination, as well as in their long continuance, proofs that our country and its benefactors are objects of His care?

ADAMS and JEFFERSON, I have said, are no more. As human beings, indeed, they are no more. They are no more, as in 1776, bold and fearless advocates of independence; no more, as at subsequent periods, the head of the government; no more, as we have recently seen them, aged and venerable objects of admiration and regard. They are no more. They are dead. But how little is there of the great and good which can die! To their country they yet live, and live for ever. They live in all that perpetuates the remembrance of men on earth; in the recorded proofs of their own great actions, in the offspring of their intellect, in the deep-engraved lines of public gratitude, and in the respect and homage of mankind. They live in their example; and they live, emphatically, and will live, in the influence which their lives and efforts, their principles and opinions, now exercise, and will continue to exercise, on the affairs of men, not only in their own country but throughout the civilized world. . . .

No two men now live, fellow-citizens, perhaps it may be doubted whether any two men have ever lived in one age, who, more than those we now commemorate, have impressed on mankind their own opinions more deeply into the opinions of others, or given a more lasting direction to the current of human thought. Their work doth not perish with them. The tree which they assisted to plant will flourish, although they water it and protect it no longer; for it has struck its roots deep, it has sent them to the very centre; no storm, not of force to burn the orb,[1] can overturn it; its branches spread wide; they stretch their protecting arms broader and broader, and its top is destined to reach the heavens. We are not deceived. There is no delusion here. No age will come in which the American Revolution will appear less than it is, one of the greatest events in human history. No age will come in which it shall cease to be seen and felt, on either continent, that a mighty step, a great advance, not only in American affairs, but in human affairs, was made on the 4th of July, 1776. And no age will come, we trust, so ignorant or so unjust as not to see and acknowledge the efficient agency of those we now honor in producing that momentous event. . . .

. . . It cannot be denied, but by those who would dispute against the sun, that with America, and in America, a new era commences in human affairs.

[1] The earth.

This era is distinguished by free representative governments, by entire religious liberty, by improved systems of national intercourse, by a newly awakened and unconquerable spirit of free inquiry, and by a diffusion of knowledge through the community, such as has been before altogether unknown and unheard of in America. America, our country, fellow-citizens, our own dear and native land, is inseparably connected, fast bound up, in fortune and by fate, with these great interests. If they fall, we fall with them; if they stand, it will be because we have maintained them. Let us contemplate, then, this connection, which binds the prosperity of others to our own; and let us manfully discharge all the duties which it imposes. If we cherish the virtues and the principles of our fathers, Heaven will assist us to carry on the work of human liberty and human happiness. Auspicious omens cheer us. Great examples are before us. Our own firmament now shines brightly upon our path. WASHINGTON is in the clear, upper sky. These other stars have now joined the American Constellation; they circle round their centre, and the heavens beam with new light. Beneath this illumination let us walk the course of life, and at its close devoutly commend our beloved country, the common parent of us all, to the Divine Benignity.[2]

[2] God.

 4   *Declaration of Rights of the Trades' Union of Boston and Vicinity,* 1834

> Long before the establishment of Labor Day, U.S. workers regarded the Fourth of July as their holiday. Employers learned to give their employees the day off (or face impromptu strikes instead), and artisans and mechanics proudly marched in Fourth of July parades displaying the tools and products of their crafts. During the 1820s and 1830s, workers organized the first U.S. labor unions and used the Fourth of July and the Declaration of Independence to promote their cause. In several cities, workers established "general trades' unions" to bring together smaller unions associated with particular crafts or industries. The Boston Trades' Union organized in 1834 and issued this Declaration of Rights shortly before the Fourth of July holiday that year.

When a number of individuals associate together in a public manner for the purpose of promoting their common welfare, respect for public opinion, the proper basis of a republic form of government, under which they associate, require that they should state to their fellow citizens, the motives which actuate them, in adopting such a course.

Source: Philip S. Foner, *We, the Other People: Alternative Declarations of Independence by Labor Groups, Farmers, Woman's Rights Advocates, Socialists, and Blacks, 1829–1975* (Urbana: University of Illinois Press, 1976), 52–54.

Now we, the Delegates of the General Trades' Union of Boston and its vicinity, deploring the humiliating state of degradation, into which the producing or working class of other countries are reduced; and fearing that in our own beloved country, unless timely arrested, the same unhappy state of society will finally prevail. We already behold the wealthy fast verging into aristocracy, the laboring classes into a state of comparative dependence, and considering that this is owing to the want of union, among Mechanics and Working men, and to their apathy and indifferences in almost entirely resigning to the not-producers, the business of legislation.

We, therefore, by and with the advice of our constituents, do declare that our object in this uniting is to give to the producing or working classes their just standing in society, by constitutional, peaceable and legal means. We expressly disavow and denounce any tendency to disorganization or anarchy. We will accomplish our objects by promoting among the working class intelligence, morality, good feelings to each other, and a just sense of their rights and duties as citizens.

With the Fathers of our Country, we hold that all men are created free and equal; endowed by their Creator with certain unalienable rights, that among these are life, liberty, and the pursuit of happiness; and we hold, that to secure to each individual, the possession of those rights, should and ought to be the principal object of all legislation; consequently, that laws which have a tendency to raise any peculiar class above their fellow citizens, by granting special privileges, are contrary to and in defiance of those primary principles.

We hold, that labor, being the legitimate and only real source of wealth, and laboring classes the majority and real strength of every country, their interest and happiness ought to be the principal care of Government and any laws which oppose or neglect those interests, ought not to exist.

Our public system of Education, which so liberally endows those seminaries of learning, which from peculiar circumstances, are only accessible to the wealthy, while our common schools (particularly in the country towns) are so illy provided for, that few who can afford to pay for their children at a private school will send them to the public one. Thus even in childhood, the poor are apt to think themselves inferior. The youth of genius is discouraged—he beholds the higher branches of learning placed out of his reach, he exerts himself but to acquire the mere rudiments of education, the science of government and legislation leaves to the more favored children of fortune, and this perpetuates those distinctions which give to wealth an undue ascendancy. . . .

We hold that it is the right of workmen, and a duty they owe to each other, to associate together and regulate the price and terms of labor, and we consider the use by our opponents of the word combination, making it synonymous with insurrection, a gross perversion of language.

To secure the working class fair remuneration and prompt payment for their labor, shall be with us a primary object. We hold that according to the immutable principles of justice the debts of actual labor should take precedence of all others, and unreasonably delaying to pay a mechanics bill ought to subject the defaulter to legal damages.

Now we as representatives of the Traders' Union, do pledge ourselves to each other, to use our utmost efforts, to support the principles of our Union, and to obtain for the working class that standing in the community to which their usefulness entitles them. Let it not be said that we are exciting the poor against the rich. We seek not to excite the passions of any, we appeal to their understandings, we invite a calm, a thorough, and candid investigation of our motives; and trusting in the justice of our cause, we persevere in it with undiminished zeal, until we behold our young men aspiring to the character and title of virtuous and intelligent mechanics, as the most certain means to obtain the respect and confidence of their fellow citizens.

5 | Excerpt from *Diary in America, with Remarks on Its Institutions*
Memoir. Frederick Marryat, 1837

Frederick Marryat was a British sea captain and writer who toured Canada and the United States in 1837–1838. He published his description of the trip in *Diary in America, with Remarks on Its Institutions* (1839), which included this description of the 1837 Fourth of July celebration in New York City.

The 4th of July, the sixty-first anniversary of American independence!

Pop—pop—bang—pop—pop—bang—bang—bang! Mercy on us! How fortunate it is that anniversaries come only once a-year. Well, the Americans may have great reason to be proud of this day, and of the deeds of their forefathers, but why do they get so confoundedly drunk? why, on this day of independence, should they become so *dependent* upon posts and rails for support?—The day is at last over; my head aches, but there will be many more aching heads to-morrow morning!

What a combination of vowels and consonants have been put together! what strings of tropes, metaphors, and allegories have been used on this day! what varieties and graduations of eloquence! There are at least fifty thousand cities, towns, villages, and hamlets, spread over the surface of America—in each the Declaration of Independence has been read; in all one, and in some two or three, orations have been delivered, with as much gunpowder in them as in the squibs and crackers.[1] But let me describe what I actually saw.

The commemoration commenced, if the day did not, on the evening of the 3d, by the municipal police going round and pasting up placards, informing the citizens of New York, that all persons letting off fireworks would be taken into custody, which notice was immediately followed up by the little boys proving

---

[1] Fireworks.

Source: Frederick Marryat, *Diary in America, with Remarks on Its Institutions* (New York: Wm. H. Colyer, 1839), 31–33.

their independence of the authorities, by letting off squibs, crackers, and bombs; and cannons, made out of shin bones, which flew in the face of every passenger, in the exact ratio that the little boys flew in the face of the authorities. This continued the whole night, and thus was ushered in the great and glorious day, illumined by a bright and glaring sun (as if bespoken on purpose by the mayor and corporation), with the thermometer at 90° in the shade. The first sight which met the eye after sunrise was the precipitate escape, from a city visited with the plague of gunpowder, of respectable or timorous people in coaches, carriages, wagons, and every variety of vehicle. "My kingdom for a horse!" was the general cry of all those who could not stand fire. In the mean while, the whole atmosphere was filled with independence. Such was the quantity of American flags which were hoisted on board of the vessels, hung out of windows, or carried about by little boys, that you saw more stars at noon-day than ever could be counted on the brightest night.

On each side of the whole length of Broadway, were ranged booths and stands, similar to those at an English fair, and on which were displayed small plates of oysters, with a fork stuck in the board opposite to each plate; clams sweltering in the hot sun; pineapples, boiled hams, pies, puddings, barley-sugar, and many other indescribables. But what was most remarkable, Broadway being three miles long, and the booths lining each side of it, in every booth there was a roast pig, large or small, as the centre attraction. Six miles of roast pig! and that in New York City alone; and roast pig in every other city, town, hamlet, and village in the Union. What association can there be between roast pig and independence? Let it not be supposed that there was any deficiency in the very necessary articles of potation on this auspicious day: no! the booths were loaded with porter, ale, cider, mead, brandy, wine, ginger-beer, pop, soda-water, whiskey, rum, punch, gin slings, cocktails, mint juleps, besides many other compounds, to name which nothing but the luxuriance of American-English could invent a word. Certainly the preparations in the refreshment way were most imposing, and gave you some idea of what had to be gone through with on this auspicious day. Martial music sounded from a dozen quarters at once; and as you turned your head, you tacked to the first bars of a march from one band, the concluding bars of Yankee Doodle from another. At last the troops of militia and volunteers, who had been gathering in the park and other squares, made their appearance, well dressed and well equipped, and, in honour of the day, marching as independently as they well could. I did not see them go through many manoeuvres, but there was one which they appeared to excel in, and that was grounding arms[2] and eating pies. . . .

I was invited to dine with the mayor and corporation at the City Hall. We sat down in the Hall of Justice, and certainly, great justice was done to the dinner, which (as the wife says to her husband after a party, where the second course follows the first with unusual celerity) "went off remarkably well." The crackers popped outside, and the champaigne popped in. The celerity of the Americans at a public dinner is very commendable; they speak only now and then; and

---

[2] Resting their guns on the ground so as to free their hands.

the toasts follow so fast, that you have just time to empty your glass, before you are requested to fill again. Thus the arranged toasts went off rapidly, and after them, any one might withdraw. I waited till the thirteenth toast, the last on the paper, to wit, the ladies of America; and, having previously, in a speech from the recorder, bolted Bunker's Hill and New Orleans,[3] I thought I might as well bolt myself, as I wished to see the fireworks, which were to be very splendid. . . .

There is something grand in the idea of a national intoxication. In this world, vices on a grand scale dilate into virtues; he who murders one man, is strung up with ignomiy; but he who murders twenty thousand has a statue to his memory, and is handed down to posterity as a hero. A staggering individual is a laughable and, sometimes, a disgusting spectacle; but the whole of a vast continent reeling, offering a holocaust of its brains for mercies vouchsafed, is an appropriate tribute of gratitude for the rights of equality and the *levelling spirit* of their institutions.

[3] An Englishman, Marryat notes that Fourth of July speeches make reference to the battles of Bunker Hill (1775) and New Orleans (1815), when outnumbered Americans put up surprising resistance to British troops.

6 *Declaration of Sentiments,* from the Woman's Rights Convention, 1848

The most famous alternative declaration of independence was the result of the first women's rights convention, held at Seneca Falls, New York, in 1848. Led by Lucretia Mott and Elizabeth Cady Stanton, the delegates at the convention protested the disabilities women suffered under the rules of coverture in U.S. law (see Chapter 7) and initiated the movement for women's suffrage, which culminated in the ratification of the Nineteenth Amendment to the United States Constitution seventy-two years later.

When, in the course of human events, it becomes necessary for one portion of the family of man to assume among the people of the earth a position different from that which they have hitherto occupied, but on to which the laws of nature and of nature's God entitle them, a decent respect to the opinions of mankind requires that they should declare the causes that impel them to such a course.

We hold these truths to be self-evident: that all men and women are created equal; that they are endowed by their Creator with certain inalienable rights; that among these are life, liberty, and the pursuit of happiness; that to

Source: Philip S. Foner, *We, the Other People: Alternative Declarations of Independence by Labor Groups, Farmers, Woman's Rights Advocates, Socialists, and Blacks, 1829–1975* (Urbana: University of Illinois Press, 1976), 78–81.

secure these rights governments are instituted, deriving their just powers from the consent of the governed. Whenever any form of government becomes destructive of these ends, it is the right of those who suffer from it to refuse allegiance to it, and to insist upon the institution of a new government, laying its foundation on such principles, and organizing its powers in such form, as to them shall seem most likely to effect their safety and happiness. Prudence, indeed, will dictate that governments long established should not be changed for light and transient causes; and accordingly all experience hath shown that mankind are more disposed to suffer, while evils are sufferable, than to right themselves by abolishing the forms to which they were accustomed. But when a long train of abuses and usurpations, pursuing invariably the same object evinces a design to reduce them under absolute despotism, it is their duty to throw off such government, and to provide new guards for their future security. Such has been the patient sufferance of the women under this government, and such is now the necessity which constrains them to demand the equal station to which they are entitled.

The history of mankind is a history of repeated injuries and usurpations on the part of man toward woman, having in direct object the establishment of an absolute tyranny over her. To prove this, let facts be submitted to a candid world.

He has never permitted her to exercise her inalienable right to the elective franchise.

He has compelled her to submit to laws, in the formation of which she had no voice.

He has withheld from her rights which are given to the most ignorant and degraded men—both natives and foreigners.

Having deprived her of this first right of a citizen, the elective franchise, thereby leaving her without representation in the halls of legislation, he has oppressed her on all sides.

He has made her, if married, in the eye of the law, civilly dead.

He has taken from her all right in property, even to the wages she earns.

He has made her, morally, an irresponsible being, as she can commit many crimes with impunity, provided they be done in the presence of her husband. In the covenant of marriage, she is compelled to promise obedience to her husband, he becoming, to all intents and purposes, her master—the law giving him power to deprive her of her liberty, and to administer chastisement.

He has so framed the laws of divorce, as to what shall be the proper causes, and in case of separation, to whom the guardianship of the children shall be given, as to be wholly regardless of the happiness of women—the law, in all cases, going upon a false supposition of the supremacy of man, and giving all power into his hands.

After depriving her of all rights as a married woman, if single, and the owner of property, he has taxed her to support a government which recognizes her only when her property can be made profitable to it.

He has monopolized nearly all the profitable employments, and from those she is permitted to follow, she receives but a scanty remuneration. He closes against her all the avenues to wealth and distinction which he considers most honorable to himself. As a teacher of theology, medicine, or law, she is not known.

He has denied her the facilities from obtaining a thorough education, all colleges being closed against her.

He allows her in Church, as well as State, but a subordinate position, claiming Apostolic authority for her exclusion from the ministry, and, with some exceptions, from any public participation in the affairs of the Church.

He has created a false public sentiment by giving to the world a different code of morals for men and women, by which moral delinquencies which exclude women from society, are not only tolerated, but deemed of little account in man.

He has usurped the prerogative of Jehovah himself, claiming it as his right to assign for her a sphere of action, when that belongs to her conscience and to her God. He has endeavored, in every way that he could, to destroy her confidence in her own powers, to lessen her self-respect, and to make her willing to lead a dependent and abject life. Now, in view of this entire disfranchisement of one-half the people of this country, their social and religious degradation—in view of the unjust laws above mentioned, and because women do feel themselves aggrieved, oppressed, and fraudulently deprived of their most sacred rights, we insist that they have immediate admission to all the rights and privileges which belong to them as citizens of the United States.

In entering upon the great work before us, we anticipate no small amount of misconception, misrepresentation, and ridicule; but we shall use every instrumentality within our power to effect our object. We shall employ agents, circulate tracts, petition the State and National legislatures, and endeavor to enlist the pulpit and the press in our behalf. We hope this Convention will be followed by a series of Conventions embracing every part of the country.

7 *What to the Slave Is the Fourth of July?*
Speech. Frederick Douglass, July 5, 1852

Frederick Douglass was an escaped slave and abolitionist, the most famous African American of the nineteenth century. As the author of a best-selling slave narrative and publisher of an abolitionist newspaper, he frequently gave speeches and acquired a reputation as a masterful orator. In 1852, he was invited to deliver a Fourth of July oration in Rochester, New York, where he lived and published his newspaper.

Fellow-citizens, pardon me, allow me to ask, why am I called upon to speak here to-day? What have I, or those I represent, to do with your national independence? Are the great principles of political freedom and of natural justice, embodied in that Declaration of Independence, extended to us? and am I,

Source: Philip S. Foner, ed., *Life and Writings of Frederick Douglass*, 4 vols. (New York: International Publishers, 1950–1955), 2:181–204.

therefore, called upon to bring our humble offering to the national altar, and to confess the benefits and express devout gratitude for the blessings resulting from your independence to us? . . .

But such is not the state of the case. I say it with a sad sense of the disparity between us. I am not included within the pale of glorious anniversary! Your high independence only reveals the immeasurable distance between us. The blessings in which you, this day, rejoice, are not enjoyed in common. The rich inheritance of justice, liberty, prosperity and independence, bequeathed by your fathers, is shared by you, not by me. The sunlight that brought light and healing to you, has brought stripes and death to me. This Fourth July is yours, not mine. You may rejoice, I must mourn. . . .

. . . My subject, then, fellow-citizens, is American slavery. I shall see this day and its popular characteristics from the slave's point of view. Standing there identified with the American bondman, making his wrongs mine, I do not hesitate to declare, with all my soul, that the character and conduct of this nation never looked blacker to me than on this 4th of July! Whether we turn to the declarations of the past, or to the professions of the present, the conduct of the nation seems equally hideous and revolting. America, is false to the past, false to the present, and solemnly binds herself to be false to the future. Standing with God and the crushed and bleeding slave on this occasion, I will, in the name of humanity which is outraged, in the name of liberty which is fettered, in the name of the constitution and the Bible which are disregarded and trampled upon, dare to call in question and to denounce, with all the emphasis I can command, everything that serves to perpetuate slavery, the great sin and shame of America! "I will not equivocate; I will not excuse";[1] I will use the severest language I can command; and yet not one word shall escape me that any man, whose judgment is not blinded by prejudice, or who is not at heart a slaveholder, shall not confess to be right and just. . . .

For the present, it is enough to affirm the equal manhood of the Negro race. Is it not astonishing that, while we are ploughing, planting, and reaping, using all kinds of mechanical tools, erecting houses, constructing bridges, building ships, working in metals of brass, iron, copper, silver and gold; that, while we are reading, writing and ciphering, acting as clerks, merchants and secretaries, having among us lawyers, doctors, ministers, poets, authors, editors, orators and teachers; that, while we are engaged in all manner of enterprises common to other men, digging gold in California, capturing the whale in the Pacific, feeding sheep and cattle on the hill-side, living, moving, acting, thinking, planning, living in families as husbands, wives and children, and, above all, confessing and worshipping the Christian's God, and looking hopefully for life and immortality beyond the grave, we are called upon to prove that we are men!

Would you have me argue that man is entitled to liberty? that he is the rightful owner of his own body? You have already declared it. Must I argue the wrongfulness of slavery? Is that a question for Republicans?[2] Is it to be settled

---

[1] Douglass is quoting here from abolitionist William Lloyd Garrison's newspaper, *The Liberator*.

[2] The Republican Party was established in the 1850s to advance the antislavery cause.

by the rules of logic and argumentation, as a matter beset with great difficulty, involving a doubtful application of the principle of justice, hard to be understood? How should I look to-day, in the presence of Americans, dividing, and subdividing a discourse, to show that men have a natural right to freedom? speaking of it relatively and positively, negatively and affirmatively. To do so, would be to make myself ridiculous, and to offer an insult to your understanding. There is not a man beneath the canopy of heaven that does not know that slavery is wrong for him. . . .

At a time like this, scorching irony, not convincing argument, is needed. O! had I the ability, and could reach the nation's ear, I would, to-day, pour out a fiery stream of biting ridicule, blasting reproach, withering sarcasm, and stern rebuke. For it is not light that is needed, but fire; it is not the gentle shower, but thunder. We need the storm, the whirlwind, and the earthquake. The feeling of the nation must be quickened; the conscience of the nation must be roused; the propriety of the nation must be startled; the hypocrisy of the nation must be exposed; and its crimes against God and man must be proclaimed and denounced.

What, to the American slave, is your 4th of July? I answer; a day that reveals to him, more than all other days in the year, the gross injustice and cruelty to which he is the constant victim. To him, your celebration is a sham; your boasted liberty, an unholy license; your national greatness, swelling vanity; your sounds of rejoicing are empty and heartless; your denunciation of tyrants, brass fronted impudence; your shouts of liberty and equality, hollow mockery; your prayers and hymns, your sermons and thanksgivings, with all your religious parade and solemnity, are, to Him, mere bombast, fraud, deception, impiety, and hypocrisy—a thin veil to cover up crimes which would disgrace a nation of savages. There is not a nation on the earth guilty of practices more shocking and bloody than are the people of the United States, at this very hour. Go where you may, search where you will, roam through all the monarchies and despotisms of the Old World, travel through South America, search out every abuse, and when you have found the last, lay your facts by the side of the everyday practices of this nation, and you will say with me, that, for revolting barbarity and shameless hypocrisy, America reigns without a rival. . . .

. . . Allow me to say, in conclusion, notwithstanding the dark picture I have this day presented, of the state of the nation, I do not despair of this country. There are forces in operation which must inevitably work the downfall of slavery. "The arm of the Lord is not shortened," and the doom of slavery is certain. I, therefore, leave off where I began, with hope. While drawing encouragement from "the Declaration of Independence," the great principles it contains, and the genius of American Institutions, my spirit is also cheered by the obvious tendencies of the age.

| 8 | *Speech*, John Wannuaucon Quinney, July 4, 1854 |

John Wannuaucon Quinney was a Mahican Indian from Wisconsin. The Mahicans originally lived in the Hudson River Valley. During the colonial era, some Mahicans amalgamated with other Algonquian peoples in that region and became known as the Stockbridge Indians, named after the town in western Massachusetts that they established. After the American Revolution, the Stockbridge Indians removed to central New York and then again to Wisconsin, where Quinney represented them in negotiations with the U.S. Congress to prevent further removals west. In 1854, the people of Reidsville, New York, invited him to deliver their Fourth of July oration.

It may appear to those whom I have the honor to address, a singular taste, for me, an Indian, to take an interest in the triumphal days of a people, who occupy by conquest, or have usurped the possession of the territories of my fathers, and have laid and carefully preserved, a train of terrible miseries, to end when my race shall have ceased to exist. But thanks to the fortunate circumstances of my life, I have been taught in the schools, and been able to read your histories and accounts of Europeans, yourselves and the Red Man; which instruct me, that while your rejoicings to-day are commemorative of the free birth of this giant nation, they simply convey to my mind, the recollection of a transfer of the miserable weakness and dependence of my race from one great power to another.

My friends, I am getting old, and have witnessed, for many years, your increase in wealth and power, while the steady consuming decline of my tribe, admonishes me, that their extinction is inevitable—they know it themselves, and the reflection teaches them humility and resignation, directing their attention to the existence of those happy hunting-grounds which the Great Father has prepared for all his red children.

In this spirit, my friends (being invited to come here), as a Muh-he-con-new [Mahican], and now standing upon the soil which once was, and now ought to be, the property of this tribe, I have thought for once, and certainly the last time, I would shake you by the hand, and ask you to listen, for a little while, to what I have to say. . . .

Two hundred and fifty winters ago . . . the Muh-he-con-new, for the first time, beheld the "pale-face." Their number was small, but their canoes were big. In the select and exclusive circles of your rich men, of the present day, I should encounter the gaze of curiosity, but not such as overwhelmed the senses of the Aborigines, my ancestors. "Our visitors were white, and must be sick. They asked for rest and kindness. We gave them both. They were strangers, and we took them in—naked, and we clothed them." The first impression of astonishment and pity, was succeeded by awe and admiration of superior art, intelligence and address. A passion for information and improvement possessed the Indian—a residence was freely offered—territory given—and covenants of friendship exchanged.

Source: Lyman Copeland Draper, ed., *Collections of the State Historical Society of Wisconsin* 4 (1859), 314–20.

Your written accounts of events at this period are familiar to you, my friends. Your children read them every day in their school books; but they do not read—no mind at this time can conceive, and no pen record, the terrible story of recompense for kindness, which for two hundred years has been paid the simple, trusting, guileless Muh-he-con-new. I have seen much myself—have been connected with more, and, I tell you, I know all. The tradition of the wise men is figuratively true, "that our home, at last, will be found in the West"; for, another tradition informs us, that "far beyond the setting sun, upon the smiling, happy lands, we shall be gathered with our Fathers, and be at rest."

Promises and professions were freely given, and as ruthlessly—intentionally broken. To kindle your fires—to be of and with us, was sought as a privilege; and yet at that moment you were transmitting to your kings, beyond the water, intelligence of your possession, "by right of discovery," and demanding assistance to assert and maintain your hold.

Where are the twenty-five thousand in number, and the four thousand warriors, who constituted the power and population of the great Muh-he-con-new Nation in 1604? They have been victims to vice and disease, which the white man imported. The small-pox, measles, and "strong waters" have done the work of annihilation. . . .

Let it not surprise you, my friends, when I say, that the spot on which we stand, has never been purchased or rightly obtained; and that by justice, human and divine, it is the property now of the remnant of that great people from whom I am descended. They left it in the tortures of starvation, and to improve their miserable existence; but a cession was never made, and their title has never been extinguished.

The Indian is said to be the ward of the white man, and the negro his slave. Has it ever occurred to you, my friends, that while the slave is increasing, and increased by every appliance, the Indian is left to rot and die, before the humanities of this model *Republic!* You have your tears, and groans, and mobs, and riots, for individuals of the former, while your indifference of purpose, and vacillation of policy, is hurrying to extinction, whole communities of the latter.

What are the treaties of the general Government? How often, and when, has its plighted faith been kept? Indian occupation forever, is, next year, or by the next Commissioner, more wise than his predecessor, re-purchased. One removal follows another, and thus your sympathies and justice are evinced in speedily *fulfilling the terrible destinies of our race.*

My friends, your holy book, the Bible, teaches us, that individual offences are punished in an existence, when time shall be no more. And the annals of the earth are equally instructive, that national wrongs are avenged, and national crimes atoned for in this world, to which alone the conformations of existence adapt them.

These events are above our comprehension, and for wise purposes. For myself and for my tribe, I ask for justice—I believe it will sooner or later occur—and may the Great and Good Spirit enable me to die in hope.

WANNUAUCON, *the Muh-he-con-new*

9   Excerpts from *A Philadelphia Perspective: The Diary of Sidney George Fisher Covering the Years 1834–1871,* Diary. Sidney George Fisher, 1864, 1866

Sidney George Fisher was a wealthy Philadelphia lawyer who kept a diary intermittently during his adult life. Like many urban elites, he preferred to get out of town on the Fourth of July so as to avoid the crowds and noise in the city.

July 4, 1864

It is the great anniversary of the birth of democracy in the western world, & is very appropriately celebrated by license & brute noise—guns, pistols, crackers, & squibs thro the day, fireworks, drunkenness & brawls at night. As a general rule, 30 or 40 houses are set on fire in town every 4th of July, and the constant noise of crackers, etc., is enough to drive a nervous person frantic. Out here,[1] we hear something of the uproar & thro the day the reports of guns were heard all around us. It was very bearable, however, compared with our experience in town, which I remember with horror.

July 4, 1866

The most hateful day of the year, when the birth of democracy is celebrated by license & noise. Every respectable person that can leaves town on this popular holiday, when the streets are given up to the rabble who appropriately express their joy by riot & brute noise. All the previous night, all day, & all the next night, there is an incessant roar of cannon, musquets, pistols, & crackers in the streets, enough to drive a nervous person mad. It was bad enough out here. All last night & all of today, the sound of guns & crackers around us never stopped. It is difficult to feel patriotic on the 4th of July.

[1] Fisher was at his country home in the Philadelphia suburbs.

Source: Sidney George Fisher, *A Philadelphia Perspective: The Diary of Sidney George Fisher Covering the Years, 1834–1871*, ed. Nicholas B. Wainwright (Philadelphia: Historical Society of Pennsylvania, 1967), 476, 518.

10 Excerpt from *The Fire of Liberty in Their Hearts: The Diary of Jacob E. Yoder of the Freedman's Bureau School, Lynchburg, Virginia, 1866–1870*, Diary. Jacob E. Yoder, 1866

Jacob E. Yoder was a Pennsylvanian who moved to Lynchburg, Virginia, after the Civil War to teach African Americans in a school sponsored by the Freedmen's Bureau. His diary of the experience included this passage about his first Fourth of July in the postwar South.

WEDNESDAY, 4 JULY 1866

A remarkable day in the history of this country. This is a day of rejoicing not only to the white people of this vast country but also to the late slaves of the Southern States. They seem to be generally inclined to select this day as an anniversary day to celebrate their emancipation. If ever it was appropriate for any people who were oppressed by a yoke like that which oxen wear, and who now are translated into the regions of civil liberty, with a sure promise that they shall have soon unlimited American political liberty of the 19th century.

I have, however, no doubt but they will do this. Their past history in slavery is noble. Why should they not do equally well in the enjoyment of partial liberty. No class of people on the face of the earth would have submitted to the outrages *they* have endured. In their present condition they need more education and independence. Ignorance and sin are their dangerous foes. If they are strong enough to conquer these then all will be right. Then the historian can with pleasure, paint a long and glorious existence among the nations of the world for them.

May this Fourth of July remind afresh every citizen of the Land of the value of our free institutions, and more especially of the duties he owes to it.

Source: Jacob E. Yoder, *The Fire of Liberty in Their Hearts: The Diary of Jacob E. Yoder of the Freedmen's Bureau School, Lynchburg, Virginia, 1866–1870*, ed. Samuel L. Horst (Richmond: Library of Virginia, 1996), 55–56.

11 *Fire-Works on the Night of the Fourth of July*
Cartoon. Winslow Homer, 1868

This cartoon and the one on the next page appeared in the same issue of a popular national magazine. In a brief comment, the editors noted their contrasting views of Fourth of July celebrations "in the town and in the country—in the North and in the South."

Source: liszt collection/Alamy.

12   *The Fourth of July in the Country*
Cartoon. Thomas Worth, 1868

Source: Harper's Weekly, July 11, 1868, 448.

13   *The Freed Slave* in Memorial Hall
Engraving. Fernando Miranda, 1876

The Centennial Exposition in 1876 generally ignored recent U.S. history, especially the Civil War and Reconstruction, but one exhibit in Memorial Hall called visitors' attention to these topics. European artist Francesco Pezzicar's *The Freed Slave* depicted a slave clad in a loincloth, holding aloft the Emancipation Proclamation, and displaying his broken chains. Not everyone was impressed by the work (one critic complained that the subject looked too much like a "Frenchy negro"), but according to contemporary reports, the sculpture drew crowds of African American viewers. This engraving by Fernando Miranda, published in the popular periodical *Frank Leslie's Illustrated Newspaper*, depicts the sculpture being viewed by an appreciative and solemn audience.

Source: The Statue of "the Freed Slave," in Memorial Hall, Philadelphia Exhibition, Engraving 1976, US, USA, America, United States, American School, (19th century)/Private Collection/Photo © Liszt Collection/Bridgeman Images.

14   Excerpt from *Lemon Swamp and Other Places: A Carolina Memoir* [of the 1890s]

Memoir. Mamie Garvin Fields, 1983

Mamie Garvin Fields grew up in Charleston, South Carolina, as Jim Crow laws formalized racial segregation in the post-Reconstruction South. During the 1970s, she recorded memories of her girlhood, which her granddaughter Karen Fields helped her publish in 1983.

"Aristocrats" lived on the Battery.[1] Some were English, some French, some Scottish, what-not. I never knew what made them "aristocrats"; maybe they just gave that name to themselves. But it was said that from Broad Street south to the Battery was where the "fine" white families lived. These families were supposed to be finer than those living other places. . . .

I don't believe the Battery was ever segregated because of a real law. That was one of the unwritten laws Charleston had. Unwritten or not, however, the policeman would come and enforce it. Or one of the black servants might even serve as the "policeman" of unwritten segregation in that part of town. . . .

Another unwritten law, or "custom," used to give the Battery over to blacks one day each year, the Fourth of July. Later on, we were allowed there no time of year. But when I was a child, oh, my, but the Fourth was a big day—although not for everybody. The old-time Southerners considered the Fourth of July a Yankee holiday and ignored it. So the white people stayed home and the black people "took over" the Battery for a day. The people were happy to be there, able to do what they felt like. I don't think the Battery was ever so alive as on the Fourth. We had food. We had music. We had a program that the children especially used to prepare for. We had all our friends. So glad to get down to where they were allowed only once a year, the mothers and grandmothers cooked up a storm, and they would bring everything for a barbecue and picnic. Some even brought fresh fish, which tasted sweetest cooked outdoors. Right up to today a "fish-fry" is a favorite Charleston version of a barbecue.

After dinner we had our program. My brother Herbert used to perform with a children's group called "the Bottle Band." That's what it really was. They would fill up bottles of different shapes and either beat them or blow across the top. Then they had "bone," beef ribs cleaned and polished until they were smooth and shiny, which they worked between their fingers. It is surprising how much music those children got out of such simple things. You could understand the songs they were playing, and they played lovely rhythms: "Toto-toto-tatee-tee-tee, Toto-toto-tatee-tee-tee!" Pretty soon the other children would get up to dance

---

[1] An upper-class neighborhood in Charleston, South Carolina.

Source: Mamie Garvin Fields with Karen Fields, *Lemon Swamp and Other Places: A Carolina Memoir* (New York: Free Press, 1983), 53–57.

and clap or sing with the band. The Bottle Band warmed up the audience. Then the trios and quartets came on, vying with each other in those performances. Certain songs, like "The Battle Hymn of the Republic," people would be asked to join in. That often introduced the speeches. One of our dignitaries generally offered a message.

The Emancipation Proclamation was always read out or some child would have it memorized for the occasion. Other children would have their "pieces" to say from Abraham Lincoln and, above all, from Frederick Douglass. On the Fourth of July many of our parents were actually celebrating their own freedom. So there were special parts of Douglass' antislavery speeches which were always said and which many people knew by heart. And then there was James Weldon Johnson's poem set to music, "Lift Ev'ry Voice and Sing."

> Till earth and heaven ring,
> Ring with the harmony of Liberty.
> Let our rejoicing rise,
> High as the list'ning skies,
> Let it resound loud as the rolling sea—
> Sing a song full of the faith that the dark past has taught us;
> Sing a song full of the hope that the present has brought us.
> Facing the rising sun of our new day begun,
> Let us march on till victory is won.

When we got through singing, we would hum, and someone recited from Douglass until everybody was really moved. You know, Douglass made a speech once despising the Fourth of July. "What to the Negro is the Fourth of July?" he said, before emancipation. Long years after emancipation, this special picnic was the Fourth of July to us.

15   *4. July. 1903* (opposite page)
Drawing. Amos Bad Heart Bull, 1903

Amos Bad Heart Bull was an Oglala Sioux who lived in South Dakota. A boy at the time of Custer's Last Stand, he came of age as his people were adjusting to lives on reservations. During the 1890s, he began drawing a pictorial record of life on the Pine Ridge Indian Reservation in a ledger book. Despite the efforts of federal agents to eradicate native culture, the Indians at Pine Ridge adopted the Fourth of July as an occasion for parading in their warrior regalia and engaging in traditional feasting and dancing. In this scene, two chiefs, Iron Bull and Bad Heart Bull (the artist), are dressed and on horseback, ready to lead a procession. A note in the Lakota language translates to "The Oglalas are still celebrating the Fourth of July in the old way."

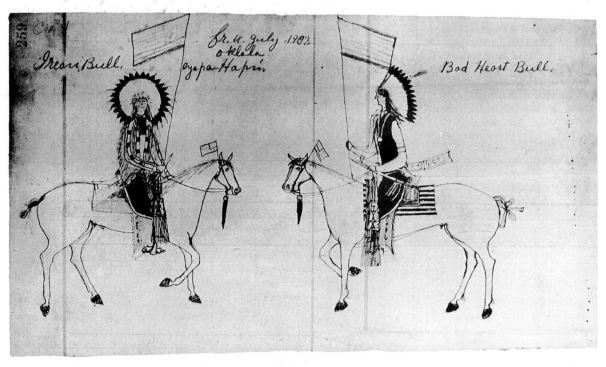

Source: Reproduced from *A Pictographic History of the Ogalala Sioux* by Amos Bad Heart Bull, text by Helen H. Blish, by permission of the University of Nebraska Press. Copyright 1967 by the University of Nebraska Press. Copyright renewed 1995 by the University of Nebraska Press.

Analyzing Sources on Fourth of July Observations

1. Where in these sources do you see evidence of nineteenth-century Americans redefining the ideas and principles expressed in the Declaration of Independence in 1776? What evidence of conflicting interpretations of those ideas and principles among nineteenth-century Americans do these sources present?

2. Which aspects of Fourth of July celebrations stayed the same and which changed over the course of the nineteenth century? How did such observations differ across class and race lines? How did groups traditionally excluded from public celebrations of the Fourth, such as African Americans and Native Americans, create their own?

3. Which of these sources offer evidence of how women experienced and participated in Fourth of July observations? Of the five types of sources presented in this chapter (speeches, alternative declarations, images, diaries, and memoirs), which do you think would be the best suited for studying gender differences in Fourth of July observations?

4. Compare these sources with your own experiences with the Fourth of July. What has changed and what has remained consistent in the way present-day Americans observe this holiday? Did the Fourth of July holiday in the nineteenth century serve any political or cultural functions that it no longer serves today? What do you think some of the authors of the sources you have read in this chapter would say about modern observations of Independence Day?

5. **Paper assignment:** The sources presented in this chapter reveal how Fourth of July observations exposed divisions within nineteenth-century American society. Pick one of these points of conflict: labor and class conflict, the women's rights movement, slavery and racial equality, or Native American rights. Using sources related to Fourth of July observations, explore how the American struggle with that specific issue changed over time.

6. **Paper assignment:** Research in greater detail American observations of the Fourth of July in the centennial years of 1876 and 1976. How did observations in 1976 compare with those in 1876? What pressing national issues shaped the bicentennial observances? What vision of the United States' future did bicentennial programs and speakers promote?

The Rest of the Story

In the late nineteenth century, observations of the Fourth of July became linked closely with debates over immigration and assimilation in American society. A tide of migration poured into the United States between 1880 and 1920, which raised nativist concerns about incorporating non-Protestants and non-English speakers into the nation's population. The Statue of Liberty, erected in 1886 in New York Harbor, the nation's busiest entry point for immigrants, became a pervasive symbol of American patriotism and opportunity. Immigrants made up a substantial portion of the workforce in U.S. factories and mines and so formed an important constituency in the labor movement, further tightening the connection between the Fourth of July and America's working peoples. During the twentieth century, administering the oath of citizenship to recently naturalized immigrants in large group ceremonies became a common civic ritual conducted on the Fourth of July.

Another modern trend in Fourth of July observations has turned the day from a public to a private celebration. The regularization of the civic calendar in the United States began in the nineteenth century but came into full form in the early twentieth, when state government and private businesses began following the federal government's lead in designating holidays for their employees. The invention of the three-day weekend and the rise of the automobile made it possible for office and factory workers to engage in what had been a time-honored practice of the rich: getting out of town for the Fourth. In this manner, observing the Fourth became more intimate, a family occasion rather than a civic one. The same trend has occurred in the modern era with Labor Day, Thanksgiving, and other national holidays originally intended to bring communities together.

Despite such changes, Fourth of July observations have remained remarkably consistent through the years. Parades, picnics, and fireworks are still the order of the day, and Fourth of July oration lives on in the speech the president usually delivers on Independence Day extolling the virtues of the Declaration of Independence. Among Native Americans, Fourth of July rodeos and powwows remain popular. Americans still fight over the legacy of the American Revolution, too, reinventing its symbols and ideas to address the issues that most concern them. If they were alive today, Daniel Webster, Frederick Douglass, and Susan B. Anthony would probably not be surprised to see how "tea party" has acquired an entirely new meaning in U.S. politics.

To Find Out More

Resources on American Fourth of July Observations

Foner, Philip S., ed. *We, the Other People: Alternative Declarations of Independence by Labor Groups, Farmers, Woman's Rights Advocates, Socialists, and Blacks, 1829–1975*. Urbana: University of Illinois Press, 1976.

"Fourth of July Orations Collection, 1791–1925." University of Missouri Digital Library. http://mulibraries.missouri.edu/specialcollections/fourth.htm.

Hawken, Henry A., ed. *Trumpets of Glory: Fourth of July Orations, 1786–1861*. Granby, CT: Salmon Brook Historical Society, 1976.

Heintze, James R. "Fourth of July Celebrations Database." American University. http://gurukul.ucc.american.edu/heintze/fourth.htm.

Secondary Sources on the Fourth of July in American Culture

Burstein, Andrew. *America's Jubilee*. New York: Random House, 2001.

Davis, Susan G. *Parades and Power: Street Theatre in Nineteenth-Century Philadelphia*. Philadelphia: Temple University Press, 1986.

Dennis, Matthew. *Red, White, and Blue Letter Days: An American Calendar*. Ithaca, NY: Cornell University Press, 2002.

Maier, Pauline. *American Scripture: Making the Declaration of Independence*. New York: Random House, 1997.

Travers, Len. *Celebrating the Fourth: Independence Day and the Rites of Nationalism in the Early Republic*. Amherst: University of Massachusetts Press, 1997.

Avoiding Plagiarism

Acknowledging the Source

If you have taken classes that involve writing, particularly writing and research, chances are good that you have heard the term *plagiarism* before. You may have received syllabi that mention plagiarism and describe the penalties for it, such as a failing grade in the course or even suspension from school. You also may have read your school's plagiarism policy, which most likely offers a brief definition of plagiarism and issues dire warnings about what will happen if you plagiarize. And if you read or watch the news, you may have noticed that plagiarism is an important issue not only within academic settings but in the larger world as well. Clearly, plagiarism is serious business, but what is it, exactly? And how do you avoid doing it?

Defined simply, plagiarism is the unattributed use of someone else's words or ideas. This apparently simple definition can be quite complicated, however. It tends to change across contexts and may be understood differently by different readers. Despite the slipperiness of the definition, every writer has the responsibility to learn how to navigate it and to attribute sources accurately and fully. Ethical researchers must acknowledge their sources because writers and readers depend on one another's honesty. To use someone else's words or ideas without sufficient acknowledgment breaks that trust. Writers in academia are interdependent, with each of us depending on everyone else to help uphold the integrity of the group. Every person engaged in academic writing, from the first-time research writer to the seasoned professor, shares this responsibility. For this reason, the penalties for an academic writer who fails to practice academic integrity are severe.

Source: Adapted from *The St. Martin's Tutorial on Avoiding Plagiarism* by Margaret Price, University of Massachusetts–Amherst.

Why Acknowledgment of Sources Is Important

Within the Western academic tradition, new ideas are built on older ones. Writers give acknowledgment in writing to their sources for a number of reasons:

- **To indicate that you are a responsible and careful researcher.** Acknowledging your sources increases your credibility as a researcher.
- **To give your writing added relevance.** When you refer to others' ideas and show how your own ideas fit into that framework, readers can see more easily what is significant about your work.
- **To help define your research project.** Sources help indicate what topic you are addressing, what approach you are taking, with whose ideas you are aligning yourself and from whose ideas you are distancing yourself, and (in some cases) what discipline you are writing in. In sum, citation helps situate *you* as a unique researcher.

Keeping Track of Source Materials: The Research Portfolio

As an ethical researcher, you should establish good research habits and stick to them. A research project, even a relatively small one involving only a few sources, quickly accumulates materials. There is no firm rule for how to keep these materials organized, but keeping some form of research portfolio is important. This portfolio should include

- photocopies or electronic copies of your source information
- your notes
- your annotated bibliography
- drafts of the paper or project you are working on
- any feedback you have received

Organize your portfolio so that it is both comprehensive (containing all your materials) and manageable (designed for easy retrieval of information). With experience, you will develop a type of research portfolio that works for you. As you collect data, however, keep in mind some basic principles that will help you organize your research materials and avoid inadvertent plagiarism. Recording your research findings precisely and accurately reduces the chances that you will unintentionally express and claim someone else's idea as your own.

1. **Create a structure for your portfolio.** One example is the folder system. Hanging file folders represent large categories that can be subdivided

using folders to represent smaller categories. As you discover more information through your research, you will add more folders or perhaps revise the categories altogether. Keep your working bibliography (see the next section) in a separate folder. Also, keep your notes and annotations for each source. Another possible structure for a research portfolio is the notebook system, in which materials are kept in a three-ring binder, with dividers separating the categories. The system you use will be governed by how much material you accumulate as well as your own organizational preferences.

2. **Keep backup materials.** Your portfolio should include backup copies of everything to guard against loss or computer failure. If a lot of your information resides on a computer, keep hard copies of everything and at least one electronic backup.

3. **Make a hard copy of each source for your own use.** You should print out any articles that you download from an online periodical database, photocopy articles or chapters of books, and print out all Web sites. (Most printouts of Web sites will automatically note the URL and date of access. If that does not occur, note this information.) These printouts will be very useful for checking quotations, paraphrases, and bibliographic information.

4. **Take notes on every source you collect.** This step is crucial. If you simply read a source over and later consult the source directly while writing your paper, your chances of plagiarizing are much greater than if you consult your notes on the source. Moreover, you cannot truly digest a source's information unless you take notes in your own words on what you read.

Maintaining a Working Bibliography

A working bibliography is a list of all the sources you consult as you work on a research project. You may not need to include every source in your project, but you should keep a list of every work you have consulted so that your records are complete. If you develop this habit, you will avoid the problem of wondering where you found certain facts and ideas. A working bibliography also may come in handy for future research projects. After you complete your research, keep your working bibliography so that you can consult it again if necessary.

Your working bibliography should include complete information for each source so that you can write your citations easily (see Appendix II, Documenting the Source). This information includes the author's name, the title of the work, the title of the book or periodical the work comes from (if applicable), the volume or issue number, the place of publication, the publishing company, the date of publication, and inclusive page numbers. Note any other information that pertains to the work's publication, such as whether it is a volume in a series, an edition other than the first, or a translation. Write down the information for each source as you begin using it. You can also keep your working bibliography on a computer file; this technique allows you to easily transfer the bibliography into your final draft later on.

Taking Notes: Knowing Where Each Idea and Word Comes From

It is easy to assume that the research process and the writing process are separate—"First I research, and then I write"—but in fact, researching and writing should be intimately intertwined. As you read and research, new ideas occur to you. Your research question begins to change shape and sometimes to change direction. The development of your own thoughts in turn leads to a different reading of your sources. Taking notes and writing drafts while you research are essential. If you wait to begin note-taking and drafting until you have "finished" your research, the rich mixture of ideas and thoughts you created while researching will never be captured on paper.

You may be surprised to learn that research involves so much writing before you begin writing your "real" paper, but note-taking is not an optional or extra step. All responsible researchers write notes before (and while) drafting their projects. They are crucial building blocks of an effective research project. A detailed note-taking system makes writing a paper much easier.

To master each source's information and argument—and avoid plagiarizing—it is best to take concise notes in your own words, including page numbers for the location in each source. When you come to a comment in the source that you think you will want to quote in your paper, be sure to write it out accurately, with quotation marks around it and the page number from the source.

Taking careful notes while you are researching also makes it easier to determine which ideas are your own. Any plagiarism policy that you read will say that plagiarism is the act of representing someone else's words or ideas as your own. Summarizing or paraphrasing requires that you take another person's idea and put it into your own words.

Clearly, then, it is better to write as you go rather than to save the writing for the end of a research project, but how do you go about doing it? Here are some concrete note-taking strategies.

- **Write an instant draft.** Before you begin researching, or as early in the research process as possible, write a draft that describes what argument you want to make or what question you want to explore. Writing professors Charles Moran and Anne Herrington call this an "instant draft." An instant draft will be a tentative, somewhat disorganized piece of writing since you have not yet done your research. Its purpose is to capture what you know about a subject before you begin consulting other people's ideas. In your instant draft, address the following questions: *What do I* *already know about this topic? Where have I gotten my information from so far? Do I have a strong feeling or stance on this topic? What questions do I have about the topic? What is (are) the main thing(s) I want to find out through my research? Where will I begin looking for this information? What do I need help with? Whom can I ask for that help?* An instant draft is a research memo to yourself and is enormously helpful in providing a recorded baseline for your knowledge. As you learn more and more through your research, you will always know where you started out and hence which ideas you have acquired through researching.

- **Annotate each source.** Before you begin taking more detailed notes, annotate each source you have just read. That is, write a brief summary of the source's main point and key ideas. It is helpful to include annotations in your working bibliography (which turns it into an *annotated bibliography*). Some instructors will ask you to turn in an annotated bibliography with your final draft.

Summarizing, Paraphrasing, and Quoting

You can record someone else's words or ideas in your notes by using three techniques: summarizing, paraphrasing, and quoting. Summarizing and paraphrasing involve putting a source's words into your own; quoting involves recording a source's exact words. After you practice these techniques independently, it is a good idea to show your notes to your instructor and to ask for his or her comments on the effectiveness of your note-taking. Is it complete? Is it accurate? When summarizing and paraphrasing, do you put other authors' ideas into your own words effectively?

1. **Summarizing.** To summarize is to rephrase a relatively large amount of information into a short statement in your own words. Although some information will inevitably be lost, your job is to record what you see as the main idea of the passage. Summarizing is useful when you want to give a reader the gist of a relatively lengthy passage without going into every detail.

2. **Paraphrasing.** To paraphrase is to restate something with your own words and sentence structure. Unlike a summary, a paraphrase is generally about as long as the original passage. Because you are changing the language, you will also inevitably change the meaning of the passage *slightly*, but your job is to keep the meaning as intact as possible. Paraphrasing is useful when you want to convey another author's exact idea but not his or her exact words, perhaps because the language is highly technical or perhaps because a quote would be distracting.

3. **Quoting.** To quote is to state a source's exact words, signaled by the use of quotation marks. If you change a quotation in any way, you must indicate

this change by including three-dot ellipsis points (when you omit part of a quotation) or square brackets (when you make a slight change or addition for clarification). In a final draft, quotations are often less useful than summaries or paraphrases because quotations break up the flow of your writing and often require fairly extensive explanation. Quotations are useful, however, when you want to capture a source's exact wording.

Knowing Which Sources to Acknowledge

Beginning researchers often ask, "Do I have to cite *everything*?" It is a good question because not every piece of information in a research paper must be cited. Figuring out what to cite can be difficult, even for experienced researchers. Generally, if you are unsure, include a citation. It is always better to have an unnecessary citation in your paper than to omit one that is necessary.

Materials That Do Not Require Acknowledgment

Here are some types of materials that usually do not require acknowledgment in research projects:

- **Common knowledge.** It is often easy to spot pieces of common knowledge. For example, the sky is blue, the United States has fifty states, and the 1996 presidential candidates were Bill Clinton and Bob Dole are all pieces of information that appear in various sources, but because they are known to just about everyone, you do not need to cite a source. Sometimes, however, recognizing common knowledge becomes tricky because common knowledge for one person may not be common knowledge for another. Identifying your audience is the key to recognizing common knowledge. If you know what audience you are writing to, you will have a clearer idea of what your readers would consider common knowledge. As always, if you are unsure, be more conservative rather than less so.

- **Fact.** Uncontested pieces of information that can be found in many different sources—particularly reference sources such as encyclopedias—do not require acknowledgment. In *The St. Martin's Handbook*, writing professor Andrea Lunsford gives an example of one such fact: that most of the Pearl Harbor military base, except oil tanks and submarines, was destroyed on December 7, 1941, by Japanese bombers. She adds an example of information on the same topic that *does* require citation: "a source that argued that the failure to destroy the submarines meant that Japan was destined to lose the subsequent war with the United States" (394). The distinction Lunsford makes here is between fact (something commonly accepted as true) and opinion (something that is arguable).

- **Your own ideas.** Recognizing that an idea is your own can sometimes be difficult, especially during the research process, when you are reading and absorbing so many others' ideas. A good way to capture your own ideas is to write a draft *before* you begin researching.

- **Your own field research.** Knowledge that you create by conducting a field study such as a survey, an interview, or an observation is considered your own work. You do not need to cite this sort of information, but another kind of ethics guides the field researcher. You should be clear about how you collected the information. In addition, you should be scrupulous about protecting your participants' autonomy (be sure to quote them accurately, and ask for their feedback when possible).

Materials That Do Require Acknowledgment

Anything that you draw from another source, unless it falls into one of the categories described above (common knowledge, fact, your own ideas, and your own field research), must be cited. Your citations should appear in two places: in the body of your paper and in a list at the end of the paper. The style of citation your instructor has asked you to use will affect the formatting of these citations. Complete bibliographic information for each source will appear in a section titled "Bibliography" (see Appendix II, Documenting the Source).

The following list is suggestive, but not exhaustive. New kinds of information are always emerging. Generally speaking, however, here are the types of materials that require acknowledgment in academic writing:

- **Another person's words.** Direct quotations must always be cited.

- **Another person's ideas.** Even if you rephrase someone else's idea by paraphrasing or summarizing it, you must cite it. Citations for paraphrases and summaries look just like citations for quotations, except that no quotation marks are used.

- **Judgments, opinions, and arguments.** Arguable information, such as the idea about the effect of the Pearl Harbor bombing discussed previously, must be cited. Whenever you offer an idea from another source that could be argued, acknowledge that it is this individual's point of view. You should do so even if you thought of the idea and *then* encountered it through your research. You can indicate in your writing that you came to the idea independently of the other author, but you cannot omit mention of the other author.

- **Visual information.** If you use a chart, graph, or picture from another source—or if you use the information from that chart, graph, or picture—acknowledge the source.

- **Information that can be attributed to a company or organization rather than a single person.** Web sites and corporate publications often do not list individual authors. In this case, the organization that sponsored the Web site or publication should be listed as the author. If the author is unknown, your citation should indicate that.

- **Information gathered from class lectures or from another aural source.** If you heard information rather than saw it, you must still cite it. You can cite information you have heard in various ways, including as a lecture, as a personal communication, or as an interview.

- **General help offered by readers.** Sometimes the feedback you receive from readers (such as your teacher, classmates, and friends) will affect the shape of your work, but not its content. For instance, a classmate might offer a suggestion for making your introduction more interesting. In this case, the best way to acknowledge your classmate's contribution is in a note of thanks appended to the paper. Such "Acknowledgments" notes generally appear at the end of academic papers or in a footnote added to the title or first paragraph. If you look at a refereed history journal, you will see examples of less formal acknowledgments of this kind.

Learning these rules and following them appropriately is one of your responsibilities as a member of an academic or writing community. Even if you plagiarize unintentionally, the penalties for plagiarism—which can be very severe—still apply to you. For more information on plagiarism, consult your school's or your department's guidelines. For more detailed and constructive information, speak with your instructor, who probably has a good idea of what sort of citation is expected. You should also find out if your school has a writing center with tutoring available. Tutors can discuss ways of citing information and often can refer you to other sources of information if you need additional help. A third resource to consider is a writing handbook that includes the rules of academic citation as well as guidelines on conducting research, managing information, and citing sources responsibly.

APPENDIX II

Documenting the Source

Whenever you use another researcher's work as a source in your own writing, whether you quote the researcher's words directly or rely on the researcher's evidence and theories to support your arguments, you must include documentation for that source. This requirement is equally true when using a map, photograph, table, or graph created by someone else. The reasons for this are twofold. First, to avoid any possibility of plagiarism, you must always include proper documentation for *all* source materials (see Appendix I, Avoiding Plagiarism). Second, a proper citation gives important information to your reader about where to find a particular source, be it on a Web site, in a book at the library, or in an archive in your local community.

When documenting sources, historians use a standard form based on the recommendations published in *The Chicago Manual of Style*. All the documentation models presented here are consistent with the guidelines published in the sixteenth edition of *The Chicago Manual of Style* (Chicago: University of Chicago Press, 2010). For each source type, you will see a citation style that can be used for either a footnote, which appears at the bottom of the page of text, or an endnote, which appears at the end of a chapter or at the end of the whole text. These model notes are indicated by an "**N**" in the margin. Each note is followed by an example of how this source type would be cited in a bibliography. Model bibliography entries are marked by a "**B**" in the margin. Two examples are provided because footnote/endnote citation style is slightly different from bibliography citation style.

The examples provided here illustrate how to cite the various types of sources that appear in *Going to the Source*, and they will help you address many of the documentation issues associated with sources that you come across in your research. This guide is not a comprehensive list, however, and as you dig further into the past, you may uncover source types that are not covered in this brief guide. For additional information about documenting sources in the *Chicago* style, please see **bedfordstmartins.com/resdoc**.

Documentation Basics

When you are wondering what to include in a citation, the question to keep in mind is, "What does my reader need to know to *find* this source?" When citing sources internally, you should use the footnote or endnote style. Footnotes and endnotes are used to document specific instances of borrowed text, ideas, or information. The first time you cite a source, you need to include the full publication information for that source—the author's full name, source title (and subtitle, if there is one), and facts of publication (city, publisher, and date)—along with the specific page number you are referencing.

> 1. David Paul Nord, *Communities of Journalism: A History of American Newspapers and Their Readers* (Urbana: University of Illinois Press, 2001), 78.

If you refer to that source later in your paper, you need to include only the author's last name, an abbreviated version of the title, and the page or pages cited.

> 4. Nord, *Communities of Journalism,* 110–12.

A bibliography is used in addition to footnotes or endnotes to list all the works you consulted in completing your paper, even those not directly cited in your footnotes. The sources included in your bibliography should be listed alphabetically, so the citation style for a bibliographic entry begins with the author's last name first.

> Nord, David Paul. *Communities of Journalism*: *A History of American Newspapers and Their Readers.* Urbana: University of Illinois Press, 2001.

BOOKS

▪ *1. Standard format for a book*

The standard form for citing a book is the same whether there is an editor or an author, the only difference being the inclusion of "ed." to indicate that an editor compiled the work.

Directory of Documentation Models

    1. Tim Johnson, ed., *Spirit Capture: Photographs from the National Museum of the*   N
American Indian (Washington, DC: Smithsonian Institution Press, 1998), 102.

Johnson, Tim, ed. *Spirit Capture: Photographs from the National Museum of the American*   B
    Indian. Washington, DC: Smithsonian Institution Press, 1998.

■ *2. Book with two or more authors or editors*

When citing a source from a book with two or three authors or editors, you
need to include the names of all the authors (or editors) in the order that they
appear on the title page. If a work has more than three authors, you need to
include all the names in your bibliography. In your footnotes or endnotes, you
need only include the name of the lead author followed by "and others" or
"et al.," with no intervening comma.

    2. Graham Russell Hodges and Alan Edward Brown, eds., *"Pretends to Be Free":*   N
Runaway Slave Advertisements from Colonial and Revolutionary New York and New Jersey
(New York: Garland, 1994), 58.

B   Hodges, Graham Russell, and Alan Edward Brown, eds. *"Pretends to Be Free": Runaway Slave Advertisements from Colonial and Revolutionary New York and New Jersey.* New York: Garland, 1994.

■ 3. Edited book

Sometimes a book will have an author and an editor. In that case, you need to include both the author's and the editor's names.

N   3. Hilda Satt Polacheck, *I Came a Stranger: The Story of a Hull-House Girl*, ed. Dena J. Polacheck Epstein (Urbana: University of Illinois Press, 1991), 36.

B   Polacheck, Hilda Satt. *I Came a Stranger: The Story of a Hull-House Girl.* Edited by Dena J. Polacheck Epstein. Urbana: University of Illinois Press, 1991.

If the edited book does not have an author, list it according to the editor's name.

N   3. Robin Wright, ed., *The Iran Primer* (Washington, DC: United States Institute of Peace Press, 2010), 59–60.

B   Wright, Robin, ed. *The Iran Primer.* Washington, DC: United States Institute of Peace Press, 2010.

■ 4. Multivolume book

If you are referring to a specific volume in a multivolume work, you need to specify which volume you used. This information should come before the page reference toward the end of the citation.

N   4. Bernard Bailyn, ed., *The Debate on the Constitution: Federalist and Anti-Federalist Speeches, Articles, and Letters during the Struggle over Ratification* (New York: Library of America, 1993), 2:759–61.

B   Bailyn, Bernard, ed. *The Debate on the Constitution: Federalist and Anti-Federalist Speeches, Articles, and Letters during the Struggle over Ratification.* 2 vols. New York: Library of America, 1993.

Sometimes individual volumes in a multivolume work have separate volume titles. When citing a particular volume, you should include the volume title first followed by the name of the complete work.

■ 5. Book with an anonymous author

Many books printed in the nineteenth century were published anonymously. If the author's name was omitted from the title page but you know from your research who the author is, insert the name in square brackets; if you do not know who the actual author is, begin the citation with the work's title. Avoid using "Anonymous" or "Anon." in citations. As originally published, the author of *The Mother's Book* was listed as "Mrs. Child," so this citation includes that information along with the full name in brackets.

5. Mrs. [Lydia Maria] Child, *The Mother's Book* (Boston: Carter, Hendee, and   N
Babcock, 1831), 23.

Child, [Lydia Maria]. *The Mother's Book*. Boston: Carter, Hendee, and Babcock, 1831.   B

SECTIONS OR DOCUMENTS WITHIN BOOKS

▪ *6. Book-length work within a book*

Sometimes, the source you are using may be a book-length work that has been reprinted within a longer work. In that case, you need to include both titles along with the editor of the longer work.

6. Álvar Núñez Cabeza de Vaca, *The Narrative of Cabeza de Vaca*, in *Spanish*   N
Explorers in the Southern United States, 1528–1543, ed. Frederick W. Hodge (New York:
Charles Scribner's Sons, 1907), 52–54, 76–78, 81–82.

Cabeza de Vaca, Álvar Núñez. *The Narrative of Cabeza de Vaca*. In *Spanish Explorers in the*   B
Southern United States, 1528–1543, edited by Frederick W. Hodge. New York:
Charles Scribner's Sons, 1907.

▪ *7. Chapter or article from a book*

If you want to cite a particular chapter from a book, you should include the title of the chapter in quotation marks before the title of the book.

7. Vicki L. Ruiz, "The Flapper and the Chaperone," in *From Out of the Shadows: Mexican*   N
Women in Twentieth-Century America (New York: Oxford University Press, 1998), 12–26.

Ruiz, Vicki L. "The Flapper and the Chaperone." In *From Out of the Shadows: Mexican*   B
Women in Twentieth-Century America. New York: Oxford University Press, 1998.

▪ *8. Published letter or other correspondence*

When citing published letters, memoranda, telegrams, and the like, you need to include the name of the sender and the recipient along with the date of the correspondence. Memoranda, telegrams, and other forms of communication should be identified as such in your citation after the recipient's name and before the date, but letters do not need to be specifically noted as such.

N   8. James Buchanan to Juan N. Almonte, March 10, 1845, in *Diplomatic Correspondence of the United States: Inter-American Affairs, 1831–1860*, ed. William R. Manning (Washington, DC: Carnegie Endowment for International Peace, 1937), 8:163.

B   Buchanan, James. James Buchanan to Juan N. Almonte, March 10, 1845. In *Diplomatic Correspondence of the United States: Inter-American Affairs, 1831–1860*, edited by William R. Manning. Washington, DC: Carnegie Endowment for International Peace, 1937.

■ *9. Table, graph, or chart*

Whenever you incorporate statistical data into your work, it is important to document your evidence. If you borrow a table, graph, or chart from another source, you must cite it just as you would quoted material in your text. Include a citation in appropriate footnote format to the source of the borrowed information directly below it. If you change the table, graph, or chart in any way (for example, eliminating unnecessary information or adding another element such as a percent calculation to it), use the phrase "adapted from" in your citation, which signals to the reader that you have altered the original. If a number is used to identify the data in the original source, that information should also be included at the end of the citation.

N   9. Adapted from Hinton R. Helper, *The Impending Crisis of the South: How to Meet It* (New York: Burdick Brothers, 1857), 71, table XVIII.

Because you would not cite any one particular table in your bibliography, you would follow the style for citing the book, periodical, or Web site where the data you consulted first appeared.

■ *10. Illustration*

When citing drawings, paintings, and other images that appear in a book, include the illustration title and author followed by the publication information for the book. In the note, include the page number for the item as well as any figure or plate number assigned to it.

N   10. Theodore de Bry, "Birds and Fish of New England," Michael Alexander, ed., *Discovering the New World: Based on the Works of Theodore de Bry* (New York: Harper and Row, 1976), 202.

B   de Bry, Theodore. "Birds and Fish of New England." In *Discovering the New World: Based on the Works of Theodore de Bry*, edited by Michael Alexander. New York: Harper and Row, 1976.

PERIODICALS

Journals are scholarly publications that are usually published a few times a year. Popular magazines are written for the general public and are most often published on a monthly or weekly basis. Most newspapers are published daily, although some small local papers are published weekly. The following examples demonstrate the style for citing each type of periodical. If you consult an online periodical, the style for citing this source would be the same, with the addition of the URL at the end of your citation.

■ *11. Journal article*

When citing an article from a journal, you need to include the volume number, issue number (when given), and date of publication.

> 11. Elizabeth A. Fenn, "Biological Warfare in Eighteenth-Century North America: N
> Beyond Jeffery Amherst," *Journal of American History* 86, no. 4 (2000): 1552–80.

> Fenn, Elizabeth A. "Biological Warfare in Eighteenth-Century North America: Beyond   B
> Jeffery Amherst." *Journal of American History* 86, no. 4 (2000): 1552–80.

■ *12. Popular magazine*

When citing material from a popular magazine, you need to include only the magazine title followed by the date of publication and the page number(s) for the material. If you are citing from a regular feature of the magazine, you should include the title of the feature in the citation. If there is an author of the magazine article or the magazine's regular feature, the author's name would appear first in your citation, followed by the name of the feature.

> 12. Benjamin Spock, "Should Mothers Work?" *Ladies' Home Journal*, January–   N
> February, 1963, 16, 18, 21.

> Spock, Benjamin. "Should Mothers Work?" *Ladies' Home Journal*, January–February, 1963.   B

■ *13. Newspaper article*

When citing newspaper articles, you must include the day, month, and year of publication, and the author if the article had a byline. *Chicago* style allows for page numbers to be omitted because newspapers often publish several editions each day and these editions are generally paginated differently.

> 13. John Dickinson, "The Liberty Song," *Boston Gazette*, July 18, 1768.   N

> Dickinson, John. "The Liberty Song." *Boston Gazette*, July 18, 1768.   B

■   *14. Letter to the editor*

For letters to the editor published in newspapers and magazines, include the letter title (if any) as well as the words "letter to the editor."

N   14. Evalyn F. Thomas, "Modern American Housewife," letter to the editor, *Ladies' Home Journal*, March 1956, 6, 8.

B   Thomas, Evalyn F. "Modern American Housewife." Letter to the editor. *Ladies' Home Journal*, March 1956.

INTERNET SOURCES

■   *15. A document from a Web site*

To cite a document found on a Web site, you need to provide as much of the following information as possible: the author, the name of the document with original date of publication, the name of the site, the sponsor or owner of the site, and the URL. Also include the date that the site was last revised or modified; if that is unavailable, include the date that you accessed the site. Sometimes a Web archive will include a document number; when available, you should include this cataloging number as well.

N   15. William Plumer, "An address, delivered at Portsmouth, N.H., on the Fourth of July, 1828," *Fourth of July Orations Collection*, University of Missouri Special Collections and Rare Books, last revised October 20, 2009, E286.P65, http://mulibraries.missouri .edu/specialcollections/fourth.htm.

B   Plumer, William. "An address, delivered at Portsmouth, N.H., on the Fourth of July, 1828." *Fourth of July Orations Collection*, University of Missouri Special Collections and Rare Books. Last revised October 20, 2009. E286.P65. http://mulibraries.missouri .edu/specialcollections/fourth.htm.

■   *16. An entire Web site*

To cite an entire Web site, you need include only the author of the site (if known), the name of the site, the sponsor or owner of the site, the date of the last revision or modification (or, if unavailable, the access date), and the URL.

N   16. University of Minnesota College of Liberal Arts, *Immigration History Research Center*, University of Minnesota, last modified December 8, 2010, http://ihrc.umn.edu/.

B   University of Minnesota College of Liberal Arts. *Immigration History Research Center*. University of Minnesota. Last modified December 8, 2010. http://ihrc.umn.edu/.

PUBLIC DOCUMENTS

▣ *17. Executive department document*

For government documents issued by the executive branch, include the name of the department or commission that created the document, the name of the document, and the publication information.

17. President's Commission on the Status of Women, *American Women: Report of the President's Commission on the Status of Women, 1963* (Washington, DC: U.S. Government Printing Office, 1963), 27, 29–30, 18, 19.   N

President's Commission on the Status of Women. *American Women: Report of the President's Commission on the Status of Women, 1963*. Washington, DC: U.S. Government Printing Office, 1963.   B

▣ *18. Congressional testimony*

Testimony given before a congressional committee is usually published in a book. The exact name of the committee is given in the title of the work in which the testimony appears.

18. United States Congress, *Report of the Joint Select Committee to Inquire into the Condition of Affairs in the Late Insurrectionary States*, vol. 2, *South Carolina, Part I* (Washington, DC: Government Printing Office, 1872), 25–28, 33–34.   N

United States Congress. *Report of the Joint Select Committee to Inquire into the Condition of Affairs in the Late Insurrectionary States*. Vol. 2, *South Carolina, Part I*. Washington, DC: Government Printing Office, 1872.   B

▣ *19. Court records*

When citing legal cases in historical writing, the name of the plaintiff appears first, followed by the name of the defendant, and both names are italicized. The first time you cite the case, you should also include the court and year in which the case was decided. Supreme Court decisions are published by the government in a series called *United States Reports*. When citing Supreme Court decisions, you need to include the name of the case in italics followed by the number of the volume that contains the particular case, the abbreviation "U.S." for *United States Reports*, page numbers, and the year of the decision.

19. *Korematsu v. United States*, 323 U.S. 242, 242–48 (1944).   N

Korematsu v. United States. 323 U.S. 242, 242–48. 1944.   B

■ *20. Online government document*

For government documents accessed online, include everything you would for a print publication, as well as the date of last modification (or your access date) and the URL.

N   20. Civil Rights Act of 1964, Document PL 88-352, *International Information Programs*, U.S. State Department, page revised August 13, 1996, http://202.41.85 .234:8000/InfoUSA/laws/majorlaw/civilr19.htm.

B   Civil Rights Act of 1964. Document PL 88-352. *International Information Programs*, U.S. State Department. Page revised August 13, 1996. http://202.41.85.234:8000/ InfoUSA/laws/majorlaw/civilr19.htm.

OTHER SOURCES

■ *21. Advertisement*

To cite an advertisement, provide the name of the company or institution, the name of the ad, and the publication information for the periodical in which the ad appeared. Advertisements should be included in notes, but not bibliographies.

N   21. Mutual of New York, "Life insurance? For a wife? That's money down the drain!" advertisement, appeared in *Newsweek*, May 6, 1968, 57.

■ *22. Audio recording*

For citing an audio recording, include information as you would for a print source. If you retrieved the recording online, include the latest modification date (or your access date) and the URL.

N   22. "Executive Committee Meeting of the NSC on the Cuban Missile Crisis," October 24, 1962, transcript and Adobe Flash audio, 37.4, *Presidential Recordings Program*, Miller Center of Public Affairs, University of Virginia, accessed February 22, 2011, http:// millercenter.org/scripps/archive/presidentialrecordings/kennedy/1962/10_1962.

B   "Executive Committee Meeting of the NSC on the Cuban Missile Crisis." October 24, 1962. Transcript and Adobe Flash audio, 37.4. *Presidential Recordings Program*. Miller Center of Public Affairs, University of Virginia. Accessed February 22, 2011. http:// millercenter.org/scripps/archive/presidentialrecordings/kennedy/1962/10_1962.

■ *23. Painting*

When citing paintings that appear in a catalog, archive, or database, you need to include the artwork's catalog or accession number if available. This documentation will help other researchers locate the original source. Generally, specific works of art are not included in your bibliography, but if a particular painting is important to your research, you may list it in your bibliography by the painter's name first.

23. George Catlin, *Shón-Ka-Ki-He-Ga, Horse Chief, Grand Pawnee Head Chief*   N
(1832, Smithsonian American Art Museum: 1985.66.99).

Catlin, George. *Shón-Ka-Ki-He-Ga, Horse Chief, Grand Pawnee Head Chief*. 1832.   B
    Smithsonian American Art Museum: 1985.66.99.

◼ *24. Photograph or other archival material*

Any material found in an archive or depository—be it a photograph, diary, letter, or map—needs to be cited just as published material would be. The name of the author (or photographer, in the case of photographs) should appear first, followed by the title of the image or document being cited in quotation marks, the date, and the name of the archive or depository. If a source from a collection is important enough to your work, you can mention that source specifically in your bibliography. If you make use of more than one photograph or other type of source from a particular collection, however, you need only cite them generally in your bibliography.

24. George P. Barnard, "Ruins of Charleston, S.C.," 1866, Beinecke Rare Book and   N
Manuscript Library, Yale University.

Photographs. Beinecke Rare Book and Manuscript Library, Yale University.   B

◼ *25. Unpublished letter or other correspondence*

Unpublished letters and those that have not been archived should include some indication of this fact, such as "in the author's possession" or "private collection." If the letter was found in an archive, the location of the depository would be included as well. (For information on how to cite material found in an archive, see the section "Photograph or other archival material," above.)

25. Jeff Rogers to William and Adele Rogers, November 10, 1968, in the author's   N
possession.

Rogers, Jeff. Jeff Rogers to William and Adele Rogers, November 10, 1968. In the author's   B
    possession.

Acknowledgments (continued)

CHAPTER 1

Pages 10–11 (Source 1): *Succarath* image caption. Schlesinger, Roger and Arthur P. Stabler. "Excerpts pp. 55–57, 140–141 and 196–197." *André Thevet's North America*, Eds. Roger Schlesinger and Arthur Stabler. Montreal: MQUP, 1986. Print.

Pages 10–11 (Source 2): *Hoga [Manatee]* image caption. Schlesinger, Roger and Arthur P. Stabler. "Excerpts pp. 55–57, 140–141 and 196–197." *André Thevet's North America*, Eds. Roger Schlesinger, and Arthur Stabler. Montreal: MQUP, 1986. Print.

Page 12 (Source 3): *Whale* image caption. Schlesinger, Roger and Arthur P. Stabler. "Excerpts pp. 55–57, 140–141 and 196–197." *André Thevet's North America*, Eds. Roger Schlesinger, and Arthur Stabler. Montreal: MQUP, 1986. Print.

Page 13 (Source 4): *Alligator* image caption. Excerpts from 43, 157, 202 [365 words] from *Discovering the New World*, edited by Michael Alexander Copyright © 1976 by Michael Alexander. Reprinted by permission of HarperCollins Publishers.

Page 14 (Source 5): *Llama* image caption. Excerpts from 43, 157, 202 [365 words] from *Discovering the New World*, edited by Michael Alexander Copyright © 1976 by Michael Alexander. Reprinted by permission of HarperCollins Publishers.

Page 15 (Source 6): *Birds and Fish of New England* caption. Excerpts from 43, 157, 202 [365 words] from *Discovering the New World*, edited by Michael Alexander. Copyright © 1976 by Michael Alexander. Reprinted by permission of HarperCollins Publishers.

CHAPTER 4

Pages 74–91 "Fashioning Moccasins: Detroit, the Manufacturing Frontier, and the Empire of Consumption, 1701–1835," by Catherine Cangany, *William and Mary Quarterly*, third series, 69 (April 2012). Reprinted by permission.

CHAPTER 11

Pages 237–240 (Source 2): Robert Penn Warren, *John Brown: The Making of a Martyr* (1929). Nashville: J. S. Sanders, 1993. Reprinted with permission of Rowman & Littlefield Publishing Group.

Pages 240–242 (Source 3): Excerpt(s) from JOHN BROWN, ABOLITIONIST: THE MAN WHO KILLED SLAVERY, SPARKED THE CIVIL WAR, AND SEEDED CIVIL RIGHTS by David S. Reynolds, copyright © 2005 by David S. Reynolds. Used by permission of Alfred A. Knopf, an imprint of the Knopf Doubleday Publishing Group, a division of Penguin Random House LLC. All rights reserved. Any third party use of this material, outside of this publication, is prohibited. Interested parties must apply directly to Penguin Random House LLC for permission.

CAPSTONE CHAPTER

Pages 321–323 (Source 7): *The Life and Writings of Frederick Douglass* by DOUGLASS, FREDERICK; FONER, PHILIP SHELDON, Reproduced with permission of INTERNATIONAL PUBLISHERS in the format Republish in a book via Copyright Clearance Center.

Page 326 (Source 9): Sidney George Fisher, diary excerpts. Sidney George Fisher Diaries, Collection 1462. Historical Society of Pennsylvania.

Page 327 (Source 10): Jacob Yoder, diary excerpt. Reproduction of these materials granted courtesy of the Library of Virginia, Richmond, Virginia, and is granted solely for the present work.

Pages 331–332 (Source 14): Reprinted with the permission of The Free Press, a Division of Simon & Schuster, Inc., from LEMON SWAMP AND OTHER PLACES: A Carolina Memoir by Mamie Garvin Fields with Karen Fields. Copyright © 1983 by Mamie Garvin Fields and Karen Fields. All rights reserved.

Index

Letters in parentheses following page numbers refer to:

(f) figures
(i) illustrations
(t) tables

Working with Sources on Your Own

Avoiding Plagiarism

See Appendix I, "Avoiding Plagiarism: Acknowledging the Source," for important information on how to work with sources effectively without unintentionally borrowing the work of another author.

Documenting Sources

See Appendix II, "Documenting the Source," for guidelines on how to cite sources you use in your papers. The following is a list of model citations included in Appendix II.

Directory of Documentation Models